Islam and Politics

CONTEMPORARY ISSUES IN THE MIDDLE EAST

Islam and Politics

REVISED, SECOND EDITION

JOHN L. ESPOSITO

SYRACUSE UNIVERSITY PRESS

First Edition 1984
Revised, Second Edition 1987
92 91 90 89 88   5 4 3 2

The paper used in this publication meets the minimum requirements of American National Standard for Information Sciences—Permanence of Paper for Printed Library Materials, ANSI Z39.48-1984.∞™

Library of Congress Cataloging-in-Publication Data

Esposito, John L.
Islam and politics.

(Contemporary issues in the Middle East)
Bibliography: p.
Includes index.
1. Islam and politics—Middle East. 2. Islam and politics—Africa, North. 3. Middle East—Politics and government. 4. Africa, North—Politics and government. 5. Political science—Middle East—History. 6. Political science—Africa, North—History. I. Title. II. Series.
BP63.A4N423 1987   320.917'671   87-9999
ISBN 0-8156-2419-0 (alk. paper)

Manufactured in the United States of America

JOHN L. ESPOSITO is Professor of Islamic Studies and Director of International Studies, College of the Holy Cross. A member of the Board of Directors of the Middle East Studies Association, he is the author of among other books, *Women in Muslim Family Law* and editor of *Islam and Development* (both published by Syracuse University Press), *Islam in Transition*, *Voices of Resurgent Islam*, and *Islam in Asia*.

Preface to Revised, Second Edition

*T*HREE YEARS have elapsed since I completed the first edition of *Islam and Politics.* "Islamic politics" have continued to influence events in the Middle East and the West. Islamic organizations and political activists from Morocco and Tunisia to Indonesia and the Southern Philippines remain a potent force for political and social change. On the one hand, moderate Islamic organizations have continued to grow and to influence many national elections. During the past few years Muslim Brotherhood candidates have successfully run for political office in Egypt, the Sudan, and Jordan while other Islamic organizations have had mixed results in Kuwait, Pakistan, and Malaysia. In the Sudan and Malaysia, leaders of Islamic organizations moved from members of the opposition to cabinet-level positions in government. Dr. Hassan Turabi of the Sudan's Muslim Brotherhood served first as Attorney General and subsequently Presidential Adviser on Foreign Affairs. Malaysia's Anwar Ibrahim, leader of the Muslim Youth Movement of Malaysia, has served as Minister of Youth and Culture, Minister of Agriculture, and most recently in the important role of Minister of Education. On the other hand, radical extremists in Lebanon, Kuwait, Bahrain, and Egypt have challenged incumbent governments, often engaging in kidnapping, highjacking, suicide bombings, and other forms of violence.

Among the more significant areas of Islamic political activity during the 1980s, not covered previously in this volume, have been the Sudan and Lebanon. In response to events which have occurred since the first publication of this volume, this revision will update major developments in several of those countries emphasized in the

v

first edition of *Islam and Politics* and extend its coverage to the Sudan and Lebanon.

Holden, Massachusetts   JLE
February 1987

Contents

For
Malcolm H. Kerr
(1931–84)
and
Jean Esposito

Foreword

$\mathscr{I}$N FEBRUARY 1979, the Islamic storm broke with full fury. It had long been brewing; now its vortex was Iran. There, the Ayatollah Khomeini, after years of exile, returned to the tumultuous acclaim of a million or more Shia Muslim followers. With his return, the Iranian Islamic Republic was born and the rule of the *Faqih*, or jurisconsult, an innovation even in Islamic political theory, was inaugurated. In short order, the Iranian polity, which had undergone forced modernization under the Shah, was theocratically restructured into what some have scoffingly dubbed a *mullacracy*. American and Soviet interests alike were challenged by a politico-religious phenomenon which both superpowers, each for different reasons, had cavalierly dismissed as incompatible with the wave of the future. Not only Iran, but the greater Middle East, felt the resultant shock waves, as national leaders in the states of the area found it prudent to propitiate increasingly assertive Islamic constituents.

The past five years have continued to witness the rippling effects of what has generically come to be termed "Islamic resurgence." In the West, confusion over the meaning of this phenomenon was compounded by ethnocentricity, prejudice, and, interestingly enough, the limitations of our modern political science technical lexicon to describe, accurately and nuancially, the dynamics of what was taking place in another cultural setting. Developments tended to be construed in Western rather than Islamic terms, often with resultant conceptual skewing.

By the end of 1979, lay elements of the conglomerate political entourage that had triumphantly returned with Khomeini had been out-maneuvered by assertive *mullahs*, who were patently more agile in manipulating the levers of Iranian popular feeling. The American embassy in Tehran had been overrun by Islamic "students," and some fifty American diplomats taken hostage in an action for which precedent would be hard to find. Washington, viewed as the most prominent purveyor of Westernization, had been excoriated by the grim-visaged leader of Iran as the "great satan." The Soviet Union, which had hoped to benefit from United States discomfiture in Iran, was to its chagrin castigated by Khomeini as a close second in the hierarchy of international peddlers of evil.

In November of that same year, the *Masjid al-Haram* in Mecca, the most sacred shrine of Islam, was seized by religious fundamentalists in an action reminiscent of the tenth-century Carmathian despoiation of that city. Only with difficulty could Saudi Arabian military forces oust the insurgents, who decried their government's policies as un-Islamic and excessively pro-Western—meaning, in the convoluted semantics of resurgent Islam, American-dominated. In quick succession, American embassies in Islamabad and Tripoli, almost 3,000 miles apart, were attacked by Muslim mobs inflamed by Khomeini charges of United States collusion in the attack on the Mecca shrine. Whether these attacks were also consciously instigated by government authorities to legitimate the role of leaders, as in Libya, or represented spontaneous demonstrations of public frustration, as in Pakistan, was essentially irrelevant.

The model of Islam's success, in wresting control of Iran, encouraged Muslims elsewhere to re-assert themselves in militant fashion. In doing so, they placed at the apex of their Islamic sense of outrage the perceived pervasive American presence. Two years later, in September 1981, President Mohammed Anwar al-Sadat of Egypt, whose close friendship with the United States outweighed in fundamentalist eyes his devotion to his Islamic faith and who had signed a peace treaty with "despised" Israel, was assassinated by uniformed Muslim fanatics.

Primary responsibility for the growing Muslim challenges to Western influence has often been attributed to the Iranian Islamic Republic's "revolution for export" concept. In fact, the link is considerably more complex than such a mono-causal explanation suggests. For centuries, Muslims everywhere have been afflicted by a deep sense of inferiority. Their once great power and civilization had over the centuries withered into relative impotence. Western political and economic intrusions into the domain of Islam had steadily eroded traditional spiritual and family values, raising the specter of ultimate cultural evanescence. True, there also existed a widespread belief that the *ulama*, the religious guardians of Islam, had over the centuries defaulted on their leadership role in the Islamic community, were often corrupt and shared blame for the low estate into which Islamic society had fallen. This, too, would have to be redressed, but the more immediate problem was Western neo-imperialism, real or imagined.

Few Muslims do not covet a better quality of life for themselves and their children. But could this not be achieved, many asked with increasing resonance, through means other than blind emulation of Western norms? That question has been fundamental to Muslim attempts at reform throughout the past two centuries. Some prominent thinkers among them have insisted that Islam, conceived as it was in the seventh century, lacks the adaptive capacity to meet the requirements of a modern age: others indignantly reject any such contention and assert in equally forceful fashion that Islam can modernize in its own way without compromising its spiritual values. For now, the latter school seems in the ascendency as leaders of Muslim states everywhere give increased status to the *Shariah* as a prime source of national legislation and, as a corollary, ban perceived symbols of Western depravity, such as alcohol.

Superficially, there appears to be a similarity of behavior in those states where smoldering Islamic discontent has erupted into open rebellion or demonstrations or threatens to do so. In fact, closer scrutiny indicates that below any surface mutuality of objectives, significant differences among Muslims persist. These are rooted in Islamic sectarianism, which even their newly regained pride cannot entirely assuage. Thus, for example, the *Salifiyyah* insurgents who seized the Great Mosque of Mecca, almost concurrently with the seizure of American diplomatic hostages in Iran, included in their litany of criticisms of the Saudi Arabian government alleged coddling of the Kingdom's Shia minority. Paradoxically, the charge came at almost same time that the Iranian Islamic Republic's Arab language broadcasts flayed Riyadh for allegedly discriminating against that same Shia minority. If further instance is needed, the Shia component of Lebanese society, now a plurality over other confessional and sectarian components in that benighted country, openly disdains the views of long-time Lebanese Sunni politicians. The Islamic *ummah*, or community, though the fastest-growing religious grouping in the world today, largely through effective, worldwide missionary activities, is in perpetual ferment not only against perceived invidious Western influences, but also because of such deep-seated organic schisms within it.

Global reactions to Islamic resurgence have been erratic and uncertain, and nowhere more so than in the United States. Occurrences in Iran and elsewhere in the Middle East, in the name of Islam, run counter to at least three ingrained American political beliefs:

First, the division between politics and religion, sacrosanct in our national ethos and one upon which most Americans have been politically weaned, has palpably been challenged. Americans tend to find it difficult to conceive of any amalgamation of politics and religion in twentieth-century political societies, even in the developing world.

Second, secular nationalism, that European import to the Middle East, which Americans sometimes decry as jingoistic and conducive to conflict, but which they comprehend and even exercise in their own ways, was the appropriate stage through which developing nations must pass on the road to nationhood. Surely, then, whatever change might have taken place in the form of government in Iran, indigenous nationalism must still play a pre-eminent role in that country, even if now garbed in Islamic trappings. I recall vividly a meeting of State Department "experts" on the Middle East, convened shortly after the Khomeini takeover, at which several senior specialists, knowledgeable of Iran, categorically insisted that nationalism remained the dominant political force in that country and that the prevailing religious fervor was but a passing fancy! They may still prove to be right, but—as the protracted Iraq-Iran war has shown—Shiism and residual Iranian nationalism seem to be interacting to develop a dialectic of their own.

Third, American modernization buffs, both in government and academia, had for years argued that religion, and especially Islam, was a barrier to socioeconomic progress. In recognition of this, they had persuaded themselves, most modernizing Muslim governments and peoples saw Islam as a vestigial, non-regulatory force, applicable at most to personal status matters. Many reputable scholars, including some from the Middle East, who should have known better, derided Islam as irrelevant to nation-building and chose to ignore it in modeling development plans for Middle East states. Now, unexpectedly, their blithe dismissal of religion as an element to be reckoned with had been thrown into a cocked hat. Had they been recklessly pushing the cause of modernization, based on Western models, to a point where they imperiled political stability in

Islamic countries by decanting economic and political counsel that disregarded Muslim sensibilities? The Iranian case seemed to suggest that they had. By underrating the sociopolitical force of Islam and overrating the views of secularists and Islamic modernists, they had thrust themselves, unwittingly perhaps but partisanly, into the omnipresent modernist versus revivalist controversy that has long sundered Islamic society.

With such flawed preconceptions characterizing the initial American analyses of the Islamic resurgence phenomenon, small wonder that its significance and durability should have been misunderstood. While many academics and government officials had for a number of years predicted the downfall of the Shah, few—very few, indeed—had predicted a clerical takeover of that country. Paradoxically, even as manyAmericans thought they perceived a monolithic quality in resurgent Islam, wherever it was reasserting itself, they also now slowly became aware of significant doctrinal differences between Sunni and Shia Islam. In fact, in the wake of the Khomeini takeover, and as part of the re-examination of the Islamic phenomenon, a torrent of academic studies of Shia Islam and the Islamic factor in the Middle East burst forth upon us. Some were valuable contributions to our knowledge of the subject; many were sensationally vapid and simply written to capitalize on the latest fad. The media, with a few notable exceptions, was generally superficial in its reportage on Islamic resurgence and added to public confusion.

Former President Jimmy Carter, in his efforts to obtain the release of the American diplomatic hostages in Iran, had the good sense to seek counsel not only from government specialists, but also from leading academic experts on Islam. From them, he learned that a considerable corpus of *Shariah,* or Islamic law, exists, dealing with the treatment of diplomats, and that this corpus is more extensive in Shia than in Sunni Islam. This prompted the thought that if an approach could be made to Khomeini by one or more widely known Muslim religious savants, pointing out the illegality of his actions in terms of the *Shariah,* it might induce the Iranian leader to release them. Regrettably, no Muslim religious leader with the stature to be received by Khomeini or the courage to undertake so delicate mission in what would patently have been in behalf of the United States could be found. Hence, the idea was never put to the test, although abortive approaches were made through various lesser lights on the religious plane. Had such an approach materialized, it might well have failed, but it suggested the need for a new religio-political level of dialogue to augment conventional diplomatic exchanges.

Some have hypothesized that Islamic resurgence has historically been a cyclical occurrence. Periods of high Islamic activism have regularly been followed by periods in which Islam appeared to be a spent political force. There is some historical evidence to support this, but we still have a great deal to learn about the staying power of Islamic resurgence. We would be well advised to recognize more than we have in the past that Islam, whether militantly assertive or seemingly passive, is omnipresent and represents a force with which we will have to come to terms. To do so requires understanding of its motivating factors.

It is precisely in this context that Professor John L. Esposito's volume, *Islam and Politics*, is so welcome an addition to the literature on the subject. A distinguished scholar who has specialized in examining the interaction between religion and politics in the Middle East, he is eminently qualified to write on this complex subject. His latest volume lays out, lucidly and concisely, the origins and evolution of Islam, beginning in the seventh century, and its rapid diffusion from Morocco to China. He describes the subsequent modernist-revivalist controversies which have for years divided Muslim thinkers and caused sharp rifts among them in Egypt, Turkey, North Africa, Iran, Libya, the Indian subcontinent, and elsewhere. His vignettes on past and present Islamic leaders in these countries illumine their philosophies, purposes, and also their divergencies. Against this background, he assesses the role of Islam in the contemporary Middle East and sets forth the issues that Muslim leaders must face in today's world at home, in the broader Islamic community, and in an increasingly interdependent world from which they, too, cannot escape.

Notwithstanding the spate of recent literature on Islam, a comprehensive work placing it in clearer historical and contemporary perspective has still been needed. The task is difficult because of the breadth and complexity of the subject and its extensive geographic as well as intellectual scope. Professor Esposito's new volume admirably fills this gap. Scholarly, yet readable, it should prove invaluable to government practitioners, academics, and students alike.

Boston, Massachusetts   HERMANN FREDERICK EILTS
Summer 1984   *Distinguished University Professor*
                                          of International Relations
                             Director, Center for International Relations
                                                  Boston University

Preface

VENTS EMANATING FROM THE MIDDLE EAST during the early 1970s brought the West into an abrupt confrontation with the Arab World: 1973 witnessed both an Arab-Israeli War and in its wake an Arab oil boycott. The magnitude and gravity of this threat to the well-being of Western industrial states was felt not only at government and corporate levels but also at gas pumps and in homes. Rationing, skyrocketing fuel costs, economy cars, and energy conservation in the home and work place became new realities, vividly driving home the economic and geo-political significance of the Middle East. Yet Saudi Arabia and Iran, let alone Kuwait, Abu Dhabi, and Oman, remained remarkably unknown and obscure to most Westerners.

During the latter half of the 1970s, a series of events once more propelled the Islamic world into Western consciousness as the mass media chronicled political upheavals in Iran, Egypt, Saudi Arabia, Syria, Pakistan, and Afghanistan under such banners as "militant Islam" or "Islamic resurgence." Despite the diversity in geography and local politics, religion emerged as a common denominator in Muslim politics.

If the average citizen knew little about the Middle East, ignorance of the greater Islamic world, which extends from North Africa to Southeast Asia, was even more widespread. Moreover, most area specialists and readers seemed especially mystified by the visible Islamic character of contemporary events. The battle cry of revolutionaries or freedom fighters from Egypt to the Moro Islands of the Philippines was *Allahu Akbar!* (God is Most Great). Islamic ideology, symbols, language, and actors became employed both by opposition movements and incumbent governments to legitimate their activities. These events were especially puzzling because, although Muslims constitute one-seventh of the world's population, are a majority in some forty-three countries, and a significant minority in others, there was little popular awareness in the West of the most basic tenets of Islam and only minimal appreciation of the role of Islam in politics, law, and society.

Ignorance of Islamic politics has been further compounded by the problem of interpretation. What is one to make of competing and, at times, contradictory appeals to Islam? While Anwar Sadat invoked Islam and used the title "president of the believers," much of his opposition, including his assassins, belonged to Islamic movements that denounced him in the name of Islam. Many in the West who supported the Islamic "freedom fighters" of Afghanistan in their resistance to Soviet aggression viewed other Islamic revolutionaries such as those in Iran as Islamic "Marxists or fanatics."

The policies of self-styled Islamic governments have raised many questions about the nature of Islamic government, the role of the clergy in politics, and the place of Islamic law. In postrevolutionary Iran, the apparent early unity of Islamic forces soon disintegrated as the clergy-dominated Islamic Republican Party wrested power from Islamic moderates like Mehdi Bazargan and Abol Hasan Bani-Sadr. In Pakistan, although the commitment of the martial law regime of General Zia ul-Haq to establish a more Islamic system of government was initially welcomed by many Pakistanis, the process of Islamization—which has come to include the banning of political parties, the postponement of elections, and media censorship in the name of Islam—has angered many religious as well as secular factions.

The diversity of actors and events in contemporary Islamic politics has raised numerous questions, among them, "Whose Islam?" In other words, who is to interpret the role of Islam and its place in state and society—rulers such as Sadat, Khomeini, or Qaddafi, religious leaders, or Islamic organizations? And secondly, "What Islam?" How does one distinguish between genuine Islamic practice and the calculated manipulation or misguided use of religion in politics to achieve questionable political goals?

Answering these and other questions raised by contemporary Muslim politics requires an appreciation of the relationship of religion to politics in Islam: both Islam's ideal and actual historical practice.

Only then can one gain a proper perspective regarding the roots and appeal of Islamic revivalism as well as the problems and issues which accompany contemporary Islamic politics.

This volume will attempt to provide the historical background and the context in which to understand Islamic politics today, describe the roles of Islam in modern Muslim politics, and analyze the major obstacles and issues which attend the establishment of Islamically oriented states and societies.

Chapter 1, "Religion, Politics, and Society," reviews the relationship of Islam to politics as reflected in early Islamic history. It is in Islam's past that Muslims find the sources of their faith and the basis for contemporary formulations of an Islamic ideology for state and society.

Chapter 2, "Revival and Reform," analyzes the formative period of modern Islamic revival and reform. The reaction of premodern revivalist movements to the breakdown of medieval Muslim empires and the socio-moral decline of the Islamic community and the responses of Islamic modernist movements to European imperialism and modernization are reviewed for both provide modern Muslim politics with an ideological legacy and an example of reformist activism.

Chapter 3, "Nationalism," investigates the role of Islam in anti-colonial, independence movements and its place in the development of nationalist ideologies in North Africa, the Arab East, Iran, and the Indian subcontinent.

Chapter 4, "The Modern State," explores the diverse paths followed by newly independent Muslim states in nation building. Five case studies (Turkey, Saudi Arabia, Pakistan, Egypt, and Iran) are used to exemplify the spectrum of modern Muslim political developments which range from secular to self-styled Islamic states. This is followed by an analysis of two Islamic organizations, the Muslim Brotherhood and the Jamaat-i-Islami, which have had and are continuing to have major influences on contemporary Islamic political activists and movements.

Chapter 5, "Contemporary Politics," discusses the sources and manifestations of the contemporary Islamic resurgence through an examination of the use of Islam by both incumbent governments and opposition movements in Libya, Pakistan, Iran, and Egypt.

Chapter 6, "Issues and Prospects," analyzes the underlying forces, questions, and issues which attend contemporary attempts to establish modern Islamic states and societies.

The geographic expanse of Islam, with its diversity of languages and political experiences, presents a complexity sometimes overlooked when Islam is simply reduced to its revelation and law. Analysis of contemporary events requires a grasp not only of the present political situation but also of the Islamic ideological framework and history (both real and ideal) which serve as a source of identity, inspiration, guidance, and legitimation for many Muslims today. I have deliberately restricted myself to the Middle East, selecting what I hope are a spectrum of positions. I had been tempted to cast my net more broadly to include the experiences of Southeast Asia and the Soviet Union. However, they are sufficiently different so that to do them justice would have required a volume twice this size.

There are many people from whom I have learned in the classroom, from their writings, and through conversation. In particular, I am indebted to Muslim friends and colleagues whose friendship, guidance, and example have been extended as freely as their hospitality. In addition I am particularly grateful to Yvonne Y. Haddad, John O. Voll, James P. Piscatori, and Laraine Carter for reading and commenting on the manuscript.

The preparation of any manuscript is a tedious process not only for the author but for his secretary. While I have the satisfaction of a finished product, Mary Cerasuolo must settle for my gratitude for a superb job—typing, proofreading, xeroxing. She suffered many of the stages of rewriting and pressures of a production schedule with a patient professionalism that characterizes all of her work. Lisa Ropple and Jennifer Carey cheerfully assisted in a variety of tasks. Finally, and most importantly, my wife Jean, as always, has been there.

Worcester, Massachusetts
Spring 1984   JLE

Islam and Politics

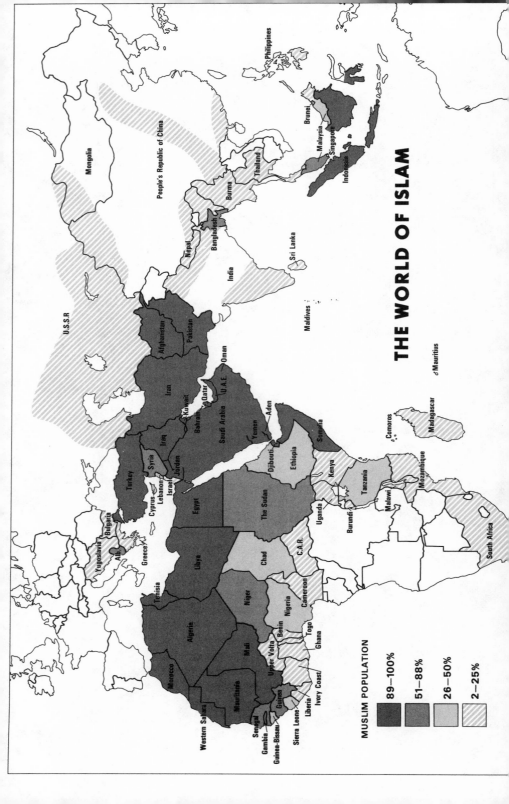

THE WORLD OF ISLAM

MUSLIM POPULATION

- 89–100%
- 51–88%
- 26–50%
- 2–25%

1

Religion, Politics, and Society

NORMATIVE IDEAL AND HISTORICAL REALITY

URING THE SEVENTH CENTURY there arose in Central Arabia (modern-day Saudi Arabia) a movement that was to sweep across the world and become the second largest of the world's religions—Islam, a religion which today has some 900 million adherents. Islam was not simply a spiritual community. Rather, it also became a state/empire. Islam developed as a religio-political movement in which religion was integral to state and society. Muslim belief that Islam embraces faith and politics is rooted in its divinely revealed book, the *Quran*, and the example *(Sunnah)* of its founder/prophet, Muhammad, and thus has been reflected in Islamic doctrine, history, and politics.

Allahu Akbar! (God is Most Great). This declaration precedes the muezzin's call to prayer five times daily; it is the traditional Islamic battle cry. *Allahu Akbar!* summarizes the centrality of God and the wedding of personal religious conviction and political life in Islam. The source and foundation of all life is Allah (God)—the One and All Powerful, Creator and Sustainer, Master of the Universe, the Merciful and Compassionate, but also the Just Judge who will reward and punish all His creatures on the Last Day. The confession of faith testifies: "There is no God but God and Muhammad is His Prophet." Any understanding of Islamic belief and practice must begin with God, who governs and intervenes in history, and with His Prophet Muhammad.

Muslims believe that throughout history, God sent Messen-

1

ger-Prophets to warn and guide humankind: Adam, Noah, Abraham, Moses, and Jesus (*Quran* 3:40–43, 2:209, 7:155–58). "We believe in God, and the revelation given to us, and to Abraham, Ismail, Isaac, Jacob, and the tribes, and that which Moses and Jesus received and [all] the Prophets were given. We make no distinction between any of them. And to God we submit ourselves" (*Quran* 2:136).

Muslims believe, however, that God's revelations, as set down in the Jewish *Torah* and the Christian Gospels, were tampered with or distorted. In His mercy, God sent Muhammad as the final Messenger, "the last seal of the prophets" (*Quran* 33:40), and gave him the *Quran*, the revelation of God's Will in its final and complete form. "It is He who sent down to you the Book with the truth, confirming what went before it; and He sent down the Torah and the Injil [Gospel] before that as a guidance to the people" (*Quran* 3:3). In the *Quran*, the transcendent God reveals his divine will for all creation. The Book and the Prophet provide the fundamental sources for the Straight Path (Shariah, or Islamic Law) of Muslim life. The Prophet Muhammad is not only the messenger who received and proclaimed God's revelation, but also the "noble paradigm," the model or exemplar of Muslim life (*Quran* 33:21). Man's vocation, then, is to surrender (*islam*), to submit and realize or carry out God's will. God has given all of creation as a trust to mankind (*Quran* 33:72, 31:20–29). Man, as bearer of this trust, is God's representative or vicegerent (*Quran* 2:30, 6:165) whose divinely mandated vocation is to be God's instrument in establishing and spreading an Islamic order, God's rule on earth.

The Islamic imperative is both personal and societal, individual and corporate. The Muslim community (*ummah*) is to be the principal vehicle for the realization of God's will. The *Quran*, the example of the Prophet, and the early Muslim community give eloquent and vivid testimony to this fact. "You are the best community ever brought forth for mankind, enjoining what is good and forbidding evil" (*Quran* 3:110).

Tribal solidarity in pre-Islamic Arabian society had represented the basic social bond. However, Islam replaced this with a community whose membership was based upon a common faith rather than male blood ties; religious rather than tribal affiliation became the basis of Islamic society. All members of the *ummah* were to be equal before God. The duties and obligations of Muslim life, as well as their rewards or punishments, fall upon men and women alike. "Whoever does a righteous deed, whether man or woman, and has Faith, we will give him (her) a good life; and we shall reward them according to the best of their actions" (16:97). "The believers, men and women, are guardians of one another; they enjoin good and forbid evil, perform the prayer, give alms, and obey God and His Prophet" (9:71).

The divine mandate of the *Quran* took on form and substance in Medina under the guidance and direction of God's messenger, the Prophet Muhammad.

Muhammad and the Muslim Community

Born in 570 but orphaned at a young age Muhammad belonged to the Hashemite clan, a respected but poor branch of the Quraysh tribe which governed the city of Mecca. Mecca was the center of commercial trade and religious pilgrimage in Central Arabia. It contained a major religious shrine with its sanctuary, Kaba, a cube-shaped structure that housed idols of the various tribal gods and goddesses of Central Arabia. Most importantly, the shrine was the object of an annual pilgrimage and, therefore, a major source of Meccan prestige and revenue.

At twenty-five, Muhammad married his first wife Khadijah, a wealthy widow and caravan owner fifteen years his senior. Combining industriousness with a reputation for trustworthiness, he became a successful, respected member of Meccan society. However, his life changed dramatically in 610 when at the age of forty on the "Night of Power and Excellence" (*Quran* 97), he received the first in a series of divine revelations which were to extend over a period of twenty-two years and which were preserved in the *Quran*. In the tradition of biblical prophets, Muhammad was a warner as well as the bearer of good tidings (*Quran* 33:44–45).

He denounced the ungodliness of his society and announced God's prescriptions for its ills. Meccan political and religious elites reacted strongly to this claimant to prophetic authority. His message was an indictment of much that they represented. It condemned polytheism and professed an uncompromising monotheism; denounced their unbridled materialism and avarice and proclaimed a sweeping program of social reform, affecting business contracts and practices, the conduct of war, and the guidelines for family relations. The prophetic call for a community of believers, the divine appointment of Muhammad as its leader, and the claim that all human activity was accountable not to a tribe's customary laws or to blind vengeance but to an overriding divine law challenged the very foundation of Abrabian society. It struck at the heart of the power and authority of Meccan political and religious elites.

Not surprisingly, Muhammad and his early converts were subjected to ridicule and rejection in Mecca. Thus, when a delegation from Yathrib invited Muhammad in 622 to emigrate (*hijra*) to their city, he accepted. The city had been torn by long-standing intertribal feuds, and Muhammad came as an arbiter or chief judge. He consolidated his political power and established a state informed by his prophetic message. Yathrib was renamed Medina (*madinat al-nabi*, City of the Prophet). The importance of the *ummah* in Islam and the significance of its establishment as a state were underscored by the fact that 622 (the beginning of the Islamic community/state at Medina) and not 610 (the year of God's first revelation to Muhammad) was reckoned as the first year of the Islamic calendar.

In the new community Muhammad was the political as well as the religious leader. He was prophet, head of state, commander of the army, chief judge, and lawgiver. His authority and its acceptance were based upon his prophetic calling and Quranic mandate: "Obey God and the Prophet" (3:32). "Those who swear allegiance/convenant to you [Muhammad], convenant with God" (48:10). "Whoever obeys the Prophet, obeys God" (4:80). "It is not fitting for any believer, man or woman, to do as he pleases, when the matter has been decided by God and His Prophet" (33:36). Moreover, the Prophet was the model upon which Muslims were to pattern their lives: "You have a good model in God's Prophet" (33:21). Throughout the years, Muhammad's exemplary character and conduct, his continued reception of divine revelations, and his effectiveness and success reinforced his position of leadership.

Under Muhammad's guidance, Islam in Medina crystallized as both a faith and a sociopolitical system. From 622 to 632, through military action and astute diplomatic initiatives, the Muslim community expanded and established its hegemony over Central Arabia. Mecca was subdued and the tribes of Arabia were united into a single polity, an Arab commonwealth with a common ideology, centralized authority, and law. However, this unity should not be overestimated. The old tribal system of loyalties and values was not simply replaced but rather reformed and modified, Islamized. For the first time an effective means had been found to unite and inspire Arabia's tribes so

that a state emerged which could challenge the neighboring established empires of Byzantium and Persia and change the political and
social life of the Middle East.

THE CALIPHATE PERIOD

The death of Muhammad in 632 plunged the community into two
successive political crises involving political authority: the issue of
succession and the problem of political fragmentation or civil war.
    The Caliphate Period (632–1258) which followed unfolded in
three phases: the Rightly Guided Caliphs (632–661), the Umayyad
dynasty (661–750), and the Abbasid caliphate (750–1258). The
Caliphate Period is particularly important both because it is the locus
for the formation and development of Islamic ideology and institutions and because it is the reference point for Muslim self-
understanding. The rule of the first four caliphs of Islam is significant
not only for what they actually did but also for the period in which
they lived, a time to which both conservative and modernist Islamic
activists return for guidance in their attempts to delineate the Islamic
character of modern states.

The Rightly Guided Caliphs

The Caliphate Period began in 632 when, as the majority of
Muslims believe, Muhammad died without designating his replacement or establishing a system for the selection of his successor. After
a brief, tense period of indecision, the leading companions of the
Prophet (and thus leaders of the community) selected one of their
own—Abu Bakr (the father of Muhammad's youngest wife Aishah)
as their leader. He had been a very close friend and adviser of the
Prophet. One of the earliest converts to Islam, Abu Bakr was a man
respected for his piety and political sagacity. Muhammad had appointed him to lead the Friday communal prayer during his absence.
Abu Bakr became the first caliph of Islam, taking the title successor or
caliph of the Prophet of God. As caliph, he was the political and
military leader of the community. Although not a prophet, he did

enjoy a certain religious prestige as head of the community. This was symbolized by the caliph's leading the Friday congregational prayer and the mention of his name in the prayer.

Having resolved the question of political leadership and succession, Abu Bakr and the Muslim community turned to the consolidation of Arabia. Muhammad's death had precipitated a series of Arab tribal rebellions. For many tribal chiefs, their political pact with Medina ceased with Muhammad's death. Tribalism, the long-standing source of political and social identity, challenged the life and unity of the new Islamic state. In a series of battles which later Muslim historians would call the *riddah* (apostasy or renunciation of Islam) wars, Abu Bakr moved swiftly. Relying on Khalid ibn al-Walid, a brilliant general whom Muhammad had dubbed "The Sword of Allah," he crushed the tribal revolt, consolidated Muslim rule over the entire Arabian Peninsula and thus preserved the unity and solidarity of the Islamic community/state.

The first four caliphs were all companions of the Prophet: Abu Bakr (632–634), Umar (634–644), Uthman (644–656), and Ali (656–661). While the crisis of political succession after Muhammad's death had been averted through the hasty selection of Abu Bakr, the Caliph Umar sought to avoid a similar problem. On his deathbed Umar appointed an "election committee" to select his successor. After due consultation, Uthman ibn Affan, from the Umayyad, a leading Meccan family, was elected and the traditional sign of allegiance (the clasp of hand which symbolized the sealing of a pact or contract) was given. A pattern was established of selecting the caliph from the Quraysh, the Prophet's tribe, through a process characterized by consultation and an oath of allegiance.

It was not long, however, before tribal factionalism and the threat of rebellion resurfaced in the community. Uthman's family had been among Muhammad's strongest foes before they converted to Islam. Many of the Medinan elites—companions of the Prophet who were early Meccan emigrants and early Medinese converts—resented Uthman's accession to power and the increased prominence and wealth of his family members. Accusations that the caliph was weak and guilty of nepotism fueled political intrigue. In 656 Uthman was murdered by a group of Muslim mutineers from Egypt. Uthman's assassination was the first in a series of Muslim rebellions and religious fratricides which were to plague Islam's political development. The caliph's assassination by fellow Muslims was to be shortly followed by another Islamic problem of equal seriousness—Muslim civil war.

Ali, a cousin and son-in-law of the Prophet, succeeded Uthman as the fourth caliph. Muhammad had been raised with Ali in the household of Ali's father, Abi Talib. Ali was devoted to Muhammad, and many of his followers believe he was the first convert. He married the Prophet's only surviving child, Fatima, his daughter by Khadijah. They had two children: Hasan and Husayn. Many of Ali's supporters, believing that political succession belonged to the Prophet's family, had viewed Ali as the legitimate successor of Muhammad. They had been frustrated by the election of the first three caliphs whom they viewed as interlopers. However, their satisfaction and vindication were short-lived, for throughout Ali's brief rule, his political authority was challenged by two opposition movements: the first a coalition led by the Prophet's wife, Aishah, and the second by the army of Muawiyah, the governor of Syria and a cousin of the caliph Uthman. Ali's failure to find and prosecute Uthman's assassins became the pretext for both revolts. In the first, Ali crushed a rebellious army led by a triumvirate including the Prophet's young wife, Aishah, whom Ali had once accused of infidelity. The "Battle of the Camel" (656), so named because fighting took place around the camel upon which Aishah was mounted, marked the first time a caliph had led his army against another Muslim army.

Of more long-range significance was Muawiyah's challenge to Ali's caliphate. Governor of Syria with a strong, standing army, Muawiyah had called for vengeance for his cousin Uthman's murder and had refused to accept Ali's appointment of another general to replace Muawiyah as governor of Syria. In 657 at Siffin (Syria), Ali led an army against his rebellious governor. When it looked as though Ali's forces would win the day, Muawiyah's men, raising *Qurans* on the tips of their spears, called for peaceful arbitration according to the *Quran*, crying out "Let God decide."[1]

The arbitration that then took place proved inconclusive militarily but had two important political results. A group of Ali's supporters, the Kharijites ("seceders"), who were disgusted with Ali's vacillation, broke with him. For the Kharijites, Muawiyah had committed a grave sin by challenging Ali's authority. Anyone who did so was no longer a Muslim and therefore the lawful object of *jihad* (holy war), given Muslim's absolute duty to do good and prevent evil.

In acquiescing to arbitration and not crushing Muawiyah, Ali had failed to perform his Islamic duty to subdue the rebels. The Kharijites were the first sect in Islam to express an uncompromising, egalitarian sociopolitical policy, namely, that leadership of the Islamic community belonged to the most observant of Muslims. Ali himself was no longer worthy of leadership since he had failed to prove himself a true believer. The Alids (followers of Ali), on the other hand, felt thwarted by Muawiyah's ruse. The rebel, Muawiyah, had not been subdued. Moreover, after Muawiyah left Siffin, he continued to govern Syria, extending his rule to Egypt. In 661, with Ali's assassination by a Kharijite, Muawiyah laid successful claim to the caliphate and established his capital in Damascus. The "golden age" of Muhammad and the Rightly Guided Caliphs of Medina came to an end.

In the Caliphate Period the pattern for the organization and administration of the Islamic state had been initiated. The model for governance had followed, in large part, the example and practice of Muhammad. The caliph exercised direct political, military, judicial, and fiscal control of the Muslim community. He was selected through a process of consultation, nomination, and election. Administratively, conquered territories were divided into provinces. In general, the Arabs did not occupy conquered cities but established their own military garrison towns such as Basra and Kufa in Iraq and Fustat (Cairo) in Egypt. From these towns, conquered territories were governed and future expeditions were launched. They were administered by a governor, usually the military commander, and centered on its mosque which served as the religious and public center of the towns.[2] An agent of the caliph, a revenue officer, oversaw the collection of taxes and other administrative activities. Revenue for the state came from the captured lands and taxes. The Islamic system of taxation took several forms: the tithe or wealth tax (zakat) and the tithe on land (ushr) paid by Muslims; the poll tax (jizya) and tribute (kharaj) later a general land tax paid by non-Muslims. All revenue was owned, collected, and administered by the state. The distribution of revenue was managed by the registry at Medina through a system of payments and pensions.

The internal civil and religious administration of conquered territories remained in the hands of local officials. Muslim society was divided into four major social classes. The elites of society were the Arab Muslims, with special status given to the companions of the Prophet because of their early support and role in establishing the ummah. Next came the non-Arab converts (mawali) to Islam. Although theoretically, all Muslims were equal before God, in fact, practice varied. The dhimmi, non-Muslim "People of the Book," were Jews and Christians who possessed a revealed scripture. In exchange for payment of the poll tax, these "protected" peoples were permitted to worship and be governed by their own religious laws and leaders and entitled to protection from outside aggression by the Muslim army. Finally, there were the slaves. Slavery had long existed among the Arabs. Although the *Quran* commanded the just and humane treatment of slaves (4:40, 16:73) and regarded their emancipation as a meritorious act, the system of slavery was adopted in modified form. Only captives in battle could be taken as slaves. Neither Muslims nor Jews and Christians could be enslaved in early Islam.

In the eyes of believers, the age of Muhammad and the Righteous Caliphs is the normative, exemplary period of Muslim life for a variety of reasons. It is viewed as the time when God sent down His final and complete revelation for humankind and his last prophet, Muhammad. Second, the Islamic community/state was created, bonded by a common religious identity and purpose. Third, the sources of Islamic law, the *Quran* and the inspired leadership of Muhammad, which provided the basic guidance for the community, originated at this time. Fourth, the importance of Muhammad's exemplary behavior *(Sunnah)* and the early practice of the community was reflected in the creation and proliferation of *hadith* (traditions) literature. These narrative stories reflect the extent to which the Prophet, his family, and companions served as models for Muslim life. Fifth, it is this period of the early companions or *salaf* ("ancestors or elders") which serves as the reference point for all Islamic revival and reform, whether traditionalist or modernist. Finally, the time of the Prophet and the early righteous caliphs was not only one of divine guidance but also one of validation. For it was here that Muslims believe the revealed message and Prophetic claims were realized and divinely validated in the full light of history by the success and power which resulted from the near miraculous victories and geographic expansion of Islam.

The Umayyad Dynasty

Muawiyah (661–80) assumed the caliphate and ushered in the Umayyad era (661–750): imperial, dynastic, dominated by an Arab military aristocracy. His move of Islam's capital from Medina to Damascus symbolized the new imperial age with its permanent shift from the Arabian heartland of Medina (religious and political center) to an established, cosmopolitan city. From this center, the Umayyads continued the expansion of Islamic rule and developed a strong centralized government, an Arab empire. Within the amazingly brief period of a hundred years, the early Islamic state had become an empire whose boundaries extended from Spain across North Africa and the Middle East to the borders of China. It was an empire greater than Rome at its zenith.

Islam provided a unity of purpose and central authority enabling Arabian tribes to achieve new levels of political organization and motivation. Driven by religious zeal and attracted by opportunities for plunder and booty, during the hundred-year period following the death of Muhammad in 632, Muslim armies overran the Byzantine and Sasanid (Persian) Empires, which were already weakened by constant warfare and internal strife. Success in this struggle (*jihad*) to spread God's rule brought religious as well as political and economic rewards. To die in battle was not to fail but, rather, to be counted among the martyrs and thus to immediately enter paradise. The conquests "were truly an *Islamic* movement. For it was Islam—the set of religious beliefs preached by Muhammad, with its social and political ramifications—that ultimately sparked the whole integration process and hence was the ultimate cause of the conquests' success."[3]

Given common misconceptions regarding *jihad*, some clarification is necessary. If Westerners are too quick to see Islam as a religion of holy war, modern Muslim apologists have tended to present *jihad* in early Islam as simply defensive in nature. In its most general sense and application in Muslim life, *jihad* refers to the vocation of Mulims to strive or struggle to realize God's will, to lead a virtuous life. This includes the Muslims' universal mission and obligation to spread God's will and rule. As Muslim armies advanced out of Arabia and penetrated new areas, the peoples they encountered were offered three choices: (1) conversion, that is, to become a member of the Muslim community with its rights and duties; (2) acceptance of Muslim rule as "protected" people; and, if neither the first nor second options were accepted, (3) battle or the sword. The expansion of Islam resulted not only from the conquest of those who resisted Muslim rule but also from those who accepted the first two peaceful options. Indeed, in later centuries, the effective spread of Islam would be due to the peaceful activities of Muslim traders and Sufi (mystic) missionaries who won converts by their example and preaching. The Muslim obligation to spread God's righteous rule or governance of the Shariah, Islamic law, came to be formulated during

Abbasid times (752–1258) in a division of the world into Islamic territory (*dar al-Islam*, land of Islam) and non-Islamic (*dar al-harb*, land of warfare).

The divisiveness of the first civil war between the caliph Ali and his general, Muawiyah, that led to the secession of the Kharijites and alienation of Ali's supporters complicated Umayyad attempts to establish effective governance. During the reign of Muawiyah's son and successor, Yazid, a second round of civil wars broke out. One of these, the revolt of Ali's son, Husayn, would shape and form the world view of Shii Islam and solidify the major division of Islam into Sunni and Shii. The repercussions of this initially minor rebellion would be magnified and felt in later Islamic history and its political potential realized in contemporary Iran in the twentieth century.

When the Umayyad caliph, Yazid, came to power in 680, Husayn, who was living in Medina, refused to recognize his legitimacy and was persuaded to lead a rebellion in Kufah. However, Husayn did not receive the expected popular support, and at Karbala, Husayn and his small army were surrounded and vanquished by an Umayyad army. The slaughter and "martyrdom" of the Alid forces gave rise to a movement of political protest centered on the martyred family of the Prophet, Ali and Husayn. The memory of Karbala provided the religio-political paradigm for Shii Islam. For Shii the injustice that had denied Ali, the cousin and son-in-law of the Prophet, his rightful succession to Muhammad had occurred again. They saw the forces of evil and injustice once more thwart the rightful rule of the Prophet's family. This outlook provided Shii Islam with its major theme—the battle of the forces of good (Shii) against those of evil (anti-Shii); its goal—the establishment of righteous rule and social justice; its model for political action—protest and martyrdom in God's way; and its model of political leadership—the Imam.

A fundamental political and legal difference between Sunni and Shii Muslims is the Shii doctrine of the imamate vs. the Sunni caliphate. In Sunni Islam the caliph is the selected/elected successor of the Prophet. He succeeded to political and military leadership of the community but had only limited religious status. For the Shii, in contrast, leadership is vested in the Imam (leader) who must be a direct descendant of the Prophet Muhammad and Ali, the first Imam. Moreover, he is the divinely inspired religio-political leader and serves both as the community's political leader and the final authoritative interpreter of God's Will, Islamic law.

As a result of its political experiences, Shii Islam also differed from Sunni Islam in its perception of the meaning of history. For Sunni historians, success and power were the signs of a faithful community and validation of Muslim belief and claims. For the Shii, history was the theater for the struggle of a righteous remnant in protest and opposition against the forces of evil (Satan) to realize its messianic hope and promise—the establishment of the righteous rule of the Imam. Yet the reign and just social order of the Imam was to remain a frustrated hope and expectation for centuries as the Islamic community developed under the guidance and rule of Sunni caliphs.

It was the Umayyads, and later the early Abbasids, who introduced and developed many of the distinctive institutions of centralized government associated with the Islamic caliphate. The basis of Umayyad unity and stability was the establishment of an Arab monarchy and reliance upon an Arab warrior aristocracy. Contrary to the practice of Muhammad and the early caliphs, legitimate succession was made hereditary and was restricted to the Umayyad house. This innovation was the pretext for later Islamic historians to condemn Umayyad rule as kingship and therefore un-Islamic. However, a form of hereditary succession continued throughout the caliphal period even under the professedly more Islamic, Abbasid caliphate.

Umayyad society, despite its Islamic character, was based upon the creation and perpetuation of an Arab aristocracy which constituted a hereditary social caste.[4] The Arabs were the heart of the Umayyad's powerful military machine, which was the source of its power and security, and the chief recipients of the fabulous wealth which poured into the empire as the Umayyads completed the conquest of the Sasanid and Byzantine empires. Arab Muslims enjoyed special tax privileges. They were exempted from the more substantial taxes levied on the non-Arab Muslims and non-Muslims and only required to pay the wealth tax and the tithe on land. This preferential system was to contribute to non-Arab Muslim discontent and the movement to overthrow Umayyad rule.

Greater unity and control were fostered through the development of a more centralized administration and the adoption of the administrative machinery (institutions and bureaucracy) and personnel of the more developed Byzantine and Sasanid empires. The caliph continued to function as the head of state, personally engaged in its supervision, and assisted by a bureaucracy composed of departments or ministries which oversaw the collection and management of taxes, lands, rents, payment of officials and the military, public works projects.[5] The progressive centralization and militarization of the state resulted in an increasingly autocratic and absolutist government supported and protected by an Arab aristocracy.

As with its government, law was an important area of increasing centralization, Arabization and Islamization, i.e., the process through which the Umayyads borrowed from existing foreign institutions and practices as well as adapting or adding to such practices. We can see this in particular in the creation of two judicial institutions: the market inspector and the judge/*Shariah* courts. The Byzantine system of government had included a market inspector. The Umayyads adapted this practice by expanding the office to include not only market inspection but also the Islamic duty of assuring that the religious/moral precepts of Islam were observed.[6] The market inspector, therefore, was also supervisor of public morals. His duties included checking for defective weights and measures, fraudulent business practices, and public observance of the fast during Ramadan.

The judge or *qadi* was one of the administrative officials introduced by the Umayyads. Originally, he was a representative/or legal secretary of the provincial governor, a member of his administration, charged with overseeing the implementation of government decrees and settling disputes. Often these tasks were carried out by government officials along with their other duties. This was the first step in the government's gaining greater control over the more *ad hoc* system of arbitration which had characterized Arab legal practice. By the end of the Umayyad period (661–750), the office had become a separate and distinct government position, that of a judge responsible for the enforcement of the *Shariah* (Islamic law). The cornerstone of the Islamic judicial system—the *Shariah* court—was laid.

Despite these developments, for many pious Muslims, Umayyad rule, with its wealth and luxury, its imperial practices, and its privileged Arab elites, seemed at odds with the Islamic message preached by the Prophet and practiced by the early community at Medina. It was not Islamic commitment and ideals but Arab power and wealth which had unified Umayyad rule. The Umayyad's Islamic critics argued that Islam was to permeate every area of life and thus should be reflected in political, social, and legal life. Could this be said of the example of many caliphs and the intrigues at the caliphal court? Were the status and authority of the new elites due to their commitment to Islam and the example of their personal lives, as had been true of the Prophet, or to privilege and wealth? For these pious Muslims, the confused and contradictory character of Umayyad rule was epitomized by the condition of Islamic legal practice. The vastness of the empire with its varying life styles and customary laws as well as the judge's ability to settle disputes on the basis of his own personal discretion or judgment, had resulted in a great diversity in Islamic legal practice.

Many asked: "Can God's will for humankind be discerned through so subjective a process; can His law for the Muslims of Medina be so different from that for Medina, Kufa, or Damascus?" These critics argued that if all Muslims were bound to submit to God's law and realize His will in their personal and public lives, then the Islamic way of life ought to be defined clearly and with more uniformity. The result was the birth of the Islamic legal system as groups of pious Muslims attempted to delineate in a comprehensive, detailed fashion the Islamic pattern for Muslim life.[7] In Medina, Kufa, and other Muslim centers, groups of like-minded Muslims began reviewing Umayyad legal practice and found it to be a testimony to the Umayyad's failure to implement Islam. They began to study the *Quran* and traditions of the Prophet in an attempt to understand and apply Islamic principles and values to Muslim life. Their goal was to discern and delineate the *Shariah*, God's revealed law which was to guide and govern Muslim life. This process, begun during the late Umayyad period, was to flourish under the Abbasids.

The elements of a growing Islamic opposition to Umayyad rule were as diverse as their motives: non-Arab Muslims who were second class citizens vis-à-vis Arab Muslims and denounced this as contrary to Islamic egalitarianism; Kharijites who continued to revolt in Mosul and Kufa; Shii or supporters of the family of Ali's claim to leadership of the Muslim community; Arab Muslims, such as those of Mecca, Medina, and Iraq, who were not among the established, favored Arab families; and finally pious Muslims, Arab and non-Arab alike, who viewed the "new cosmopolitan life" of luxury and social privilege as a departure from pristine Islam. For this last group, in particular, the renewal of Muslim society meant a return to the early normative period, to the example of Muhammad and the Rightly Guided Caliphs, and a restoration of the "Medinan ideal."

All opposition factions shared a common discontent with Umayyad rule and a tendency to couch their critique and their response in Islamic terms: "From being a society of Arabs who happened to be bound together by Islam, it must become a society of Muslim who happened to use the Arabic tongue and respect parts of the Arabic heritage."[8] The result was a broad-based, diverse anti-Umayyad sentiment which grew increasingly strong during the last decades of Umayyad rule (c. 720–50). The opposition's justification and legitimation were cast in ideological terms: condemnation of Umayyad policies and practices as un-Islamic innovations; the call for a return to the *Quran* and the practices of the Prophet and the early community. Their agenda called for implementation of political, social, and legal reforms in the name of Islam, reforms that would establish a system of Islamic governance and social justice.

From 730 onwards, a series of Kharijite, Shii, and tribal revolts occurred. By 747 one insurrection in particular had survived—that of Abu Muslim, a freed slave of the Abbasid leader, Ibrahim, who was a descendant of the Prophet's uncle al-Abbas. With strong Shii assistance, Islamic opposition groups gave their support. In 750 the Umayyads fell and Abu-l-Abbas, the brother of Ibrahim, was proclaimed caliph. Islam's capital moved from Syria to Iraq, from the long-established city of Damascus to the newly created Baghdad, the City of Peace. This royal citadel was to serve as the political, economic, and cultural center of the Islamic empire. Under Abbasid rule (750–1258), the empire would be the seat not only of political power but also of great cultural activity and the flowering of Islamic civilization.

The Abbasid Caliphate

The Abbasids came to power under the banner of Islam: "The ideology of a restoration of primitive Islam, with variants reflecting different trends, had conquered the masses, and, with the support of a majority of the learned men, became part of the programme of all, or nearly all, the leaders of parties. It triumphed when the Abbasids adopted it as their slogan."[9]

Their revolution was justified by condemning Umayyad rule as impious and un-Islamic and by promising a more Islamic sociopolitical order. While Abbasid caliphs were fully as autocratic as their predecessors and were not hesitant to use ruthless force to crush their opposition, they took care to align their government and policies with Islam. They became patrons of the Islamic religious establishment, supported the development of Islamic disciplines, built mosques, and established schools.

The Abbasids adopted and refined Umayyad practice by borrowing heavily from the Persian tradition with its divinely ordained system of government. The caliphs' claim to rule by divine mandate was symbolized by the altering of his title, "successor" or "deputy" of God's Prophet to "Deputy of God" and the appropriating of the Persian-inspired title "Shadow of God on Earth." The ruler's exalted status was further reinforced by his magnificent palace, retinue of court attendants, and the introduction of court etiquette appropriate for a monarch or emperor. For the religiously minded, the court at Baghdad was a far cry from the Medinan ideal.

From a community of believers, all equal before God and submissive to His divine will, headed by its elected, pious leader, Islam had now become an empire ruled by a caliph who inherited an office now cast in a royal mold. Although Muslims were only to submit to the one, true God alone, court etiquette required subjects to "bow" before the caliph, kissing the ground, a symbol of the caliph's absolute power and autocratic rule. Nothing could be farther from the Quranic ideal in which all power and homage belonged to God alone and all Muslims, as God's representatives on earth, were to constitute an egalitarian community.

The caliph enjoyed absolute power. If not in Islamic belief, in practice his word was law. He retained his position as the commander of the believers. He was the leader of the Friday, community prayer and of the community's armies in warfare and was to insure rule according to the Islamic law. Thus, the caliph possessed both religious prestige and political power and the duty to enforce Islamic law, defend the Islamic state and guarantee internal security and peace.

Governmentally, there was a shift from the Arab, especially Syrian, dominated administration and military to a more broad based, egalitarian, system in which the non-Arab Muslims, especially the Persians, played a major role. The Abbasids relied on a strong military and an intricate, hierarchic bureaucracy through which they attempted to directly oversee and supervise every province of their empire. The central administration in Baghdad, building on previous Umayyad and Persian traditions, was highly structured. The government was organized into a system of ministries: treasury, army, intelligence, etc., headed by the chief minister, the vizier, who served as head of the caliphal cabinet, supervising the large army of administrators and their staffs. In effect, the caliphs increasingly delegated the conduct of government to the vizier and his ministers.

The empire was divided into provinces. Each province was administered by a governor and a superintendent of revenue, an agent of the caliph responsible for the collection and management of revenue (land and taxes) as well as other administrative tasks. The

Islamic tax system became more equitable since Arab and non-Arab Muslims alike paid the same taxes just as they enjoyed the same socioeconomic status and opportunities. Under Abbasid rule, Muslim society approximated more closely the early Islamic division of the *ummah:* Muslim and non-Muslim.

The development of Islamic law, the *Shariah,* constitutes the Abbasid Period's most significant contribution to Islam. Since part of the indictment against the Umayyads had been their failure to implement an effective Islamic legal system, the Abbasids gave substantial support to legal development. The work of the early law schools which had only begun during the late Umayyad period (c. 720) flowered under caliphal patronage of religious scholars (*ulama,* learned men.) Islam has no clergy or priesthood. However, by the eighth century, the *ulama* had become a professional class of religious leaders. Their prestige and authority were based upon a reputation for knowledge of Islamic learning: *Quran,* prophetic traditions, law. As jurists, theologians, and educators, they became the interpreters and guardians of Islamic law and tradition.

A second motivation for legal development was the desire of many religious scholars to set forth clearly an Islamic ideal and mandate which all too often was not to be found during the rule of less pious caliphs. In this way the path to be followed, the Islamic charter for state and society, could be preserved independent of a caliph's moral character or political power. If the religious scholars could not control their caliph, they could attempt to get their way indirectly by delineating and preserving their interpretation of Islam in its law.

Although Muslims were enjoined to submit, i.e., realize God's will, until the eighth century there had been no systematic delineation of Islamic law. The *Quran* is not a law book. Rather, the *Quran* sets forth general legal and ethical principles which are to guide and govern Muslim life. For the early Muslims, law consisted of *Quranic* prescriptions, Prophetic traditions, and decisions by the early caliphs and judges. These superceded and supplemented but did not replace Arab customary practice, or law. Under the Umayyads, as seen above, law continued to develop in the legal opinions of *qadis* (*Shariah* court judges). Critical of Umayyad practice, the early schools of law had reviewed the Umayyad legal system in light of the *Quran.* However, the bulk of Islamic law developed as a self-conscious, systematic attempt by Muslim jurists to understand and apply revealed Islamic principles and values to the many exigencies of Muslim life. Thus was born Islamic jurisprudence or the science of law which by the end of the ninth century produced a detailed, systematic body of law that provided the established blueprint for Islamic state and society throughout subsequent centuries.

According to classical Islamic jurisprudence there are four sources or roots of law: (1) the *Quran;* (2) the *Sunnah* (example or model behavior) of the Prophet as preserved in the traditions; (3) analogical reasoning *(qiyas),* i.e., where a revealed prescription is lacking, a new regulation may be deduced by reasoning from a similar or analogous situation in scripture or the Prophetic traditions; and (4) the consensus or agreement *(ijma)* of the Islamic community on a point of law. The authority of consensus is based upon the Prophetic dictum: "My community will never agree upon an error." In practice, the consensus was usually that of the religious scholars in a particular generation and not that of the entire community.

In fact the actual development of Islamic law was far more complex and creative than this idealized version preserved by Islamic jurisprudence. The classical statement of the sources of law overlooked the important roles played by the personal interpretation or judgment *(ijtihad)* of early judges and jurists. Even more important was the bulk of customary practices which, if judged not contrary to Islam, were adopted and incorporated in the law books.

During the first two centuries of Abbasid rule (750–950), schools of law (groups of scholar-jurists) could be found in major centers of the empire. It was here, not in the courts, that Islamic law developed. Thus Islamic law was not the product of judicial decisions and review. There is no recognized case law system of legally binding precedents. Rather, given the Muslim's divinely revealed vocation to submit to and realize God's will, groups of jurists or legal scholars, not judges, sought to discover and delineate God's Will for mankind in light of the *Quran* and example of Muhammad. As a result, Islamic law is as much a system of ethics as it is law, for it is concerned with what the Muslim "ought" or "ought not" to do. To violate the law is not only to risk legal sanctions on earth but divine judgment in the hereafter, for law in Islam is viewed as God-ordained, not man-made. This is why all acts or duties were ethically categorized as: (1) obligatory, (2) recommended (3) indifferent or permissible, (4) reprehensible, (5) forbidden or prohibited.

While there is a general unity in Islamic law, differences in approach and geographic location (and thus customary practice) among the law schools resulted in a legal diversity amidst this unity. Although there had been many schools of law, four major Sunni

schools (Hanafi, Shafii, Maliki, and Hanbali) and one Shii school
(Jafari) endured the test of time. The differences among law schools
affect such questions as grounds for divorce, inheritance rights, and
taxation. And, of course, a major difference between Sunni and Shii
concerns leadership (caliphate vs. imamate) of the Muslim community. The content of Islamic law was seen as comprehensive since it
set forth the divinely revealed blueprint for Muslim society. The law
encompassed such areas as prayer and fasting as well as international
and family laws. Muslim jurists divided all law into two general categories: duties to God (worship including prayer, tithing, pilgrimage,
fasting); and duties to one's fellow man (social transactions which
encompass public as well as personal life: civil, penal, commercial,
and family laws).

By the tenth century, Islamic law, in the opinion of the *ulama*,
was finalized and institutionalized. The consensus of legal scholars
was that Islam's way of life had been adequately delineated. The task
of future generations was to follow God's path as set forth in the
authoritative legal manuals. Individual, independent reasoning or
personal judgment was no longer deemed necessary or permissible—
the door of *ijtihad* (personal interpretation) was henceforth closed.
Jurists were not to write law books but commentaries. While individual religious scholars like Ibn Taymiyya (1263–1328) and al-Suyuti
(1445–1505) demurred, the majority position resulted in the traditional belief prohibiting substantive legal development by jurists:
"The power of absolute *ijtihad* was completely abolished; a 'relative'
ijtihad was allowed. This meant either that one was allowed to reinterpret law within one's own school of law or, and this was the highest
point of legislation, one could carry on an eclectic and comparative
study of law of different schools and thus find some scope for limited
expansion in details."[10] The task of the judge and his Islamic law court
was the "application" not "interpretation" of law. Judges were organized under the direction of a central authority or chief judge, appointed by the caliph. Assisting the courts were legal specialists
whose task was the interpretation of law as set forth in the legal
manuals of the schools. They communicated their findings in legal
opinions which both the judge and litigants could utilize. In general,
the judiciary was dependent upon the caliph. Judges were appointed,
paid, and dismissed by the government. In addition, the caliph or his
provincial governor retained the right to review all decisions rendered by the courts.

While in theory the *Shariah* was the only recognized law and judicial system of the Islamic empire, in practice a parallel system of caliphal law and courts developed for a variety of reasons. First of all, the idealism of the *Shariah* was often deemed impractical. For example, in criminal law, where two adult Muslim witnesses are lacking, the rules of evidence require the court to accept an oath sworn in God's name. Moreover, *Shariah* rules of procedure exclude circumstantial evidence and the cross examination of witnesses. Second, and perhaps of greater influence, was the caliph's desire to personally regulate and govern society. However there was a problem. Although, in practice, the caliph might exercise absolute power, in theory God was the only lawmaker. In order to resolve this seeming contradiction, through a series of legal fictions, a parallel system of caliphal jurisdiction was introduced, the *Mazalim* (complaint) court system. Initially, the court of *Mazalim* enabled the caliph to hear complaints against senior government officials (whose status or power may have inhibited the judge) or even against the judges themselves. In time, the *Mazalim* became a system of courts whose scope and function were defined by the sovereign. An Islamic rationale for this dual legal system (*Shariah* and *Mazalim*) was established to justify such legal practices. In Islam, the primary task of the caliph is to maintain a society governed by the Islamic law. However, in order to assure the proper implementation and administration of *Shariah* rule, the government was permitted to issue regulations or ordinances as long as these regulations were not contrary to the *Shariah*. Thus, in the name of Islam and the upholding of the *Shariah*, the right of the sovereign to issue ordinances, not laws, was justified. This method continued down through Islamic history and can be seen today, in countries such as Saudi Arabia which have employed this rationale in introducing "regulations" such as the Mining Code (1963) and the Civil Service Law (1971) which supplement the *Shariah*.

Thus, the Islamic empire had two complementary jurisdictions: the *Shariah* courts which increasingly were restricted to matters of personal law: family law (marriage, divorce, and inheritance) and religious endowments and the Mazalim (complaint) courts which dealt with public law: criminal, land, taxation, and commercial regulations. Given the centrality of law as a blueprint for the ideal Islamic society and its function as the basis for Islamic government, the place of Islamic law remains a major issue in Islamic politics.

The Abbasid period is remembered by Muslims not simply for its power and wealth or its completion of the process of state organization and law but especially for the development of Islamic culture and civilization. The Abbasids were committed patrons of culture and the arts. In addition to law, religious disciplines such as *Quran* interpretation, tradition, criticism, history, and biography were developed. The process of Arabization which had begun during the late Umayyad period was completed by the end of the ninth century. Arabic language and tradition had interacted with, modified and eventually dominated the peoples and cultures of the conquered territories. Arabic displaced Syriac, Aramaic, Coptic, and Greek, becoming the language of common discourse, government, and literature throughout much of the empire. Translation bureaus were established. Manuscripts were obtained from the far reaches of the empire and translated from their original languages (Greek, Syriac, Latin, Sanskrit, Persian) into Arabic at state supported translation bureaus. Thus, the best of literature and the sciences was made available. The period of translation and assimilation was followed by one of Muslim intellectual and artistic creativity in which significant contributions were made in many fields: literature and philosophy; art and architecture; science, medicine and mathematics.[11] As Islam had challenged the world politically, it now did so culturally. This brilliant period, which Muslims came to view as "The Golden Age" of Islamic civilization, with its urban cultural centers in Cordova, Baghdad, Cairo, Nishapur, and Palermo, eclipsed Christian Europe, mired in the Dark Ages. As with the conquests and expansion of Islam, Muslims then (and now) regarded this phenomenal period as a sign of God's blessings and validation of Islam's message and the Muslim community's mission.

　　　　The Golden Age of Islamic civilization paralleled the progressive political fragmentation of imperial Islam. Abbasid political unity deteriorated dramatically after 950. Despite a strong central government, controlling a vast empire extending from the Atlantic to Central Asia with so many competing groups proved impossible. From 861 to 945 religious (in particular Kharijite and Shiite) and regional differences and competing political aspirations precipitated a series of revolts and secessionist movements. In Morocco and Tunisia local rulers, while continuing to give nominal allegiance and to pay tribute to the caliph, exercised *de facto* rule over their territories, establishing their own local hereditary dynasties. Egypt saw the rise of the Shii Fatimid dynasty (909–1171). In Iran, Syria, and Iraq itself, local governors, who were often army commanders, increasingly asserted their independence as heads of semi-autonomous states. By 945 the disintegration of a universal caliphate was evident as the Buyids, a family that ruled several such independent states in western Iran, invaded Baghdad and seized power. The Buyids assumed the title commander-in-chief or commander of the commanders. Although Shiite, they did not change the Sunni orientation of the empire and left the caliph as nominal head of a fictionally unified empire. The Abbasids continued to reign but not to rule. From that time on, with an Abbasid on the throne as a symbol of legitimate government and Muslim unity, real power passed to a series of Persian (Buyid) and then Turkic (Seljuq) military dynasties or sultanates. The sultan ("power," ruler), as chief of the commanders, governed a politically fragmented empire. Finally, in 1258 the Mongols, under Hulagu, swept across Central Asia, conquered Persia, and descended upon Baghdad. They captured the capitol and killed the Caliph, al-Mutasim, who left no heir. The Islamic caliphate was terminated; the first stage of Islamic political history had come to an end.

While politically the Mongol conquest of the Abbasid Caliphate may seem to be nothing more than the estabishment of one more usurper dynasty, its Islamic significance was far more profound. Whatever the merits of the Persian Turkic sultans that had seized power and governed from 945 to 1258, they were *Muslim*. The *ummah* continued to exist as a religio-political community/state with the caliph as its symbolic head and governed by Islamic law. Thus, the ideological prerequisites for Muslim life remained intact; Muslims continued to live in an Islamic state, following the straight path (the *Shariah*) of Muslim life. Whatever the changing fortunes of Islamic history, for Muslim historical consciousness, the message and mission of the Islamic community had been validated from its Medinan beginnings in 622 by a long period of remarkable expansion, power, and wealth. Success and power were viewed as signs of God's pleasure and His reward for a faithful community. Muslim usurpers might come and go, but Islamic presence and rule had remained. However, the conquest by Mongol invaders who were unbelievers meant the destruction of the land of Islam. It was a challenge to Muslim life, faith and identity. In this sense, the Mongol threat was as traumatic and Islamically significant as that of European imperialism in the eighteenth century. Whatever the response, a successful resolution would entail the incorporation of Islam ideologically and politically once again in Muslim life.

Throughout the first six centuries of Islamic political history, despite the character of individual rulers and competing claims of various factions, religion provided the basic identity and ideological framework for political and social life. The world was divided into Islamic and non-Islamic territory. All Muslims were to strive to extend Islamic rule (the Pax Islamica), wherever possible. Thus, merchants, traders, as well as soldiers were the early missionaries of Islam. Islam was part and parcel of the state's institutions: caliphate, judiciary, taxation, education, and social welfare systems. It affected the definition of citizenship and social classes and was symbolized in the new coinage system introduced by the Umayyads to replace that of the Byzantines. Coins were struck using Quranic phrases or images of Muhammad's lance or a *mihrab* (the prayer niche indicating the direction of Mecca). Islamic identity and ideology were so basic to politics that anti-caliphal opposition movements—such as Muawiyah's challenge to Ali, Kharijite and Shiite revolts, social discontent, and the Abbasid revolution—also appealed to Islam to legitimate their actions. The political and social institutions, and especially Islamic law, which represented an ideological synthesis of the Islamic way of life, would continue to constitute the essentials of Islamic government for future generations.

Medieval Muslim Empires: The Sultanate Period

The fall of Baghdad in 1258 did not sound the death knell of Islamic rule. Islam proved resilient. The post-caliphal period was both a dynamic and expansionist period of Islamic history. The political unity of the caliphate gave way to a burgeoning number of Muslim sultanates which governed an area that eventually extended from North Africa to Southeast Asia as Islam progressively penetrated East, West, and Central Africa, Central and Southeast Asia, and Eastern Europe. The continued expansion of Islam was accompanied by Muslim rule and large scale conversions inspired both by the message of Islam as presented by Muslim preachers, especially the Sufi orders, as well as conversions due to the socio-economic advantages of full membership or citizenship in the *ummah*. Despite the political fragmentation of the caliphate, or lack of a universal central authority, during the sultantate period, an underlying unity of faith and culture continued to exist. Muslim citizens of a particular state also maintained an awareness of a broader affiliation and identity with the more universal community. For Islamic faith and culture went hand in hand: "Whichever way Muslim faith and rule came, once it had endured any length of time there tended to follow the whole Islamicate civilization as found in the area from which Islamization had come."

By the sixteenth century three major Muslim empires had emerged in the midst of the many sultanates: the Sunni Ottoman in West Asia and Eastern Europe, the Shii Safavid in Persia, and the Sunni Mughal in the Indian subcontinent. Harnessing gunpowder technology, these "gunpowder empires," whose central governments were supported by a blend of religious ideology and military strength, dominated the heartlands of the Islamic world: North Africa, the Middle East, and South Asia. Reminiscent of Abbasid times, great sultans like the Ottoman Sulayman the Magnificent (1520–1605), Shah Abbas in Persia and the Mughal emperor Akbar in India, were patrons of learning and the arts. The Islamic character of the state was reflected by the Ottoman conquerors who, after conquering the capital of the eastern Roman world and renaming Constantinople Istanbul, "crowned the hills with monumental mosques."[12] Their political and military achievements were accompanied by a dazzling cultural florescence. With the dynamic expansion of Islam during the sultanate period and the emergence of three Muslim empires, history continued to witness the vitality, success, and divine guidance of Allah's commonwealth. Baghdad's successors were now Istanbul, Isfahan, and Delhi.

While there were significant differences between the three great medieval Muslim empires, they each carried over the basic features of Islamic state and society. Islam provided legitimation, political ideology, and law; it informed the principal institutions of government. The head of state, the sultan, although temporal ruler, derived his authority as emperor from God and was the defender/protector of Islam. He was an absolute monarch, ruling his empire as head of its military through a strong central government. While sovereign, the sultan often delegated the civil administration of his government to his grand *vizier*, his chief minister or steward, who oversaw an elaborate network ministries.

The *Shariah* played a major role in all three empires. The *Shariah* was the official law of the empire. It was the source of Islamic legitimation and identity and defined the norms of life. However, the ruler also maintained his *Mazalim* courts and, in the name of *Shariah* governance, promulgated ordinances which in effect constituted much of the state's public law. The *Shariah* courts were generally restricted to matters of personal status: marriage: divorce, inheritance, and religious endowment.

The *ulama* often were a significant presence among the army of officials who served as government advisors and administrators. As in earlier Islamic history, they were the guardians of law and tradition and thus dominated the judicial, education and social service systems. They were indeed a religious establishment. Although the emperor retained absolute authority, the religious scholars through tacit alliance (Ottoman and Mughal) or independence (Safavid) wielded a great deal of influence. Their power and prestige can be appreciated if we recall the extent to which their activities impacted upon their societies. Legally, they were the judges and legal advisers *(muftis)* of the state responsible for the administration and application of law. In addition to the office of chief judge, the religious institution was further centralized and administered from the capital by a chief religious functionary (head of religious affairs) known in the Ottoman empire as a chief *mufti* or *Shaykh al-Islam* and in the Safavid and Mughal empires as the *Sadr al-sudir.*

The *ulama* also controlled the educational system, serving as its administrators and scholar-teachers. Royal patronage of learning resulted in a marvelous system of schools and universities which provided the education required for all who aspired to public as well as religious office. This system of education reinforced both the prestige of the religious scholars and the Islamic identity and character of the state. Finally, they exercised considerable influence and power through their control over a broad range of social services. The income for such activities was generated from royal land grants, religious endowments and religious tithing. These funds were applied to the construction and maintenance of a variety of public services: mosques, hospitals, schools, lodges for travellers, and roads and bridges.

In conclusion, despite differences between the caliphate to sultanate periods and among the medieval Muslim Empire sultanates themselves, there was a continuity rooted in their Islamic legacy and tradition. Islam constituted the basic ideological framework of meaning for political and social life. Moreover, whether the state was headed by a pious or impious caliph/sultan, or a usurper dynasty, none directly challenged the *Shariah* governance of the state. Thus, for the believer, there was a continuum of Muslim power and success which, despite the vicissitudes and contradictions of Muslim life, validated and reinforced the sense of a divinely mandated and guided community with a purpose and mission.

ISLAMIC POLITICAL THOUGHT

The integral relationship of religion to politics in Islam and its emphasis on the Muslim vocation to realize God's rule were reflected in the tendency to view political and social revolts (the apostasy wars, the social rights of non-Arab converts, the political secession of the Shiites and Kharijites) as not simply political but religious issues. The rebellion of Arabian tribes after Muhammad's death was not just treason but apostasy. The systematic expression of the Islamic ideal had been preserved in Islamic law. However, as we have seen, the historical reality was often at odds with the normative ideal. The early extraordinary expansion and development of Islam as a state necessitated immediate decisions by caliphs and generals rather than reflective planning by scholars and policy makers. The political and social infrastructure of the Umayyad and Abbasid empires did not grow out of the systematic interpretations and application of Islamic ideology but rather from the *ad hoc* policies of successive regimes which drew heavily from Byzantine and then Sasanid practice.

Given the comprehensive claim of the Islamic vision and the diverse nature of Islamic governments, the sharp discrepancy between revealed ideal and political reality posed a challenge to Muslims' consciences, in particular to that of the *ulama* who saw themselves as the guardians of Islam. The Kharijites had been among the first to address the question: "What is the proper response to a conflict between the ideal and the real in Muslim political life?" Belief that a grave sinner was no longer a Muslim and was, in fact, the legitimate object of *jihad* had motivated their secessionist movement and been used to justify subsequent rebellions against caliphal authority. For others, Umayyad authority and rule was based not upon the Medinan example of selection of a caliph through consultation but upon force and dynastic succession. Such a policy was un-Islamic and therefore a justification for the Abbasid revolution. Consequently, Islamic theories on the nature of the caliphate developed not as deductions or speculations on the nature of Islamic government but rather as justifications for a political reality often at odds with norma-tive Islam. Sunni apologists responded to Shii and Kharijite objec-tions to the actions of early Sunni caliphs (e.g., Ali's arbitration with Muawiyah or Yazid's rout of Husayn).

Other scholars addressed the disparity between Umayyad and Abbasid dynastic rule and the early normative practice of the Rightly Guided Caliphs. They responded to questions such as (1) What constitutes an Islamic government? (2) To what extent is an Islamic government dependent upon the virtuous character of the caliph or the manner of his selection? (3) How should a Muslim re-spond to seemingly un-Islamic rulers or governments? Whatever the belief concerning the unity of religion and politics, the historical expe-rience of the community often contradicted the Islamic ideal. The issues raised by this discrepancy between faith and practice gave rise to the development of Islamic political thought.

Classical Sunni Islamic political theory took shape during Ab-basid rule. Heavily indebted to and therefore influenced by royal patronage, Muslim jurists and theologians had a twofold purpose: to maintain the divine origin and purpose of the Islamic community and to legitimate the claims and the rule of Abbasid caliphs.[13] During succeeding centuries, a wide variety of positions resulted, but no single theory was universally adopted. For some, the true caliphate was restricted to the first four Rightly Guided Caliphs. Others, like the great historian Ibn Khaldun (d. 1406), pragmatically accepted the possible compatibility of caliphate and kingdom: "Government and kingship are a caliphate of God amongst men, for the execution of his ordinance amongst them."[14] The jurist, al-Mawardi (d. 1058), in his treatise *Al-Ahkam al-Sultaniyah (The Ordinances of Government)*, which became a classic exposition on Islamic government, presented a theoretical, idealized view of the caliphate. Many other jurist-theologians, like al-Ghazali (d. 1111) and al-Baqillani (d. 1013), fol-lowed suit. These scholars were not drafting government regulations or guidelines but rather delineating a moral ideal. By the end of the Abbasid period, the essentials of Islamic political theory were formed with a number of common themes. God is the absolute sovereign and ruler of the universe and the ultimate authority of the state. Through a covenant, authority is delegated to mankind as God's instrument in the world. The institution of the caliphate is based upon revelation, the Quranic designation to serve as God's vicegerent, and not simply upon reason. The caliph is elected or nominated by a group of in-fluential community leaders "the people who loose and bind." He may also be designated by his predecessor (the incumbent caliph). Election or designation of a caliph is followed by community acceptance or public acclamation. The moral idealism of caliphal political theory was especially evident in the qualifications for office: justice; knowledge to interpret and apply the law; virtuous character; courage to wage war; good physical health; and finally, descent from the Quraysh—the Prophet's tribe. As the Commander of the Faithful he leads the community in war. The caliph's primary task is to uphold and enforce the *Shariah*. He is the guardian or protector of Islam, Defender of the Faith.

The disintegration of the Abbasid caliphate during the tenth century raised an additional question for Islamic political thought: If the caliph in Baghdad was reduced to nominal head of state, often restricted to his palace by the ruling army commander, were Muslims bound to revolt against a now un-Islamic usurper government? Al-Ghazzali and Ibn Khaldun provided justifications for the acceptance of harsh political realities, maintaining that order was better than political chaos. Necessity or public interest legitimated acceptance of such sultan usurpers. Moreover, as long as the sultan acknowledged the caliph as the spiritual and temporal head of the community, continued to mention the caliph's name at the Friday community prayer and pledged to uphold *Shariah* rule, Islamic government continued to exist. Through such a legal accommodation, the symbol of Muslim unity and identity was preserved.

Despite the diversity of Islamic political thought, a common denominator emerged: The minimal requirement for an Islamic government was not the character of the head of state but rule according to the *Shariah*. Acknowledgement by the ruler that the *Shariah* was the state's official law preserved both the unity of the community and its Islamic framework or character. Islamic law, not the religious commitment or moral character of the ruler or government, was the criterion for the legitimacy of an Islamic state.

CONCLUSION

A review of the role of religion in politics and society in early Islam reveals a rich and complex history. Islam proved to be a faith in which religion was harnessed to political power. The Islamic community was both spiritual and temporal, church and state. Religious faith and ideology provided the ideological and motivational glue that united Arabian tribes and inspired and gave direction to the early period of expansion and conquest. Religion provided the world view, the framework of meaning for both individual and corporate life. Whether under the Righteous Caliphs or Umayyad and Abbasid rulers, the ideological foundation of the community/state was Islam. The legitimacy and authority of the ruler, the officially acknowledged law of the state, its judicial, educational, and social institutions were rooted in Islam. Though the historical and political realities of caliphal life were often at odds with its Islamic ideals, nevertheless the primary principle of political identity and social cohesion continued to be public and popular commitment to the *Shariah.* The Islamic ideal remained intact and authoritative though often circumvented. For the believer, the Islamic character of Muslim history and political life was not belied by the disparities of history. Later generations of Muslims inherited the romantic, idealized understanding of the nature of Islamic political history and law that had been developed by the early *ulama,* transmitted and perpetuated in their writings, educational institutions, and religious instruction. This ideal, though it obscured many of the realities of Islamic history, provided the Islamic paradigm which inspired subsequent generations, from pre-modern revivalist movements to contemporary Islamic political activists, who would seek to emulate and realize an Islamic religio-political vision.

2

Revival and Reform

ODERN ISLAMIC REFORM is often depicted simply as a reaction and response to Western imperialism—political and cultural domination by European colonial powers. However, the roots of modern reform lie in both Islamic and Western sources. Understanding twentieth century Islamic politics requires an understanding of the character and legacy of both pre-modern Islamic revivalism which addressed the internal weakness of Muslim society as well as Islamic modernism which responded to the challenge of Western colonialism. Pre-modern revivalism was primarily a response from within Islam to the internal socio-moral decline of the community. In many cases it led to the creation of Islamic states in Saudi Arabia, the Sudan, and Libya. Islamic revivalist movements such as th Wahhabi in Arabia, Mahdi in the Sudan, and Sanusi in Libya were forerunners of both twentieth century Islamic modernism and contemporary Islamic revivalism. As such, they reveal much of the pattern of modern Islamic movements: their world view, ideology, language, and methods.

Islamic modernism broadened and built on the pre-modern revivalist legacy. By the mid-nineteenth century concern for the internal weakness of the Islamic community was compounded by the threat of subjugation to the Christian West. European colonial domination of much of the Muslim world constituted for many Muslims the end result of a long period of decline. The political and religio-cultural threat of western imperialism brought forth a variety of Muslim responses ranging from conservative religious militant rejectionism to wholesale western-oriented adaptationism, from *jihad* movements to modernist reform movements. As we shall see, Islamic modernism represented an Islamically rooted response to unite and strengthen a demoralized community. Its method was a reinterpretation of Islam which drew on Islamic tradition but also attempted to assimilate the best of modern science, thought, and institutions.

PRE-MODERN ISLAMIC REVIVALISM

Islamic history offers many examples of Muslim responses to the glaring disparity between God's revealed will for humankind and the historical development of the Islamic community. Among those were the early Kharijite and Shiite rebellions, the development of Islamic mysticism (Sufism) and law in the face of alleged "un-Islamic" Umayyad practice, the "Islamic rationale" for the Abbasid revolution, as well as the reformist activities of great individual religious figures like the theologian Abu Hamid al-Ghazali (d. A.D. 1111) and the jurist Taqi al-Din Ahmad Ibn Taymiyyah (d. 1328). All had claimed to be responding to the socio-moral corruption of Muslim society; all had called for a return to the fundamentals of Islam to restore and revivify an errant community. Herein lies the historical roots for the long tradition of Islamic revival, a process of renewal and reform which have inspired both pre-modern and modern Muslim reform movements.

Throughout the eighteenth and nineteenth centuries a wave of Islamic religio-political movements occurred from the Sudan to Sumatra. In the core areas of the Islamic world, the imperial sultanates (Ottoman, Safavid, and Mughal) had peaked in the sixteenth century; by the eighteenth century their power and prosperity were fading into a period of decline. Among the common indices of imperial decline were internal political disintegration (the decline of central authority and the rise of semi-autonomous regional and provincial governments), military losses, social dislocation and disruption, and a worsening economy, affected by European competition in trade and manufacturing. Political and economic decline were accompanied by a growing concern for spiritual and moral decay in eighteenth century Islamic societies. While there were distinctive differences due to local conditions, all reflected a similar pattern of revival and reform.

Within Sunni Islam, there developed an awareness that the

continued vitality of the Islamic community would require renewal and reform from time to time. This belief in the need for a recurrent process of revitalization was crystallized in the development of a revivalist tradition and a belief in a "renewer" or reviver of Islam. In addition experience of the disparity between public life and the Islamic ideal contributed to the popular expectation of a messianic figure, the Mahdi.

The renewer of Islam is sent at the beginning of each century to restore true Islamic practice and thus regenerate a community which tends, over time, to wander from the straight path. Belief in these renewers is based upon a tradition of the Prophet: "God will send to this *ummah* at the beginning of each century those who will renew its faith."[1]

The Mahdi, "the guided one," in Sunni Islam is a popular rather than doctrinal belief in an eschatological individual who will come in the future to deliver the community from oppression by the forces of evil and to restore true Islam and with it a reign of justice on earth. This popular Sunni belief, never formally included in Sunni theology, should be distinguished from the Shiite theological doctrine of the Mahdi which refers to the awaited return of the Hidden Imam. The Shiite Mahdi is the divinely inspired religio-political leader of Shii Islam, the successor of Muhammad and Ali. He will come to inaugurate a New Age of peace and justice in the world. He is an absolute, infallible guide and interpreter of revelation who rules by divine right.

Among the principal ingredients of Islamic revivalism were a sense that something had gone wrong in Islam and a diagnosis that decline in Muslim fortunes was due to a departure from the straight path of Islam. Revivalists maintained that Islam had become corrupted through its historical accretions from foreign (i.e., un-Islamic) influences. Nowhere was this debilitating eclecticism believed to be more clearly evident than in Sufism's absorption of popular religious practices.

Sufism was an ascetic, mystical movement which had developed during the early centuries of Islam. It had swept across the Islamic world in the twelfth and thirteenth centuries, serving as an enormously effective missionary movement. Islamic reformers maintained that in becoming a mass movement, Sufi syncretism and eclecticism had resulted in the assimilation of many innovations: ecstatic trances, saint/tomb worship, and a passivity and fatalism that resulted from the mystics' denigration of worldly affairs. The cure followed from the diagnosis. Muslims must "return to Islam," that is, the correct practice of Islam with its emphasis upon active realization or implementation of God's will in this world. This purification was the prerequisite for a strong, powerful society as well as a requirement for eternal life. Muslims must reclaim the original Islam revealed in the *Quran* and the example of the Prophet and embodied in the life and practice of the early Medinan community.

Islamic revivalist movements sought to transform not only the religious, but also the political and social life of the community. Their goal was nothing less than a moral reconstruction of Muslim society to restore its Islamic center. To accomplish this, they reasserted the right of individual reinterpretation. As discussed earlier, the majority of religious scholars had determined that individual interpretation of Islamic law was no longer necessary. Rather, Muslims were to follow the path of Islam as set forth in the regulations of the law manuals. Eighteenth and nineteenth century Islamic revivalists rejected this blind following of Muslim legal or theological teachings, believing that medieval law had been infiltrated by un-Islamic, historical accretions. They asserted their right to go back directly to the only immutable authority, the revealed sources of Islam in order to rediscover and restore true early Islam. However, in contrast to later Islamic modernism, premodern revivalism simply sought to restore and implement an existing ideal, not to reformulate or reconstruct *new* Islamic responses to modern change.

The Islamic rationale for change which views the nature of Islam and the basis of religious renewal as both an individual and communal affair provided a religio-political ideology that inspired pre-modernist Islamic movements and provides a paradigm for many contemporary Islamic movements today. Islamic ideological slogans and beliefs were harnessed to provide a legitimacy and a framework of meaning by which Islamic actors and movements mobilized popular support. We can see this approach to Islamic reform in several of the more prominent revivalist movements in Arabia, India, and Africa.

Arabia: Muhammad ibn Abd al-Wahhab

Muhammad ibn Abd al-Wahhab (1703–92) was the son of a learned jurist and theologian. He was educated at Mecca and Medina in Hanafi and Shafii law. He studied with teachers of the Hanbali school, the strictest of the Sunni law schools, and took Ibn Taymiyyah (d 1328) as his exemplar. Disillusioned by the moral laxity and spiritual malaise of his times, Muhammad ibn Abd al-Wahhab set out to reform his society, to return it to the practice of the Prophet. He denounced the ills of his society and called upon the people to abandon many popular religious beliefs and practices which he compared to pre-Islamic Arabian practice, the period of ignorance. The historical additions that overlay pure Islam constituted idolatry. In particular, he attacked the superstition and idolatrous practices of Sufism, denouncing them as "innovations," unwarranted deviations from true Islam. He called for a literal interpretation of the *Quran* and *Sunnah*. Muslims must return to the pure Islam of the first generation of Muslims, the righteous ancestors.

Muhammad ibn Abd al-Wahhab joined forces with a local tribal chief, Muhammad Ibn Saud (d. 1765) of Dariyia, and from this alliance the so-called Wahhabi movement was born. Religious zeal and military might merged in a religio-political movement that waged holy war with a zeal reminiscent of the early Kharijites, viewing all Muslims who resisted as unbelievers. The tribes of Arabia were subdued and united in the name of Islamic egalitarianism. The Wahhabi forces' self-designation as Muwahiddun ("Unitarians", i.e., those who believe in and practice monotheism) was reminiscent of early Islamic radical monotheism and its iconoclasm. As Muhammad in Mecca had cleansed the Kaba of the tribal gods, so Abd al-Wahhab rejected all popular religious practices that smacked of idolatry—saint worship, pilgrimage to sacred tombs, devotional rituals: "to worship anyone or anything whether it be a king, prophet, sufi saint, sacred tomb or tree is to create idols" (*Majmu'at al-rasa'i* 4:5). Since many of these practices were attributed to Sufi cultural accommodation, Sufism was suppressed: shrines, tombs, sacred objects were destroyed. In imitation of the Prophet's cleansing of the Kaba, Wahhabi iconoclastic zeal led to the destruction of sacred tombs in Mecca and Medina including that of Muhammad and his early companions as idolatrous shrines. Wahhabi forces destroyed Karbala, a major Shiite pilgrimage site in Iraq, which housed the tomb of Husayn. These latter actions have never been forgotten by Shii Muslims and have contributed to their negative attitude toward the Wahhabi of Saudi Arabia.

Abd al-Wahhab respected tradition but rejected an uncritical following of past authority. All post-prophetic tradition, including the time honored formulations of Islamic law, were subject to selective criticism since the law itself had taken on un-Islamic customary practices. The starting point was to return again to a purified Islam. However, his interpretation was not that of twentieth-century Islamic modernism who sought to reinterpret Islam in order to formulate solutions for new situations. His was a literalist interpretation; the revealed sources offered the immutable pattern of life which must be reclaimed and implemented in order to purify Islam, regenerate Muslim society, and restore its past glory.

India: Shah Wali Allah

In India the decline of Mughal power had spurred a number of revivalist movements. Among the most influential was that of Shah Wali Allah of Delhi (1702–62) and his disciples. Wali Allah rejected the moral corruption of Indian society, indicted popular Sufiism's indiscriminate syncretism, and called for a purification of Islam. Yet, unlike Muhammad ibn Abd al-Wahhab, Wali Allah's surgery was less radical. Rather than reject the present to restore the past, he sought to modify present Muslim belief and practice in light of early Islamic practice. Thus, he set out to reform or purify Sufism rather than to suppress it. Similarly, he advocated use of interpretation to reform medieval Islam. Wali Allah believed that the rectification of Islamic belief and practice would lead to a revitalization of Muslim society and the restoration of Mughal power. Under the leadership of his son, Shah Abdul Aziz (1746–1824), and then Sayyid Ahmad Barelewi (1786–1831), the sociopolitical implications of Wali Allah's teachings were developed and applied.

For Sayyid Ahmad, effective response to both the interior decay of the community and the external thrust of the Sikhs, and later the British, required *jihad*. Loss of political power meant that India was no longer an Islamic territory but an "abode of war," or non-Islamic territory. He and his followers, holy warriors, combined preaching and military power in a *jihad* movement whose goal was the establishment of a purified Islamic state based upon social justice and equality. Sayyid Ahmad saw the Muslims' loss of political power as due to their failure to follow the law. He emphasized the centrality of monotheism and denounced those polytheistic practics (Sufi, Shii, and popular customs borrowed from Hinduism) which were contrary to it.[2] With a band of followers, he made the pilgrimage to Mecca in 1823. At Hudabiyya, the place where Muhammad's companions had made a pact to fight the Meccans, Sayyid Ahmad administered an oath of *jihad* to his followers.[3]

Sayyid Ahmad Barelewi was revered by his followers as a renewer of Islam. There was a belief that in each century God sends a leader who would strengthen Islam. The commitment of the holy warriors was reflected in their 3,000-mile trip in 1826 to the Northwest Frontier Province (Pakistan). This area was viewed as a proper area for *jihad* and the creation of a new Islamic state since a predominantly Muslim population was ruled by an oppressive non-Muslim Sikh regime. The holy warriors defeated the Sikhs at Balakot and established a religio-political state. Like the early caliphs, Sayyid Ahmad was proclaimed commander of the believers. In 1831 Sayyid Ahmad was killed in battle; his scattered movement continued until 1860.[4]

Africa: Jihad Movements

The general sense of Muslim decline and the desire for Islamic renewal were nowhere more evident than in nineteenth-century Africa. A series of *jihad* movements led to the establishment of Islamic states, including those led by Uthman dan-Fodio (1754–1817) in Northern Nigeria, the Grand Sanusi in Libya (1787–1859), and the Mahdi of the Sudan (1848–85). A distinctive characteristic of most African revivalist movements was its leadership: reformist, militant, and politically oriented Sufi orders. Libya and the Sudan provide striking examples of Sufi led *jihad* revivalist movements.

In Africa, as in most of the Muslim world, the Sufi orders had been the greatest missionaries of Islam. Sufism's openness and flexibility regarding indigenous African beliefs and practices subjected African Sufism to sharp criticism for opening the door to idolatrous superstition and an attitude of passive withdrawal which resulted from an other worldly orientation. Reformers sought to realign Sufism with the more orthoprax path, that is, to bring the inner path of Sufism into harmony with the more exterior path of Islamic law. This approach was more like that of Shah Wali Allah than that of

Muhammad ibn Abd al-Wahhab. Sufi reformers did not eradicate but rather redefined Sufism, emphasizing a spirituality that stressed a this worldly, activist Islam. The sociopolitical dimension of Islam was reintroduced as African Islamic movements, led by Sufi brotherhoods, fought to establish Islamic states. Prayer and political action were joined together in the earthly pursuit of God's will.

Among the major early African reformers was the Moroccan Ahmad ibn Idris (d. 1837), a jurist as well as a Sufi, who established his order, the Tariqa Muhammadiyya (Path of Muhhamad), in Arabia. As with Muslim reformers throughout the Islamic world, he denounced tribal and regional particularism in the name of Islamic unity and solidarity as well as the moral and social abuses of a debilitated society. He called for Sufi reform through a return to the Quran and teachings of Muhammad. The finality of medieval Islamic teachings was rejected and the need for interpretation affirmed.

It was Shaykh Ahmad's disciples who were to successfully transform his teachings into religio-political organizations. Among his more illustrious disciples was Muhammad Ali ibn al-Sanusi (1787–1859), founder of the Sanusiyyah Order, a movement which would lead to the establishment of modern-day Libya.

Born in Algeria, the Grand Sanusi, as he was later known, studied in Cairo and Mecca, earning a reputation as a scholar of law and *hadith*. Al-Sanusi preached a purification of Sufism through a return to the *Quran* and *Sunnah*. He rejected much of Islamic law which had been based upon the reasoning and consensus of the *ulama*. For this and his claim to practice *ijtihad*, he earned their enmity. After the death of his teacher, Ahmad ibn Idris, al-Sanusi moved to modern-day Libya where he established the Sanusiyyah religious brotherhood. The Order was both a reformist and missionary movement whose members penetrated areas of Central and West Africa establishing a network of settlements based upon the Sanusi ideology.

The Sanusi were militant activists who united tribal factions in the name of Islamic solidarity and brotherhood. Their Sufi devotional lodges served as religious, educational and social centers, places for prayer and religious instruction as well as social welfare and military training. They were commited not only to establishing their own Islamic state and society but also to spreading Islam through extensive missionary activity in West and Central Africa. Although not seeking political conflicts, the Libyan descendants of al-

Sanusi resisted European colonial expansionism: first French, and later Italian occupation and rule. Sayyid Muhammad Ali ibn Idris, grandson of the Grand Sanusi, led the Sanusi resistance to Italian colonial rule (1911–51) and, at independence in 1951, became King Idris I of Libya.

In contrast to the Grand Sanusi of Libya, who had steadfastly resisted attempts to declare him caliph or Mahdi, the *jihad* movement of the Sudanese Mahdiyya Order was led by Muhammad Ahmad (1848–85) who did proclaim himself Mahdi in 1881—the divinely selected and inspired guide for renewal, sent to restore God's rule and justice. Like Muhammad ibn Abd al-Wahhab, the Mahdi united his followers against fellow Muslims, in this case the Turks—Ottoman Egyptian rulers, whom he, too, declared infidels who "disobeyed the command of His messenger and his prophets . . . ruled in a manner not in accord with what God has sent, . . . altered the Sharia of our master, Muhammad, the messenger of God, and . . . blasphemed against the faith of God."[5] The corruption of Sudanese Islamic society was based upon the adoption of foreign (Turko-Egyptian and local non-Islamic) influences and practices: prostitution, gambling, tobacco, alcohol, music.

The Sudanese Mahdi shared with leaders of other Islamic revivalist movements the belief that they were re-enacting the paradigmatic drama of early Islam—establishing as the Prophet had done in the seventh century the rule of God on earth. Moreover, the "Mahdi and his Ansar [followers] had seen the taking of Khartoum as but one in a series of conquests throughout the Muslim world."[6]

The Sudanese Mahdi, like Sayyid Ahmad Barelewi in India, Uthman dan Fodio in Nigeria, and Muhammad Ali ibn al-Sanusi in Libya, became the religio-political leader of an Islamic movement which sought to establish a theocratic state that would recreate the ideal, early Islamic community/state. In common with other reformers, the Mahdi called for a purification of Islamic belief and practice which had been corrupted by alien, un-Islamic customs and beliefs. Sufism was not rejected but reformed. However, unlike other revivalists, his view of normative Islamic practice did not rest upon asserting his right to exercise *ijtihad* but his claim as Mahdi to divine inspiration and guidance. As with the early Islamic victories of Muhammad, Mahdist victories were interpreted as divine validation of his mission. In 1885 the Mahdist movement successfully conquered the Sudan's Egyptian occupiers. A theocratic state, governed by Mahdist religious ideology, was created. The Mahdi had supreme power as God's delegate, with the *Shariah* as its only law. The Mahdist state ruled for fourteen years until it was finally defeated in 1899 by Anglo-Egyptian forces under Sir Herbert Kitchener.

Conclusion

Premodernist revival movements of the eighteenth and nineteenth centuries contributed to the pattern of Islamic politics and provided a legacy for twentieth-century Islam. Unlike Islamic modernism, it was motivated primarily in response to internal decay rather than external, colonial threat. As had been true from the early Islamic centuries, political disunity as well as socio-moral decline was viewed as due to digression from the straight path since success and power were God's rewards for a faithful community. If Muslims had wandered then they must renounce their society with its foreign (i.e., alien or non-Islamic) practices reform Sufism, and return to Islam as lived during the early normative period of Muhammad and the Rightly Guided Caliphs. This purification process of renewal and reform was underscored by the growth of popular religious beliefs regarding the coming of renewers and of the Mahdi, the "rightly guided one."

Despite their individual differences and characteristics, premodern revivalist movements provided a common legacy to modern Islam both in their ideology and methodology: first, they brought into sharp focus the weakened and disorganized condition of the community. Second, they provided the diagnosis and cure: departure from true Islamic belief/practice and thus the need for a return to Islam. Third, they reasserted a belief that Islamic monotheism meant the unity and totality of God's will for both the individual Muslim and the Islamic community. Religion is integral to all areas of life: political, social, and moral. Fourth, Islamic reform required the rejection of a blind acceptane of tradition, i.e., a recognition that the medieval synthesis of Muslim life, contained in the corpus of Islamic law, included un-Islamic historical accretions. Fifth, they maintained that the restoration of true Islam necessitated personal interpretation which was based on the sole authoritative foundations of Islam—the *Quran* and prophetic practice as found in the early community. Sixth, they reemphasized the belief that the socio-moral revival of Islamic society required political action, an activism epitomized by *jihad*, the exertion to realize God's will through moral self-discipline and, when necessary, military combat or warfare.

ISLAM AND THE WEST

At the beginning of the eighteenth century many areas of the Islamic world had felt the impact of the economic and military challenge of an emerging modernizing West. A major shift of power was taking place as declining Muslim fortunes reversed the relationship of the Islamic world to the West—from that of an expanding offensive movement to a defensive posture. The dominant role Islam had played in world history was fast disappearing, while Christian Europe "was experiencing a prolonged period of outstanding creativity which was to prove historically decisive for all the world."[7] As Marshall Hodgson observed: "The most central Muslim areas were rapidly becoming a backwater."[8]

By the late nineteenth and early twentieth centuries, European imperial penetration of the Islamic world extended from Morocco to Indonesia. Military and economic presence often culminated in foreign political domination or rule: the French in North, West, and Equatorial Africa, and the Levant (now Lebanon and Syria); the British in Palestine, Transjordan, Iraq, the Arabian Gulf, and the Indian subcontinent; the Dutch in Southeast Asia. Where Muslims retained self rule, as in the Ottoman Empire and Iran, they, too, were forced into a defensive posture against Western political and economic expansionism. British, French, and Russian ambitions chipped away at the territory and political stability of both empires.

Muslim responses to Christian Europe's power and dominance ranged from rejection to adaptation, from Islamic withdrawal to acculturation and reform. For many, colonial rule transformed the Islamically governed territory into a land of war, that is, non-Muslim territory. Although Christians had always been regarded as believers, "People of the Book," European colonizers were now denounced as unbelievers, enemies of Islam. Some Muslim leaders adopted the tradition-honored responses to foreign intrusions were holy war or emigration to a Muslim territory. In nineteenth-century India, Shah Abdul Aziz, the son of Wali Allah, issued a legal opinion or ruling on a point of Islamic law, declaring British India a land of war in which holy war or emigration were appropriate responses.[9] While some Muslims emigrated to Muslim territories,[10] a greater number joined *jihad* movements. Yet the majority of traditionalists advocated a policy of cultural isolation: withdrawal and non-cooperation. They equated any form of political cooperation with the West or adaptation to Western culture as betrayal and surrender.

A third major Muslim response to the West emerged during the nineteenth century. It was led by reform minded Muslims who sought to respond to, rather than simply to react against, the challenge of Western imperialism. Muslim reform was both secular and Islamic. The initial impetus for reform came from the West; Muslim governments during the nineteenth century sought to strengthen themselves by looking to Europe to modernize their military and bureaucracy. Modernization soon came to include the gradual Westernizing of politics, law, and education. Two major examples of secular reform occurred in the Central Ottoman Empire and Egypt. By the late nineteenth and early twentieth centuries Islamic modernist movements also developed, seeking to bridge the gap between tradition and modernity by offering an Islamic rationale for modern political, legal, and social change.

Modernization in The Central Ottoman Empire

Modernization in the Muslim world began in the nineteenth century. Since the source of European power was its modern armies, Muslim rulers like the Ottoman Sultan Mahmud II (1808–39) and his vassal in Egypt, Muhammad (Mehmet) Ali (1805–49), tried to emulate the West. They created military training schools staffed by Europeans. Delegations were sent to Europe to study languages, sciences, and politics. Translation bureaus and printing presses were established to make technical information more accessible. Military modernization was accompanied by government attempts to modernize their central administration, law, education, and economy. Rather than turning, as traditionalists did, to their Islamic past and to the *ulama* for advice, this new generation of reformers looked to Europe, to the West.[11] Like the Umayyad and Abbasid rulers, they were open to a selective, pragmatic process of assimilation, appropriating "foreign" ideas, methods, and techniques to develop a modern army and administration. However, early nineteenth century modernization efforts were not extended to all areas of society in general. Westernizing modernization had its primary impact on the military-bureaucratic institutions of the state. Change was adopted by the state and implemented by a small political elite. These reforms were initiated, formulated, and imposed from above by ruling elites. They were responding to the external threat of European expansionism not to internal, societal pressures for social change.

During the latter half of the nineteenth century, modernization progressively expanded into other spheres of life. Early attempts to strengthen military defense were followed by a more widespread modernization program in the Ottoman empire under the Sultans Abdulmejid (1839–61) and Abdul Hamid II (1876–1909) and in Egypt under Khedive (Viceroy) Ismail. The piecemeal modernization initiated in the Central Ottoman Empire under Mahmud II was developed and systematized by his son, Abdulmejid (1839–61), through an ambitious series of reforms known collectively as the Tanzimat (reorganizations). Islamic institutions were challenged by the establishment of state-supported, modern, European-inspired counterparts: new secular schools to train not only the military but a new bureaucratic corps; land reforms; new, European inspired legal codes and courts to regulate civil, commercial and penal affairs. Traditional institutions of the Islamic state succumbed to a gradual process of secularization: the separation of religion from the institutions and functions of the state. Opposition to the Tanzimat reforms came from conservative religious elements who viewed such innovations as unwarranted deviations (bida) from religion which undermined the traditional Islamic basis of the Ottoman Empire and would lead to the westernization and secularization of society. Even modern oriented political leaders like Ahmed Vefik seriously questioned the grafting of these new "imported" concept and institutions, fearing that: "An attempt to introduce, wholesale, European institutions into Turkey, and to engraft European civilization upon the ancient traditional Turkish political system, before it was prepared for so great an innovation, could not possible prove successful, and must inevitably so weaken the Ottoman Empire that it would lose the little strength and independence that it still possesssed."[12]

Under Abdul Hamid II's (1876–1909) grand vizier Midhat Pasha, the Tanzimat reforms were extended to introduce western political institutions. The promulgation of the First Ottoman Constitution in 1876 was based upon French and Belgian models and included a constitutional monarchy with a two chamber parliament. However, it quickly became apparent that Abdul Hamid's commitment to modernization was more military and technological than political. He refused to surrender the sultan's absolute power and, in fact, despotically set about crushing liberal reforms and eliminating reformers through persecution and exile. In order to mask his true intentions, Abdul Hamid appealed to religion; he resurrected the title of caliph and tried to set a pan-Islamic movement in motion. He sought to rally Muslim support within and without the Ottoman empire by appealing to Muslim unity against Christian nationalist movements that had sprung up among his Christian Balkan subjects in southeast Europe. However, political dissent among Muslim as well as non-Muslims Ottoman subjects culminated in the revolution of 1908, led by the Committee of Union and Progress. Some of the revolutionaries advocated a liberal political ideology, "Ottomanism," based upon a multinational concept of the state. However the CUP, reacting in part to the wave of Balkan revolts, espoused an empire united by a policy of pan-Turanism or Turkification which sought to force all Ottoman subjects, Christians as well as Arab Muslims, to become Turks. Both Balkan Christian ethnic groups (Armenian, Greek, Romanian, Bulgarian) and Arabs (Muslim and Christian) reacted by pressing for greater decentralization and autonomy as nationalist sentiments grew. Among Arab Christians the nationalist movement was spurred by a literary revival in centers like Beirut, Damascus, and Aleppo which emphasized Arabic language, literature, and history rather than religion as the sources of Arab national pride and identity. Societies such as the Arab Society of Arts and Sciences (1847) and the Syrian Scientific Society (1857) fostered Arab consciousness and group feeling. In 1875 Christian Arabs organized an Arab nationalist secret society in Beirut. However, though they sought support from among the Arab Muslim majority, most Arab Muslims remained wary of Arab Christians because of their close ties with Western Christian missionaries who were viewed as an arm of European imperialism. As we shall see, the British occupation of Egypt in 1882 would unite a nascent Islamic modernist movement with nationalism. Islamic modernism would serve as a catalyst in the development of Egyptian and Arab nationalism.[13]

Modernization in Egypt

In Egypt, the Khedive Ismail (1863–79) had initially sought the cooperation of the *ulama* in modernizing Egyptian society. However, when the religious scholars proved intransigent, he adopted the policy of his predecessor, Muhammad Ali, of establishing new, Western secular institutions parallel to their traditional Islamic counterparts. Modern national secular schools were set up alongside the traditional religious system. Islamic law and courts were restricted to family law (marriage, divorce, inheritance) as the state adopted new legal codes based on French prototypes, which were applied by civil courts. The new skills required in a modern society bred new social groups such as engineers, lawyers, doctors, and journalists which were the products of the modern, secular national schools and "now challenged the political, intellectual, and social leadership the *ulama* had always enjoyed and forced them ever farther away from the center of the political arena."[14] The process of modernization was also accompanied by the emergence of nationalist sentiments which developed in opposition first to French and then to British dominance of Ismail's successor, the Khedive Tawfiq. The result was an anticolonial revolt in 1881 led by Urabi Pasha, Egypt's Minister of War. This act provided the pretext for British military occupation of Egypt in 1882 and their *de facto* if not *de jure* rule of Egypt.

As a result of nineteenth-century government reform, the traditional Islamic basis of Muslim states was altered by a progressive secularization of society in which the ideology, law, and institutions of state were no longer Islamically legitimated but were indebted to imported models from the West. The net result was a growing bifurcation of Muslim society, epitomized in its educational as well as its legal system. The coexistence of traditional religious and modern, secular schools, each with its own constituencies, trained two classes with divergent outlooks or worldviews: a Westernized elite minority and a more traditional, Islamically oriented majority. The process of modernization also contributed to the erosion of the traditional bases for the power and prestige of the religious establishment as new classes of professionals assumed positions in education, law, and government, positions which had previously been the province of the *ulama*.

Islamic Modernism: Afghani and Abduh

The modern Muslim response to modernization was twofold. The progressive secularization by governments was accompanied in the late nineteenth century by the emergence of Islamic modernist movements in the Arab world and the Indian subcontinent. Secular reformers had tended to restrict Islam to the personal, moral sphere of life and turned to the West to rejuvenate the sociopolitical areas of life. However, during the latter half of the nineteenth century there emerged a generation of Islamic reformers who sought to unite and strengthen Muslim communities through a reform of Islamic belief and society. Recognizing the scientific and political power of the modern West, they eschewed the rejectionist tendency of religious conservatives as well as the secularist policies of Western-oriented elites. For Islamic reformers, modernity posed no serious threat to an Islam that was correctly understood and interpreted. They maintained that the original message of Islam which had provided the "ideal" pattern for traditional Muslim society remained eternally valid.

Unlike conservative Muslims, however, Islamic modernists asserted the need to revive the Muslim community through a process of a reinterpretation or reformulation of their Islamic heritage in light of the contemporary world. Though they shared with pre-modern Islamic revivalist movements a call for renewal and reform through *ijtihad*, Islamic modernists did not simply seek to restore the past, i.e., early Islamic practice. Rather they advocated a reinterpretation and reformulation of their Islamic heritage to respond to the political, cultural, and scientific challenge of the West and modern life. They attempted to show the compatibility (and thus acceptability) of Islam with modern ideas and institutions, whether they be reason, science and technology or democracy, constitutionalism, and representative government.

Jamal al-Din al-Afghani (1838–97) was a major catalyst for Islamic reform and change and the Father of Muslim nationalism.[15] As he roamed across the Muslim world from India to Egypt, Afghani called upon Muslims to unite in order to regenerate their community and culture. He appealed to their faith and pride. He reminded them of Islam's divinely revealed mandate and mission and of its past Islamic historical and cultural accomplishments: the conquests and expansion of Islam, the establishment of the Islamic empire and the flourishing of Islamic civilization.

Although Afghani did not espouse the rejectionist position of many conservative religious leaders, his call for a return to Islam, for Muslim unity and political autonomy made him acceptable to them. Afghani's espousal of modern science, his assertion that Islam was a religion of change and progress, his call for Muslim unity, solidarity and political action in the face of European imperialism proved an attractive alternative for many of the younger generation. Afghani came at a critical juncture in Muslim history. He identified and brought into sharp focus the major concerns and issues facing the Islamic world, the causes of its weakness, and the major challenge to its very survival. He warned that the inner weakness of the Muslim community, coupled with the external political and cultural threat of European imperialism, threatened the very survival of the Islamic community. His genius was to serve as the catalyst which fired the imaginations and moved the wills of a generation of Muslims.

Born and educated in Iran and then British India, where he first encountered modern education and sciences, Afghani travelled throughout much of the Muslim world (Afghanistan, India, Persia, Egypt and the Ottoman Empire) as well as London and Paris. He has been described as the "agent provocateur par excellence."[16] He was more a political activist than a philosopher or theorist. In many ways he embodied his belief that: (1) Islam was a comprehensive, cohesive way of life encompassing politics and society as well as worship; (2) the true Muslim carried out God's will in history. Whether in Persia, India, Afghanistan, Istanbul or Egypt, his preaching was accompanied by an active involvement in local politics. While he taught Islamic philosophy, theology, and jurisprudence to those that gathered around him, he also implanted his political message: "the danger of European intervention, the need for national unity to resist it, the need for a broader unity of the Islamic peoples, the need for a constitution to limit the ruler's power."[17]

Afghani was distrusted by Muslim as well as British rulers. Invited to serve as an adviser to Iran by Shah Nasir al-Din, he was deported in 1891 for initiating the political agitation that led to the Tobacco Revolt. In 1892 he travelled to Istanbul at the request of Sultan Abdul Hamid. However, after Shah Nasir al-Din of Iran was assassinated in 1896 by a follower of Afghani, Sultan Abdul Hamid restricted his movement and activities.

Attributing the weakness of Muslim society to its stagnation and tendency to blindly follow and cling to past authority, Afghani emphasized the dynamic, creative, and progressive character of Islam. Islam was no simple imitation of the past or complacent passivity but rather the religion of reason and action. True Islam encompassed worship of God as well as active realization or implementation of His will in state and society. Afghani stressed that Islam was more than just a religion in the Western sense of the term.

It was a religion and civilization. Moreover, Islam was an ideology, supplying the *raison d'être* for Muslims both as individuals and as a sociopolitical community. The future strength and survival of the community was dependent upon the reassertion of Islamic identity and the re-establishment of Islamic solidarity. Afghani believed that Muslim revitalization of a subjugated community could be achieved not by ignoring or rejecting the West but by direct, active engagement and confrontation.[18] Muslims could claim and reappropriate the sources of Western strength (reason, science, and technology) since, he asserted, they had also been part of their Islamic heritage as witnessed by the past contributions of Islamic civilization in philosophy, medicine, science, and mathematics. Thus, he exhorted Muslims to look to their own glorious Islamic past as the source for their inspiration, identity, and unity.

For Afghani, Muslim renewal and reform had but one ultimate political purpose, liberation from the yoke of colonial rule. While acknowledging the importance of language and regional ties, Afghani maintained that Islam provided the common, most fundamental bond and basis for Muslim solidarity. Afghani's legacy continued in the Salafiyya movement of his disciples Shaykh Muhammad Abduh (1849–1905) and Rashid Rida (1865–1935). Afghani did not choose between Islamic solidarity and the more local nationalist aspirations. He supported both Muslim nationalism and pan-Islamism. The reassertion of Muslim identity and solidarity were prerequisites for the restoration of political and cultural independence, and unity and solidarity were essential at both national and transnational levels.

Muhammad Abduh received a traditional religious education. When Afghani came to Cairo in 1871, Abduh became his most enthusiastic disciple. After qualifying as a religious scholar, Abduh joined the faculty at Cairo's Al-Azhar University, renowned as the principal center of Islamic learning and orthodoxy. He also taught at Cairo's Dar-al-Ulum, a new college which provided modern education for Al-Azhar students who wished to qualify for government positions. During the 1970s Abduh published newspaper articles reflecting Afghani's theories of political and social reform. Abduh became involved with Afghani in a nationalist opposition movement that culminated in Urabi Pasha's unsuccessful nationalist revolt in 1882 against British and French influence in Egypt. Britain occupied Egypt, and Abduh was sent into exile. He joined Afghani in Paris where they organized a secret society and published *Al-Urwa al-wuthqu* (The Indissoluble Link), a newspaper which embodied Afghani's message of resistance to European expansionism through Muslim solidarity and the revival of a dormant Islam through reinterpretation and reform.

However, after Abduh's return to Cairo from exile in 1888, he accepted the existing political framework and channeled his energies into religious, educational, and social reform rather than politics and agitation against political rule. Abduh was convinced that the transformation of Muslim society required both a reinterpretation of Islam and its implementation among the Egyptian people through national educational reform. Muslims must shed the dead weight of scholasticism and selectively appropriate what was best in western civilization. His knowledge of the West resulted from his reading of modern European authors and travel in Europe. In 1898 Abduh and his disciple, Rashid Rida, published the first issue of the journal, *al-Manar* (The Lighthouse) (1898–1935), which propagated Islamic reform. He worked to implement his ideas. In 1899 Abduh became Mufti of Egypt, head of the nation's *Shariah* law court system. He pioneered court reform. His legal opinions as Mufti of Egypt had the character of authoritative rulings. Abduh reinterpreted Islamic law in light of modern conditions. His rulings ranged from the lawfulness of Muslims wearing European clothing to the permissibility of bank interest. Through his writing, teaching, preaching, and legal opinions, Abduh championed the cause of reform in Islamic law, theology, and education. His influence both in his own time and on successive generations of Muslims earned him the title, "Father of Islamic Modernism."

Rejecting the blind following of tradition, he called for a new interpretation of Islam which would demonstrate its relevance to contemporary thought and life in the modern world. Abduh maintained that there was no inherent conflict between religion and reason or modern science. Change in Islamic practice was both possible and necessary. The renewal of Islam and Muslim society should be based not simply on Western secular modernization. Abduh sought to provide the rationale for the selective integration of Islam with modern ideas and institutions. Thus, the needs of modern Muslim society cound be accomplished through Islamic legal and social change.

Abduh argued that the Islamic basis for change was the division of Islamic law into two spheres: duties to God and social duties to other persons. Abduh maintained that the former, which included beliefs and practices such as prayer, fasting, and pilgrimage, are immutable duties to God. However the latter, social regulations such as criminal, civil, and family laws, are open to and subject to change. Thus, for example, Abduh advocated educational and legal reforms affecting the status of Muslim women. Recognizing the discrepancy between *Quranic* reforms, which had greatly improved women's status, and her social status in the nineteenth century, Abduh had criticized the waywardness of Muslim society: "To be sure, the Muslims have been at fault in the education and training of women, and of acquainting them with their rights; and we acknowledge that we have failed to follow the guidance of our religion, so that we have become an argument against it."[19]

Abduh was especially critical pf polygamy and its deleterious effect on family life. The *Quranic* argument that Abduh developed regarding polygamy was adopted by most modern reformers and used by Muslim states to justify reforms in Muslim family law curtailing polygamy. According to Abduh, polygamy had been permitted in the Prophet's time as a concession to prevailing social conditions. The true intent of the *Quran* (4:3 and 4:129) was monogamy because it said that more than one wife was permissible only when equal justice and impartiality were guaranteed.[20] Since this is a practical impossibility, Abduh concluded that the *Quranic* ideal must be monogamy.

Abduh's associate, Qasim Amin (1863–1908), developed the social dimension of the modernist movement by focusing on the plight of Muslim women as a cause for the deterioration of the family and society. For Amin the emancipation of women was integral to national development. He argued that true, uncorrupted Islam recognized the equality of both sexes. He criticized as un-Islamic customs such as the veiling and social seclusion of women, arranged marriages, the wife's lack of power to divorce, and the husband's unlimited rights of divorce. He believed that all these perpetuated the bondage of women. Following Abduh, Amin re-emphasized the original *Quranic* intent that divorce be viewed as reprehensible although permissible when necessitated by failure of the marriage and of attempts at arbitration. As a step toward providing some relief, he recommended that women have equal rights of divorce with men.[21]

Reactions to Amin's feminist books, *Tahrir al-Mar'ah* (The Emancipation of Women) and *al-Mar'ah al-jadidah* (The New Woman), and his ideas were swift and harshly critical. Conservative religious as well as some nationalist leaders dismissed Amin's stand as a desire to ape the West which would undermine the family and weaken Egyptian society. However, his writings became a source of inspiration to many feminists. Madame Huda Sha-arawi, a leader of the feminist movement in Egypt a generation later, hailed him as "the hero of the feminist awakening and its founder."[22]

During the nineteenth and twentieth centuries, modernization was introduced into the Arab world in the military, bureaucracies, politics, law, economics, and education. The traditional Islamic ideological basis of state and society was progressively altered under the impact of Western, secular nationalism. Muslims found themselves between two norms: (1) the traditionalist belief that religion ought to determine the nature of political organization and that Islamic law provided the necessary standard and guidance for society, and (2) the secular modernist Muslim preference for Western political concepts and institutions. With Afghani, an Islamic movement arose which sought to take a middle position between the rejectionist tendency of many religious leaders and the unquestioned accommodationist proclivities of Westernizing, secular Muslim elites.

Islamic modernism emphasized the political and cultural ascendency of Islam's past; the dynamic spirit and character of Islam and the acceptability of political, legal, and social modernization. Its purpose was twofold: (1) to reawaken the Islamic community and restore its strength through Islamic reform, a modern reformulation of Islam; (2) to overthrow European imperialism in the Muslim world and regain autonomy and independence. Islamic modernism dispersed in many directions. It influenced variety of Muslim leaders from Islamic to secular nationalist reformers and contributed to the development and acceptance of Egyptian and Arab nationalism alongside traditional pan-Islamism. What Fazlur Rahman had observed regarding pan-Islamism and nationalism in Afghani is true of the Islamic modernist legacy in general: "actual influence has been in both directions of pan-Islamism and nationalism, sometimes in conflict with one another. Although the pan-Islamic idealism has not been successful in concrete terms, it continues to inspire various activist groups in different lands and lives so patently, if amorphously, in the aspirations of the people."[23]

Although it did not produce a unified movement, the reformist/activist spirit of Islamic modernism provided a renewed awareness and sense of pride in Islamic history and identity, an Islamic rationale for modern reforms and an anti-colonialist, ideologized Islam which reasserted Islam's relatedness to politics and society. It inspired Islamic reformist and national independence movements in other Muslim areas such as North Africa and contributed to the ideological basis of Islamic activism today.

Islamic Modernism in the Indian Subcontinent

For Muslims of the Indian subcontinent, 1857 was a turning point in their political history. From the sixteenth century, India had become a primary object of companies British, French, and Portuguese trade companies. By the nineteenth century, British military, economic, and political dominance in India was a reality. The Mughal emperor remained on the throne in Delhi more a figurehead than ruler of a Muslim India. The "Indian Mutiny of 1857" (what some Indian historians prefer to call the first war for independence) provided the occasion for the declaration of formal British *raj* (rule) in India. Although both Muslims and Hindus had participated in the uprising, Muslims received the bulk of the blame and retribution. The Mughal emperor was dethroned. The centuries-long Indian Muslim empire came to an end as the British government asserted direct rule over the subcontinent. Earlier Muslim debates as to whether the colonial dominated Mughal empire was a *dar al-harb* were no longer necessary. The *dar al-Islam* had clearly ceased to exist as a non-Muslim government seized power; colonial control of a Muslim empire gave way to the establishment of an Imperial empire in India.

Just as the eighteenth and early nineteenth centuries India had produced Islamic revivalists like Shah Wali Allah and Sayyid Ahmad Barelewi, the post-1857 period generated Islamic movements in the Indian subcontinent. As the Middle East had had Afghani and Abduh, Indian Islam produced, among others, Sayyid Ahmad Khan (1817–98) and his Aligarh movement. Ahmad Khan had come from an established Delhi family and worked for the East India Company. Although he knew many of those who had participated in the mutiny, he had withheld his support and remained loyal to the British. Initially overwhelmed by the chaos and destruction of the War of 1857, he considered emigrating from India. However, he soon committed himself to the regeneration of a devastated Muslim community. Unlike Afghani, Sayyid Ahmad was convinced that Islamic revolts and pan-Islamism were useless. He confined his attention to the Indian Muslim community and espoused a "realpolitik loyalism."[24] Indian Muslims should accept the reality of foreign rule and within its limitations/boundaries restore and revivify their identity and community. Like his Middle East counterparts, Ahmad Khan was convinced that the decline in Muslim fortunes was a sign that Islam was not being correctly understood and practiced; Islam was in need of reform. In the tradition of earlier Islamic revivalists like Wali Allah, he too rejected the unquestioned acceptance of medieval formulations of Islam and claimed the right to a fresh reinterpretation of Islam. In this way, Muslims might see that Islam was not only enduringly relevant to modern society but also not in conflict with Western science and technology. For Khan modern science and modern education were critical for the renewal of Indian Islam. He believed it was imperative to demonstrate that there was no inherent conflict between religion, reason and science: "If people do not shun blind adherence, if they do not seek the Light which can be found in the *Quran* and the independent Hadith, and do not adjust religion and science to the science of today, Islam will be extinct in India."[25]

In 1864 Ahmad Khan founded the Scientific Society which translated important Western texts into Urdu. In 1874 he established the Muhammadan Anglo-Oriental College at Aligarh (renamed Aligarh Muslim University in 1920) and modelled it on Cambridge University which he had visited. Its purpose was to educate Muslim leaders in both Western disciplines and their Islamic heritage. Much like Abduh, Sayyid Ahmad Khan devoted the major portion of his energies to a theological reinterpretation of Islam. This was motivated both by the internal needs of the Muslim community as well as a desire to respond to the attacks of Christian missionaries and the distortions of orientalist scholars. He published a journal, *Tahdhib al-akhlaq*, which provided his modernist Islamic perspective on a broad range of topics. In addition he wrote a commentary on the *Quran* and a biography of Muhammad, *Essays on the Life of Mohammed*, in 1870. Ahmad Khan saw the problem of Indian Islam quite clearly: "Today we need, as in former days, a modern theology by which we either render futile the tenets of modern sciences or [show them to be] doubtful, or bring them into harmony with the doctrines of Islam."[26] He was equally sure of his goal to "justify without any wavering what I acknowledge to be the original religion of Islam which God and the Messenger have disclosed, not that religion which the *ulama* and preachers have fashioned. I shall prove this religion to be true and this will be the difference between us and the followers of other religions."[27] Whereas Abduh maintained that there was no necessary contradiction between true religion and science, Khan, more strictly influenced by nineteenth century European rationalism and natural philosophy, maintained that Islam was the religion of reason and nature. There could be no contradiction between the Word of God (*Quran*) and the Work of God (Nature). Since Islam was in harmony with the laws of nature, it must be compatible with modern scientific thought. Employing a rationalist interpretation of Islam, he felt free to interpret texts symbolically rather than literally in dealing with such questions as evolution, the existence of angels, and miracles.

Ahmad Khan, like Muhammad Abduh, also distinguished between *Quranic* injunctions concerned with religion in the strict sense and those relating to social matters. The former were immutable, the latter subject to change. This distinction enabled Sir Sayyid and followers like Mumtaz Ali and Chiragh Ali to view medieval formulations of Islamic legal and social practice as transient and to advocate widespread social and legal change.

Mumtaz Ali championed the social aspect of Ahmad Khan's reformism in India. Ali's special concern for women's rights led to the publishing of the journal *Tahdhib al-niswan*, through which he asserted the need for equality of women with men in marriage and social customs. Like his Egyptian counterpart, Qasim Amin, he stressed the right of equal educational opportunities for women, arguing it would make for better marriages between intellectually equal companions. Ali refuted the anti-feminist exegesis of many classical Muslim scholars, maintaing that their interpretations reflected not the meaning of the *Quranic* text but the customs and mores of the exegetes' own times. In language strikingly similar to the Egyptian Qasim Amin, Mumtaz Ali maintained that the inferior position of Muslim women was due to their lack of education and subjection to marriage laws and customs that needed fundamental reform. He criticized child marriages and arranged marriages, asserting that marriage must be based on love and free choice. Ali also followed Ahmad Khan's *Quranic* interpretation (*Quran* 4:3, 129) regarding polygamy as a tolerated institution which must in contemporary society give way to the *Quranic* ideal—monogamy.

While Mumtaz Ali provided the modernist critique for social reform, Chiragh Ali, a close protégé of Ahmad Khan, spoke more directly to the need for legal reform to implement needed social changes. For Chiragh Ali, Islam is distinct from any particular social system. However, the law books of the four Sunni schools reflect the social system of Muslim society during the period of their formation. Failure to recognize this had led Muslims in the past to identify their social system and its institutions with the *Quran*, and thus to regard them as ideal. Since society has changed, Chiragh Ali argued, Muslim law must also be updated to meet new social needs. The legal manuals of the law schools are not immutable sources to be blindly imitated. Ali argued that reform in Muslim family law was both desireable and Islamically possible. In many ways such change would continue the process of reform begun in early Islam. If Muslim family law is viewed in the proper historical context, vis-à-vis pre-Islamic practices, Ali believed *Quranic* reforms regarding women's position in marriage, divorce, inheritance, would be judged truly fundamental and forward looking: "Islam . . . changed the attitude towards women to one of respect, kindness and courtesy. The Muslim Law of inheritance, giving a women exclusive right to her own property, compares favourably with the British law. Man's superiority is recognized by the *Quran* only in matters relating to his natural physical attributes."[28]

However these *Quranic* intents and commands (the spirit and letter of its laws) were diverted through the ages by jurists who, in areas such as polygamy and divorce, developed laws which reflected customary practices often at odds with the *Quran*. Thus, Ali believed, an overhauling of traditional Islamic law to eliminate anachronistic customary practices alien to the *Quran* was essential to the modernization of the Muslim community.

Ahmad Khan's Aligarh movement, with its positive orientation towards modernization, served as a catalyst for the development of modernism in the Indian Muslim community. When Indian nationalism emerged during the late nineteenth century, he urged Muslims not to participate in the nationalist movement. He believed that even in a secular Indian nation, the Hinda majority would rule and thus threaten the continued existence and strength of the Muslim community. At first, many Muslins did not follow his example. However, by the 1930s, Ahmad Khan's modernist legacy informed the Muslim nationalism of Muhammad Iqbal and Muhammad Ali Jinnah, leaders in the call for a separate Muslim state—Pakistan.

CONCLUSION

Islamic modernists were trailblazers for they did not simply seek to return to the straight path of Islam but to chart its future direction. They were pioneers who planted the seeds for the acceptance of change, a struggle that has continued. While their secular counterparts simply looked to the West, Islamic reformers attempted to establish a continuity between their Islamic heritage and modern change. On the one hand, they based their principal arguments on revelation and Islamic history and identified themselves with their pre-modernist Islamic revivalist predecessors. On the other, they borrowed freely from Western thought and institutions. However, as with secular political elites, Islamic modernists were a minority. They sought to inspire and motivate a more conservative religious majority. The religious establishment was often alienated with reformers' rejection of the status quo, i.e., the unquestioned acceptance of traditional religious authority, and their assertion of a right to reinterpret and refashion Islam to meet the needs of the contemporary world.

As previously noted, modernist interpretation was not that of pre-modern revivalist leaders who had wished simply to reclaim and implement the teachings of the *Quran* and *Sunnah* of the Prophet. Rather than a restoration of early Islamic practices, modernists advocated an adaptation of Islam to the changing conditions of modern society. This process would result not simply in the reaffirmation of the past but in new laws and attitudes towards religious, legal, educational, and social reforms. Traditionalists criticized such changes as unwarranted innovations, an accommodationism which permitted un-Islamic, Western Christian practices to infiltrate Islam. Reforms were condemned as *bida* (deviation from Islamic tradition), a term akin to heresy. Reformers' criticism that the *ulama* were out of touch with the modern world and in need of reform deepened the resistance of many, though not all, of the religious establishment to Islamic modernism. What then can we say specifically regarding the accomplishments and contribution of Islamic modernism?

First, Islamic modernism implanted an outlook or attitude toward the past as well as the future. Pride in an Islamic past and the achievements of Islamic civilization provided Muslims with a renewed sense of identity and purpose. This countered the sense of weakness and religio-cultural backwardness fostered by the reality of subjugation to the West and by the preaching of many Christian missionaries. At the same time, emphasis on the dynamic, progressive, and rational character of Islam enabled new generations of Muslims to more confidently embrace modern civilization.

Second, belief in the absolute relevance of Islam, its compatibility and adaptability to modernity, inspired reformers throughout much of the Islamic world.

Third, reformers' espousal of an assimilative and creative

process of reinterpretation fostered a transformation of the meaning of traditional beliefs and institutions to accommodate and legitimate modern political and social change. As a result, future generations of Muslims, whether modernist or traditionalist oriented, have come to speak of Islamic "democracy", to view traditional concepts of community consensus and consultation as conducive to parliamentary forms of representative government, to accept forms of Muslim nationalism and Islamic socialism. Moreover, the use of *ijtihad* to formulate fresh responses to modern conditions came to be used quite readily by the religious establishment itself. In the name of Islam nationalist ideologies such as the Arab nationalism/socialism of Egypt's Gamal Abd al-Nasir, Libya's Qaddafi and Algeria's Islamic socialism, were initially legitimated by *ulama*. Governments obtained *fatwas* to justify new policies regarding land reform, nationalism of banks or critical industries, and birth control.

Fourth, the anti-colonial thrust of both Afghani and later Rashid Rida's Salafiyya thought, their emphasis on Islam as a self sufficient alternative to the West, assured their continued influence among Islamic activists from Egypt's Muslim Brotherhood to contemporary Islamic revivalist organizations.

However, the Islamic modernist legacy is a mixed one. Neither Muhammad Abduh nor Ahmad Khan produced a systematic, comprehensive theology or reformist program. As we shall see, their disciples later travelled in many directions. The examples of both Muslim family law reform and the development of modern nationalism exemplify the diffuse and, at times, inconsistent nature of the modernist legacy.

The spirit of Islamic modernism was a major factor in the development of early women's emancipation movements among upper and middle class Muslim women and the subsequent reform of Muslim family law which provided the major theater for modernist activity.

Although Islamic law had been displaced by European based civil and criminal codes, Muslim family law had remained intact. However, during the post-World War I period, governments in Muslim countries enacted modern Muslim family law legislation which had a two-fold purpose: (1) to improve the status of women (2) to strengthen the rights of nuclear family members vis a vis more distant members of the extended family, favored by traditional law. Reforms occurred in three major areas: marriage, divorce and inheritance. Thus, for example, legislation was enacted to eliminate child marriages, restrict polygamy, curtail a man's unfettered, unilateral right to divorce his wife, and to increase a woman's grounds for divorcing her husband.

The Islamic modernist legacy was employed in drafting and justifying reform legislation. Governments cited reformist concepts such as the right to *ijtihad* and the public interest to justify legal changes for the betterment of Muslim society. The main argument for restricting polygamy was specifically based upon Muhammad Abduh's and Ahmad Khan's modernist reinterpretation of the *Quran.* However, because of the *ad hoc* use of modernist teachings, and the drafting of modern legislation by modern political elites, not by the traditional religious authorities, legal reforms were resisted. Traditionalists often viewed such reforms as an Islamic facade employed by westernized, secular elites to justify their desire to further ape the West. The state's unwillingness to directly challenge the continued strength of traditional Islam could be seen in the fact that, except for Tunisia, failure to observe modern family law reforms in most Muslim countries renders the act illegal but not invalid. Should a man, for example, ignore reform legislation in contracting a polygamous marriage, he is subject to prosecution for violating state law, but his marriage is not invalidated!

A second example of the failure to develop a united Islamic modernist movement and to provide a systematic reformist program is the differing paths followed by the disciples of early modernists. As will be seen in the next chapter, the Afghani-Abduh legacy took a more conservative turn in Rashid Rida's Salafiyya movement. At the same time, it also contributed to the development of Egyptian and Arab nationalism. Under other Abduh followers, like Lutfi al-Sayyid, Ali Abd al-Raziq, and Taha Hussein, it resulted in a secular, Egyptian, nationalism.

Islamic revivalist and modernist movements provided a variety of Muslim approaches to the regeneration of a debilitated and subjugated community. This reformist legacy was often linked to the development of nationalism in the Arab East, Arab West (North Africa), and the Indian subcontinent.

3

Nationalism

A S WE HAVE SEEN, a major crisis in Islamic history and in
Muslim identity had been precipitated by the advent of
European colonialism. By the end of the nineteenth century the Islamic world had in large part succumbed to Western Christendom—economically, militarily, and, finally, politically. The
disintegration of the traditional Islamic political order and the struggle against European colonialist intervention and rule provided both
an identity crisis and a political purpose for Muslims in the twentieth
century. The ground had been prepared by Muslim reformers like
Jamal al-Din al-Afghani, with his call to resist imperialism, seek political liberation, and undertake an intellectual reawakening rooted in a
return to Islam.

Two major political trends, often interrelated, predominated:
anti-colonial independence movements and the emergence of modern nationalism. Islam played an important role in each. First, in
independence movements in North Africa and the Indian subcontinent, Islam served as a unifying rallying cry, providing an identity
and allegiance, ideology and symbols, leadership and mosque-based
communications centers. Second, the development of modern Muslim nationalism was indebted to Islamic modernist as well as secular
nationalist leaders. Given the transnational religious ideology of
Islam, the shift in loyalty from the pan-Islamic community to the
more limited modern nation state required a process of ideological
redefinition and legitimation. Islam was integral to the development
of nationalist ideologies: Egyptian, Arab and Iranian nationalism as
well as Tunisian, Algerian, Moroccan and Pakistani nationalism.

THE ARAB EAST: FROM ISLAMIC REFORM TO ARAB NATIONALISM

The Arab Christian Literary Movement and the Young Ottoman Turkification program had stirred early nationalist sentiments in the Ottoman Empire. However, Arab and Egyptian nationalism in the Middle East did not really develop until after World War I and as the result of three major influences: (1) the break up of the Ottoman Empire after World War I and the emergence of modern states which no longer shared a common (Islamic) religiously rooted ideology and religiously legitimated sociopolitical order; (2) the intensified struggle for independence from the political and religio-cultural dominance of European imperialism and (3) the ideological influence of the Salafiyya movement of Afghani's disciples—Muhammad Abduh and Rashid Rida.

In retribution for Ottoman support for Germany during World War I, the European Allies in the Treaty of Sèvres of August 1920 dismembered the Ottoman Empire, placing a major portions of the empire under a mandate (Great Power) system of government. The Arab provinces were placed under France and Britain. France took control of Syria and Lebanon; Britain governed Iraq, Palestine and Transjordan. In Egypt, British control had been tightened in response to Ottoman entrance into World War I on Germany's side; Britain declared Egypt a protectorate and deposed the Khedive, Abbas Hilmi II.

By the end of World War I a strong independence movement led by Saad Zaghlul (1857–1927), a former disciple of Afghani, friend of Abduh and leader of the "Egypt for Egyptians" movement, forced the British to end the protectorate in 1922. Egypt was granted a limited conditional form of independence; Egypt refused to accept anything but complete independence. Not until 1956 was the British occupation of Egypt finally terminated. In Egypt, as in the mandate areas, resentment toward continued European political, military, and economic hegemony fueled nationalist fervor and provided a common goal for opposition movements otherwise divided by class, region, tribe, or degree of religious (vs. secular) commitment.

Three ideological orientations emerged during this period: the Salafiyya reformism of Rashid Rida, Egyptian nationalism, and Arab nationalism. All were influenced by the Islamic reformist spirit of Afghani and Abduh which continued through the Salafiyyah (*salaf*, ancestors) movement, i.e., a reform based upon a return to the practice of Muhammad and the early Muslim community. However, as the twentieth century unfolded, Abduh's disciples and friends took a number of directions ranging from the increasingly conservative position of Rashid Rida to the more acculturationist, secular nationalism of Saad Zaghlul, Lutfi al-Sayyid, Taha Hussein and others. Thus, the legacy of Islamic modernism, though diffuse, informed nationalist leaders and ideology from Salafiyyah reformism to Egyptian and Arab nationalism.

The Salafiyyah Movement of Rashid Rida

Rashid Rida (1865–1935) has been called the "mouthpiece of Abduh."[1] While this describes his reverence for Muhammad Abduh and their close relationship, during the thirty-year period after Abduh's death (1905), Rida developed his own distinctive position and legacy. With Rida, Islamic reformism took a more fundamentalist turn. Born in Tripoli (then Syria and now Lebanon) after an early education at a local *Quranic* school, he studied at the Ottoman government school and at Shaykh Husayn al-Jisri's school in Tripoli where he was exposed to modern learning as well as the Islamic classics. Here Rida met Muhammad Abduh and first became acquainted with Afghani and Abduh's *Urwa al-wuthqa*. Rida's strong attraction to Afghani and Abduh and the extent to which their reformist ideas seemed to penetrate his very being are revealed in the following recollection:

I found several copies of the journal among my father's papers, and every number was like an electric current striking me, giving my soul a shock, or setting it in a blaze, and carrying me from one state to another. . . . My own experience, and that of others, and history, has taught me that no other Arabic discourse in this age or the centuries which preceded it has done what it did in the way of touching the seat of emotion in the heart and persuasion in the mind.[2]

Rida became a devoted disciple of Abduh from 1894 until his death in 1905. In 1897 he joined Abduh in Cairo and in 1898 the first edition of their jounal, *al-Manar*, was published. It remained the primary vehicle for Salafiyya reformist thought. The contents of the many volumes of *al-Manar* reflect the broad range of its concern for Islamic reform: doctrine and spirituality, *Quran* and *Tafsir* (commentary), political and legal modernization.

The departure point for Salafiyya thought was the legacy of Afghani and Abduh. Islamic reform was a *sine qua non* for the revitalization of the Muslim community and the restoration of its lost political power and prosperity. Like Afghani, Rida attributed the decline in Islam to stagnation and blind imitation which impaired the ability of Islam to respond to changing needs through modern political and legal reform. Following Muhammad Abduh, Rida believed that the return of Islam to a central position in public life required the restoration and reform of Islamic law. The development of a modern Islamic legal system was a fundamental priority and starting point. He rejected the authority of medieval law, distinguishing between matters of ritual and worship which were fixed and those related to social laws which are subject to adaptation and change by successive generations of Muslims where public welfare requires reform:

> Creed and ritual were completed in detail so as to permit neither additions or subtractions, and whoever adds to them or substracts from them is changing Islam and bring forth a new religion. As for the rules of *muamalat* [social laws], beyond decreeing the elements of virtue and establishing penalties for certain crimes, and beyond imposing the principle of consultation, the Law Giver delegated the affair in its detailed applications to the leading *ulama* and rulers, who, according to law, must possess knowledge and moral probity, to decide by consulting one another what is more beneficial for the Community according to the circumstances of the times.[3]

Therefore, Islamic legal reform requires an Islamic government, i.e., the restoration of the caliphate. For Rida the true Islamic political system is based upon consultation between the caliph and the *ulama* who are the guardian interpreters of Islamic law. However, like most modernists, he believed that the *ulama* were backward and ill-equipped to reinterpret Islam in light of modern exigencies. Therefore, Rida advocated the development of a group of Islamic progressive thinkers who could bridge the gap between the conservative *ulama* and Westernized elites.

The political realities of the post-World War I period forced Rida into reluctant political compromises as well as a shift in his reformism to a more assertive conservative position. His long support for a universal caliphate gave way to a grudging acceptance of an Arab nationalism informed by Islam.

Turkey, the sole remnant of the former Ottoman Empire, emerged as a nation state, led by Mustapha Kemal (Ataturk) who, in rapid succession, abolished the caliphate (1924) and set Turkey on a Western, secular path of political, social, and legal development. Therefore, without a caliph/sultan and the Ottoman Empire, who was the just Muslim ruler? Where was the pan-Islamic unity of the *ummah*? Like Afghani, Rida proved a political pragmatist. Although he advocated the ultimate restoration of the universal caliphate and a transnational Islamic community, he also accepted the reality of the new separate Muslim states, the importance of Muslim unity, and the need to avoid anything which might weaken that unity and make Muslims even more vulnerable to continued European rule. While some of Abduh's disciples turned to an Egyptian nationalism, Rashid Rida linked Islam with a broader Arab nationalism. For Rida, as in its early formation, the revitalization of the community was dependent upon Arab Muslim leadership. God's revelation had been in Arabic and the Arabs had constituted the vanguard of Islam, spreading and uniting all under the banner of Islam. So, too, Muslim unity would only be restored again through the Arabs.[4]

Although pragmatically accepting nationalism and the nation state, he also reminded Muslims of the transnational identity of the Islamic community. Both Rida's position on nationalism and its relationship to pan-Islamism as well as the influence of the Salifiyya movement beyond the Middle East are reflected in a legal ruling given by Rida in the 1930s in response to an inquiry from an Indonesian Muslim as to whether or not patriotism and nationalism were un-Islamic. In it Rida stated:

> All the jurisprudents have declared that holy war is a duty incumbent on all individuals when an enemy commits aggression against Muslims or occupies any of their lands. . . . The contemporary notion of patriotism expresses the unity of the people of different religions in their homeland and their cooperation in defending the homeland they share. They cooperate to preserve its independence. . . . The type of patriotism that should adorn Muslim youth is that he be a good example for the people of the homeland no matter what their religious affiliation, cooperating with them in every legitimate action for independence. . . . In his service of his homeland and his people he must not, however, neglect Islam which has honored him

and raised him up by making him a brother to hundreds of millions of Muslims in the world. He is a member of a body greater than his people, and his personal homeland is part of the homeland of his religious community. He must be intent on making the progress of the part a means for the progress of the whole.[5]

Thus, Rida accepted the reality of patriotism and nationalism provided that national unity not overshadow or replace Muslims' identity and solidarity as members of a transnational religious homeland and community which remained the Islamic ideal. In *The Caliphate or Imamate*, written in 1923 in response to the caliphate crises, he declared: "The Muslims consider in fact that their religion does not really exist unless an independent and strong Islamic State is established which could apply the laws of Islam and defend it against any foreign opposition and the domination."[6]

Despite Rida's commitment to Islamic reform and the important role of *al-Manar*, after World War I his Islamic modernism gave way to an increasing conservatism. Reacting to the growing influence of Western liberal nationalism and culture in Egyptian life, Rida became more critical of the West. Unlike Abduh and many of Egypt's elites who were iñenced in their studies and travel by Europe, Rida had had only limited contacts. He believed the threat to be both religious and political: "The British government is committed to the destruction of Islam in the East after destroying its temporal power."[7] He also saw how Abduh's moderate liberal reformism had led other disciples, like Qasim Amin, Lutfi Al-Sayyid, and Saad Zaghlul, to espouse a secular, liberal Egyptian nationalism which restricted religion to private, moral life. Alarmed at what he perceived as the growing danger of Westernizatin, Rida drifted toward a more conservative position.

He had also become an admirer and staunch supporter of Abdul Aziz ibn Saud's revival of the Wahhabi Movement in Arabia. As had Muhammad Abd al-Wahhab, and pre-modern Islamic revivalism in general, Rida emphasized the comprehensiveness and self-sufficiency of normative Islam. The fundamental sources of Islam provided a complete code of life. Thus, Muslim reformers must not look to the West for answers but singledmindedly return to the sources of Islam—the *Quran*, *Sunnah* of the Prophet and the consensus of the Companions of the Prophet. Rida's increasing conservatism was reflected in his restricted understanding of the term *salaf* (ancestors). For Abduh it was a general reference to the early Islamic centuries. For Rida, however, as for pre-modern Islamic revivalism, *salaf* was restricted to the practice of Muhammad and the first generation of Muslims.

As Muslim politics unfolded in the post- World War I Arab world, Islam was only a factor but not the dominant factor in the development of Egyptian and Arab nationalism. Rida's primary commitment to an Islamic state and society increasingly made him less amenable to more secular-oriented modernists than to the religious establishment whose backwardness he had earlier criticized. He feared that modernist rationalism would lead to the Westernization and secularization of society as was occurring under Egyptian nationalism. Increasingly he defended Islam against Westernizing Muslim intelligentsia, many of whom had been Abduh's disciples, rather than against the intransigence of the *ulama*. In the end he became "an ideologist bound by traditional idealism rather than a practical reformer."[8] Ironically he had come full circle from his early days with Abduh when the majority of the members of the *al-Manar* circle were young laity and the majority of the *ulama* were critics. From being an Islamic modernist, Rida had become an Islamic fundamentalist ideologue. His emphasis on the comprehensiveness and self sufficiency of Islam as well as his more critical attitude toward the West would prove acceptable to Islamic movements like Eqypt's Muslim Brotherhood and many Islamic activist organizations today.

Egyptian Nationalism

For much of Islamic history, Egypt had retained its sense of separateness and regional identity. Throughout the caliphate period and later under the Ottomans, Egypt's rulers paid homage to the caliph, but Egypt functioned as a semi-autonomous state at some distance from the central imperial capital and its authority. This strong sense of separate identity was reflected in the development of Egyptian nationalism. Although Egypt has come to be viewed as a leader of Arab nationalism, the early development of the nationalist movement in Egypt focused on a local, territorial Egyptian patriotism which was influenced by Western liberal, secular nationalism and rooted in a sense of separate Egyptian history, identity, and therefore nationhood. Though many Egyptian nationalist leaders were early disciples of Afghani and Abduh, Islamic modernism gave way to a more secular oriented nationalism. The relationship of Islam to state and society was reinterpreted so as to restrict religion to personal not public life. Ahmad Lutfi al-Sayyid, Taha Husayn, and Ali Abd al-Raziq, who were influenced by Afghani and Abduh, are representative of this understanding and approach.

Ahmad Lutfi al-Sayyid (1872–1963) was born in Lower Egypt and received an early traditional religious education. Subsequently, he undertook his modern secondary and legal education in Cairo where he met Afghani and became a close associate of Muhammad Abduh. After a short stint in government, Lutfi al-Sayyid and a group of Abduh's followers formed the Peoples Party and founded a publishing house. In March, 1907 he edited the first issue of their newspaper *al-Jaridah*. In later life he served as a professor and then as the Rector of the Egyptian (Cairo) University. Although strongly influenced by Abduh, Lutfi al-Sayyid, like many other disciples of Abduh, espoused a more liberal secular response. He emphasized national identity, the separation of religion from politics, as well as a process of selective appropriation and accommodation of European political and social ideas.

For Lutfi al-Sayyid traditional notions of the Islamic community had no real relevance to the political realities of the modern Muslim world:

> Among our forefathers were those who maintained that the land of Islam is the fatherland of all Muslims, however, that is a colonialist formula used to advantage by every colonizing nation that seeks to expand its possessions and to extend its influence daily over neighboring countries. . . . In the present situation, the [traditional Islamic] formula has no *raison d'être* because it fits neither the present state of affairs in Islamic nations nor their aspirations. One option remains to replace this formula by the only doctrine that is in accord with every Eastern nation which possesses a clearly defined sense of fatherland. The doctrine is nationalism.[9]

Lutfi al-Sayyid believed that the reality of the modern Muslim world was neither that of a pan-Islamic community nor a pan-Arab nation but a local, territorial nationalism. Each nation must seek to preserve its very identity and existence to gain independence. The Egyptian nation was based on common love and loyalty for a territorial homeland—Egypt: "Their love for Egypt must be free from all conflicting associations. . . . They suppress their propensity for anything other than Egypt because patriotism, which is love of father-land, does not permit such ties."[10] For Lutfi al-Sayyid, as for many of his contemporaries, primary emphasis or loyalty was shifted from the community with its religious, Islamic, solidarity to the Egyptian fatherland, the country, and the nation: "Our Egyptian-ness demands that our fatherland be our *qibla* [the direction to which a Muslim turns in prayer, i.e., Mecca] and that we not turn our face to any other."[11] Islam, while not rejected as a religion, was restricted to private life and to informing the moral life of society.

Taha Hussein (1889–1973), an associate of Lutfi al-Sayyid, reflected the European orientation of Egyptian nationalism. This was especially evident in his attempt to establish the cultural roots of Egyptian identity as well as chart its future course, not in its Arab, Islamic past but, in the West. Although a childhood accident had left him blind, after an early education in his village's religious school, Taha Hussein went to Cairo. He studied at al-Azhar University for ten years, and attended the Egyptian (Cairo) University. He then spent four years (1915–19) studying in France. A member of Lutfi al-Sayyid's circle of intellectuals and politicians who had founded *al-Jaridah*, Taha Hussein quickly became a dominant and, at times, controversial figure in Egyptian intellectual and academic life, serving as a university administrator in Cairo and Alexandria and then as Minister of Education (1950–52). In 1938 Taha Hussein published *The Future of Culture in Egypt* which epitomized the Western orientation of many emerging Middle East elites for whom the acquisition of strength and prosperity was to be accomplished not by a return to an Islamic past or by Islamic modernist reform, but by a liberal, secular reform program which drew heavily on the West. To a great degree their diagnosis judged Islam as either the cause of Muslim decline or as incapable of meeting the new demands of modern life. Their cure was modernization based in large part upon Western models of polit-ical, social, and legal change.

In *The Future of Culture in Egypt,* Taha Hussein addressed the fundamental question: "Is Egypt of the East or the West?" He found the two closely linked in both their political and cultural heritages. In contradistinction to both Islamic modernism and Arab nationalism, while acknowledging Egypt's Islamic past and her Arabic language, Taha Hussein denied the distinctive uniqueness of Muslims' Arab/Islamic past. He asserted that from very early times Islam and the state were separated: "Muslims have been well aware of the now universally acknowledged principle that a political system and a religion are different things, that a constitution and state rest on practical foundations."[12] Hussein closely aligned both Islam and Egypt with Christian Europe in the past and especially in Egypt's modern political, educational, and legal development.

According to Hussein Islam and Christianity had shared the same essence and source; therefore there are no cultural or intellectual differences among Mediterranean peoples. Similarly, he maintained that Egypt's modern renaissance was based upon Europe: "So far has the European ideal become our ideal that we now measure the material progress of all individuals and groups by the amount of borrowing from Europe" (p. 75). Egypt's system of government emulated European administrative and political systems. Similarly, Egypt's entire modern education system had been based on European models. Dependence on European modernization had even penetrated the religious establishment. Islamic institutions, the *Shariah* courts, and al-Azhar University itself, had been so modernized, Hussein maintained, that if God were to resurrect Azhar scholars of the past "they would beg Him in all sincerity to return them to their graves so they would not have to look upon the great innovations, deviation, unorthodox practice that have already been introduced into the university" (p. 76).

For Taha Hussein Egypt had become an integral part of Europe and so he urged: "The world has struggled for hundreds of years to attain the present stage of progress. It is within our power to reach it in a short time, woe to us if we do not seize the opportunity" (pp. 76–77). Such enthusiasm completely overshadowed, both for his contemporaries and his critics today, Taha Hussein's claim that he advocated "a selective approach to European culture, not wholesale and indiscriminate borrowing" (p. 77). Taha Hussein represented the very Western, secular nationalism that Rashid Rida had reacted against. His Islamic critics, both then and now, saw him as an example of the excesses which resulted from many educated Muslims' infatuation with the West. This Western orientation is characterized by contemporary activists as "Westoxification."

Ali abd al-Raziq (1888–1966) took the Western, liberal, secular tendency to its logical conclusion. A disciple of Abduh, he was educated at al-Azhar and studied for a year at Oxford University. Abd al-Raziq was a religious scholar and a judge in the *Shariah* courts. In 1925, he published *Islam and the Principles of Goverment*,[13] which became a political *cause célèbre* in Egypt and led to his condemnation by a council of Al-Azhar *ulama*.[14] As a result he was dismissed from his job as a judge and prohibited from holding any public office.

Abd al-Raziq's book was written in response to the crisis over the caliphate which surfaced after World War I (1914–18). With Allied occupation of Constantinople, world wide Muslim concern for the future of the Ottoman Empire and its caliph had mounted. Whatever the difference in inter-Muslim politics, Christian Europe threatened the centuries-old center of Muslim power and the symbol of pan-Islamic unity. In the Indian subcontinent the Khilafat (Caliphate) Movement (1919–25) was created to promote preservation of the caliphate. Rashid Rida wrote *The Caliphate*, advocating the necessity and restoration of the caliphate.[15] Abolition of the caliphate in 1924 by the newly established Turkish nation brought the caliphate issue to a head. Several Arab monarchs eyed the title for themselves among them King Fuad of Egypt. In 1925, after Rida published an article on the importance of the caliphate in *al-Manar*, Abd al-Raziq's book appeared, denying that Islam required the fusion of religion and political power. Abd al-Raziq's repudiation of this traditional Islamic religio-political position became a lightning rod for orthodoxy.

In 1926 al-Azhar, the center of Islamic learning, convened a Caliphate Congress to address the problem. The Congress reasserted the traditional mainstream belief that the Caliphate is legitimate and necessary. However, it acknowledged that a caliph with both spiritual and temporal authority was not possible, given the prevailing political situation, and so the issue remained unresolved.

Abd al-Raziq denied the necessity and bases of Islamic government. He maintained that, contrary to traditional belief, there were no clear *Quranic* or Prophetic texts prescribing an Islamic government and that none had been established by Muhammad at Medina:

> Muhammad was solely an apostle. He dedicated himself to purely religious propaganda without any tendency whatever towards temporal sovereignty, since he made no appeal in favor of a government . . . the Prophet had neither temporal sovereignty nor government. He established no kingdom in the political sense of the word nor anything synonomous with it; . . . he was a prophet only, like his brother prophets who preceded him. He was neither a king nor the founder of a state, nor did he make any appeal for temporal empire.[16]

Abd al-Raziq argued that the *Quran, Sunnah,* reason, and the very nature of Prophetic mission "forbids us to believe that the Prophet, besides his religious preaching, engaged in propaganda with a view to constituting a political government" (p. 33). He argued that the caliphate, even that of the first four caliphs, was simply a political phenomenon. Monarchs had simply used or exploited religion to protect their thrones. Flying in the face of what he acknowledged as Muslim dogma from its early days, Abd al-Raziq espoused a thoroughly secular revisionist position which completely separated Islam from the political order: "This institution [the caliphate] has nothing in common with religious functions, no more than the judiciary and other essential functions and machinery of power and state. All these functions are purely political; they have nothing to do with religion" (p. 36).

The controversy surrounding Ali Abd al-Raziq's book is significant not only within its limited historical context but also because it crystallized many of the issues which the modern secularism raises regarding the nature of prophecy and the Prophet Muhammad's mission, and by extension the meaning and purpose of Muslim life. It strikes at beliefs, practices, and institutions which have been integral to mainstream Islam from its earliest period: the religio-political nature of Islam (the nature of the community and its divinely mandated mission) and the fundamental importance of the *Shariah* in providing guidance and certitudes in social life. Abd al-Raziq's position, like liberal secularism today, was viewed by many as simply acquiescing to Western secularism. Emulating the secular West, it sacrificed the totality of the Islamic world view for the restricted vision of Christianity, and contributed to the further weakening of Islamic power vis à vis the West. The secular option was then, as it is today, a religio-political issue for many Muslims.

Arab Nationalism

Within Egypt, the Islamic modernist legacy of Afghani and Abduh had taken two major paths: the increasingly conservative reformism of Rashid Rida and the liberal, secular nationalism of Egyptian elites such as Lutfi al-Sayyid and Taha Hussein who, though they demanded political independence from Europe, looked to her as the

paradigm to be emulated in nation building. However, Arab nationalism proved to be the more enduring and pervasive Middle East ideology. Arab nationalists emphasized the Arab nation, a national
identity and solidarity rooted in the common language, history, culture, and geography of the Arab peoples.

Although Arab Christians of the Ottoman Empire had fostered Arab nationalist identity and pride through their literary revival
and secret societies in the late nineteenth century, it had failed to
become a popular movement or ideology. For Arab nationalism to
become a popular ideology, Arab nationalists had to address the
question of the role of Islam in Arab nationalism. This issue was
inescapable given the traditional role of Islam in providing the common ideology and legitimacy for the Middle East's sociopolitical order, the Islamic subculture of the Arab masses as distinct from that of
the new Western-oriented elites. Arab history, identity, pride, and
language had been closely linked to Islam. Historically, Arabism and
Islam had been intimately connected: the language of the *Quran*, the
Prophet Muhammad, early Islamic conquests and heroes all sprang
from Arabia. Arab nationalist writers and organizations, whether
from genuine conviction or political pragmatism, were inevitably
forced to address the relationship of Arab nationalism to Islam. This
need was accentuated by the rejection by most traditional religious
leaders of any form of nationalism as a particularism contrary to the
universal message, mission, and nature of the transnational Islamic
community. Thus, for example, during the 1920s both the Rector of al-
Azhar University, Muhammad al-Jizawi, and the Mufti of Egypt, Abd
al-Rahman Qurrah, had condemned nationalism. Similar denuncia-
tions came from Muslim revivalist groups such as Egypt's Muslim
Brotherhood and Pakistan's Jamaat-i-Islami. If Arab nationalism or
indeed any ideology was to be effective, its positive relationship to
Islam, and thus its legitimacy, had to be established. Among those
who addressed the question of Islam and Arab nationalism were
Shakib Arslan, Sati al-Husri, and Abd al-Rahman al-Bazzaz.

Shakib Arslan (1869–1946) was a close friend and associate of
Rashid Rida. He devoted much of his life to the Arab nationalist cause
in the Middle East and North Africa, and remained a convinced advocate of the Islamic nature of Arab nationalism. Born into a leading
Lebanese Druze family, Shakib Arslan studied at the American school
in Shwayfat and then at al-Hikma in Beirut. A visit to Cairo in 1889
brought him into contact with Muhammad Abduh and his circle. He
was elected to the Ottoman parliament in 1913, but after World War I

spent much of his time in Europe where he published *La Nation Arabe* and was a proponent of Arab causes at the League of Nations. He also served as a link between Middle Eastern and North African Islamic nationalist movements in Algeria, Morocco and Tunisia. For Arslan, the strength and inspiration of the Arabs, their history and civilization, had been Islam. Their decline was due to the fact that the: "zeal of our ancestors, their fervor and their devotion to their faith, has disappeared from among the Muslims."[17] Arslan condemned both "ultra moderns" and "conservative conventionalists" for "ruining Islam between themselves" (p. 63). He castigated conservatives for their "blind obstinacy," "maintenance of hackneyed conventions," "reducing Islam to a religion of mere other-worldly preoccupations" and because they had "declared war on natural science, mathematics, and all creative arts [and] condemned them as practices of infidels and thereby deprived Muslims of the fruits of science" (pp. 63–64). He characterized the "ultra moderns" as those who, upon encountering a Muslim who advised holding fast to the *Quran*, religious traditions, Arabic language, and ethics, "would yell like lunatics 'Down with your traditionalism. . . . How can you progress like others with outworn traditions and customs of the Middle Ages?'" (p. 63).

For Arslan, Islam provided the basis for Arab nationalism, Muslim nationalism, and Islamic reform. He moved easily, if facilely, from one to the other. Islam had provided the unity, strength, and prosperity of the past, so: "If Muslims will resolve and strive, taking their inspiration from the *Quran*, they can attain the rank of the Europeans, Americans and the Japanese . . . nay more . . . we would be better qualified for progress than others" (p. 64).

Sati al-Hursi (1880–1964) moved beyond the generalities of Shakib Arslan and addressed a more specific manner the issues that were generated by the formulations of Arab nationalism, Egyptian nationalism, and pan-Islamism. He brought both wide learning and years of practical experience in politics to this task. Although born in Aleppo, Syria, Sati al-Hursi was raised and education as an official in the Ottoman Empire at Istanbul. Here he became familiar with European political philosophy in the new Ottoman schools. He served in the Ottoman Ministry of Education and after World War I became committed to the Arab nationalist movement, serving King Feisal in education posts in Syria and then Iraq until 1941. He went to Cairo where he became Director General for Cultural Affairs for the Arab League and then Dean of the Institute of Higher Arab Studies.

For Sati al-Husri nationhood is not simply based upon the

will of the people in forming and identifying with a group. Rather, it has an objective basis in reality. First and foremost, nationalism is rooted in language, followed by shared history and culture. For al-Husri the Arab nation is an objective fact, reaching across regional territories and encompassing all those whose mother tongue is Arabic. Language then provides the primary national bond which history and religion may support and strengthen. Sati al-Husri argued against the separatism of Egyptian nationalists like Taha Hussein who looked to Europe rather than the Arab world. Without sacrificing their regional ties (such as Egyptian, Syrian, Iraqi) all Arabs constituted a single Arab union or nation: "the idea of Arab unity is a natural idea . . . a natural consequence of the existence of the Arab nation itself. It is a social force drawing its vitality from the life of the Arabic language, from the history of the Arab nation, and from the connectedness of the Arab countries."[18]

Sati al-Hursi also addressed the problem of the relationship of Arab unity to Muslim unity, or Arab nationalism to Islamic universalism. He argued that, given the vast geographic expanse and the diversity of languages and races of the Muslim world, Muslim unity cannot be realized (p. 66). Al-Husri maintained that a careful study of Islamic history showed that "the political unity which existed in the beginning of its life was not able to withstand the changes of circumstance for any length of time" (p. 67). In fact, Muslim unity was more symbolic than real. He distinguished between "the principles of Islamic brotherhood, in its moral sense, and the idea of pan-Islamic political unity, in its political sense" (p. 68). Fidelity to the Arab nation did not exclude a more universal, religious solidarity with a worldwide Muslim community.

Finally, although al-Husri did not accept the idea of Islamic unity, in order to counter conservative religious forces, in particular the *ulama*, he argued that acceptance of Arab unity did not preclude a continued long range commitment to bringing about Islamic unity which is wider and more inclusive. Arab unity would be a necessary stage in establishing any later pan-Islamic unity.

While Sati al-Husri tried to make secular Arab nationalism religiously acceptable by maintaining that there was no necessary contradiction between Arab unity and Islam, Abd al-Rahman al-Bazzaz (1913–72) argued that Arab nationalism and Islam were in perfect harmony because Islam is the national religion of the Arabs. Abd al-Rahman al-Bazzaz was born and raised in Iraq. Lawyer, historian, and man of politics, he became Dean of the Law School at

Baghdad in 1955 and was Iraqi Prime Minister 1965–68. After the Baath *coup* in 1968, he was imprisoned and died subsequently in exile.

As Sati al-Husri, al-Bazzaz had to address those critics who not only rejected Arab nationalism as un-Islamic but also denounced it as a Western secular ideology. For al-Bazzaz, the Arab nation was not an artificial creation formulated in response to or as a result of European influence. Al-Bazzaz, like al-Husri, believed that Arabism was a natural objective reality based upon language, history, and culture. "Language, then, is the primary tenet of our national creed; it is the soul of our Arab nation."[19] However, as with Rida and Arslan, he also believed that the religious dimension was integral to Arab nationalism. Those who had missed this point were influenced by Western thinkers who confuse the "comprehensive nature of Islam" with the more limited nature of Christianity. Unlike Christianity, according to al-Bazzaz, Islam consists of more than devotional beliefs and ethical values: "Islam, in its precise sense, is a social order, a philosophy of life, a system of economic principles, a rule of government in addition to its being a religious creed in the narrow Western sense" (p. 84–85). Al-Bazzaz maintained that the dualism (spiritual vs. temporal) of Western Christendom is unknown to true Islam.

For al-Bazzaz, Arabism and Islam are inextricably intertwined since the Arabs have been the backbone of Islam—the *Quran* was first revealed to the Arabs, its language is Arabic, its heroes and early conquests were Arab: "In fact, the most glorious pages of Muslim history are the pages of Arab Muslim history" (p. 87). Islam is the "reflection of the Arab soul and its inexhaustible source" (p. 90). Although al-Bazzaz sounded like such Islamic reformers as Rashid Rida, in fact he shifted the primary emphasis from pan-Islamic unity to Arab, Islamic unity. His primary focus was on Arab nationalism as informed by Islam whereas he viewed pan-Islamism as a pious desire which was unattainable. Like al-Husri, he courted the support of pan-Islamic advocates by writing that if pan-Islamism was ever to be attained, Arab nationalism was a necessary prerequisite.

THE ARAB WEST: NORTH AFRICAN NATIONALIST MOVEMENTS

Colonialism, as did national independence, came to North Africa (Algeria, Morocco, and Tunisia) later than most other parts of the Muslim world. French control over the Maghreb (the Arab "West") was established in the late nineteenth century and early twentieth centuries—Tunisia in 1881, Algeria 1847, and Morocco in 1912. If European imperialism had posed a threat to Islamic identity, French policies in North Africa often exemplified its most extreme form. Through a concerted and sustained program, total political and cultural assimilation was attempted and promoted under the French policy of "naturalization" or naturalized citizenship. French language was imposed as the official language and the language of instruction in schools. Arabic was reduced to a foreign status. The most extreme expression of French policy and their "mission to civilize" occurred in Algeria where they attempted "to eradicate Islam and impose French culture. Most of the Koranic schools and madrasas [high schools] were shut down. Mosques were turned into churches. Those who wanted an education had to turn to the French, and the French opened their schools only to a small number of Algerian children, who thus learned about their cultural heritage—their ancestors the Gauls, Racine, Corneille, and the French Revolution."[20]

Key issues in the struggle for independence in North Africa, which transcended the traditional Berber-Arab rivalry, were identity and authenticity. North Africa's Islamic heritage and past provided a natural, indigenous starting point. Islam offered a common history and a set of beliefs, symbols, and language, which Islamic reformers and early nationalists required in order to restore identity and pride; Islam was also an effective means for mass mobilization in opposition to colonial rule. Islamic reform leaders and organizations played an important role in North African independence.

The initial reaction of the Muslim community to the French protectorate was varied. The ulama and Sufi brotherhoods, though resistant to the religious and ideological challenge of the West, made their political accommodation with French rule. While the traditional religious elites held fast to their medieval world view and resisted reform, they accepted French governance and, at times, even cooperated with the government. In Algeria, for example, the head of the Sufi Tijaniyya Order assisted the French in an attempt to legitimate their colonial rule by obtaining a legal ruling from al-Azhar University regarding the permissibility for Muslims to live in a Christian-ruled country.[21]

Given the acquiescence of traditional secular and religious elites, resistance to Western imperialism in North Africa tended to come from young, modern, educated reformers. In its early stages it was an Islamic reform rather than a nationalist movement. Faced with a French policy of total assimilation to things French, cultural as well as political, young educated Muslims saw the need to reassert their own, indigenous identity. Their Arab Islamic heritage was a natural starting point. Their agenda was the defense of Islam, the preservation of Muslim identity and values in the face of a French policy of assimilation, through the revitalization of Islam. Muslims must see that Islam and the modern world were indeed compatible. The primary method would be educational reform.

The inspiration for Muslim reformers in the Arab West was the Salafiyya movement of the Arab East. The influence of Afghani and Abduh upon the thought and outlook of reformers like Morocco's Bonchaib al-Doukkali and Allal al-Fasi, Tunisia's Abd al-Aziz al Thalibi, and Algeria's Abd al-Hamid Ibn Badis (Ben Badis) was such that Islamic reformism in North Africa is often simply referred to as a Salafiyya or neo-Salafiyya movement. This designation is misleading if understood as an organic, organizational linkage with the Egyptian Salafiyya or a single, unified refrom movement within North Africa. However, the ideological influence of Afghani and Abduh certainly had its impact and served as a catalyst for North African Islamic reform. While there was some direct contact between reformers in the Maghreb and those in Egypt, the more extensive influence came indirectly through the writings of Afghani and Abduh, in particular the Salafiyya journal, al-Manar (The Lighthouse). In addition, North African reformers were inspired to publish similar journals such as al-Islah (Reform), al-Shihab (The Meteor), and al-Muntqid (The Critic).

Despite differences in each country's experience, Islamic reform in North Africa did display common features.[22]

First, in opposition to French cultural assimilation, the reassertion of a national identity was rooted in an indigenous Islamic heritage.

Second, in addition to the external threat from French imperialism, Muslim survival was also threatened by an internal decay of the Islamic community attributed in large part to Sufism. As in many other parts of the Muslim world, although the mystical orders of Islam were credited with the initial spread of Islam, Sufi eclecticism was blamed for the "vulgarization" of Islamic practice. Popular superstitions, beliefs, and practices such as saint worship, passivity, and fatalism had been incorporated and had undermined the purity and vitality of Islamic orthodoxy. In addition, the Sufi orders were criticized for their acquiescence to and collaboration with the French protectorate.

Third, the restoration of the unity and vitality of Islam required not only a cleansing but a reappropriation of Islamic learning coupled with modern sciences. Muslims were exhorted to see and accept the modern world, learn from the West, and thus be better prepared to respond to the ideological challenge of the West. Educational reform became the common vehicle for the reformist movement. In an attempt to counter both the modern secular French lycée and the traditional Islamic system, modern *Quran* schools (free schools) which incorporated both Islamic studies and modern disciplines were established. A network of schools that provided a modern Islamic alternative sprang up in major cities of the Maghreb. Within sixteen years of the establishment of the first modern *Quran* school in Fez in 1927, a network of schools extended to major cities and towns throughout Morocco. At the same time attempts were made to reform the curriculum at major Islamic universities such as Qarawiyin in Fez and Zaytunna in Tunis. A noteworthy aspect of reformist activity was its leadership which tended to be modern, educated Muslims rather than the traditionally educated religious establishment.

A fourth aspect of Islamic reformism was its call for reform in Muslim personal life and practice. Following Afghani and Abduh, emphasis was placed on the dynamic progressive character of Islam; the presence of a "Protestant work ethnic" in Islam was rediscovered. Hard work and social responsibility, abstention from alcohol, and the discipline of the Ramadan fast were re-emphasized. Islamic values and morality were an integral part of Islamic reform.

During the post-World War I period, Islamic reformism was transformed into a nationalist movement as religion and nationalism were joined together. Concern to preserve a sense of identity in the face of cultural absorption and to reform the Protectorate gave way to formal calls for national independence. Islamic reformist groups that were relatively small organizations of dedicated elites became linked with emerging nationalist movements. As nationalists of differing political orientations sought to build a mass political movement capable of effectively mobilizing popular support, Islam provided the common denominator that transcended all other political and tribal differences. Their Arab Islamic heritage was a source of basic identity, solidarity, pride, history, and values. Islamic symbols and language offered an alternative rallying point and ideology capable of reaching out to the masses of Muslims and their religious leaders to unite them with elites in an opposition movement. Morocco provides a vivid example of this process.

Morocco

At the turn of the century most observers would have viewed Morocco as a country under foreign control with a weak monarch, quiescent religious elites, and a centuries old division between Arab and Berber tribes. French attempts to exploit the adversary relationship between Arab and Berber Muslims provided the issue for political activists. Though religious elites were open to occasional collaboration with their colonial masters, they remained aloof from any attempts at cultural absorption, continuing to maintain their own schools, Sufi centers, and way of life. The fiercely independent Berbers had resisted Arabization and were deemed casual in their Islamic observances. French administrators viewed them as likely candidates for their policy of cultural assimilation as a means for dividing their Berber and Arab Muslim subjects. In 1930 the French-promulgated Berber Decree declared that Berber tribal areas would be under French and tribal law rather than Islamic law. The decree provided the event that Moroccan activists needed for political agitation, an issue which would join Arabs with their Berber co-religionists. Mosques and religious preachers were pressed into service to denounce the French policy as a direct threat to Islam and to the unity and identity of the Islamic community. The traditional Islamic rallying cry of "Islam in Danger" seemed most appropriate. The issue took on an international Islamic character when Shakib Arslan, a friend of Rashid Rida and a supporter of North African Islamic reformism/nationalism, used his journal *Le Nation Arabe* to spread an awareness and concern for the problem. Thus, the Berber Decree and its opposition served to crystallize a nationalist movement whose programs and language continued within a religious framework.[23]

Islam also played an important role in the development of Morocco's major political party, Istiqlal (Independence) which was organized in 1931 by the Salafiyyah leader Allal al-Fasi. It remained a small group of young, educated, Islamically reform-minded urbanites from Fez and Rabat until Istiqlal adopted the organization and nomenclature of Sufi orders. The result was the transformation of Istiqlal into a mass political movement whose membership grew to 10,000 by 1947 and to 100,000 by 1951. As John Waterbury has noted regarding the Islamic impact on Moroccan nationalism: "Nationalism made no real and important progress until it took the form of a religious brotherhood, the 'nationalist *zawiya*,' and until Allal al-Fasi became Shaykh Allal."[24]

Algeria

Algeria's struggle for independence also displayed influences of neo-Salafiyya thought and the use of Islam in building a nationalist movement. During the 1920s, a number of Islamic reform groups were established by young educated Muslims influenced by Abduh and Rida. Their reformist ideas were presented in newspapers and journals such as *al-Islah* (Reform) and *al-Muntqid* (The Critic).

Among the most important Islamic reformers was Abdul Hamid Ben Badis (1890–1940), a scholar at the Zaytunna Mosque University in Tunis. After *The Critic* was banned, he and others published *The Meteor* whose banner read: "Our goal is the reform of religion and all that relates to the things of this world." In 1931 reformers joined with some *ulama* and founded the Algerian Association of Ulama (AAU) whose motto was: "Islam is my religion; Arabic is my language; Algeria is my Fatherland." The AAU combined Islamic reformism and nationalism and disseminated its brand of Algerian Muslim nationalism through the creation of a network of schools and centers. The AAU escaped French suppression by avoiding direct political action. At the same time, through its educational work and the direct involvement of *ulama*, Algerian nationalism was firmly planted in the minds of a new generation. Modern reformers were able to gain support and Islamic legitimacy by joining with the traditional religious leadership in developing and spreading an Algerian nationalism that was not simply Arab but Muslim.

The Algerian nationalist use of Islam found fertile ground in popular culture. The Islamic consciousness of Algeria's non-elites was reflected in the popular poems, especially those recited by wandering bards. The major themes found in these works are a celebration of the past glories of Islam: the portrayal of the enemy as a powerful demon, an unbeliever (Christian France) who violates the law of Islam; the belief that the current humiliation in Islam at the hands of the unbeliever will be avenged by the Prophet's son-in-law, Ali. The French historian Desparmet concluded that such views " . . . have nourished and brought to birth primitive impulses that accord with national consciousness that the *ulama* are today transferring into nationalism."[25] As Islam was integral to Algerian nationalism, so too it would inform the revolution: "The Revolution was to be a struggle both for entry into the modern world and for a revitalization of Islamic values."[26] The slogan of the revolution would be "Algerie Musulmane" not "Algerie Arabe." It was declared a *jihad*, its leaders were called *mujahidun* (holy warriors), and its journal *El-Moudjahid* (The Holy Warrior). Thus, Islam was the basic impulse in Algerian Arab nationalism.[27]

Tunisia

Tunisian nationalism received a major impetus from the Islamic reformer Abd al-Aziz al-Thalibi, an early nationalist who organized the Destour (Constitution) Party in 1920. Thalibi was influenced by Abduh and the Salafiyyah; however, though he advocated Islamic reform, his energies were devoted more to political independence. The Destour emphasized a national identity based upon Tunisia's Arab and Islamic heritage, Arabic language, and Islamic values. Tunisia was to be modern but to resist French colonial cultural absorption. Nationalists used the fear of loss of identity to assert their role as the defenders of Islamic identity and culture. Islamic symbols became an important tool in mass mobilization of national identity and political agitation. French attempts in 1923 to absorb Tunisian Muslims by offering them citizenship ("naturalization") were rejected on Islamic grounds. To do so would be apostasy since such citizenship meant transferral from Islamic jurisdiction to French. In 1932, a Tunisian *mufti* issued a legal ruling prohibiting the burial of such French "naturalized" Tunisians in Muslim cemeteries. Similarly French attempts to outlaw Muslim women's wearing of the veil were rejected by modernist as well as conservative Muslims as an encroachment on their Islamic way of life and a threat to a symbol of their national identity.

Throughout the independence movement in the Maghreb, Islam informed and complemented Moroccan, Tunisian, and Algerian nationalism. What had begun as neo-Salafiyya Islamic reform in the early decades of the twentieth century turned into a nationalist movement after World War I. Islam was a basic component of national identity and provided the ideological framework and symbols for mass politicization.

IRAN: SHII ISLAM AND POLITICAL PROTEST

The Iranian nationalist movement developed during the late nineteenth and early twentieth century (1870–1914). Whereas in the Ottoman Empire and Egypt the power of the *ulama* had steadily decreased with government modernization, the Iranian *ulama* did not experience a similar loss of power. The Qajar shahs (1794–1925) had not established a strong central government. Under the long rule of Nasir al-Din Shah (1848–96) little effective modern reform had taken place: provinces remained relatively autonomous; tribal chiefs with their own standing armies remained strong; and the *ulama* enjoyed popular respect and power. They maintained their own private armies and their own sources of revenue (religious endowments and Islamic taxes). When necessary, they assumed an effective oppositional role in government politics.

To appreciate the role of the *ulama* in both Qajar and contemporary Iranian politics, the distinctive Shii religio-political ideology which informed the *ulama* attitude toward government, as well as their perception of their role and function in society, must be recalled. Shii belief maintained that the mantle of leadership of the Islamic community belonged rightfully to the family of the Prophet. The institution of the imamate meant rule by the descendants of Muhammad, Ali and his successors were to be the Imams, religio-political leaders of the Islamic community. However, the political aspirations of Ali's party had been consistently thwarted: first by the election of the first three caliphs and later by Umayyad and Abbasid dynastic rule and finally for Twelver Shiism by the "occultation" or seclusion of the twelfth Imam. Shiism had divided into several communities based upon differences in recognition of the specific number of Ali's successors as Imam. Twelver (Ithna Ashari, "Twelve") Shiism, which constitutes the majority community in Shii Islam, accepted twelve Imams. The twelfth Imam is believed to have gone into seclusion in 874. His return in the future as a Mahdi or messianic guide was awaited. He would return at the end of time to bring an end to corruption and tyranny, and to initiate a reign of justice and righteousness.

However, until the return of the Imam as the Mahdi, how was the community to proceed? Who would lead the Islamic community during the absence of its infallible guide? Into the void created by the seclusion of the Imam stepped the *ulama* and the shah. Although they did not claim the infallibility or the esoteric knowledge of the Imam, the *ulama* asserted their leadership as deputies of the Imams. Contrary to Sunni Islam, the Shii religious scholars retained the right to interpret Islam. As official interpreters, they were the religious guides, charismatic leaders who served as a "source of emulation" for the community during the absence of the Imams. However, the shah also claimed to be the deputy of the Imam until his return from seclusion. Shah Ismail Safavi, founder of the Safavid Dynasty (1501–1742), alleging descent from one of the Imams, asserted both religious and temporal authority.[28]

The establishment of the Safavid dynasty (1501–1742) had brought Shii Islam its first major realization as the official religion of an Islamic empire. The Safavids skillfully used Islam, and were relatively successful in subordinating the religious establishment. In practice Shii *ulama* accepted the shah as a representative of the Imam, acquiesced to the royal title "Shadow of God on Earth," and willingly accepted government appointments. However, despite imperial success, Shii doctrine, unlike Sunni political thought, never developed a theological or juridicial justification for the religious legitimacy of temporal rulers.[29] Though the religious scholars were coopted by the state, Shii political theory continued to affirm the Imam as the only legitimate ruler and to maintain an ambivalent attitude toward the state and its representatives. While a temporal ruler might be accepted as necessary for public order until the return of the Imam, ultimate legitimacy was denied him.

Iranian nationalism developed during the nineteenth century both as a response to the increasing threat to Iranian independence and to Islam by the penetration of Western (non-Muslim) colonial powers and as an attempt to introduce formal constitutional limits on an autocratic and, at times, despotic Qajar government. Under Qajar rule (1794–1925), the relationship of the *ulama* to the government changed as they reappropriated their oppositional role as guardians, protectors, and defenders of Islam rather than government advisors and administrators. The relative weakness of the Qajars, both internally and before the Western colonialist forces of Russia and Britain, fostered a reassertion of the Islamic religious establishment's independence, its role as a curb and a check on the state. Religious leaders joined with intellectuals and merchants in forming political opposition movements and in political action. They formed particularly strong ties. Both represented traditional classes with power and prestige and a certain independence from the government. The merchants looked to the *ulama* for religious guidance. After religious endowments, donations, and payments of religious tithes provided a major source of revenue and hence independence for the *ulama*. Both the traditional religious and the merchant classes found their self interests threatened by European modernization which brought new modern institutions and new professional elites as well as European intervention and control of commercial markets. Two such European attempts at market monopolization, in 1872 and again in 1890, served as catalysts for early nationalist activity as Iranians united in resistance to foreign control.

The Tobacco Protest

In 1872 the Shah Nasir al-Din sold a concession to Baron deReuter, a British citizen, which gave him exclusive rights in developing banking, railroads, irrigation works and mining. Both Russian and popular Iranian opposition led to its cancellation of the concession. However, in 1890 the Shah again sold a concession to a British company which gave them a monopoly on the sale and export of tobacco.[30] Popular Iranian protest was initiated and religiously legitimated in 1891 when Ayatollah Hasan al-Shirazi, a leading spokesman of the *ulama* issued a legal ruling against smoking tobacco. The Tobacco Protest (1891–92) received strong support from Jamal al-Din al-Afghani, who was serving as an advisor to the Shah. He wrote a letter appealing to the religious scholars to resist such economic concessions which could only be a prelude to foreign rule.[31] Afghani's role in popular political agitation led to his expulsion from Persia in 1891. A nationwide boycott (1891–92) was led by the religious scholars and the merchants. Smoking was prohibited, the bazaars were closed, and political opposition and demonstrations grew. In December 1891 widespread opposition and fear of Russian intervention, if civil war ensued, caused the Shah to capitulate and cancel the tobacco concession.

The arbitrary actions of the Shah and the success of the boycott inspired the constitutional movement through which Iranian nationalists sought to curb the power of their rulers. A combination of intellectuals, religious leaders, merchants, tribal leaders, and land owners demanded liberal reforms to control the abuses of the monarchy. The core of the movement came from Islamically oriented groups—intellectuals, merchants, artisans, and craftsmen. Shii ideology, symbols, and leadership played a central role in a movement that was both nationalist and Islamic and would become the constitutionalist revolt.

The Constitutional Revolution (1905–11)

After Shah Nasir al-Din's assassination in 1896 by an associate of Jamal al-Din al-Afghani, Iran continued to degenerate. Semi-secret societies supporting liberal reform were established, drawing heavily from the *ulama* for membership and religious inspiration.[32] These societies sought religious legitimacy by claiming that the first such group was founded by the Imam Husayn, Ali's martyred son.[33] The *ulama* became leaders of a popular protest movement, with the mosque serving as a center for political organization. Sermons proclaimed the danger to Islam and compared the tyranny of the Qajars to that of the Umayyads who had martyred the Imam Husayn.[34] Moreover, the alliance of religious leaders and merchants, the mosque and the bazaar, constituted the backbone of the opposition movement. Both took refuge or asylum in the Shah Abd al-Azim shrine, demanding the dismissal of the Belgian customs director and the governor of Teheran and the establishment of a ministry of justice to assure legal equity. Although imperial promises of constitutional reform were forthcoming, implementation was not. The religious leaders once more denounced the government, riots broke out, and the bazaars were shut down. Once again religious leaders, merchants and others took refuge. More than a thousand leading *ulama* from Teheran sought asylum in Qum while merchants flocked to the British embassy in Teheran. On August 5, 1906, the Shah capitulated and an imperial order was issued establishing a National Consultative Assembly.

The *ulama* returned to Teheran from Qum in Triumph. Because of the religious character of the constitutional revolution, the liberal reform measures achieved were seen as restoring a more Islamic government and system of laws. However, as the constitution movement passed from simply one of opposition to that of actually drafting a constitution, the differing visions of religious traditionists and modern Western oriented reformers surfaced quickly. The majority of the religious scholars had expected a return to Islamic law in its entirety. Modern reformers, who included some *ulama,* offered a compromise, the establishment of a parliamentary committee of five *ulama* who would determine whether legislation was compatible with Islam. The essential incompatibility of religious traditionists' and modernists' positions and viewpoints opened a rift which would grow wider. Leading *ulama,* themselves, divided on the issue of constitutionalism as religious leaders like Shaykh Fadlullah Nuri (1842–1909) withdrew their original support, denouncing it as an "innovation and a downright aberration because in Islam no one is allowed to legislate." Nuri concluded that "constitutionalism is against the religion of Islam . . . . It is not possible to bring this Islamic country under a constitutional regime except by abolishing Islam."[35]

The debate among the religious scholars produced one of the most influential defenses of constitutionalism, *An Admonition to the Community and an Exposition to the Nation Regarding the Foundations and Principles of Constitutionalism,* written by Shaykh Muhammad Husayn Naini (1860–1936) in 1909. Naini argued that, in the absence of the Imam, complete implementation of the *Shariah* was impossible. Care had to be taken to develop a means to limit and circumscribe the powers of the temporal or secular ruler and thus protect against the tyranny and oppression of an authoritarian despot: "This sort of rulership is called bound, limited, just, conditioned, responsible and authoritative." Its basis is the "performance of duties for the sake of public benefit."[36] For Naini the establishment of such a responsible government was based upon two principles—a constitution and a consultative national assembly. The constitution should set forth the rights of the people and establish the limits of government. The consultative assembly, composed of the "wise ones of the country and the good intentioned," should serve as guardians and overseers to guard against oppression. The constitution could have no law which was contrary to Islam; the assembly would include a number of leading *ulama* or their delegates to assure that no provisions or draft laws were un-Islamic. However, the *ulama* continued to be divided; the question remained unresolved.

The constitutional period was short lived. In 1907 Britain and

Russia signed an agreement recognizing their mutual spheres of influence—Russia in northern Iran and Britain in the south. With Russian support, the new Shah was able to close the National Assembly in June 1908. Although reopened in 1908, it was disbanded in December 1911. The West's presence and threat to Iranian national identity and independence as well as indigenous demands for constitutional reform would re-emerge during the Pahlavi period. Islam had played an important role in the formative development of Iranian nationalism. The issue of constitutionalism and the place of Islamic law in the state would resurface again after the Iranian Revolution (1979). The pattern of a religious-lay alliance under the banner of Islam would be resurrected in the late 1970s in Iran's Islamic revolution.

THE INDIAN SUBCONTINENT:
FROM INDIAN TO MUSLIM NATIONALISM

In the Indian subcontinent the development of an independence movement and Indian nationalism began during the nineteenth century. Shah Abdul Aziz's legal ruling that British rule made India an un-Islamic territory in which *jihad* or emigration were appropriate Muslim responses and the Mutiny of 1857 demonstrated Muslim engagement in anti-British politics. While Sayyid Ahmad Khan had preached loyalty to British rule in the aftermath of the 1857 Mutiny, it was not long before anti-British sentiments led to the development of an Indian nationalist independence movement. By 1885 the Indian National Congress had been founded, and in 1906 the Muslim League was established. Although some Muslim leaders had concerns about Muslim rights in a Hindu majority movement, in general, during the early decades of the twentieth century, Muslim elites joined with the congress either formally or through informal cooperation in seeking national independence.

The *ulama* travelled in differing directions from each other. In addition to the choices of emigration and holy war during the latter half of the nineteenth century a number of religious scholars, although theologically at odds with Sayyid Ahmad Khan's modernism, had adopted a somewhat similar attitude of political accommodation toward the British. The Deobondi School of religious scholars, although descendants of Shah Wali Allah and Shah Abdul Aziz, nevertheless eschewed politics and devoted themselves to educational and scholarly activities. In Lucknow, scholars at Nadwat al-Ulama went further when they accepted British patronage and even tried to integrate Western disciplines into their traditional Islamic curriculum.

However a series of events between 1911 and 1913 brought together Muslims of differing political orientations, Western educated and *ulama*, against the British in a common concern for preservation of Muslim identity and political rights. The first event occurred in Bengal in 1911. Under pressure from Hindu anti-partition groups, the British revoked the partition of Bengal. As a result, the separate Muslim majority province of East Bengal and Assam was lost and with it a major source of Muslim political influence and administrative jobs. During the same period the Balkan War of 1912 had broken out in the Ottoman Empire. For many Indian Muslims, the revolt of "Christian" Balkans was an attempt to overthrow the Ottoman Empire and with it the caliph of Islam. These events were seen as simply part of the historic confrontation between Christianity and Islam, dating back to the Crusades. This situation was further exacerbated by the Russian bombardment of the Shii holy city of Mashhad in 1912 and an Italian threat to bomb the Kaba in Mecca which further stirred Muslim emotions and concern for the safety of Islam and its holy cities. Shawkat Ali, the brother of Muhammad Ali, and Mawlana Abd al-Bari, leader of the religious scholars of Firangi Mahal, the oldest conservative religious school in India, established the Society for the Servants of the Kaba to unite Muslims in defense of the holy cities of Mecca, Medina, and Jerusalem.

It was the "Kanpur incident" of 1913 that sparked the real confrontation between a united Indian Muslim community and its British colonial rulers. In realigning a road in the town of Kanpur, a corner of the local mosque, used for ritual washing before prayers, was demolished. Arguing that this area was part of the mosque, a group of *ulama* issued a ruling condemning the government's action as an act of desecration and, thus, a threat to Islam. After a gathering of Muslims was told by a prominent religious leader that Islam was in danger and that Muslims must be prepared to make whatever sacrifice was required, the group moved on to the Kanpur mosque to pray. They were confronted by armed police who fired upon them and a riot broke out in which several Muslims were killed.[37] This essentially local incident became a national Indian Muslim cause. Leading Muslim newspapers, like Abul Kalam Azad's *al-Hillal* and Mohammad Ali's *Comrade*, bitterly denounced the central government for permitting this infringement upon Muslim rights by the local municipality. Under pressure from a united Muslim front, the British viceroy traveled to Kanpur to resolve the issue.

The Caliphate Movement

The events and lessons of 1911–13 left their impact upon Muslim leaders like Azad, Ali, and the traditional *ulama*. First, they reinforced the distrust of European colonial powers and stirred anti-British sentiments. Second, both the effectiveness of Hindu agitation in Bengal and of Muslim political action at Kanpur confirmed the belief that the British were more responsive to action than to acquiescent accommodation. Third, these incidents and the appeals to Islam succeeded in the uniting and mobilization of modern Western oriented Muslims along with traditional *ulama*. Finally, Kanpur strengthened the resolve of many Muslims to join with Hindus in pressing demands for more political autonomy. In 1916 the Muslim League and the Indian National Congress formed an alliance with the signing of the "Lucknow Pact." Muslim cooperation in the Indian nationalist movement was accompanied by a growing pan-Islamic sentiment after World War I which culminated in the Khilafat (Caliphate) Movement (1919–25). Indeed the two movements became intertwined in Muhammad Ali and Abul Kalam Azad.

Muhammad Ali (1878–1931) was educated in India and then at Oxford. After a brief career as a civil servant, he turned to journalism, founding and editing *Comrade* (English) and later *Hamdard* (Urdu). When Turkey entered World War I on the side of Germany in 1914, Ali wrote a provocative article, "The Choice of the Turks," for which he was arrested by the British and, like Abul Kalam Azad, imprisoned for the remainder of the war.

Abul Kalam Azad (1888–1958) was born in Mecca where his Indian father, Mawlana Khayruddin, had emigrated from Delhi at the time of the Mutiny. In 1890 the family returned to Calcutta, where Azad received a traditional religious education. Despite his father's objections, he secretly learned English in order to study modern subjects. Azad began writing newspaper articles at eighteen and quickly gained recognition. At the age of twenty two he founded his own weekly *al-Hillal* (1912) which soon encountered problems with the British government for its criticism of Muslim loyalist attitudes toward the British. In 1915 with the outbreak of World War I *al-Hillal* was confiscated. Azad then published *al-Balagh* which was closed down by the government in 1916. Azad was interned in 1919 and again sporadically from 1920 to 1945 for his political activities.

Despite Muslim-British clashes, the majority of Indian Muslims had remained pro-British during World War I while the Ottomans sided with Germany. However, after Germany's defeat, fear of the European allies (in particular Britain and France) dismemberment of the Ottoman Empire and its consequent threat to the institution of the Caliphate, a last symbol of Muslim power and unity, provided the seeds for mass politicization of Indian Muslims. The caliphate issue was used by Muhammad Ali and Abul Kalam Azad to develop a political movement that reached beyond Muslim elites to the masses. Because the Caliphate Movement appealed to pan-Islamic sentiments, it attracted religious leaders who otherwise remained aloof from Indian politics. Muslims rallied to the preservation of the caliphate and the protection of the holy places. Early support came from the *Jamiyyat-i-Ulama-i-Hind* (The Organization of Indian Ulama). They were followed by others. Azad, like Muhammad Ali, recognized the need for the religious scholars to join with Westernized modernists if an effective mass political organization was to be formed. This did not blunt Azad's criticisms of both segments of Muslim leadership:

> It drives me mad to see the deplorable sight that today among the Muslims there are only two kinds of leaders. For the traditionalists there are the *ulama*; for the modernist group, the Western-educated intellectuals. Both are ignorant of religion and both are paralyzed limbs of the community. . . . The first group is beset by religious superstititions, prejudices and stagnancy while the other is caught in atheism, imitation of the West and love of power and position.[38]

However, given the place of the *ulama* in Muslim society, Azad was convinced that mass mobilization and the political revitalizatin of Indian Muslims was dependent upon the assertion of the *ulama's* traditional right to lead the community politically as well as religiously.

The Caliphate Movement eclipsed the Muslim League, and it became a means for mass politicization of the Indian Muslim community both for the survival of the caliphate against European imperialism and in the struggle against the British for national independence.

Muhammad Ali and Abul Kalam Azad brought Muslims into both the Caliphate Movement and political alliance with the Indian National Congress under the leadership of Mahatma Gandhi. But the caliphate movement was short lived. The European Allies ignored Muslim concerns and partitioned the Ottoman Empire.

The Treaty of Sévrès (August 1920) set up a mandate system: Britain controlled Iraq and Palestine (including Jordan); France governed Syria (and what is now Lebanon); the Hijaz was to be independent. The Ottoman Empire ceased to exist. Attaturk, who had emerged as the leader of an independent Turkey, set the new nation on a Western secular path. In 1924 the Turkish National Assembly abolished the caliphate and effectively removed the *raison d'être* of India's caliphate movement. While the battle for the caliphate had been lost, the struggle for independence continued. Islam and the Khilafat Movement had served Muslim leaders like Ali and Azad as a symbol for mass political mobilization and participation of the *ulama* and the Muslim masses who were drawn into India's independence movement. Once in, they would remain so. Moreover, the Caliphate Movement served as an example to Muslim League politicians of the strength of Islamic symbols in politics.

Islam and the Birth of Pakistan

The Central Caliphate Committee lingered on until the early 1930s working in concert with Gandhi and the Indian National Congress. Its demise coincided with the progressive withdrawal of major Muslim involvement in the Indian National Congress. Renewed tensions and communal fighting between the Hindu and Muslim communities resurrected Muslim separatist sentiments. Leaders like Muhammad Iqbal and Muhammad Ali Jinnah of the Muslim League became increasingly concerned about the future of a Muslim minority in an independent, Hindu-dominated secular state. Given a long history of communal differences and distrust, could Muslims be sure that communal rather than national identity and concerns would not become an overriding factor in Indian politics? The provincial elections of 1937 seemed to confirm the worst fears of many Muslims. The Congress Party routed Muslim League candidates in a landslide victory and refused to establish coalition governments in Muslim majority areas. By the late 1930s both Muhammad Iqbal and Muhammad

Ali Jinnah of the Muslim League would call for the creation of a separate Muslim state. At this point three differing Muslin positions regarding independence and nationalism had crystallized.

More traditional religious leaders like Sayyid Abul Hassan Ali Nadwi of the Nadwat-i-Ulama seminary in Lucknow, Mawlana Abul Ala Mawdudi, who would later found the Jamaat-i-Islami in Pakistan, and the majority of India's *ulama* argued that nationalism and Islam were antithetical ideologies. Nationalism was condemned as a particularism which conflicted with Islamic universalism. It was a Western-bred phenomenon rooted in "a narrow national feeling, racial prejudice, and an exaggerated regard for geographical division [which] are the characteristics of the Western mind."[39] In contrast, Islam, they maintained, teaches that all belong to a single, universal community governed by God's law: "Be it in the sphere of economics or politics or civics or legal rights and duties or anything else, those who accept the principles of Islam are not divided by any distinction of nationality, of class, or country."[40] Therefore, any form of nationalism, even Muslim nationalism, was rejected.

A second Muslim position was that of Abul Kalam Azad (1888–1958) who had been the major theoretician of the Caliphate Movement and remained a staunch supporter of the Congress Party, serving as its president. With the abolition of the caliphate and the end of the Caliphate Movement, Azad's political philosophy shifted to a "composite nationalism," based upon the Hindu and Muslim communities' shared history and experience in the subcontinent.[41] Although for different reasons, he would later agree with Nadwi, Mawdudi and the majority of the religious scholars in their opposition to the establishment of Pakistan as a separate Muslim state. To the end Kalam Azad remained committed to Indian nationalism.

Finally, a third position, Muslim nationalism evolved under the influence and leadership of Muhammad Iqbal, the Islamic reformer, and Muhammad Ali Jinnah, the politician, in the Muslim League. As noted previously, communal conflicts had led to a growing concern that the historic divisions between the Hindu and Muslim communities would seriously affect the rights of Muslims in a Hindu dominated state. At the same time the dismal failure of the Muslim League in the elections of 1937 convinced Ali Jinnah and the leadership of the Muslim League that if they were to obtain mass support from the Muslim populations, a formal appeal to religion was the only effective means for building a national, All-India, Muslim movement. Islam provided a common denominator that bridged tribal, linguistic, provincial, regional, and class differences which otherwise divided Muslims and competing Muslim parties. It was the one element that had proven effective in uniting Muslims—modern elites, *ulama* and the masses in the Caliphate Movement.

Muhammad Iqbal (1875–1938) embodied much of modern Muslim India's dilemma. Iqbal's early Islamic education was followed by years of study in England and Germany at Cambridge and Munich where he earned a doctorate in philosophy and a law degree. He was enough of a religious romantic to revere the glories of his Islamic past but was also a realist who could appreciate the necessity and desirability for change and Islamic reform. Iqbal was a product of Indian Islam and could celebrate both the Islamic and Indian aspects of his heritage equally. He was India's leading poet-philosopher, respected and admired by Hindu and Muslim alike. Yet, his realism moved him to turn from the dream of a united India, espouse Muslim nationalism and join with Jinnah, the secularist, in calling for a separate Muslim state. Iqbal provided the political philosophy and Jinnah the political leadership. They would come to be viewed by later generations as Pakistan's poet-philosopher and politician-founder respectively.

For Iqbal, questions posed by secular nationalism for the Islamic world took on special significance in India where Muslims were a minority: "Is it possible to retain Islam as an ethical ideal and to reject it as a polity in favour of national politics in which religious attitude is not permitted to play any part?" Iqbal believed such a nationalist option was impossible since the revealed "religious ideal of Islam . . . is organically related to the social order which it has created."[42] That Islamic social order included a state and a law, the *Shariah*. Any nationalism which challenged Islamic solidarity and life was unacceptable. Iqbal was convinced that attempts in India to discover a principle of internal Hindu-Muslim communal harmony had failed and that the object of Hindu political leaders was Hindu dominance in India. Standing before the All-India Muslim League in Lahore in 1930, Muhammad Iqbal issued a call which was to progressively dominate Muslim politics in India, to subside only in 1947 with the establishment of Pakistan: "I would like to see the Punjab, North-Western Frontier Province, Sind, and Baluchistan amalgamated into a single state. Self government within the British Empire or without the British Empire, the formation of a consolidated Muslim state in the best interests of India and Islam."[43]

Muhammad Ali Jinnah (1876–1948), like Iqbal, had initially been an Indian nationalist. He began his political career as a member of the Indian National Congress and later joined the Muslim League in 1913, influenced by Muhammad Ali. Jinnah remained active in the Indian nationalist movement until the 1930s. However, he left the Congress Party and the Indian nationalist movement in 1932 disillusioned by communal strife and the inability of Gandhi and Nehru to control Hindu militancy. Jinnah turned to Muslim separatism and nationalism, sharing Iqbal's concern for the future of Muslims at the hands of a Hindu majority. Although a secularist, he revived the Muslim League during the late 1930s by consciously turning to religion as a primary tool in the mass politicization of Muslims in the subcontinent. Religious language, symbols and slogans, such as "Islam in Danger" and the traditional battle cry "Allahu Akbar!" became an integral part of the Muslim League's political ideology and rhetoric. Local religious leaders and mosques played an important role in bringing the mass of Muslim peasants and artisans into the Pakistan movement. Though religious leaders like Abul Kalam Azad, Mawlana Mawdudi, and the *ulama* of the JUI did not support the call for Pakistan, they were soon a minority voice.

By 1940 the Muslim League, with its popular appeal to Islam, emerged as the major Muslim political party, displacing competing Muslim organizations. In that year Jinnah set forth his "Two Nation Theory" in which he argued that Islam and Hinduism were two separate and distinct cultures. Jinnah espoused a theory of religio-cultural nationalism which maintained that, despite centuries of coexistence, there had never been a single nation in India but, instead, many nationalities and peoples. While Hindus and Muslims lived side by side, they neither "intermarry nor interdine together . . . they belong to two different civilizations which are based on conflicting ideas and conceptions. Their aspects on life and of life are different. . . . [They are] different and distinct social orders, and it is a dream that the Hindus and Muslims can ever evolve a common nationality."[44]

For Iqbal and Jinnah, the religious reformer and the secular politician, the path of national independence had shifted from a united India to a separate Muslim state. On March 20, 1940, the Muslim League held its annual meeting and passed a resolution calling for the creation of Muslim states in the northwest and eastern (Bengal) Muslim majority areas. By 1947 Pakistan was established as as Muslim nation state, encompassing the areas of present-day Pakistan and Bangladesh.

As in many other parts of the Muslim world, Islam played an important role in the modern political development of the subcontinent. Its vitality was witnessed in the Indian nationalist movement and, in particular, the use of Islam to legitimate a Muslim nationalism which led to the creation of Pakistan as a modern nation based upon Indian Muslims' common Islamic identity and cultural heritage.

CONCLUSION

The evolution of nationalism in the Muslim world provides forceful examples of the role of Islam in mass mobilization and sociopolitical change. The twentieth century brought the Islamic world to a political crossroads. After a long period of colonial rule, Muslims mounted a series of efforts to respond to the political and cultural dominance of the West. Given the centuries long history of Islamic power as well as its continued presence and strength in the lives of the Muslim masses, Islam played an important role in Muslim reaction and response to Western imperialism. It inspired the development of Islamic modernism and contributed to Muslim independence and nationalist movements. Appealing to their Islamic legacy and heritage, Islamic reformers attempted to restore Muslim pride and self-confidence, to revitalize the community politically and socially. Their brand of Islamic reform called for a new interpretation, a reformulation of Islam which reasserted the compatibility of Islam and modernity; reaffirmed the comprehensiveness and relevance of Islamic ideology to politics, law and society.

Despite Islam's role during independence movements and its influence on the early development of nationalism, for younger generations of modern, educated nationalists, religion had been a means, not an end in itself. Once political independence had been achieved, Islam tended to recede from public life as political elites set about the process of nation building.

4

The Modern State

T HE PATTERN of modern political nation building in the Muslim world reveals three general orientations in the governments of Muslim countries: secular, Islamic, and Muslim. Turkey chose a totally secular path, separating Islam from the state and thus restricting religion to private life. States like Saudi Arabia and Pakistan formally proclaimed the Islamic character of their state and the primacy of Islamic law; this Islamic commitment was used not only to legitimate domestic rule, but also to strengthen foreign policy with other Muslim countries. The vast majority of Muslim countries emerged as Muslim states. While indebted to Western models for their political, legal, and social development, they incorporated certain Islamic constitutional provisions. For some, Islam is declared the state religion, and the *Shariah* is said to be a source of law whether or not this is true in reality. Most require that the head of state be a Muslim and provide some state control over religious affairs. Countries such as Tunisia, Algeria, Egypt, Syria, Iran, Jordan, and Malaysia reflect this approach.

Islam was not only a factor in modern state building but also a catalyst in the formation of modern Islamic movements or organizations.

Two of the most important were the Muslim Brotherhood of Egypt and the Jamaat-i-Islami (Islamic Society) of Pakistan. Both offered Islamic alternatives to what they viewed as an increasingly Westernized and hence un-Islamic society. Both organizations have played significant roles within their countries of origin and internationally. The Brotherhood's Hasan al-Banna and Sayyid Qutb and the

Jamaat's Mawlana Abul Ala Mawdudi have become ideologues of contemporary Islamic revivalism.

TURKEY

Once the heart of the Ottoman Empire, Turkey provides the sole example of an attempt to establish a totally secular state in the Muslim world. Turkey's war of liberation in 1919, led by Mustafa Kemal, sought to create in the Turkish fatherland a nation state. Although Kemal initially appealed to Islam, his goal was to counter Western imperialism and establish a modern secular state, not to restore an Islamic empire. Islamic religion and culture were not denied, but the foundations of the new state of the "People of Turkey" was to be the "national will," "national sovereignty." The dismemberment of Ottoman territory and the flight of Ottoman minorities had left a culturally and ethnically homogeneous culture of 97.3 percent Turkish Muslims, so common language, culture, and territory could provide the ingredients for Turkish nationalism.[1] From 1924 to his death in 1938, Mustafa Kemal implemented a series of secular reforms which progressively created a state characterized by the institutional separation of religion from politics. In 1922 the sultanate was abolished; in 1924 the Turkish National Assembly also abolished the caliphate. At the same time the chief religious office of the state, Shaykh al-Islam, and the Ministry of Religious Affairs and Pious Endowments were terminated. Passage of the Law on the Unification of Education made all education secular, thus eliminating the state's traditional Islamic educational system. The ultimate purpose and orientation of Mustafa Kemal's program was formalized in 1928 when a constitutional amendment deleted the phrase, "The religion of the Turkish state is Islam," as well as other references to Islam. Moreover, the constitution declared that the Turkish Republic was a "secular" state.

In terms of classical political thought, the movement to the secular state was effected with the displacement of the *Shariah* by civil or man-made law. In April 1924 the *Shariah* court system was abolished, its judges retired, and its jurisdiction absorbed by the secular court system. In February 1926 Islamic law was totally replaced by a Swiss and Italian based legal system. The centuries-long practical criterion for the existence of an Islamic state—governance according to the Shariah—had been removed. The radical nature of this change was reflected in the new laws affecting women and the family. The *Quranically* permitted and traditionally sanctioned practice of polygamy was simply abolished. A husband's unilateral right to divorce his wife was radically restricted by the requirement that all divorce was subject to the courts. Women received the right to vote and to be elected to public office. In addition, they were given greater access to education and the professions.

Kemalist reforms effectively controlled and suppressed the traditional religious establishment of the *ulama* and the heads of Sufi organizations. The secularization of law and education and state control of religious endowments struck at the very heart of the power and authority of the *ulama* who had served as judges, legal experts and advisers, educators, and administrators of religious endowments with their related social services. Most of these jobs were now abolished and their revenues sharply curtailed. In addition, seminaries were closed, the use of religious titles forbidden, the wearing of ecclesiastical clothing prohibited outside mosques, and religious education in state schools was discontinued.

The Sufi brotherhoods had long provided popular religious leadership and guidance, enjoying great support and influence among the masses. However, if the religious scholars were seen as medieval obscurantists, the Sufi leaders were perceived by the government as purveyors of superstition and backwardness, the causes of passivity and fatalism. Moreover, Sufi brotherhoods, especially the Naqshbandi and Tijaniyya, had joined in opposition movements against Ataturk's secularization of the state. When two shaykhs of the Naqshbandi Order organized tribes in the Seyh Site Rebellion in 1925, the government responded by outlawing all Sufi brotherhoods. The net result of Turkey's new secularism was the disestablishment of the two major wings of the religious establishment, the *ulama* and Sufism.

The attempt to establish a Turkish nation state also extended to the Turkification of Islam. The purpose was to replace Arab Islam, which was viewed as conservative and backward and more interested in a romanticized past than in the present, with a modern, Turkish Islam. Reforms were introduced to have Turkish replace Arabic as the language of religion. Having rejected its Ottoman pan-Islamic past, Islam in Turkey was to be a *national* religion. Ataturk encouraged the translation of the *Quran* into Turkish. Turkish replaced Arabic in the muezzin's five times daily call to prayer as well as the Friday congregational prayer and sermon in the mosque.

The creation of modern Turkey included a broad attempt to purify its history and culture of foreign influences by cutting itself off from much of its Ottoman past. An attempt was made to start afresh and root Turkish identity and nationalism in a reclaimed, if not at times rewritten or fabricated, past. Turkey's capital was changed from Istanbul to the heartland of Anatolia—Ankara. Arab and Persian influences were rejected as backward and conservative. Perhaps the most radical reform was the replacement of Arabic script with the Latin alphabet. This change effectively cut off younger generations of Turks from the religious and literary heritage of their Islamic, Ottoman past which was preserved in its official, religious, and literary language, Arabic. The change in script required a massive program of re-education in order to read and write in Turkey's new script. Turkish was the only language taught in the schools and in which official documents, publications could be printed. An attempt was even made to purge Turkish of its many Arabic and Farsi loan words.

The fez and turban were outlawed as symbols of the decadent social class system of an Ottoman past. Instead, wearing a brimmed or visored hat was made compulsory since, for Mustafa Kemal, the hat symbolized the modernization of Turkey. For traditional Muslims, however, this "Western or European hat" symbolized apostasy, cooperation with foreign, infidel powers. Kemal made wearing of the hat a constitutional provision and, therefore, compulsory. Villagers objected that the brim interfered with their religious duties since the prostration in the performance of prayers required that the forehead touch the ground. Kemal toured the villages, wearing a straw Panama hat to introduce and impose his new system. When traditional religious opposition took the form of violent disorder in the village of Rize, several of its religious leaders who had preached against the hat law were executed.[2]

In order to strengthen the sources of national identity and pride, the Turkish Historical Society (1925) and Turkish Language Society (1926) were established to assist in the process of rooting and buttressing Turkish nationalism. Turkish history was rewritten to foster Mustafa Kemal's theory that Central Asia, the original homeland of the Turks, was the origin of man, the cradle of human society and civilization and, thus, Turkish was the mother of all languages. Kemal's concern was less with historical accuracy than with providing a pre-Ottoman and pre-Islamic past upon which a strong Turkish nationalism might rest.

Kemal's ambitious program of political and social transformation owed much of its success to his total political control of the parliament and government. Only one political party was permitted, the Republican Peoples Party, which Kemal created in 1922. This situation changed only in 1946. The introduction of a multi-party system and consequent greater competition for votes, strengthened sensitivity to the power of Islam in the lives of most Turks: "a kind of rediscovery of the continuing attachment of the peasant majority to traditional Islamic values and rituals."[3] Many middle class Muslims had also remained religiously observant. Although committed to the secular, nationalist ideals of the Turkish state, many Turks were concerned that the pendulum had swung too far, inhibiting Islam from playing its role in personal life and from providing the basis for social morality. While modern nationalism and secularism were the cornerstones of public political life, Islam still remained the "practical criterion for Turkishness," commanding loyalty and providing internal unity.[4] The continued strength of Islam in the majority of Turkish Muslims' lives made politicians and political parties more open to concessions that eased restrictions on religious practice. For the political opposition, religion offered an effective appeal to a strong, widespread popular sentiment.

During the post-World War II period, when the Democratic Party came to power, the restrictive secularist policies of the state were somewhat loosened. Religious education was reintroduced in Turkish schools first as an elective (1949) and then as a requirement unless parents objected (1950). The faculty of divinity was restored at the University of Ankara to train religious leaders. New mosques were built and old ones repaired. By 1960 some 15,000 new mosques had been erected.[5] Mosque attendance and participation in the pilgrimage to Mecca increased to the extent that today Turkey ranks among the leaders (third in 1982) in the size of its delegation to the annual pilgrimage to Mecca. The prayer leader-preacher training schools which had ceased to exist in 1932 were revived. They grew rapidly from seven in 1951 to 506 by 1980. Indeed, voluntary associations that support such activities as *Quran* courses and mosque building grew from 237 in 1951 to 2,510 in 1967.[6] Restrictions on Sufi brotherhoods and their activities were lifted. Public performance of Sufi rituals were permitted as were visits to tombs of saints. The growth of Sufi organizations and religious gatherings quietly increased. However, these concessions did not mean that the state had departed from its secular commitment. When Naqshbandi and Tijaniyyah Sufi leaders became politically disruptive, the government responded quickly by passing a law which forbade the use of "religion to obtain political or personal gain."[7]

The easing of religious restrictions after World War II was also accompanied by the increased involvement of religious groups in politics. The Democratic Party, having found religious appeals useful in its defeat of the Kemalist RPP in 1950, forged an alliance with an Islamic group, "The Followers of Light," led by Said Nursi (1867–1960). Nursi favored the re-establishment of an Islamic state based upon the *Shariah* and guided by the *ulama*. At the same time a number of religiously oriented political parties began to appear. In 1948, the Nation Party was created, advocating private enterprise, economic planning, and a greater role of Islam in the state. Outlawed in July 1953 for using religion to attempt to subvert the republic, it was later restored as the Republican Nation Party.

In response to Sunni Muslim activity, the Alawi (Shii) organized their own political party, the Party of Union, in 1966, to protect their rights as a religious minority. After receiving only 3 percent of the vote in the 1969 elections, they broadened their platform and base of support to include other minority groups as well as the Turkish left. Shortly thereafter a Sunni political party, the National Order Party, was established in 1970 by Professor Necmeddin Erbakan. Outlawed for its anti-secular religious and political activities, it was replaced by the National Salvation Party in 1972. The NSP argues that the failure of Turkey's modern, secular identity to provide a sense of history, pride, and values for society can only be rectified by a reappropriation of Turkey's Islamic heritage. Its ultimate goal is an Islamic state. Critical of Turkey's Europeanization, its emphasizes Turkey's more independent, authentic Islamic past. The NSP advocates the Islamization of Turkish life: politically, economically and socially and closer political ties with Middle East countries.

During the 1970s Turkish public life was often dominated by political extremism, pushing the state toward anarchy. Ethnic separatism, terrorism (attributed to both radical secularist and Islamic fundamentalists), and religious sectarian conflicts between Sunni and Shii increased dramatically. The Iranian revolution of 1979 fueled religious tensions and secularist apprehensions. Demonstrations by supporters of Erbakan's National Salvation Party increased along with demands for an Islamic state. In September 1980 a military junta seized power. The generals, committed to Kemalist secularism and to heading off political anarchy, moved quickly, clamping down on all "radical" elements. Erbakan was arrested and imprisoned for violating Turkey's law prohibiting the use of Islam for political purposes.

The impact of Turkey's secularist program under Mustafa Kemal cannot be underestimated. The abolition of the caliphate and the rapid modernization of the new Turkish state through a fairly comprehensive policy of secularization and Turkification brought substantive change. Yet despite Kemalist secular reforms in politics, law, and society, during the post World War II period Turkey's secular path was somewhat modified, reflecting its political, religious, and social realities. In a state which is 99 percent Muslim and in which Islam retains its vitality among the majority of the population, Turkish governments, though committed to a secular republic, have often judged some accommodation with Islam desirable. Whether its moderated secularism will be sufficient to mute the activism of more militant Muslim critics remains, as yet, unanswered.

SAUDI ARABIA

Saudi Arabia has long provided the example of a modern self-proclaimed Islamic state. The Saudis proudly affirm and their history and practice mirror an Islamic character.

During the post-World War II period, the discovery of oil enabled Saudi Arabia to be transformed from an underdeveloped sheikhdom into a rapidly developing modern state with international status. Although the kingdom of Saudi Arabi was officially established in 1932, its origins date back to the eighteenth century. Modern Saudi Arabia is a product of an alliance struck in Central Arabia between the Islamic revivalist Muhammad ibn Abd al-Wahhab and a local ruler, Muhammed ibn Saud of Diriyah in the Najd (near modern-day Riyadh). In 1744 the religious reformer and the prince wedded spiritual vision and temporal ambition, producing a successful religio-political movement that occupied Mecca and Medina in 1802 and united the disparate tribes of Arabia in what seemed to its followers a re-creation of Islam's seventh century beginnings under the Prophet Muhammad.[8]

Once again there was a unified Islamic community which included the holy cities of Mecca and Medina and was commanded by its Imam, Muhammad ibn Saud. Muhammad ibn Abd al-Wahhab provided the religious guidance and legitimation. They called themselves Unitarians, followers or believers in the unity of God. Affirming the absolute unity of God, a radical monotheistic position, they rejected the veneration of all else as polytheism or idolatry which is the only unforgivable sin according to the *Quran*. Local religious practices, especially those of Sufism, were repudiated. Wahhabi armies destroyed saints' shrines and tombs, sacred temples, and trees. Strict observance of prayer and *Quranic* laws and punishments were enforced.

However, for many other Muslims Wahhabi expansion and establishment of centralized rule over Arabia was cause for alarm rather than thanksgiving to Allah. Within Arabia, local tribal leaders resented the Saud clan's infringement on their power. Shii, incensed at the destruction and desecration of their holy site at Karbala in 1802, struck back through a series of assassinations. The Ottoman sultan, threatened by these "upstarts" who challenged Ottoman control of the Meccan pilgrimage, sent Muhammad Ali of Egypt at the head of an army to drive the Wahhabi out of Mecca and Medina. They razed Dariyah, the Saudi capital, in 1819. Prominent members of the Saud and al-Shaykh (descendants of Muhammad ibn Abd al-Wahhab) families were exiled, and thus the core of Saudi power in the Najd destroyed in 1819–22. Although the House of Saud reestablished itself at Riyadh, by the end of the nineteenth century continued Ottoman opposition in the Hijaz and Eastern Province, the assertion of British influence in the Arabian Peninsula, a successful challenge by the rival Arabian dynasty of Muhammad ibn Rashid, as well as fraternal rivalries within the House of Saud, seemed to spell the end of Saud fortunes. The Saud family fled to Kuwait for refuge. However, at the turn of the twentieth century, Abd al-Aziz ibn Abd al-Rahman al-Saud (1879–1953) reasserted the Saud family's claims and undertook the reconquest of Arabia. Appealing once more to Islam, he led a religious and political movement which rapidly captured and established control over the Najd (1906), al-Hasa (1913), Asir (1920), and the Hijaz (1925). By 1932 the territorial state now called Saudi Arabia had superimposed a central government upon the tribes of Arabia.

Abd al-Aziz had used Islam skillfully to legitimate his claims and achieve his goals. First, the banner of Wahhabism enabled him to justify his seizure of Mecca and Medina from fellow Muslims as well as his battles with other Muslim tribal leaders. By the standards of the Wahhabi upholders of God's Unity, or monotheism, the practice of the other Muslim communities could be denounced as polytheism; such un-Islamic behavior constituted unbelief. They were no longer brothers in faith but enemies; *jihad* was not only permissible but also obligatory in order to re-establish a true Islamic territory. Second, appeals to Islamic unity and solidarity were grounded in orthodox belief and symbols; the establishment of a unified Islamic state was reminiscent of the creation of the Medinan state by Muhammad and his early followers. As in the days of Muhammad, the religious solidarity of the Islamic community provided the one basis for uniting otherwise fiercely independent Arab tribes. It was this Islamic rationale that enabled Abd al-Aziz to recruit a Bedouin army. Islamic symbolism was employed to describe the process by which nomadic tribes were convinced to join in a Brotherhood of believers. As Muhammad and his companions had had to emigrate to establish the first Islamic community at Medina, tribesmen emigrated to sedentary agricultural communities where they might better live as members of a virtuous Islamic community under their rightly guided leader. Here they trained militarily and religiously. By 1930 there were as many as two hundred brotherhood settlements that provided as many as 30,000 warriors. Like their seventh-century predecessors, they were committed to spread Islamic rule in Arabia. Often this took the form of armed conflicts as missionary zeal and military might were combined in what were viewed as holy wars approved or legitimated by the religious authorities. To die in battle was to become a martyr and thus gain paradise; victory meant not only the triumph of virtue but also the rewards of plunder and booty.

Controlling his Bedouin forces proved difficult for Abd al-Aziz as intertribal attacks among the brotherhoods of believers broke out during the mid-1920s. Rebels mounted an ideological attack, repudiating Abd al-Aziz's dealings with the infidel British army, his curbing of their right to wage *jihad* (and thus gain booty) against British protected tribes, and his introduction of such Western devices as the automobile and telegraph. Abd al-Aziz crushed the revolt, eliminating his brotherhood opposition in 1929–30; tribal stability was restored.[9]

The traditional Islamic world view had been used to buttress and give meaning to the Saud movement. Through force, statesmanship, and ideological mobilization, the tribes of the Arabian peninsula were united by the Saud tribe, and in 1932 the kingdom of Saudi Arabia was proclaimed. The union of the twin forces of Islam and the Saud family was vividly symbolized in the Saudi flag which combines the confession of faith with the crossed swords of the House of Saud and Abd al-Wahhab.

Islam has continued to provide the ideological basis for Saudi rule and its legitimacy. Although kingship is not an Islamic institution, the monarchy has been rationalized by the claim that all, even the king, are subservient to Islamic law. The *Quran* and *Shariah* provide the basis and fundamental structure of the state—its constitution, law, and judiciary. Moreover, this policy has also provided great flexibility since the royal family is free to regulate all areas which are not specifically covered by the *Quran* and *Shariah*. The Saud attitude toward the complete adequacy of the *Shariah* and thus superfluousness of a written constitution was reflected in a speech of Prince Faisal in 1963, one year prior to his becoming king: "What does a man aspire to? He wants 'good.' It is there, in the Islamic *Sharia*. He wants security. It is there also. Man wants freedom. It is there. He wants remedy. It is there. He wants propagation of science. It is there. Everything is there, inscribed in the Islamic *Sharia*."[10]

In many ways the king symbolizes the union of sacred and secular power. He is head of the Saud family of some 4,000 princes, the leading shaykh in a tribal society, leader of the *ulama* who serve as his religious advisors, Protector of the Holy Cities of Mecca and Medina, and head of state. Unfettered by a constitution, legislature or political parties, the House of Saud enjoys political power exceeded only by its oil wealth. The executive, legislative, and judicial activities of the state are overseen by the king, assisted by the Council of Ministers (created in 1953) and the bureaucracy.

A Consultative Council was created in 1926 on the basis of Chapter 42 of the *Quran* which commands consultation. In fact, little happened. It was not until the early 1950s that oil revenue and the consequent growth of development projects made the creation of modern administrative infrastructure critical during the early 1950s. Government agencies proliferated. However, no national assembly or parliament has ever been created. In times of grave crisis, talk of a national assembly has surfaced, only to recede in time. For example, during the early sixties when the House of Saud faced internal dissent from elements demanding liberalization as well as the external threat of radical Arab nationalist condemnations of "feudal Arab monarchies," Prince Faisal spoke of national and regional assemblies. However, after Faisal became king in 1964, nothing happened.

Despite his power, the king is not an absolute monarch since he is ultimately subject to the Shariah. He does not rule by divine right but is informally elected by a council of Saud princes. Deviation from the Shariah is grounds for his removal from office as exemplified by the case of King Saud. Saud ibn Abd al-Aziz ruled from 1953 to

1964. He proved an inept ruler given more to indulging his extravagant tastes than to governance. In 1964 a council composed of senior princes, *ulama* and government officials forced the king to resign. They obtained a legal ruling from the *ulama* which Islamically justified the deposing of Saud and the transferral of power to his brother, Faisal who ruled until 1975. This judgment cited the Islamic legal principle of "public interest."

Islam has also been used to validate many other government actions and policies. The *ulama* serve as advisors in the drafting of royal decrees; their legal opinions are sought to justify, on Islamic principles, important political actions. Where official religious opposition to apects of modernization has occurred, appeals to Islam have been utilized by the Saud family to win over the religious establishment and the masses. For example, Prophetic history and traditions concerning the employment of non-Muslims in early Islam were cited by Abd al-Aziz to justify the importing of oil technicians in the 1940s. Furthermore, Kings Abd al-Aziz and Faisal advanced Islamic rationales to gain religious support for such innovations as radio, telephone, automobiles, TV, and women's education.

Although Saudi rulers have differed from time to time with the *ulama*, they have generally taken great care to court the support of these guardians of Islam who serve as the consciences of the community. From the early alliance of Muhammad Abd al-Wahhab and Muhammad ibn Saud, the Saudi monarchy has cultivated and maintained close ties with its religious establishment, especially the Al-Shaykh family, the descendants of ibn Abd al-Wahhab. Intermarriage between the Sauds and the al-Shaykhs and royal patronage of the *ulama* have resulted in a close, supportive working relationship. In general, Saudi monarchs have been careful to consult with and establish a basic agreement with the *ulama* on religious affairs as well as those political matters that require or benefit from religious sanction. As Muhammad ibn Saud had always consulted with Muhammad ibn Abd al-Wahhab, so in the twentieth century Abd al-Aziz obtained legal opinions from the *ulama* whenever he led the Ikhwan (believers) warriors into a battle. Saudi monarchs' deference to Islam and the religious scholars was dramatically evident in 1944 when Abu Bahz, an old Ikhwan, publically criticized Abdul Aziz for importing oil technicians (Americans) who were unbelievers. The king brought Abu Bahz before a group of leading *ulama* at his royal court in Riyadh. After Abu Bahz repeated his denunciation, insisting that a good Muslim ruler's duty before God was not to aid non-believers in the making a profit from Muslims:

> the King left his throne seat and stood beside Abu Bahz and said, "I am now not the King, but only a Muslim, like you a servant of the Prophet, Abdul Aziz, appealing for judgment to the *ulama*, the judges of the Islamic law which binds us both equally." . . . Showing a thorough knowledge of the Prophet's life and traditions, the King cited several well-attested cases when the Prophet employed non-Muslims individually and in groups. "Am I right or wrong?" The judges replied unanimously that he was right. "Am I breaking the Sharia law, therefore, when I follow in the footsteps of the Prophet, and employ foreign experts to work for me? The Americans at El Kharj, and the other foreigners who operate machines, are brought here by me and work for me under the direction to increase the material resources of the land, and to extract for our benefit the metals, oil and water placed by Allah beneath our land and intended for our use. In so doing, am I violating any Muslim law?" The judges returned a verdict of not-guilty.[11]

The basic law of Saudi Arabia is the *Shariah* which is administered by *Shariah* Courts whose judges and legal advisors are *ulama*. Just as the use of the *Quran* in the place of a formal constitution has allowed the royal family great leeway in most areas which are not covered by scripture, a similar flexibility has existed in the Saudi judicial system's use of Hanbali legal tradition. Hanbali law is the strictest, most rigid of the Islamic law schools; yet where the written law is silent, change is possible. Moreover, though clearly circumscribed, unlike other Sunni law schools, reinterpretation has remained open in principle of Hanbali jurists. Thus the Saudi government has claimed the right to introduce modern regulations in areas not covered by Hanbali law.

The history of Islamic jurisprudence provides vast resources which a shrewd Saud leadership has used in rendering legal and social change. A judicious use of Islamic legal principles of jurisprudence such as independent reasoning or interpretation, selection or the right to select from varying teachings of accepted law schools, and the public interest or welfare of society have provided the rationale and means for substantive legal modernization where the *Quran* and Sunnah are silent. Furthermore, while the *Shariah* is the law and thus

human legislation is technically proscribed, yet classical Islamic jurisprudence recognized Muslim governments' power to enact "regulations" by administrative decree in areas not covered by Islamic law.
The result is an Islamic rationale which has enabled the Saudi government to promulgate various modern codes in the form of Royal Decrees such as: The Regulation on Commerce (1954), The Mining Code
(1963), The Labor and Workman Law (1970), The Social Insurance
Law (1970) and The Civil Service Law (1971).

Shariah courts constitute the basic judiciary of Saudi Arabia.
As in classical Islam, the judges have had full jurisdiction to apply
Shariah law. However, this has not prevented change in the judicial
system. Reforms have been introduced which resulted in the creation
of a Ministry of Justice, in place of the traditional religious office of
Shaykh al-Islam, which supervises the administration of the judiciary
and a tiered system of Shariah courts. A complementary judicial body
handles extra-Shariah matters. The Board of Grievances or Complaint
Court was established by Royal Decree in 1955 to hear complaints
against government officials. It found its Islamic rationale and
justification in a similar system, the Complaint (Mazalim) Court,
which had been established during the Abbasid period. Originally
created to hear grievances against senior government officials, the
Complaint Court soon became a system of courts whose scope and
functions were determined by the caliph. Saudi Arabia has adopted a
similar rationale. Just as the early Complaint court system enabled the
ruler to establish an alternative judicial body alongside the Shariah-
qadi system to hear cases involving extra-Shariah areas (such ruler-
initiated laws or regulations), so too Saudi Arabia's Board of
Grievances handles disputes resulting from Royal Decrees or modern
legislation. Thus, Saudi Arabia's legal system is a combination of
Hanbali and modern law, of Shariah and grievance courts.

Finally, Saudi Arabia utilizes another traditional but informal
Islamic institution for law enforcement—the religious police. Originally created during the Abbasid Caliphate as inspectors of markets,
charged with checking on equitable business practice, these officials
developed a broad jurisdiction roughly the equivalent of a supervisor
of public behavior and morality. Saudi Arabia introduced this institution in 1929 when the Committee for Encouragement of Virtue and
Suppression of Vice was established. Its members check on public
Islamic behavior: that business establishements close during prayer
periods, that the Ramadan fast is publically observed, that alcohol is
not consumed, that people are modestly dressed.

Islam has also played a role in Saudi Arabia's foreign policy. The House of Saud's emphasis on its position as guardian of Islam's holy cities and overseer of the pilgrimage provided a basis for prestige and leadership in the Islamic world. The challenge of Arab revolutionary regimes, particularly that of Egypt's charismatic leader, Gamal Abd al-Nasser, served as an impetus for Saudi Arabia to expand its role in international Islamic politics. The late 50s and early 60s had been a troubled time for Arab monarchs. Egypt and Iraq's monarchies had been toppled by a military *coup* in 1958; radical socialist governments had also come to power in Syria and Algeria. In 1962, Yemeni Republican forces, inspired and aided by Nasser, staged a successful *coup d'état* defeating the royalists and deposing the Imam of Yemen which borders Saudi Arabia.

In the early 1960s, Nasser sought to extend his influence beyond Egypt and assert his leadership of a pan-Arab movement. Espousing Arab socialism, Nasser bitterly condemned conservative Arab countries like Saudi Arabia, charging them with cooperating with Western imperialism and distorting Islam in order to perpetuate their feudal regimes. He presented his socialist brand of Arab nationalism as an "Islamic socialism" which embodied the true revolutionary spirit of Islam, with its emphasis on solidarity, equality, and social justice. The fiscal irresponsibility and official corruption that had led to King Saud's forced abdication in 1964 had provided fuel for Nasser's propaganda. King Faisal responded to the threat of Nasser's pan-Arab challenge by advancing the cause of pan-Islam. Faisal sought to give an Islamic alternative to Nasser's Arab socialism. Thus, Egypt and Saudi Arabia were pitted against each other in an ideological war in which both appealed to Islam.

Faisal's pan-Islamic leadership took several forms. First, during the 1962 pilgrimage Faisal persuaded a group of leading *ulama* to condemn socialism. At the same time the Muslim World League was organized with support from forty-three countries. The League sponsored Islamic conferences and programs and was a mouthpiece for the Saudi interpretation of Islam. It emphasized the universal Islamic community and Islamic unity over any form of nationalism: "the Islamic world forms one collectivity united by Islamic doctrine. . . . In order for the collectivity to be a reality, it is necessary that allegiance will be to the Islamic doctrine and the interests of the Muslim *ummah* [community] in its totality above the allegiance to nationalism or other isms."[12]

Second, the 1965 King Faisal joined with the Shah of Iran in calling for an Islamic summit or conference of heads of Muslim states in Mecca. Nasser, viewing this as a threat to his pan-Arab nationalism denounced this "Islamic Pact" before his own Supreme Council of Islamic Affairs as the plan of "reactionary governments which are imperialist agents exploiting and falsifying Islam."[13]

In March 1970 Faisal convened the first Islamic conference of foreign ministers in Jeddah. The result was the formation of a permanent body, the Organization of the Islamic Conference (OIC), with its secretariat in Jeddah. This body constituted the first official pan-Islamic institution of inter-governmental cooperation among Islamic governments. Since that time Saudi Arabia has served as a catalyst for the creation of many other transnational Islamic organizations such as the International Islamic News Agency, the Islamic Development Bank, the International Center for Research in Islamic Economics, and the Institute for Muslim Minority Affairs. All have their headquarters in Saudi Arabia and receive major funding from the kingdom. Saudi Arabia has also used its oil wealth to fund Islamic conferences, subsidize the publication and massive distribution of Islamic materials, encourage and assist Muslim countries in the Islamization (to render more Islamic) of their governments and societies, and support Muslim organizations such as the Muslim Brotherhood in Egypt and Syria and Pakistan's Jamaat-i-Islami.

A third and major part of King Faisal's pan-Islamic policy centered on Saudi leadership in calls for the liberation of Jerusalem. The quick and decisive rout of Arab (Egyptian, Syrian and Jordanian) forces and the loss of Jerusalem, Islam's third holiest city, in the Arab-Israeli war of 1967 offered the opportunity for Faisal to effectively counter Nasser's bid for transnational leadership and to enhance Saudi prestige in the Islamic world.

The ignominious Arab defeat of 1967 dealt a heavy blow to Arab pride and caused a great deal of soul-searching regarding the causes of Arab weakness and decline. It challenged the credibility of radical Arab nationalism and socialism in general and Nasser's claim to pan-Arab leadership in particular. Faisal seized the opportunity. Saudi Arabia led other Arab oil countries in providing financial aid to the defeated Arab countries, successfully pressured Nasser to remove his troops from Yemen, and committed itself to the liberation of Jerusalem. Whereas prior to 1967 Saudi Arabia had been wary of the Palestine Liberation Organization (PLO), from 1967 onwards the kingdom became a major source of its financial support.

The liberation of Jerusalem and the creation of a Palestinian state became a major component of Saudi foreign policy and an Islamic issue to which Faisal rallied world-wide Muslim support. When the al-Aqsa Mosque in Jerusalem was burned in 1969, Faisal called for a *jihad* against Israel and organized an Islamic summit conference which was attended by representatives of twenty-five Muslim states. Faisal managed to combine his pan-Islamism with Arabism and establish Saudi Arabia as a leader for both Islamic and Arab world interests.

When Faisal died in 1975, King Khalid was quick to assert its Arab/Islamic leadership, reiterating Saudi Arabia's commitment to its first pillar, Islam, and its second pillar, Arab solidarity.

If Saudi Arabia's Islamic ideology has proven flexible and viable thus far, its use of Islam may prove to be a mixed blessing. The appeal to Islam can be a two-edged sword. The strong identification by the House of Saud with Islam to validate the monarchy also invites its use by critics as a standard for judgment. Indictment of the government in the name of Islam by an Islamic opposition occurred dramatically on November 20, 1979. As Muslims prepared to celebrate a New Year's Day that ushered in the fifteenth Islamic century, the kingdom was rocked by the seizure of the Grand Mosque in Mecca by a group of militants, one of whom declared that he was the long-awaited Mahdi: "The Mahdi and his men will seek shelter and protection in the Holy Mosque because they are persecuted everywhere until they have no recourse but the Holy Mosque."[14]

Juhayman ibn Muhammad al-Utayba and Muhammad ibn Abdullah al-Qahtami led a group of several hundred followers who repudiated the House of Saud for impiety and the unwarranted innovation of modernization, condemned the *ulama* for having been coopted by the government, and sought to establish a true Islamic state. The seige lasted two weeks and was finally terminated after the government obtained a legal ruling from the *ulama*, calling upon government forces to rescue the mosque and restore order.

While reeling from the Meccan turmoil, the kingdom was rocked by a second eruption which occurred at the same time. Riots broke out among the 250,000 Shii Muslim living in the oil-rich Eastern Province. Although Sunni Islam predominates throughout Saudi Arabia, Shii constitute a significant minority in the Eastern Province where they make up 35 percent of the workers in the oil fields. The Shii minority have long felt that they have been discriminated against by their Sunni rulers in terms of their share in the country's economic prosperity and development projects. Pent-up feelings had exploded earlier in the year in response to the success of the Iranian revolution and the Ayatollah Khomeini's triumphant return to Iran. These new riots occurred on Ashura, the tenth day of the annual mourning period commemorating Husayn's martyrdom at Karbala and the tyranny, injustice, and slaughter of Shii forces at the hands of their Sunni (Umayyad) oppressors.

Both the seizure of the Grand Mosque and the Shii disturbances focussed attention on the question of pockets of dissatisfaction and political unrest within Saudi Arabia. Despite the successes of the Saudi monarchy in economic development and modernization and a social policy which provided housing, education, and health care services for all its citizens, did these disruptions signal serious potential problems?

While the use of arms and violence in the sacred area of the Grand Mosque alienated many, criticism of the government and the royal family in particular had been mounting. For many, rapid modernization undermined Saudi Arabia's Islamic way of life. In particular, questions of public morality became increasingly sensitive. Reports regarding the un-Islamic personal behavior of the royal family were as common within the kingdom as they were in the media abroad. Drinking, gambling, and living ostentatiously, all ran counter to the Puritan-like spirit of Wahhabi reform. Stories of official corruption in government and business contracts leading to enormous windfalls and "billionaire princes" were common. There were signs in the late 1970s of government recognition of these problems. Regulations were hastily passed banning women from working alone and from working with men, enforcing dress regulations, restricting members of the royal family from vacationing abroad during Ramadan (and thus avoiding the month-long fasting period). In the much publicized incident reported in the film "Death of a Princess," a member of the royal family was executed for adultery.

After resolving the mosque incident, King Khalid announced plans for a consultative assembly in 1980. Historically, when the Sauds have felt challenged, talk of a consultative assembly has resurfaced. In 1982 King Fahd, successor to Khalid, reiterated a commitment to an assembly. He has also announced the formation of a committee to develop a uniform code of Islamic law for the Gulf states. At the same time, there has been a growth of religious revivalism among students at university campuses, increased activity by Saudi religious police of public morality and steady pressure from the *ulama* upon the government to preserve their traditional Islamic way of life.

If the government does not effectively counter criticisms regarding royal corruption, the undermining of Islam by rapid Westernizing, modernization and failure to expand political participation in a system based on royal patronage, the traditional moral authority of the House of Saud may be sufficiently eroded to undermine its political legitimacy.

PAKISTAN

While most nations are based primarily on a common territory, ethnic background, or language, Pakistan was expressly founded in 1947 as a homeland for a people who shared a common religious heritage—it was to be a Muslim nation. Though juridically one nation, Pakistan was in fact a composite of people who were divided by many spoken languages (five major linguistic families with thirty-two distinct languages), strong regional sentiments, and distance (the two major provinces of West and East Pakistan were separated by more than a thousand miles of Indian territory).

During Pakistan's first decade, questions of national identity and ideology were overshadowed by basic issues of national survival. The process of nation building was severely constrained by the harsh practical realities of the post-partition period: settlement of vast numbers of Muslim refugees who had migrated from India, conflict with India over Kashmir, Muslim-Hindu communal rioting in the Punjab, and, as a result, mass migrations of Hindus from West Pakistan to India—political and social upheavals which caused vast carnage, destruction, and a breakdown of law and order. Such events rendered the situation of the new state precarious at best. Thus it is not surprising that the energies of the first years were devoted not to a realization of Islamic identity but rather to practical concerns assuring the survival of the state.[15]

Early attempts at the consolidation of political power and establishment of a viable political and economic system were further frustrated by the untimely death of Pakistan's founder-architect,

Mohammed Ali Jinnah, in 1948, barely one year after independence, and the assassination of Jinnah's protégé and Pakistan's first Prime Minister, Liaquat Ali Khan, in October 1951—events which intensified the fragile condition of the new state.

Although religious ideology and symbols had been utilized by the Muslim League to mobilize and unite Muslims during the independence movement, there was no clear understanding or consensus about the positive content of Pakistan's ideology and its application to the new state's structure, programs, and policies. Put quite simply, the ideological questions faced by the new nation were: What does it mean to say that Pakistan is a modern Islamic or Muslim state? How is its Islamic character to be reflected in the ideology and institutions of the state?

During the first decade of Pakistan's existence, two major events—(the drafting of the Constitution of 1956 and the anti-Ahmadiyya disturbances)—provide insight into the problems and issues associated with the quest to articulate Pakistan's Islamic identity. The process of framing the first constitution lasted about nine years. The constitutional debate provided an arena for a protracted battle between conservative religious leaders and modern secular factions—the former were inclined to a revival of a past ideal, the latter to modernization and reform through the adoption of Western-based models of development. The Constitution of 1956 reflected the long years of debate and the sharp differences between religious traditionalists and modernists.[16] The resulting document was substantially that of a modern parliamentary democracy to which several Islamic clauses or provisions were added in response to the expectations and demands of religious leaders. Among the principal Islamic provisions were: the title of the state was the Islamic Republic of Pakistan[17] Pakistan was a democratic state based upon Islamic principles; (Preamble); the head of state must be a Muslim (Part IV, Art. 32); an Islamic research center was to be established to assist in the "reconstruction of Muslim society on a truly Islamic basis" (Part XII, Art. 97); and finally, the so-called repugnancy clause, the stipulation that no law contrary to the *Quran* and Sunnah of Prophet could be enacted (Art. 198).

The Constitution of 1956 demonstrated the early failure of the government to articulate and implement Pakistan's distinctive ideology, a Muslim nationalism that transcended ethnic ties and provided a sense of national unity and solidarity. It skirted the question of the Muslim or Islamic character of the state for it lacked any systematic statement and implementation of an Islamic rationale. Modernists had a document whose few Islamic provisions caused a minimum of difficulty. While religious leaders had called for an Islamic state based upon the full implementation of Islamic law, they had settled for a legal system in which no law could be repugnant to Islam. The relationship of modern constitutional concepts such as democracy, popular sovereignty, parliamentary political party system, and the equality of all citizens to Islamic principles was asserted but not delineated. These unresolved constitutional questions and inconsistencies illustrate the ideological quandary which has continued to resurface throughout Pakistan's subsequent history.

A second event during Pakistan's formative period also concerned the issue of the Islamic identity and character of the state, the 1953 anti-Ahmadiyyah disturbances. During the constitutional debates, religious leaders had sought to have the Ahmadiyyah, a modern Islamic sect, declared a non-Muslim minority maintaining that their founder, Mirza Ghulam Ahmad (1835–1908), had claimed the mantle of prophethood and had thus denied an essential Islamic belief—that Muhammad was the final or last of the prophets. Furthermore, these religious leaders demanded that Zafrullah Khan, Pakistan's Foreign Minister, and other Ahmadi government officials be dismissed from office. They argued that a non-Muslim minority could not be fully committed to the state's Islamic ideology, and so non-Muslims should not hold key policy-making positions. The tragic result of this agitation was widespread rioting and murder of Ahmadis in the Punjab province.

A national court of inquiry was established to investigate the causes of these disturbances, and in 1956 it issued a report, commonly referred to as the *Munir Report*, named after Justice Muhammad Munir, President of the Commission. This report is significant because it provides insight into several problems which have been and continue to be central to Pakistan's quest for its Islamic identity. While the religious leaders could join in declaring the Ahmadis non-Muslims, those interviewed by the commission were unable to agree on the most fundamental questions: What is Islam? Who is a Muslim? What constitutes a believer? What is the nature of an Islamic state? As in the past, agreement could be reached in resisting a perceived deviation or threat to Islam, but consensus about the positive content of Pakistan's Islamic ideology, even the most fundamental questions of Islamic belief, seemed to be beyond those who were the self-proclaimed experts and the strongest advocates of an Islamic state.

The commission addressed itself to the inherent danger of this situation for Pakistan in the future, identifying two key issues: (1) the lack of any clear understanding or consensus regarding Islamic belief and ideology as well as the absence of a centralized teaching authority; and (2) the necessity for a bold reorientation, through a process of reinterpretation and reform of Islam, to meet modern needs and demands.[18]

Discussion among the religious leaders regarding Pakistan's identity had existed from pre-partition days. As previously noted, prior to the Partition of 1947, the *ulama* of the Indian subcontinent had been divided in their political responses to the Muslim League and the Pakistan Movement. Abul Kalam Azad had remained a staunch supporter of a joint or composite (Muslim-Hindu) nationalism. Other *ulama* such as those at Deoband and the Ulama Organization of India (Jamiyyat i-Ulama-i-Hind) also supported a political alliance. A second group of *ulama* who supported the Pakistan movement created The Ulama Organization of Islam (Jamiyyat i-Ulama-i-Islam or JUI). These religious leaders had joined with the Muslim League in the struggle for Pakistan. A third position was represented by men like Mawlana Mawdudi of the Society of Islam (Jamaat-i-Islam) and Abul Hasan al-Nadwi of the Nadwat-i-Ulama Seminary who objected to any form of nationalism, even Muslim nationalism. Their conviction that nationalism was antithetical to Islamic revivalism resulted in opposition to both Indian and Pakistani Muslim nationalists like Azad and JUI as well as the Muslim League.

After the creation of Pakistan, all religious leaders accepted the political reality and a number of religio-political parties became active, providing organized outlets for the *ulama*. Among the three most important Islamic parties were the Jamaat-i-Islam (JI), Jamiyyat i-Ulama-i-Islam (JUI) and the Jamiyyat i-Ulama-i-Pakistan (JUP). Although Mawlana Mawdudi and his Jamaat-i-Islam were not an *ulama* organization, they were often joined by them in demanding and working for full implementation of an Islamic ideology and state in Pakistan.

Moreover, the religious landscape remained further divided. Unity of faith did not mean a common interpretation or understanding of Islamic belief and practice. In addition to a sizeable Shii minority, the Sunni Muslim community included many schools of thought—the Deobandi, Brelevi, Wahhabi, Ahl al-Hadith. While most might agree on the non-Islamic status of the Ahmadiyya or might unite in opposition to modernist innovations, their individual theological orientations constituted a form of sectarianism and remained an obstacle to any consensus on an Islamic vision and program for state and society. These differences in thought, exacerbated by the differing and competing personalities of their leadership, have remained a continuing problem.

The conflict between religious leaders and the government in defining Pakistan's ideology continued during the Ayub Khan era. In October 1958 Muhammad Ayub Khan led a military *coup d'état*. While Ayub's government sought primarily to rebuild a strong centralized national government and to foster rapid socio-economic reforms, Islam continued to be a factor in Pakistan's political development. Ayub was himself a Western-oriented modernist Muslim in understanding and approach. He stressed the need to "liberate the spirit of religion from the cobwebs of superstition and stagnation which surround it and move forward under the forces of modern science and knowledge."[19] Ayub's modernist outlook was reflected quite clearly in the new Constitution of 1962, the establishment of the Advisory Council on Islamic Ideology and the Islamic Research Institute, as well as the reforms embodied in the Muslim Family Laws Ordinance (1961). However, once again, the struggle between modernist and traditionist factions resulted in minimizing the potential of these mechanism of reform.

While the new Constitution of 1962 generally adopted the Islamic provisions of the 1956 constitution, there were some significant changes. The new document omitted "Islamic" from the official name of the republic and the divine sovereignty phrase, which limited the power of the state, "within the limits prescribed by Him." However, under strong public pressure, these Islamic provisions were again restored by the first Amendment Bill of 1963.

Perhaps the most notable Islamic provisions of the new constitution occurred in "Part X Islamic Institutions" which, following the lead of the Constitution of 1956, called for the establishment of an Advisory Council of Islamic Ideology and an Islamic Research Institute, the former concerned with legislation and the latter with research, especially on Islam in the modern world.

The functions of the Advisory Council of Islamic Ideology were: (1) to make recommendations to the government regarding provisions that may better enable Muslims to lead their lives in conformity with the tenets of Islam; (2) to advise the government as to whether proposed legislation is repugnant to Islam.

The Central Institute of Islamic Research had been mandated

by Article 197 of the Constitution of 1956. Its Charter reflected a modernist approach, emphasizing its role as defining Islamic fundamentals in a "rational and liberal manner" so as to "bring out the dynamic character in the context of the intellectual and scientific progress of the modern world."[20] A connection between the Research Institute and the Advisory Council of Islamic Ideology existed since the Council could request the Research Institute to gather materials and submit an opinion on a particular legislative proposal.

However, the effectiveness of these Islamic institutions was compromised by their status as strictly advisory bodies. For example, in addition to the fact that the legislature could ignore a recommendation from the Ideology Council, it could even pass new legislation prior to consulting the Council. Furthermore, both the Ideology Council and the Research Institute were government-sponsored and supported, and their directors and members served at the pleasure of the executive.

Resistance to Ayub Khan's attempts to define Pakistan's Islamic identity in liberal modernist terms can be quite forcefully seen in two events: the agitational politics that forced the Director of the Central Institute of Islamic Research from office, and the bitter debate surrounding passage of the *Muslim Family Laws Ordinance*.

Dr. Fazlur Rahman, a scholar educated both in Pakistan and at Cambridge University, was appointed Director of the Central Institute of Islamic Research in 1962 by Ayub Khan. In addition, he served as a member of the Advisory Council on Islamic Ideology. The research conducted under his leadership and many of the publications in the Institute's journal, *Islamic Studies*, reflected modernist, reconstructive themes that alarmed many traditionalists. Opposition intensified with the publication of Rahman's book, *Islam*, which contained several modernist interpretations objectionable to traditional religious leaders who seized this opportunity to rally their forces against the government of Ayub Khan. Throughout Pakistan, the religious leaders directed mass demonstrations against Rahman. These eventually led to his resignation. Their struggle, however, was more with Ayub Khan than with his appointee, Dr. Rahman.

Traditionists took strong exception not only to Ayub Khan's modernist positions but also to his methods. Since Ayub viewed the *ulama* as chiefly responsible for the retrograde state of Islam and as generally ill-prepared to meet the demands of modernity, he had severely limited their powers and participation in government. Although the *ulama* were, according to tradition, the protectors of the law and therefore advisors to the government, Ayub minimized their role within the Ideology Council, the Research Institute or the Commission for the Reform of Muslim Family Laws, which were all dominated by lay people. The tension between Ayub Khan and traditionist religious leaders was especially evident in the debate surrounding the reform of Muslim Family Law. In many ways it crystallized two major questions associated with the long struggle to articulate Pakistan's Islamic identity: "Who shall have primacy in this process?" and "How shall change be brought about?"

The Commission on Marriage and Family Laws was established in 1955 and issued its report in 1956 with recommendations for reforms in the laws governing marriage, divorce, and inheritance. The Commission had consisted of seven members: three men, three women, and one representative of the *ulama*. From its inception, the work of the Commission was surrounded with controversy. The religious establishment bitterly resented the government interference in their province; they objected to the "lay dominance" of the Commission; they denied the need for substantive change in the Shariah. Moreover, given the centrality of the family in Islamic society, Muslim family law had enjoyed pride of place as the heart of the *Shariah*. While other areas of Islamic law had been replaced in many Muslim countries as part of the process of modernization, family law had remained relatively secure. Therefore, potential changes affecting such areas as polygamy, divorce and inheritance rights were viewed with great dismay by most traditional religious leaders. Moreover, family law reform also became politicized because it provided a major test case: confrontation between Ayub Khan's policy of imposing his modernist interpretation of Islam with little regard for a religious establishment whom he viewed as part of the "problem" rather than integral to the solution.

Predictably, the Commission on Marriage and Family Law split between its modernist lay majority and its single religious leader, Mawlana Ihstisham-ul-Haq. The arguments advanced in the majority and minority reports reflect basic differences in outlook between modernists and conservative religious leaders. Moreover, these differences regarding the authority of traditional law, the need for social change, and the sole authority of the *ulama* as official interpreters of Islam remain contested issues throughout much of the Islamic world today. The modernist majority of the Commission argued that since the *Quran* and Sunnah of the Prophet had not, indeed, could not, "comprehend the infinite variety of human relations for all occasions

and for all epochs, the Prophet of Islam left a very large sphere free
for legislative enactments and judicial decisions. . . . This is the principle of *ijtihad* or interpretive intelligence working within the broad
framework of the *Quran* and Sunna."[21] Echoing Islamic reformers like
Jamal al-Din al-Afghani, Muhammad Abduh, Ahmad Khan and
Muhammad Iqbal, the modernists advocated an on-going legal process freed from simple dependence upon medieval legal interpretations and open to continued development in light of changing
historical and socio-economic conditions. Of equal significance, the
report rejected the *ulama's* monopoly of Islamic learning and interpretations, maintaining that all informed Muslims have the right to exercise interpretation since "Islam never developed a church with
ordained priests as a class separate from the laity . . . some may be
more learned in the Muslim law than others, but that does not constitute them as a separate class; they are not vested with any special
authority and enjoy no special privileges" (p. 202).

    In his minority report, Mawlana Ihstisham-ul-Haq ques-
tioned the competence, motives, method, and recommendations of
his colleagues on the Commission. How could the Commission's majority "whose members have neither the detailed knowledge of Islamic teachings and injunctions nor are . . . versed in the
interpretation and application of those laws" assume "the position of
an expert authority on the *Shariah* and an absolute *mujtahid* [one who
practices interpretation]"? (p. 205). He accused the modernist majority of "contravening the Holy *Quran* and the Sunna and . . . ridiculing
Muslim jurisprudence" (p. 205). He reasserted the role of the *ulama* as
religious guides for it is the "pious *ulama* who possess knowledge of
Shariah and act upon it" (p. 206). Finally, Mawlana Ihstisham-ul-Haq
rejected the reform recommendations of the modernist report as an
attempt to blindly copy the West. Thus, he portrayed the attempt to
limit polygamy as due to an "inferiority complex against the West and
a desire to copy it blindly" (p. 206).

    In many ways Mawlana Ihstisham-ul-Haq's minority report
served as the religious establishment's indictment of the government's legislative attempt at Muslim family law reform. Strong religious opposition forced a prolonged national debate which lasted five
years. However, with support from the Ayub government and
women's organizations, led by the All Pakistan Women's Organization, the Muslim Family Laws Ordinance of 1961 was finally enacted.
The religious opposition did affect the final draft of the law which had

been weakened by a series of deletions and qualifications of the original Commission majority report.

The year 1971 marked a turning point in Pakistan's history. As previously noted, although a sovereign state, Pakistan lacked many of the characteristics of a nation—common language, ethnic background, geography. Nowhere was this more evident than in Pakistan's eastern wing. East Pakistan was Bengali, ethnically and linguistically. The sole rationale for national unity between East and West Pakistan had been their common bond, Islam. However, for many Bengalis this ideal was far from the reality. A persistent complaint of less developed East Pakistan was the belief that their interests were subordinated to those of West Pakistan. As the capital remained in the West (first in Karachi and later in Islamabad) so, too, West Pakistan dominated the government, military, and economy. In such a situation Mujibur Rahman was able to mobilize Bengali support for his Awami Party on the basis of Bengali ethnic nationalism. The disastrous Civil War of 1971, with its brutality and carnage, shocked West Pakistan as it had the world community. With assistance from India, Pakistan's erstwhile enemy, East Pakistan seceded and was reconstituted as an independent nation, Bangladesh.

The loss of the eastern wing and 55 percent of the population stood as a direct challenge to Pakistan's very *raison d'être*. What had happened to that common Islamic bond which was the basis of national unity and solidarity? What then was the source of Pakistani identity?

As one reviews the first two decades of Pakistan's existence and quest to give shape to its Islamic aspiration, several conclusions emerge. First, while there was general agreement regarding the need for a Muslim homeland, what that meant was far from clear. For some it was simply a nation of Muslims, for others it was an Islamic state. Second, profound differences in education, outlook, and approach between modernists and traditionalists presented formidable obstacles—as witnessed in the drafting of the 1956 Constitution and the *Muslim Family Laws Reform Ordinance* of 1961. Third, as a consequence of unresolved differences, *ad hoc,* piecemeal approaches were taken to reach an acceptable compromise. No systematic attempt had been made to define and implement Pakistan's Islamic identity and ideology. The net result of this approach is exemplified by constitutions for an Islamic state whose Islamicity was established by the inclusion of a few Islamic provisions; by Islamic institutions (the Advisory Council on Islamic Ideology and the Central Islamic Research Institute) whose independence and effectiveness were seriously hampered by their excessive dependence upon the executive and whose power was at best advisory; and finally by a major piece of family law reform legislation whose passage was surrounded by controversy and whose final form was compromise both in its substantive provisions and its legal methodology.[22]

IRAN

Nothing could be farther from our present-day views of Iran than prerevolutionary Pahlavi Iran. Prior to the Khomeini era, Iran seemed to be an oasis of stability in an otherwise volatile Middle East—a staunch political ally and a seemingly insatiable market for the products of the American military-industrial complex. In fact, the reality was far more complex than its facade which was the product of both Western ignorance and imperial public relations.

Mohammed Reza Shah Pahlavi ascended the peacock throne in 1941, succeeding his father Reza Khan Shah, a military commander who had taken control of Iran's government in 1925. Reza Khan, an admirer of his Turkish contemporary, Mustafa Kemal, had moved quickly to modernize Iranian state and society. However, unlike Ataturk, he did not singlehandedly attempt a total secularization of society. As in Egypt, Reza Khan sought to modernize Iran politically, militarily, economically, and socially. Rather than eliminating traditional institutions, he sought to limit or control them. Politically he built a strong central government, a dynastic monarchy rather than a republic. His choice of Pahlavi, the language of pre-Islamic Iran, and the adoption of symbols such as the lion and the sun were proof to his religious opponents of the non-Islamic (equated with anti-Islamic) character of the Pahlavi dynasty. Zoroastrianism was re-established with Islam as the state's religion. Streets and public places were renamed in honor of pre-Islamic heroes such as Cyrus the Great. Furthermore, while Reza Shah paid lip service to Islam and Iran's Islamic heritage, his modernization program progressively alienated many of the *ulama*. Two areas, law and education, are indicative of Reza Shah's approach.

Western-based legal codes were enacted. Though incorporating some *Shariah* regulations, they were essentially secular laws applied by state, not religious courts, and administered by a Western-oriented bureaucracy. Even the *Shariah* court which continued to apply Muslim family law came under the ministry of justice. In effect, much of the power and revenue of the *ulama* as judges, legal experts, notary publics, and registrars of deeds was now under government control and in the hands of modern judges and lawyers and civil servants.

A second area in which the power of the *ulama* was eroded is education. The modern secular school system received strong royal patronage and thus was greatly expanded while the religious educational system was taken out of the administrative hands of the *ulama* and brought under state control. The Ministry of Education set the curriculum, oversaw examinations, and certified teachers.[23]

A special irritant to the *ulama* and traditional classes in general was passage of the Uniformity of Dress Law (1928) which mandated Western dress for men and shedding of the veil by women. In addition to these state-enforced modernization reforms, "the regime sustained a day to day harassment concerning efforts to conduct moralistic passion plays, public homilies, pilgrimage to shrines, etc."[24] This, then, was part of the legacy of Reza Shah to his twenty-two year-old son, Mohammed Reza Shah, in 1941, a legacy that had alienated most of the religious establishment and traditional classes in society and which had effectively weakened the *ulama*.

During the first decade of Mohammed Shah's reign, the young monarch was less a ruler than a survivor. Because of Reza Shah's strong ties with Nazi Germany, Britain and Russia had reoccupied Iran in 1941 and forced Reza Shah to abdicate in favor of his son. For the remainder of World War II, Iran was occupied and controlled in great part by England, Russia, and the United States. During the early post–World War II period the young Shah was caught between Western colonial powers and domestic opposition forces. Anglo-Soviet occupation forces were reluctant to leave due to Iran's vast oil wealth. However, in 1946 the Soviets withdrew from northern Iran due to United States and United Nations pressure. At the same time the American presence in Iran grew as the United States began to develop its close ties with the Shah's regime.

Within Iran there were many who, as in the nineteenth-century Tobacco Revolt, objected to foreign presence and control. Dr. Mohammed Mosaddeq organized a coalition, the National Front, and mounted a campaign to nationalize the British owned Anglo-Iranian

Oil Company (AIOC). Britain's presence and the Shah's protection of the foreign (non-Muslim) economic domain proved a popular cause. Mossadeq's coalition included support from "the traditional middle class—the bazaar—formed of small merchants, clerics and guild elders; and the modern middle class—the intelligentsia—composed of professionals, salaried personnel, and secular educated intellectuals."[25]

By 1951 religious leaders who had been politically subdued by Reza Shah were issuing decrees calling for the nationalization of the Anglo-Iranian Oil Company. With passage of the Nationalization Bill in 1951, Britain and the West boycotted Iranian oil. Mossadeq emerged as a popular hero, a symbol of national unity and independence in the face of foreign intervention. The Shah could not prevent his becoming prime minister. When he did try to dismiss Prime Minister Mossadeq in 1953, popular reaction and support for Mossadeq resulted in the Shah's flight from Iran. However, within six days, the continued loyalty of the army and strong U.S. support, including that of the Central Intelligence Agency, enabled the Shah to return.

Re-established on his throne, the Shah sought to consolidate his power. Aware of his weak position and more sensitive to the religious and traditional classes in Iranian society, he realized the need for greater cooperation with the clergy. The religious leadership had been divided over the question of direct involvement in politics. Although some had been issuing rulings on political matters and other religious leaders had been among Dr. Mossadeq's staunch support in parliament, a majority, under the leadership of Ayatollahs Muhammad Musavi Bihbihani (d. 1965) and Muhammad Husayn Burujirdi (d. 1961), had been against political activism. In 1949 Ayatollah Burujirdi had held a conference of two thousand *ulama* in Qum and issued an injunction banning clergy from joining political parties or acting in politics. Disturbed by secularist and leftist extremism, in particular that of communism, Burujirdi and Bihbihani followed a policy of political quietism while the Shah crushed the Fidaiyan-i-Islam, a militant Islamic organization that had often been critical of the religious leaders as well as of the communists. Similarly, they did not voice objections to Iran's reinvolvement with the Western oil companies. In exchange, the Shah made religious concessions: more coverage of Islamic topics in the state-run press and media, observance of the Ramadan fast in government offices, greater funding for mosques and schools. Moreover, Qum, under Ayatollah Burujirdi emerged as the center of Shiism to which even the government was careful to pay deference. Its religious schools thrived as student enrollment rose sharply from thirty-two hundred in 1952 to five thousand in 1956. However, the Shah was walking a tightrope. The *ulama's* attempt to ban the Bahai provides a primary illustration of the complexity of clergy-state relations.

In 1955 the *ulama* mounted a campaign against the Bahai, a nineteenth-century Iranian religious movement whom the Shii regarded as heretics and enemies of the state. A bill was introduced in parliament declaring the Bahai faith illegal, stipulating imprisonment for its members, and seizure of Bahai property and its distribution by the government to Islamic religious schools and activities. The Army Chief of Staff and the Governor of Tehran had participated in the destruction of the main Bahai center in Tehran. Although communicating sympathy for the concerns of the *ulama*, the Shah finally side-stepped the legislation, fearful of international repercussions. However, the uneasy tactical alliance between the Shah and the clergy was broken in 1959 over two issues—women's suffrage and land reform.

In January 1959 a government draft bill for women's enfranchisment drew heavy criticism from the religious establishment, causing the regime to back down. However, it was the land reform bill which proved to be a turning point in state-clergy relations as well as a catalyst for broader-based opposition politics.

The Land Reform Bill, which called for the redistribution of large tracts of and to peasants, drew strong criticism from the religious establishment. Indeed, Ayatollah Burujirdi issued his only decree against the regime's policy on this issue. Objection to the Bill was based less on its economic merits than its religious and political implications. Land reform affected religious endowments as well. The revenue from these endowed lands provided for support of mosques, schools, seminaries, and the salaries and income of religious personnel as well as students. Withdrawal of this revenue would seriously undercut the independence of the clergy from the state—an independence which was to prove crucial during the revolution of 1978. In addition, the *ulama* charged that the bill violated the *Shariah*-mandated principle of private property. Although ratified in 1960, the law remained inoperative.

In 1961 the Shah suspended the parliament and announced

his decision to rule by royal decree. Under pressure from the U.S. government, he moved to implement land reforms. His edict drew fire from a coalition of religious and secular leaders. Critical of his growing authoritarianism, they demanded the reinstatement of parliament. Anti-government street demonstrations culminated in riots at Teheran University in January 1962. Demonstrators were brutally crushed by the army and police; several protestors were killed and scores arrested.

In 1963, subservience to the West was added to the bill of indictment against the Shah as Iran contracted a $200 million loan with the United States for military equipment. In addition, the government proposed to grant diplomatic immunity to U.S. personnel (military and non-military advisers) in Iran. Amidst the renewed political agitation, the Ayatollah Khomeini emerged a leader in Iranian politics.

After the death of the Ayatollah Burujirdi in 1961, no single individual proved capable of succeeding him as the country's Shiite leader. Instead, people were guided by a number of respected ayatullahs. From among the more prominent, Ruhollah Khomeini of Qum emerged in 1963 as a leading critic of the Shah's regime. Although considered a junior colleague to men like Ayatollah Muhammad Kazim Shariatmadari of Qum and Ayatollah Hadi Milani of Mashhad, Khomeini became a symbol of resistance to the Shah. Khomeini delivered a series of provocative sermons at the principal seminary of Qum, Madrasah-i-Fayziyah, in which he criticized "the Shah's autocracy, corruption, social inequity and injustice, foreign domination, the regime's enfranchisment of women and the Family Protection Law, and the government's land tenure policies."[26]

In March 1963 the Shah's secret police (SAVAK) arrested Khomeini. Released within several days, he again spoke out, criticizing Iran's close ties with America which he denounced as an enemy of Islam for its imperialist control over Iran and its support of Israel.[27] By June 1963 the situation came to a head. On the tenth of Muharram (the anniversary of Husayn's martyrdom at Karbala), Khomeini was arrested for his continued fiery attacks against the Shah. In response to the Shah's accusation that the *ulama* were parasites on society, Khomeini had retorted: "Am I a parasite . . . or are you, O Shah, the parasite, who have erected towering palaces and filled foreign banks with your untold wealth."[28] As news spread, the religious processions commemorating Husayn's martyrdom turned into political protest marches. During the following days, demonstrations (led by religious leaders) spread from Qum to other provinces. The government responded swiftly and harshly: thousands were killed; in Qum, seminarians were thrown from the roof of the seminary to their death. Khomeini proved an indefatigible critic. Upon his release from prison in August, he denounced the Shah's plans for elections and called for a boycott. He was again imprisoned and finally in 1964 deported to Turkey.

During the late 60s and early 70s the Shah consolidated his power with major military assistance from the United States both in weapons sales and training for his military and secret police. The economic and selective social reforms of the Shah's "White Revolution" were pursued with great fanfare. They were often plagued by corruptions and mismanagement. They seemed to benefit the cities more than the rural areas and the new entreprenurial, industrial, and bureaucratic classes rather than the traditional merchants and artisans. For the more traditional populace, the impact of a rapid and often indiscriminately imposed modernization policy meant enduring the trauma and dislocation engendered by the urbanization, industrialization, and Westernization of their traditional way of life and values. Another kind of burden was borne by religious leaders and liberal intellectuals. While friends of the regime were rewarded lavishly and enjoyed the good life, its critics were silenced through surveillance, harassment, arrest, torture and even death. The government also harassed the *ulama*: defaming religious leaders like Khomeini, monitoring sermons, attempting to control seminaries and schools, introducing a corps of state-certified, secular, university-trained teachers to fill positions in rural elementary religious schools which were the province of the clergy. From his exile in Turkey and later in Iraq, the Ayatollah Khomeini denounced the monarchy and became the primary symbol of political protest. However, by the 1970s Mohammed Reza Shah Pahlavi had gone from a figurehead in an Allied-occupied nation during World War II to an autocratic monarch who had stilled many of the voices of dissent and ruled what appeared to many outsiders as a modern, progressive, stable society in the Middle East. Though charges of authoritarianism, political oppression, and corruption could be found, the voices of dissent had been silenced. In October 1971 a Muslim ruler, the second generation of a dynastic monarchy in which Islam was the state religion, held the celebration of the 2500th anniversary of his Pahlavi dynasty at Persepolis, Persia's ancient pre-Islamic Zoroastrian capitol!

EGYPT

Unlike Saudi Arabia and Pakistan, Egypt has never proclaimed itself to be an Islamic state. From the nineteenth century reforms of Muhammad Ali and the Khedive Ismail, Egypt pursued a Western, secular path in its political, military, and socioeconomic development. While Islam was acknowledged as a "source" of Islamic law, Egyptian law, as its constitution and system of government, was Western in its origins and outlook. When the Free Officers overthrew King Farouk on July 20, 1952, Egypt continued, under Gamal Abd al-Nasser (1918–70) along its secular path, respecting Islam but generally separating religion as far as possible from the state. The agenda of the July Revolution was summarized in the preamble of the Constitution of 1956. "The eradication of all aspects of imperialism; the extinction of feudalism; the eradication of monopolies and the control of capitalistic influence over the system of government; the establishment of a strong national army; the establishment of social justice; and the establishment of a sound democratic society."[29] Nowhere was Islam mentioned in this early statement of the goals of Nasserism. When referred to, as in his *Philosophy of the Revolution,* published in 1955, Islam meant simply Egypt's Islamic heritage which constituted one of the three geographic historical circles to which she belonged: Arab, African, and Islamic."[30]

During the late 1950s and early 1960s, radical Arab regimes had come to power in Syria, Iraq, and Algeria as well as in Egypt. Western inspired liberal governments were indicted for the continuance of feudal societies in the Middle East. The failure of liberal nationalism and the influence of Western capitalism and imperialism were denounced by the new regime with promises of a social revolution to redress the profound socioeconomic inequities of their societies. Rejecting a "feudal past" and a Western, capitalist present, the Baath Party in Syria and Iraq, the Front de Liberation Nationals (FLN) in Algeria and Nasser in Egypt advocated an Arab nationalist/socialist future—Arab socialism. From the mid 1950s Nasser merged Egypt's local nationalism with the broader identification of Arab nationalism and, in the process, sought to be both president of Egypt and an Arab leader. In 1956 Nasser seized control of and nationalized the Suez Canal. His "victory" in the Suez War of 1957 over British and French colonial forces made him a popular hero throughout the Islamic world and enhanced his bid for Arab leadership. Egyptians were both children of the Nile Valley and members of the Arab family/

nation. Article 1 of the constitution of 1956 described Egypt as a "sovereign independent Arab state . . . part of the Arab nation."

Nasser's bid for leadership in the Arab world led to his progressive use of both the Arab and Islamic aspects of Egypt's heritage. These twin aspects of Egyptian identity often were intertwined as important components of "Nasserism," its ideology and politics.

While Nasserism had been an essentially secular movement in its early stage, internal and external political realities led Nasser to selectively employ Islam to legitimate his Arab socialist ideology and to muster popular support at home and abroad. Thus, Islam increasingly became a factor in Egypt's domestic and foreign policy. During the 1960s Nasser had competition from several Arab socialist regimes: Syria, Iraq, and Algeria in addition to the newly emerging, oil-rich, conservative Arab monarchy in Saudi Arabia.

Domestically, Nasser faced the disruptive challenge of the Muslim Brotherhood, an Islamic movement which rejected the Western secular path of modern Egypt, and advocated a return to Islam and the *Shariah* in charting Egypt's future. Although originally supportive of the Free Officers Revolution, the Brotherhood felt alienated from Nasser when it became clear that he was not going to join with them in the creation of an Islamic state. The Brotherhood increasingly became an opposition movement which resorted to violence in achieving its goals. After several assassination attempts had been made against him, Nasser suppressed the Brotherhood. Nasser's need to counter the Muslim Brotherhood's Islamic appeal and challenge to his legitimacy and to mobilize the Arab masses behind his Arab socialist revolution at home and abroad influenced him to turn to Islam to achieve his political goals: "the regime seemed to recognize more and more that Islam remained the widest and most effective basis for consensus despite all efforts to promote nationalism, patriotism, secularism, and socialism."[31]

Although he had refused to acquiesce to the demands of religious leaders that the Egyptian Charter of 1962, which set forth Nasser's socialist blueprint for society, include a clause declaring Islam the state religion, by 1964 the clause was placed in Egypt's constitution. Nasser also involved the government in Islamic affairs when he nationalized al-Azhar University, the oldest Islamic university and a major center of religious authority. Key administrative positions went to government officials and curriculum reform was imposed by the government. The justification given was the need to counter a reactionary conservatism and train a new generation committed to and capable of contributing to modernization and development. As a result, the university lost much of its independence both academically and politically. Government control of al-Azhar as well as those mosques whose *imams* (prayer leaders) were appointed and paid by the Ministry of Awqaf (Endowments, Religious Affairs) enabled Nasser to marshall religious support for such socialist policies as land reform and nationalization of public utilities. For example, the Rector of al-Azhar, Mahmud Shaltut (1892–1963), declared that Islam and socialism were completely reconcilable because Islam was more than just a spiritual religion; it regulated "human relations and public affairs with the aim of ensuring the welfare of society."[32] Basing his interpretation upon the *Quran*, Shaltut justified government policies such as the religious acceptability of expropriation of land in the public welfare since "If worldly possessions are the possessions of God . . . then wealth, although it may be attributed to a private person, it should also belong to all the servants of God, should be placed in the safekeeping of all, and all should profit from it."[33] Shaltut could conclude: "Can man find a more perfect, more complete, more useful, and more profound socialism than that decreed by Islam? It is founded on the basis of faith and belief, and all that is decreed on that basis participates in the perpetuation of life and doctrine."[34]

The government obtained *fatwas* from religious authorities to support programs such as birth control or land reform.[35] Moreover, the Supreme Council for Islamic Affairs, a government created and funded agency, published such decrees in its journal *Minbar al-Islam* (The Pulpit of Islam) which also included articles written by lay intellectuals on Arab socialism and Islam on such topics as "Socialism in Islam," "Arab Socialism is in the Spirit of Islamic Belief," and "The Cause of the National Charter is the Cause of Islam." *Minbar al-Islam* became "the single most important attempt by a group of writers to lay out the major concepts of a socialist ideology drawn from Islamic principles."[36]

The use of Islam to legitimate Arab socialism also enhanced Nasser's foreign policy since the vast majority of Arabs to whom he was appealing were Muslim. Moreover, as indicated earlier, in the rivalry that developed between Egypt and Saudi Arabia, Islam became important because Faisal used Islam to condemn Arab socialism and to advocate a pan-Islam that countered pan-Arabism. When Faisal obtained a decree from his *ulama* condemning socialism, Nasser obtained decrees from Egyptian *ulama*, especially leading scholars of al-Azhar, legitimating his ideology and programs. While Faisal argued that pan-Islam included Arabism, Nasser proclaimed that Arab socialism was rooted in Islam: "Islam is the first religion to call for socialism, the first religion to call for equality." Countering his conservative Arab critics, Nasser declared: "Our enemies say that socialism is infidelity. But is socialism really what they describe by this term? What they describe applies to raising slaves, hoarding money and usurping the people's wealth. (Nasser's criticism of the Saudi regime). This is infidelity and this is against religion and Islam. What we apply . . . is the law of justice and the law of God."[37]

Many forces during the 1950s and 60s resulted in the re-emergence of religion in Egyptian politics. Nasser's use of Islamic politics was a testimony to the widespread presence and influence of Islam in the lives of the majority of the population—in all classes of society and across educational levels and a testimony to the capacity of Islamic history and belief to include political and socioeconomic aspects of life within its normative boundaries.

The Egyptian experience challenged underlying assumptions of modernization and development theories. Despite the century-long commitment of Egyptian leaders to modernization, reforms imposed from above did not guarantee their acceptance by the vast majority of the people. The orientation of the state, its institutions, laws, and policies reveals more about the ideals and goals of Egyptian rulers than it did about the realities of Egyptian society. Modern elites constituted a small fraction of an otherwise tradition-oriented majority. Thus, if modernization is equated with the beliefs, values, and attitudes—with the total world view of a people—Egypt, like most Muslim countries, was not truly a modern (secular oriented) state. The institutions of a modern state had been transplanted from West to a society whose historical experience and values were not the same. These differences account for the failure of political institutions (parliaments, political parties, free elections) to function despite their official existence in constitutions. The continued presence and importance of religion was reflected both in the politicizing of religion under Nasser and the activities of the Muslim Brotherhood. Indeed, as Muslim states in nation building had tended to ignore, downplay, or control religion in their general pursuit, two major Islamic organizations—the Muslim Brotherhood in Egypt and the Jamaat-i-Islami in Pakistan advocated a return to an Islamic alternative to Western inspired political systems. Their influence would in time extend beyond their national origins as they became international Islamic organizations which have had a major impact on contemporary Islamic politics from Algeria to Indonesia.

ISLAMIC ALTERNATIVES

The Muslim Brotherhood

Hasan al-Banna (1906–49), the founder of the Muslim Brotherhood, was born in Mahmudiyya, a small town northeast of Cairo in the Nile delta. His early traditional religious education was combined with some exposure to modernist thought through his father, Shaykh Ahmad Abd al-Rahman al-Banna, who had been a student at al-Azhar during the time of Muhammad Abduh. After study at a local Teacher Training College, al-Banna went to Cairo to study at Dar al-Ulum College. In Cairo, he came into contact with Rashid Rida and his Salafiyya movement. An avid reader of *The Lighthouse*, he absorbed the reformist spirit of Afghani and Abduh. However, he was particularly influenced by Rida's writings on the political and social aspects of Islamic reform, the need for an Islamic state and the introduction of Islamic law. It was the later, more conservative Rida that al-Banna knew. He was attracted by Rida's emphasis on the complete and total self-sufficiency of Islam and the dangers of Westernization.

In addition to the influence of al-Banna's father and early teachers, two other factors played a significant role in his formation: the anti-British revolt of 1919 and membership in several Islamic associations. Although al-Banna had become deeply involved in Sufi mystical practice, he responded immediately to the political crisis of 1919: "Despite my preoccupation with Sufism and worship, I believed that duty to country is an inescapable obligation—a holy war."[38] The aborted revolt and British occupation of al-Banna's hometown, reinforced his sense of British hegemony in Egypt and the political as well as cultural threat of Western colonialism. The conclusion he drew as a thirteen-year old regarding the relationship of religion to politics would become a foundation stone of the Muslim Brotherhood.

During his school days, Hasan al-Banna belonged to a num-

ber of Islamic associations such as the Society for Ethical Education
and the Society for the Prevention of Prohibited Actions. These associations emphasized individual religious and moral reform and a
commitment to preach and spread the message of Islam to other
Muslims in coffee houses and other public gathering places as well as
mosques. Al-Banna would comment later: "There is no doubt that
such an association has more influence in forming character than
twenty theoretical lessons."[39] Both the political and religious moral
activities of his youth were major influences on the formation of his
own Islamic society with its emphasis upon organization and its religious rationale for political and socio-moral reform.

After completing his studies in 1927, Hasan al-Banna accepted a teaching post at a primary school in Ismailiyya. Convinced
that only through a return to Islam (by following the *Quran* and
Sunnah of the Prophet) could the Muslim world be awakened from its
lethargy and decline, he organized religious discussion groups and
committed himself to Islamic renewal. A man of great religious zeal
and charisma, al-Banna quickly attracted followers and in 1928 established the Muslim Brotherhood or Muslim Brethren (Ikhwan al-
Muslimun).

During his studies in Cairo and in Ismailiyya, which was at
the heart of the British occupied Suez Canal Zone, Hasan al-Banna
experienced both Western political presence, or occupation, as well as
its religious and cultural challenge to traditional Egyptian society. The
threat of Westernization came both from the British and from
Westernized Egyptian elites who sought to implement Western-based
models in political, social, and economic development. Hasan al-
Banna, as Rashid Rida, concluded that Westernization was a major
threat to Egypt and Islam, the source of much of Egypt's political,
social and economic problems. Thus, as he viewed the political disunity, the profound socioeconomic disparities, the social dislocation, the
growing indifference to religion in Egyptian society, Western secularism and materialism stood out as major causes of Muslim impotence
and decline. The cure for this "disease"—a return to Islam. However,
unlike Islamic modernists, who looked to the West and provided an
Islamic rationale for the appropriation of Western learning, Hasan al-
Banna emphasized the perfection and comprehensiveness of Islam
and hence its self-sufficiency. Following the methodology of
nineteenth-century Islamic revivalism, al-Banna called for a return to
the *Quran* and Sunnah of the Prophet as the primary sources for the
re-establishment of an Islamic system of government. In addition to

rejecting Western sources, he also differed from the general tendency of the *ulama* to rely on their medieval formulations of Islam. Like Muhammad ibn Abd al-Wahhab and other revivalists, al-Banna believed that Muslims must go back beyond all historical accretions, and return to the early normative period of Islamic history—the time of the Prophet and the first caliphs of Islam.

During the first decade of its existence, the Muslim Brotherhood concentrated on moral and social reform, attracting popular support for their educational and social welfare projects. They ran small hospitals, built neighborhood mosques and schools, established cottage industries, and opened local social clubs. By 1949, the Brotherhood had some two-thousand branches spread across Egypt, with an estimated membership of five-hundred thousand and an equal number of sympathizers. Each branch consisted of a center, mosque, school, and a club or home industry.

In 1933 Hasan al-Banna decided to move the center of activities to Cairo, where he devoted himself to the organization and communication of the Brotherhood's mission and message. The comprehensive nature of the Brotherhood's organization and program was reflected in his description of the movement as "a Salafiyya message, a Sunni way, a Sufi truth, a political organization, an athletic group, a cultural-educational union, an economic company, and a social idea."[40] It was in Cairo that the Muslim Brotherhood's weekly magazine *Majallat al-Ikhwan al-Muslimun* (The Journal of the Muslim Brothers) and its press, which would play an important role in the development and dissemination of Muslim Brotherhood ideas throughout the Muslim world, were established.

Under the leadership of its charismatic guide, the Brotherhood developed into a well-knit religious and political organization with a network of branches that were further divided into secret cells. Its members underwent a program of training and ideological indoctrination emphasizing moral and physical fitness in order to defend Islam. Membership spread beyond its rural, lower-class origins to the urban middle class. It attracted merchants, teachers, physicians, lawyers, judges, civil servants, the military, and university students.

The Brotherhood became progressively embroiled in politics, in particular through its anti-British and anti-Palestine activities. Its goal was the establishment of an Islamic state in Egypt. The situation came to a head in December 1948 when the government of King Farouk, reacting to a series of violent incidents, including the assassination of Cairo's chief of police, banned the Brotherhood and imprisoned many of its key leaders, excepting Hasan al-Banna. Shortly afterward Egypt's prime minister, Nurashi Pasha, was murdered by a twenty-three year-old veterinary student and Muslim Brother. Although al-Banna denied either his or the Muslim Brothers' involvement, the government blamed the Brotherhood and the estimated one million members of the Brotherhood were driven underground or into exile. On February 12, 1949, in retaliation, Hasan al-Banna was himself assassinated by Egypt's secret police as he left his Cairo office.

When martial law was finally abolished in May of 1952, the Brotherhood re-emerged. As noted previously, the Brotherhood's initial support of Gamal Abd al-Nasser's July 1952 "Revolution" was withdrawn when it became clear that Nasser was not going to establish an Islamic state or share power with the Brotherhood. The conflict between the Brotherhood and Nasser's government climaxed in 1954 with an abortive assassination attempt against Nasser by several of its members. Although there was no proof that this was anything more than the act of several individuals, the government used it as a pretext to crush the entire Brotherhood organization. Its headquarters in Cairo and the provinces were sacked, thousands of members arrested, and a number of its leaders executed.

The Muslim Brotherhood's understanding of the nature of Islamic state and society has been particularly influenced by the teachings of Hasan al-Banna and the writings of Sayyid Qutb (1906–66). Like Hasan al-Banna, Sayyid Qutb graduated from Dar al-Ulum and was a schoolteacher. He then became an inspector in the Ministry of Education. In 1948 he published *Social Justice in Islam*, after which he spent two years in the United States studying educational organization. On his return to Egypt, Sayyid Qutb joined the Muslim Brothers and became its major ideologue. Qutb was a prolific author, writing some twenty-four books and a host of articles primarily on religion but also on literary criticism and education. Among his religious writings were *Social Justice in Islam; This Religion of Islam; Islam the Religion of the Future; Signposts on the Road;* and a commentary on the *Quran.*

Although initially attracted to the West, like many Egyptian intellectuals, Sayyid Qutb became disillusioned during the 1940s. Western complicity in the establishment of Israel and his stay in the United States convinced him of the moral decadence of Western civilization and its anti-Arab bias. Qutb's increasingly militant Islamic writings and activities catapulted him into a position of leadership in the Brotherhood and made him a target in Nasser's crackdown in 1954. He was sentenced to fifteen years in prison, where he continued to write. Released in 1964 through the intervention of Iraq's president, Abd al-Salam Arif, Qutb was again arrested only a few months later and executed with two other Brothers suspected of plotting against the government. Like Hasan al-Banna, Sayyid Qutb is often referred to as the martyr of the Islamic revival. Both their writings not only have had a formative influence upon the Muslim Brotherhood, but also have been a major influence upon Islamic revivalism today.

Sayyid Qutb's thought was strongly influenced by Hasan al-Banna and the writings of Pakistan's Mawlana Mawdudi. He borrowed frequently from Mawdudi in his exposition on such themes as God's governance, *jihad*, and the revolutionary character of Islam. Because he wrote more extensively than al-Banna, he provided more of a blueprint for the Muslim Brothers. Moreover, although Qutb drew from Mawdudi, he took many of these beliefs to their more literal, militant conclusion. Qutb himself moved from an early phase which spoke of an Islamic alternative to Western systems to a latter stage in which an Islamic alternative became *the* Islamic imperative which all Muslims were obligated to implement, for which the true believers should be willing to live and die.[41] As a result, he appealed to the more radical elements among his contemporaries in the Brotherhood and has been a strong formative influence on militant Islamic organizations today, including Egypt's Takfir wal Hijra (Excommunication and Emigration) and al-Jihad (The Holy War Society) the assassins of Anwar al-Sadat.

Like pre-modern revivalists and modern Islamic reformers, for al-Banna and Qutb the early Islamic state of Muhammad and the first four caliphs constitute the ideal period. After that time, pure Islam declined as kingship was introduced by the Umayyads, and tribal factionalism re-emerged and wracked the history of the Islamic empires. Despite political and cultural success, the Islamic ideal was not being fully realized and, therefore, the Islamic community remained vulnerable to outside attack and penetration from the Crusades to European colonialism. Internally, un-Islamic practices infiltrated Islamic belief and practice. This degeneration was evident in medieval Islamic law and the extremes of sufism. The net result was a weakened, disintegrating Islamic community whose decayed state made it an easy victim of European imperialism. Muslim governments succumbed politically, militarily, intellectually, spiritually, and culturally to the West.

Muslim leaders had failed their community. Sufism had become corrupted through its absorption of superstitious practices. The *ulama*, clinging to their medieval ways, had become irrelevant as they proved incapable of responding to the demands of modernity. Islamic modernists had also failed. Primarily concerned with charting an Islamic response to the West through religious, intellectual, and educational reform, they sought an Islamic rationale for learning from the West. As a result, they were too Western-oriented. More importantly, they did not undertake mass political organization and action. Finally, the most influential and destructive force among the Muslims was its secular, elite leadership. Islamically uncommittted, they turned to the West in politics, economics, law, and education. Secular elites constituted indigenous, domestic colonizers, responsible for the Westernization of Muslim society. As Muhammad al-Ghazzali, a Muslim Brother, wrote: "The faction which works for the separation of Egypt from Islam is really a shameless, pernicious, and perverse group of puppets and slaves of Europe."[42]

Yet, the Brotherhood charged that faith in the West was misplaced; the West had failed miserably. Parliamentary government and democracy were simply manipulated by the upper class to control the masses. Concentration of political power was accompanied by that of wealth and resources. Western democracy had not countered but contributed to continued economic exploitation, corruption and social injustice by landlord, as well as by new "modern" elites. Western secularism and materialism undermined religion and morality and thus weakened the fabric of society in general and the Muslim family in particular. Finally, despite Egypt's uncritical dependence upon and subservience to the West, the West had betrayed the Arabs in its support for Israeli occupation of Palestine.

The Brotherhood believed that neither Western capitalism nor atheistic communism could cure the diseased condition of the Muslim community. The only answer is a return to Islam which provided the revealed ideological alternative for Muslims.

There are two huge blocs: the Communist Bloc in the East and the Capitalist Bloc in the West. Each disseminates deceptive propaganda throughout the world claiming that there are only two alternative views of the world, Communism and Capitalism, and that other nations have no alternative but to ally themselves with one bloc or the other. . . . We have recently experienced in Palestine that neither the Eastern Bloc nor the Western Bloc give any credence to the values they advocate, or consider us ourselves as of consequence. . . . We will receive no mercy from either bloc.[43]

The Islamic alternative is: "a divine vision that proceeds from God in all its particularities and its essentials. It is received by man in its perfect condition. . . . He is to appropriate it and implement all its essentials in his life."[44]

Implementation of the Islamic model is an imperative which demands the restoration of Islam through a return to the *Quran* and the Sunnah of the Prophet. For both Hasan al-Banna and Sayyid Qutb, the task of modern Muslims is nothing less than a great *jihad* against the enemies of Islam to re-establish a true Islamic territory or rule, which is the prerequisite for following the Islamic way of life. Such an Islamic revival would assure the restoration of Islamic ascendency in the world. Any other form of government, whether foreign dominated or under Muslim control, is illegitimate and thus a non-Islamic territory, an object of holy war. Muslims who stand in the way of implementing an Islamic government are themselves unbelievers and therefore enemies of God and the state, objects of *jihad*.

Ideologically, the Brotherhood emphasized the union of religion and society in Islam. This belief was grounded in the unity of God and his supreme sovereignty over all His creation: "If Islam is to be effective, it is inevitable that it must rule. This religion did not come only to remain in the corners of places of worship. . . . It has come that it may govern life and administer it and mold society according to its total image of life, not by preaching or guidance alone but also by setting of laws and regulations."[45]

God's will for his creation is embodied in the *Shariah* which provides the comprehensive blueprint for Muslim society. Emphasizing the universality of the Islamic community and its mission, the Muslim Brotherhood rejected nationalism, whether liberal nationalism or Arab nationalism, and called for an Islamic state governed by the *Shariah*. While open to modern science and technology, the Brotherhood renounced the dependence of Muslim intellectuals and of Muslim governments upon the West. Instead of Westernization and secularization, the renewal of Muslim society must be rooted in Islamic principles and values: "Until recently, writers, intellectuals, scholars, and governments glorified the principles of European civili-

zation . . . adopted a Western style and manner. . . . Today, on the
contrary, the wind has changed. . . . Voices are raised . . . for a return
to the principles, teachings, and ways of Islam . . . for initiating the
reconciliation of modern life with these principles, as a prelude to a
final Islamization."[46]

For many the Brotherhood critique of both the West and
Egyptian society rang true and seemed a ray of hope in a society
gripped by disillusionment and cynicism. They appealed not only to
the religiously devout but also to those Egyptian elites whose initial
faith in liberal nationalism had been deeply shaken. The disastrous
defeat of the Arabs in Palestine, the establishment of the Israeli state
with U.S. support, the continued failure of the Egyptian government
to rid itself of its British occupiers, the massive unemployment and
poverty of post–World War II Egypt and rampant political corruption
moved many former protagonists of Western culture to reassess their
position, so much so that by the 1940s "the whole Egyptian literary
endeavor came to be dominated by works on Muslim subjects."[47] In
particular, authors looked to Muhammad, the heroes and the victories of early Islam for inspiration and values. Native rather than
foreign soil became the source for historic identity, pride, and values.
In this climate of disillusionment and disaffection, the Muslim
Brotherhood offered a well-organized and politically mobilized viable
opposition movement.

Traditional Islamic categories were used to describe the two
options open to mankind today: ignorance and Islam. The former,
which had been used by Muslims to describe pre-Islamic Arabian
society, was extended to apply to the blind condition of non-Muslims
and Western-oriented Muslims who had compromised themselves.
They uncritically emulate everything they see. The other option, Islam, is the divinely mandated alternative to Western capitalism and
Eastern communism: "Islam alone has remained preserved in its principles. Its sources have not been polluted, nor has its truth been
superimposed on falsehood."[48] The Islamic vision is divinely ordained
and unique: "of such comprehensiveness and breadth, of precision
and depth, of authenticity and integratedness that it rejects every
foreign element."[49]

The Muslim Brotherhood called for an Islamic revolution; it
offered a theology of liberation. If Muslims were to restore Islamic
ascendency, they must return to Islam, to the straight path of a comprehensive way of life. The task at hand required nothing less than a
holy war against the enemies of Islam. These included both the forces

of Western Christian imperialism and of Muslim Westernizers—both were the oppressors, both were guilty of unbelief. The faithful Muslims, the true soldiers or holy warriors of Islam must band together in groups or societies for the struggle to implement Islam. Such Islamic societies or organizations are the leaven that will bring about the Islamization of the community.

The Brotherhood believed that, given the un-Islamic and anti-Islamic condition of modern Muslim societies, Islamic societies or organizations at first would, of necessity, be small vanguards of true believers. Like the early Muslims who were forced to withdraw from Mecca and emigrate to Medina, they also would experience oppression and would be compelled to withdraw from modern day un-Islamic society. During this interim period of struggle, the Islamic societies must form their own separate community or family where, in a true, Islamic milieu, members can study and be formed to constitute the saving remnant, the nucleus of actors who are the agents of change, the implementors of the Islamization process. The true soldier of God must expect adversity as seen in the example of Muhammad and of all God's prophets. *Jihad* is a necessary component in the struggle against the enemies of God. Indeed, Qutb came to divide society into two camps: the Party of God and the Party of Satan, those committed to the rule of God and the remainder who followed all other, un-Islamic, systems. Qutb was critical of Islamic modernists as well as those members of the religious establishment who downplayed *jihad* as armed struggle preferring to restrict it instead to moral self-discipline. Qutb reminded Muslims that the *Quran* mandated the waging of war where God's enemies prevented Islamic governance. Though they experience persecution and martyrdom because God governs all creation, ultimate victory would be realized, that is, a new Islamic political order will be established based upon Islamic brotherhood and social justice and governed by God's law.

The Brotherhood believed that the introduction of the *Shariah* makes a government and society Islamic; therefore, implementation of Islamic law was a primary goal. The Muslim Brotherhood's understanding of *Shariah* was quite flexible. Muslims were not restricted to the formulations of the four Sunni law schools. These interpretations were themselves conditioned by their historical context and therefore open to revision. Sayyid Qutb distinguished between the eternal principles of the *Shariah* and the law regulations contained in the law books which were made by men who applied the *Shariah* to specific historical and social situations. True renewal was not based on blind imitation of tradition, but was open to fresh interpretation to meet the needs of the community. Thus, while eternal in nature and universal in scope, Islamic law remains flexible and open to development.

A guiding principle in Islamic legal reform is the general welfare of public interest. In addition the ruler can enact regulations to assure Islamic government. What assures the authenticity of Islamic law is its reference point, God, as opposed to temporal social needs or desires, as in the human legislation of secular societies. The *Shariah* of God provides the guiding principles which check all new interpretations. Moreover, the restoration of Islamic law will overcome the alienation from law which necessarily results from the adoption of Western codes which were "inspired in an alien environment, with a different history, religion, conditions and needs. Unless the law is a response to the ethos and need of the masses, they will not be led by it nor will they be faithful to it."[50]

Because the Muslim Brotherhood is often characterized as a fundamentalist movement, it has been depicted as desiring to recreate a seventh century Islamic state or government. In fact, this is a gross distortion. The Brotherhood is fundamentalist in the sense that it called for a return to Islamic principles which are timeless, but it did not necessarily advocate adopting a specific form of government. Both in its conception of government and law, due recognition was given to the fact that specific institutions and regulations were created to meet particular socio-historical situations. "The Islamic system is not restricted solely to a replica of the first Islamic society. . . . The Islamic system has room for scores of models which are compatible with the natural growth of society and the new needs of the contemporary age as long as the Islamic idea dominates these models in its expansive external perimeter."[51] Thus whether a particular form of government is Islamic is determined by implementation of the *Shariah* which provides the framework for state and society.

In general, the Muslim Brotherhood gave little attention to the specific form of an Islamic state. Rather, it provided general principles. Discussions of Islamic government tend to be theoretical, marked by a moral idealism, rather than practical. God is the sovereign ruler of the universe, the only true legislator. The *Quran*, therefore, is the fundamental constitution of the state. The temporal ruler receives his authority and power from God and is to administer and supervise, i.e., to assure that society is governed by the *Shariah*.

The ruler must be Muslim, male, sane, virtuous, and knowledgeable in Islamic jurisprudence. The method by which he is chosen by the people (direct or indirect selection or election) is not fixed, nor is his tenure in office, which may be for a fixed term or for life. In governing, the ruler must follow the *Quranic* principle of consultation of the people (3:159). Thus, there is a covenant or social contract between ruler and ruled, who have delegated authority to him. In this sense, Islamic government is democratic. However, the form that such consultation would take has not been given and therefore may vary. The consultative assembly may consist of a select number of Muslims or all Muslims, directly or indirectly selected or elected. Obedience is due a Muslim ruler who governs according to the *Shariah*. If he does not do so, then the covenant between the ruler and the people ceases. Such a ruler becomes an unbeliever and, according to the *Quran* (5:44), must be resisted.

Islam's comprehensive system includes the social as well as the political and legal aspects of life. While affirming that there is an Islamic social system, again the Brotherhood offered guidelines or limits rather than detailed models, principles rather than specific institutions.

At the heart of Muslim society is the family. The Brotherhood believed that the strength of the nation begins with the individual, is nurtured in the family, and blossoms into a strong and powerful nation. The central importance of the family was based upon the attention given to the Prophet's family and that of Ali as a paradigm for society and in the historic primacy of Muslim family law as the very heart of the *Shariah*. Given the family's role as the cornerstone of Muslim society, the Brotherhood viewed the status and role of women with special concern. It espoused the traditional Muslim position that Islam had improved the status of women in Arabia, giving her marriage, divorce, and inheritance rights. Women were viewed as equal to men before God, but different. Because they believed men are generally endowed with superior mental ability and emotional stability, men exercise political and social leadership and are responsible for women and the family. Women's primary sphere of activity is home and family. Therefore, education is important but with emphasis on those areas that best prepare Muslim women for their roles as wives and mothers. With this view of human nature, the Brotherhood deemed separation of sexes rather than coeducation preferable. Women may have careers in engineering, medicine, law where necessary, but special care must be given to a woman's dignity and modesty. Most importantly, career development should not obscure or hinder the realization of woman's natural and primary role: "The woman's natural place is in the home, but if she finds that after doing her duty in the home she has time, she can use part of it in the service of society, on condition that this is done within the legal limits which preserve her dignity and morality."[52]

For the Muslim Brotherhood, economic reform was imperative, both to assure Islamic social justice and to repel the forces of imperialism. Muslims caught between the twin fallacies of capitalism and communism, must turn to the creation of an Islamic economic order. An Islamic economic system is based neither on unfettered individualism and conspicuous consumption nor on state socialism, but upon Islam's integration of the material and the spiritual aspects of life. As in politics, so too in economics—God is the point of origin. All wealth, as all power, belongs to God. Man has a *Quranic*-mandated role as God's steward or trustee. Muslims do not enjoy an absolute, unfettered right of ownership and wealth. This belongs to God alone. Individual rights are limited by God's law and the broader needs of the Islamic community. Certain means of acquiring wealth such as usury and gambling are prohibited, as are hoarding and the monopoly of natural resources. The Brotherhood strongly affirmed the right of private property in Islam as well as differences in wealth based upon personal initiative, hard work, and an individual's natural endowments and skills. However, wealth involves social duties as well. Muslims have a social obligation to assist fellow Muslims who are in need. The *zakat*, i.e., wealth tax on capital as well as profits, is "the social pillar of Islam," the fundamental principle of Islamic social justice. Payment of the wealth tax is not simply a discretionary, charitable act but based upon the right of the poor to assistance from their more fortunate co-believers. Where social justice demands, the state may even limit the individual's right of private ownership in the public interest through government land reform and nationalization of public utilities, banks, mineral resources. Thus, the Muslim Brotherhood maintained that Islam provided its own distinctive approach and basis for a social revolution which would bring about true social equity.

However, the political and social program of the Brotherhood was never realized. Indeed the ruthless suppression of the Brethren by Nasser in 1965 led many to believe that the movement had been effectively extinguished. Few would have anticipated its return and revival in Egypt nor its influence upon contemporary Islamic activists throughout the Muslim world.

The Jamaat-i-Islami

In South Asia a second major Islamic organization, the Jamaat-i-Islami (Islamic Society), developed under a contemporary of Hasan al-Banna, Mawlanda Mawdudi (1903–79).[53] Abul Ala Mawdudi was born in Aurangabad, in central India. His early upbringing and education were dominated by his father, who supervised his son's traditional religious education (*Quran, hadith, Shariah*, Islamic languages, history). Modern education was assiduously eschewed, so that it was only later that Mawdudi learned English and studied modern subjects. Mawdudi pursued an early career as a journalist and at twenty one he became editor of *al-Jamiah* (1924–27), the newspaper of India's Jamiyyat-i-Ulama (Association of Ulama). Like many other Indian Muslims, Mawdudi was active in the Khilafat and the All-India National Congress. However, he progressively became convinced that the future of Indian Muslims was threatened not only by British imperialism but also by Hindu and Muslim nationalism.

Two particularly important events served as catalysts that motivated Mawdudi to assume an independent role as an Islamic leader and attempt to be a spokesman for an Islamic alternative for state and society. In 1925 Swami Shradhanand, leader of a Hindu revivalist movement (the Shudhi) was assassinated by a Muslim extremist who claimed it was a religious duty to kill non-believers. In the public controversy that followed there were charges that Islam was a religion of the sword. As Ahmad Khan had responded to similar claims after the war of 1857, Mawdudi came to the defense of Islam. He wrote a series of articles which were published as a book, *War in Islam*, in 1927. Mawdudi not only discussed the Islamic attitude towards warfare but also presented in seminal form many of the themes that he would develop and explicate in his later writings on the Islamic state and society.

A second formative influence on Mawdudi was the Indian independence movement and, in particular, the question of Indian or Muslim nationalism. As previously discussed, during the 1930s when Hindus and Muslims strongly pressed for independence from Britain and the establishment of a separate state, Mawdudi had become increasingly critical of the options presented to Indian Muslims by both the Gandhi-led Congress Party and the Jinnah-led Muslim League. Aware of the reality of religious communalism in India, he shared the growing concern of most Muslims for the survival of their identity and way of life in a Hindu dominated, albeit secular, state. He regarded Mahatma Gandhi's increasing reliance on Hindu beliefs such as truth-force, and self-rule to express the ideology of the Indian nationalist movement as well as the Hindu communal approach to the 1937 elections as proof of fundamental Hindu-Muslim differences. In language strikingly similar to the "Two Nation Theory" of Mohammad Ali Jinnah, Mawdudi asserted that Muslims were a permanent community "based on specific moral and civic rules. We have some basic and inherent disagreements with the majority [Hindu] *gawm* [community] . . . so it is not possible to join ourselves into a single whole. . . . Their path and ours can run parallel, and can even come together in places, but they can never coincide."[54]

However, Mawdudi was equally critical of the Muslim nationalism of the Muslim League. As noted earlier, he viewed nationalism as an imported ideology from the West, alien to Islam and ill suited as the basis for a so-called Muslim state. Muslim nationalism was ultimately idolatrous since nationalism emphasized popular sovereignty rather than divine sovereignty as well as secularism or the separation of religion from the state. Moreover, its narrow particularism was contrary to the universalism of Islam and would further divide an already fragmented Islamic community. In addition, Mawdudi objected to the potential Muslim League leadership of the proposed Muslim state since he regarded Jinnah and his associates as secular, "Westernized" Muslims incapable of true Islamic leadership. Thus, neither in its ideology nor in its leadership would the proposed Muslim state be Islamically acceptable. Mawdudi's convictions placed him at odds with most of India's leadership: secularists as well as Hindu and Muslim nationalists. He rejected the two dominant positions in the Indian subcontinent: Congress' call for an independent, united, secular Indian state as well as the Muslim League's proposal to partition India and establish Pakistan as a separate Muslim state.

Judging the nationalist options offered Indian Muslims unacceptable, Mawdudi believed that an Islamic revolution was necessary to establish an Islamic state and society. He advocated a gradual societal, rather than a violent, political, revolution. The Islamization of society was a prerequisite for establishing a true Islamic state. From the late 1930s onwards, Mawlana Mawdudi committed himself to the task of Islamic revivalism, in particular the training of Islamic leaders who might bring about the transformation of society. He developed and dissemininated his interpretation of an Islamic alternative in the journal *Tarjuman al-Quran* (Exegesis of the *Quran*), whose editorship he assumed in 1934. The journal remained a major vehicle for his thought during subsequent years. Mawdudi's purpose and vision were reflected both in his exposition and interpretation of Islam in that journal and in his founding of the Jamaat-i-Islami (The Islamic Society) in 1941. In the former he set forth the principles of Islamic state and society; through the latter he hoped to produce a band of committed and well-trained Muslims, a righteous society capable of implementing true Islam in the Indian subcontinent.

Mawdudi had moved from India to the Lahore area of what is now Pakistan in 1938 at the invitation of Muhammad Iqbal, to establish the Dar al-Islam Academy at Pathankot. In 1941, joined by seventy-five followers, he founded the Jamaat-i-Islami. Like the Muslim Brotherhood, the Jamaat was an ideological rather than a political party. Membership was strictly limited to those "righteous" Muslims whose understanding of Islam and religious integrity were proven and acceptable. Major emphasis was placed upon the formation and indoctrination of members. Mawdudi's interpretation of Islam provided the basis for instruction and guidance. In the prolific writings of Mawdudi one finds the authoritative source of the Jamaat's Islamic ideology and its program. He was in every sense the Amir (leader) of the Jamaat.

Although Mawdudi had objected to the establishment of Pakistan as a separate Muslim nation, after the partitioning of India, he accepted political reality and remained in what had become Pakistan. The Jamaat proceeded almost immediately to assert a position of leadership in the debate (1948–56) surrounding Pakistan's first constitution. As the new country's leaders sought to define and institutionalize Pakistan's ideology and system of government, the Jamaat pressed for the establishment of an Islamic state. In this effort, Mawdudi shared a common cause with most of the *ulama*, in particular, with their organization—the Jamiyyat-i-Ulama-Pakistan (The Association of Pakistan's Ulama) and with the general public for whom Jinnah's Muslim homeland and an Islamic state were interchangeable terms. From 1948 to the present, Mawdudi and the Jamaat-i-Islami have remained active in Pakistan's politics, often, as we shall see in the next chapter, in opposition to the government, pressing for its vision of an Islamic state. At the same time, the Jamaat's mission and influence of the Jamaat has extended beyond Pakistan. Through distribution of its literature and its widespread activities, it has advocated and disseminated its message internationally. Mawdudi, like Sayyid Qutb, who borrowed extensively from Mawdudi, has been a major influence on contemporary Islamic revivalism.

Mawdudi's outlook and method differed from that of both Muslim secular elites and Islamic modernists. Unlike the former, he did not look to the West for the models of modern political and social development. In contrast to the latter, Mawdudi did not seek an Islamic rationale for the appropriation of Western science and technology. Rather like Rashid Rida and the Muslim Brotherhood, he asserted the self-sufficiency of Islam as the source for Islamic renewal and reform. Mawdudi emphasized the universalism of Islam and the comprehensiveness of Islamic life. This position was at the heart of his rejection of nationalism and secularism. Unlike the Muslim Brotherhood, the Jamaat-i-Islami, through the writings of Mawdudi, has attempted to provide a theoretical blueprint for what Mawdudi saw as a revival or "Islamic revolution" in Muslim society. The character and extended parameters of this blueprint are reflected in the titles of such works as: *The Process of Islamic Revolution, Nationalism in India, The Islamic Way of Life, First Principles of the Islamic State, Islamic Law and Constitution, Economic Problem of Man and Its Islamic Solution*. Mawdudi's writings have been translated and distributed across the Islamic world and may be found in book shops and stalls from Cairo to Jakarta. Given the propagation of Mawdudi's vision of Islam throughout much of the Muslim world and its impact on contemporary Islamic revivalism, an understanding of his interpretation of Islam is essential.

For Mawdudi, the foundational principle of Islamic state and society is the doctrine of the unity and universal sovereignty of God. "The belief in the Unity and the sovereignty of Allah is the foundation of the social and moral system propounded by the Prophets."[55] As the creator, sustainer, and ruler of the universe is one, so too is God's law which governs all creation. All of reality—all areas of life—come from God and are subject to his sovereign law, Shariah: "The Shariah is a complete scheme of life and an all embracing social order."[56] Thus, the comprehensiveness of the Islamic way of life is rooted in the unity and totality of God's law revealed in the *Quran* and the example (Sunnah) of the Prophet. It is this organic relationship between religion, politics and society which distinguishes Islam and the Islamic community from the West. Separation of religion from the state for Mawdudi represents the inherent fallacy of Western secularism where the withdrawal of divine guidance has been the basis for its moral decline and its ultimate downfall. Western culture and all who do not follow Islam, God's revealed straight path, exist as did pre-Islamic society in a state of ignorance and darkness.

Mawdudi emphasized that Muslims' vocation must be to live within the limits and according to the precepts of the *Shariah* in its entirety. A *Shariah*-governed community constitutes an Islamic state. While Muslims such as the great Islamic jurists of the law schools may discern and apply God's law, God alone is the supreme lawgiver, the source of all authority and law. Thus, there can be no human lawgiver. However, despite an interdict on human legislation, Mawdudi does acknowledge the role of the state to not only enforce but also create laws in areas not covered by the *Shariah*. The state can do this by virtue of its role as God's agent or vicegerent. For Mawdudi the *Quranic* teaching regarding man's vicegerency (*Quran* 24:55) encompasses both the individual and communal Muslim mission on earth. All Muslims are God's vicegerents or representatives (caliphs). Thus, an Islamic state may quite accurately be called a "Caliphate." The ruler (Caliph, Imam, Amir) is the one whom the community has delegated as their leader. The head of state or Amir receives his authority from God and exercises his power on behalf of the people. As with the Rightly Guided Caliphs, he may be elected or selected by the people, directly or indirectly, through their representatives. He is the representative of both God and his fellow Muslim: "answerable to God on the one hand and on the other to his fellow caliphs who have delegated their authority to him."[57] The ruler oversees the conduct of state: the executive, legislative and judiciary. His power would include that of both the president and prime minister of a modern state. Yet, because the ruler is bound to observe and enforce God's law, he does not have an absolute power and authority. He is neither monarch nor dictator.

According to Mawdudi, the legal qualifications for head of state are that he must be Muslim, male, adult, sane, and a citizen of the Islamic state. More importantly, he should be the best man, i.e., the most committed and virtuous Muslim. The idealism of Mawdudi's approach is further reflected in his assertion that this "best man" can neither seek office nor undertake a political campaign. Rather, suitable candidates will be identified by some kind of election or selection committee. The utopianism of Mawdudi's thought is strikingly evident in his assertions that in the time of the early caliphs there was no dissension, only complete harmony: "the Ministers and the Head of State were all along working in complete cooperation and harmony and the question of anybody resigning in protest never arose at all."[58]

Mawdudi's Islamic idealism also gave rise to an "Islamic totalitarianism." Given the comprehensive nature of the Islamic state's divinely revealed law, "no one can regard any field of his affairs as personal or private."[59] Is this not totalitarianism? Mawdudi answered with a qualified "yes." The totalitarianism of an Islamic state is a good form of totalitarianism since it requires and enforces God's precepts. Unfortunately, Mawdudi did not indicate how Muslims can safeguard against rulers who falsely use the banner of Islam to legitimate their rule, impose their will, and stifle dissent.

The Islamic state was viewed by Mawdudi as the "very antithesis of secular Western democracy."[60] Western democracy is based upon popular sovereignty, with the people or nation enjoying absolute powers of legislation and thus able to make laws which are even contrary to religion and morality. For this reason, "Islam has no trace of Western democracy. . . . [It] repudiates the philosophy of popular sovereignty and rears its polity on the foundations of the sovereignty of God and the vicegerency (Khilafah) of man" (p. 160).

Mawdudi concluded that the Islamic system might best be called a theo-democracy. He used this term to distinguish the Islamic state as the "Kingdom of God" from the Western meaning of theocracy which also implies rule by a religious class or clergy. Here Mawdudi rejected any notion of ulama governance of the state. Furthermore, as a theo-democracy, while affirming the political role of all Muslims, the state was protected from, what Mawdudi called, the "tyranny of the masses" permitted by Western democracy. Since Islamic democracy must function within the limits of God, no law that is contrary to the Shariah may be passed even though it may enjoy mass support. Mawdudi was skeptical about the ability of most people to transcend their narrow self interest: "the great mass of the common people are incapable of perceiving their own true interests." (p. 134) He cites the repeal of the Prohibition Act in America as an example. Despite alcohol's proven danger to physical and mental health, those who voted for prohibition subsequently revolted against it and so, Mawdudi asserted, the law was finally repealed by the very people who had voted for it. (p. 137) Mawdudi believed that this problem could not occur in an Islamic state which is governed by religious norms, not societal whims.

Popular vicegerency in an Islamic state is reflected especially in the doctrine of mutual consultation (*shura.*) Since all sane adult Muslims, male and female, are vicegerents (agents of God), it is they who delegate their authority to the ruler (Caliph, Imam, Amir) and whose opinion must also be sought in the conduct of state. This may be done, directly or indirectly, through an elected representative body or assembly. Thus, the head of an Islamic state is not free to do as he likes. According to Mawdudi the consultative assembly or parliament should consist of adult, Muslim males who are good Muslims and sufficiently Islamically trained to interpret and apply the *Shariah* as well as to draft laws which are not contrary to the *Quran* and Sunnah of the Prophet.

The functions of the parliament are fourfold: (1) to enact legislation which embodies the explicit directives of God and Muhammad as well as regulations which will assure their proper enforcement; (2) where differing interpretations of the *Quran* and Sunnah exist, to decide which interpretation is to be enacted; (3) when no explicit directives exist, to deduce rules from the *Quran* and Sunnah or where previously enacted laws are found in the legal manuals to adopt one of them. (4) Finally, where "even basic guidance is not available" to formulate laws provided such legislation is not contrary to the letter and spirit of the *Shariah*.[61]

Given the ideological nature of the state and the functions of the parliament in an Islamic state, Mawdudi believed the vast majority of its members should be Muslim. While non-Muslims may elect their own representatives, this should be done through a system of separate electorates so that non-Muslims would be excluded from the selection of Muslim representatives. Mawdudi suggested another possible alternative for both non-Muslims and Muslim women, who were not eligible for election. Each might have their own consultative assembly; each could then advise the ruler and the parliament on those issues which affected their lives and welfare.

Mawdudi's notion of citizenship in an Islamic state and the rights of non-Muslims followed rigorously from early Islamic practice and medieval Islamic political theory. There are two categories of citizenship in a modern Islamic state: Muslim and non-Muslim. Non-Muslims are "protected people" (*dhimmi*). In return for payment of the poll tax, they enjoy protection and have certain rights and duties.

They may worship but not proselytize. In religious matters they are governed by their religious leaders. However, in all other areas of life, Islamic law prevails since it is the "Law which commands the approval of the majority alone [which] has the right to become the Law of the Land."[62] Since an Islamic state is an ideological state, only those who accept that ideology should run the state. Therefore, non-Muslims would be barred both from key administrative positions as well as policy-making posts. Moreover, they should not serve in a standing army since, as believers, they could not be expected to defend Islam.

For Mawdudi herein lies the difference between a national state and an Islamic state. For the former, citizenship is based upon belonging to a nation, race, ethnic group. For the latter, citizenship is determined by ideology (belief or unbelief). Therefore, citizenship is not equal and the same for all. Rather, citizens are classified as Muslim or non-Muslim and, as a result, differ in their rights and duties.

Preservation of an Islamic state may necessitate and even require a holy war. Mawdudi believed that *jihad* is an obligation for the faithful Muslim citizen. Mawdudi began with the broad definition of *jihad* as the duty of all Muslims to strive or struggle to actualize God's will. "Those who believe fight in the cause of God, and those who disbelieve fight in the cause of force" (*Quran:* IV:76). He viewed two kinds of warfare as permissible: defensive *jihad* and corrective *jihad*. These become necessary when Islamic belief and practice are threatened by an external enemy, by disruptive internal forces, or by non-Muslim rulers in a non-Islamic state. While many modern Muslims prefer to simply emphasize the meaning of *jihad* as an internal struggle to lead a virtuous Muslim life, Mawdudi did not shrink from affirming the continuing division of the world into Islamic and non-Islamic territory and the right, indeed duty, of a good Muslim to wage war when Islam and the Islamic way of life were threatened.

For Mawlana Mawdudi and the Jamaat-i-Islami, as for the Muslim Brotherhood, the Islamic community in the twentieth century was at a critical crossroads. Like secular modernists and Islamic reformers, they acknowledge the internal weakness of the Muslim community, the external threat of Western imperialism, and accept science and technology. However, unlike secularist and Islamic reformers, the Brotherhood and the Jammat were more sweeping in their condemnation of the West and their assertion of the total self-sufficiency of Islam. While secularists might reject Western political hegemony, they looked to the West in charting their future. Islamic reformers sought to provide an Islamic rationale for a selective borrowing from the West. However, Islamic movements like the Brotherhood and the Jamaat tend to view their options more clearly and simply. Both capitalism and Marxism represented man-made Western secular paths which were alien to the God ordained, straight path of Islam. If Muslims were to remain faithful to God and His divine will, they must reject Western secularism and materialism and return solely to Islam whose perfection assured guidance in all aspects of life.

CONCLUSION

During the post-independence period, newly emergent Muslim states faced a formidable task. For most, the process of modern nation building followed a long period of colonial political and military domination and economic dependence. Their recent Western colonial experience had been preceded by a centuries-long Islamic imperial past. For modern elites their Islamic heritage was, though perhaps still valid for spiritual life, no longer relevant to the needs and requirements of modern politics and society. Since modernization and industrialization had originated in the West, Western nations had had several centuries to grapple with questions of religious reform and modern nation building. Issues of national identity and ideology, the development of appropriate institutions of government and law were hammered out, if not fully then at least adequately. Despite the strains of post enlightenment rationalism and the industrial revolution, change had occurred within the context of Western history and tradition. However, Muslim leaders were faced with a compressed time frame of decades rather than centuries and with models for modern development which were indeed "alien", of foreign origin. Ataturk's secular path and Saudi Arabia's "Islamic" path provided polar solutions, enforced by autocratic rulers. For many other Muslim countries such as Egypt, Syria, Libya or Pakistan, inherited colonial patterns were carried over, augmented by those alterations which suited the state's needs or the personal preferences of their rulers. Though heavily indebted to Western models, Islam was selectively employed where deemed necessary or useful. However, for Islamic organizations such as the Muslim Brotherhood and the Jamaat-i-

Islami, modern states in the Muslim world were doomed to failure so long as they looked to the West and failed to root their identity and sociopolitical development directly in Islam. Thus they spoke of the third Islamic alternative. Indeed it is an imperative. Few people would have guessed the decade of the 70s would see Islam re-emerge in Muslim politics across the Islamic world to such a marked degree that scholars, journalists and government analysts would employ phrases like Islamic resurgence, Islamic revival, and the rise of militant Islam to describe this new and unexpected phenomenon.

5

Contemporary Politics

*P*OLITICAL EVENTS in the Muslim world during the 1970s dramatically drew attention to the political and social potential of Islam. Contrary to accepted norms of political development, with its secular presuppositions, and the expectations of many analysts, religion did not recede in the Muslim world but rather reemerged in the politics of countries such as Iran, Pakistan, Egypt, Afghanistan, Saudi Arabia, Syria, and Malaysia.[1] Islamic ideology, symbols, slogans, and actors became prominent fixtures in Muslim politics. Iran established an Islamic Republic and Pakistan recommitted itself to the implementation of a more Islamic system of government. Islamic laws, dress, taxes, and punishments were introduced in many Muslim countries. Both incumbent governments and opposition movements often competed with one another in declaring their allegiance to Islam and commitment to a more Islamic way of life. Islamic politics, economics, law, and education became hotly contested issues. Amidst the diversity of Islamic revivalism there are common sociopolitical concerns and themes, rooted in a general consensus among many that Muslims have failed to produce a viably authentic political and social synthesis which is both modern and true to their indigenous (Islamic) history and values. Among these shared concerns were: (1) the continued impotence of Muslim society, i.e., the failure and ineffectiveness of Muslim governments and nationalist ideologies; (2) a disillusionment with the West; and (3) the desire to articulate a more authentic identity.

If Islam's glorious political and cultural past had been reversed by European colonial rule, many believed that political

152

independence had not significantly improved the political and socioeconomic condition of Muslim countries. Most continued to be subservient to the West both politically and culturally. European colonialism was replaced by American neo-colonialism as represented by America's foreign policies, military presence and multi-national companies. Moreover, political leaders failed to establish a legitimate, effective public order and to adequately address the profound socioeconomic disparities in wealth and class in most Muslim countries. This sense of disillusionment and failure was reflected in Muslim literature in the late 1960s, in its growing criticism of the West and its concern to reclaim historical and cultural identity.[2] For the religiously oriented, the problem had always been clear—departure from the straight path of Islam was doomed to failure. For Western-oriented intellectuals and elites, the disillusionment was more unsettling. They had embraced the West as both an ally and a model for modern development. The establishment of Israel, continued massive American economic and military aid for Israel, support for regimes like that of the Shah of Iran, as well as the failures of Muslim governments posed a direct challenge to those Muslims who had espoused Western oriented positions.

The complete and decisive nature of the Arab defeat at the hands of Israel in 1967 shattered faith and confidence in the West and in Arab nationalism. The defeat in 1967 was the most vivid confirmation, in Muslim eyes and before the world, of political and military impotence. Despite national independence, the centuries-long decline of Muslim power and prestige had not been reversed but, in fact, seemed to have reached its nadir. From the establishment of Israel, Arab forces had lost in a series of military confrontations. However, Egyptian and Syrian forces were now defeated with lightning speed by Israel's pre-emptive strike which destroyed much of the Arab forces before they could even respond and left Egypt and Syria in a state of debilitated paralysis. The trauma of the '67 war in the Arab world was vividly reflected by its common reference in literature as "the disaster."

The result was protracted period of soul-searching self-criticism: What had gone wrong? Why did Muslim countries remain weak and subservient to the West and Israel, its "Middle East Colony." For the Islamically oriented, there were two questions: "What had the Muslims continued to do wrong that Divine guidance seemed so absent?" "Could it be that Islam was the cause of Muslim backwardness, that it was unable to respond to modernity?" For Western-oriented Muslims the questions were different but no less troubling:

"Despite their confidence in the West, why had they remained so impotent?" and "Why did the West continue to favor Israel over the Arabs?"

The self-criticism and disillusionment with the West was accompanied by an increased emphasis on the need for greater self-reliance, a desire to reclaim one's past and to root individual and national self-identity more indigenously, to find pride and strength in an Islamic past and cultural tradition that had once been a dominant world civilization. This quest for greater authenticity was reflected in popular and intellectual as well as religious literature where there was a confluence of concerns on such topics as religion, tradition, and values, politics and ideology, language and education.[3] All became part of a general call for a religio-cultural revival, reform, or renaissance.

The year 1973 proved to be decisive, providing a sign that Muslim fortunes were indeed changing. The Arab-Israeli War of 1973 and the Arab oil boycott became major sources of Muslim pride. The Arab defeat of 1967 was reversed by the "Islamic victory" of 1973's October War with Israel. For Arabs, the ability and success of Egyptian forces were established even if final victory had been thwarted by massive American assistance to Israel. The war and thus the "victory" had been placed in an Islamic context. Islamic symbols and slogans were emphasized; from its name, the Ramadan War; its battle cry (*Allahu Akbar!*—"God is Most Great"); its code name (*Badr*), Muhammad's first victory over his Meccan opponents. For many, the victory, coupled with the oil boycott's demonstration of Arab (Muslim) economic power, instilled a new sense of pride and strengthened a commitment to their Islamic identity. The return of power and wealth, lost during the colonial period, seemed a sign from God and the revival of Islamic ascendancy.

While there are distinctive differences among Islamic revivalists, they share both a common Islamic heritage and confrontation with Western political and cultural imperialism. Common themes in Islamic politics and sociopolitical thought may be identified: (1) the failure of the West, i.e., the inappropriateness of transplanted, imported Western models of political, social, and economic development. The need to throw off Western political and cultural domination which foster secularism, materialism, and spiritual bankruptcy; (2) the need to "return to Islam" in order to restore a lost identity, moral purpose, and character (3) an emphasis on the unity and totality of Islam, rooted in the doctrine of the unity of God, i.e., belief that religion is integral to politics and society because Islam is both religion and government; (4) a call for the reintroduction of *Shariah* law as the *sine qua non* for establishing a more Islamic state and society.

Despite the unity of faith and commonality of general concerns, the character and manifestations of the Islamic resurgence have varied significantly, reflecting each country's specific history and politics. The examples of Libya, Pakistan, Iran, and Egypt amply illustrate the complexity of contemporary Islamic politics. Islamic vision is translated into reality. Differences in context as well as understanding and interpretation have resulted in divergent experiences.

LIBYA

On September 1, 1969, the government of King Idris (1890–1983) was overthrown by a clique of junior military officers headed by a young army lieutenant. Since that day Muammar Qaddafi (1942–) has been the principal architect of modern day Libya.[4]

Libya had been a monarchy ruled by the grandson of Muhammad ibn al-Sanusi (1780–1859), founder of the Sanusiyyah Sufi Order. As discussed in Chapter 2, the Sanusiyyah, like other eighteenth- and nineteenth-century Islamic reform movements such as the Wahhabi in Saudi Arabia and the Mahdi in the Sudan, had united tribes in what today is Libya, Chad, and western Egypt into a movement that sought to purify Islamic practice and establish an Islamic state and society. However, during the early twentieth century (1911–30) Italy progressively extended its colonial rule over Libya. Under Idris, the grandson of the Grand Sanusi, the Sanusiyyah led the resistance to Italian forces, with encouragement from Great Britain. Although Italy had effectively subdued Libya by 1930, the Sanusiyyah continued to fight on as an Islamic resistance movement. To counter their Islamic opposition, the Italians cultivated the non-Sanusi religious establishment, providing generous government support for the *ulama* and for Islamic education. Moreover, in 1937 Benito Mussolini even proclaimed himself "the protector of Islam."[5] The *ulama*, who had fared less well under their Sufi Sanusi competitors, cooperated with the Italians.

After Italy's defeat in World War II, its hold in Libya waned;

Libya gained its independence in 1951. Idris, who had been living in exile in Cairo, returned as Idris I, king of an independent Libya. Although King Idris was a descendant of the founder of the Sanusiyyah, Libya was in fact more a Muslim than an Islamic state. While the legitimacy of the monarchy and its Islamic character rested upon King Idris' position as head of the Sanusiyyah Brotherhood, yet with few exception, Libya's law as its government was inspired by the West. Libya's legal system was based upon French and Italian legal codes not Islamic law. The Islamic courts were absorbed under a united national judicial system. Only Muslim family law remained in force. The religious establishment *(ulama)* which was viewed as having collaborated with the Italians, was incorporated within the bureaucracy and thus controlled by the state. The royal family was assisted by a small coterie of prominent families and Sanusi religious leaders in governing Libya.

Libya's modern development has been profoundly affected by two events. In 1959 oil was discovered, and so this poor nation of one million inhabitants, which had been economically dependent upon Britain and America, became a leading oil producer within a decade. The second dramatic event was the *coup d'état* in 1969 that brought Muammar Qaddafi to power. As with similar revolutionary movements during the late 1950s and early 60s in Egypt, Syria, Iraq, and Algeria, the rationale for seizure of power was socioeconomic reform necessitated by the failure of Libya's liberal, Western influenced monarchy.

Muammar Qaddafi had long been strongly influenced by Egypt's Gamal Abd al-Nasser. For Qaddafi Nasser was the hero of Arab nationalism who rejected Western imperialism, called for Arab unity, re-established Egyptian and Arab pride and identity on its own cultural foundations, and tried to right the socioeconomic inequities of Arab feudalism through planned socialism. Nasser and Egypt provided a model for the early stages of the Libyan revolution as seen in its self-designation as the "Free Officers" revolution, its Nasserite slogan of "freedom, socialism, unity," its provisional constitution, and its single party—the Arab Socialist Union. It was not long before Qaddafi, at the head of the Revolutionary Command Council, turned to Islam for popular support and legitimation. Given Qaddafi's personal piety and the religious character of Libya's Sanusi history, such a move was not surprising.

In late 1969, Qaddafi announced his intention to reinstitute Islamic law as a first step in what appeared to be the Islamization of state and society. Qaddafi seemed to be placing Libya on a path of Arabization and Islamization. In addition, Nasser's untimely death in 1970 at the age of fifty-two created a void which Qaddafi has tried to fill. Qaddafi combined Arab nationalism and socialism with his own brand of Islamic fundamentalism. Qaddafi took up the banner of Arab socialism and relied heavily upon an Islamic rationale both to legitimate his domestic reforms and to assert his pan-Arab as well as pan-Islamic leadership. During the 1970s, both within Libya and abroad, the new "Arab Republic of Libya" was viewed as an Arab Islamic state. The early statements of the new government placed Libya on an Islamically legitimated, Arab socialist path. Distinguishing itself from Marxism, Qaddafi declared that the state's social policy was the socialism of Islam: "a socialism emanating from the true religion of Islam and its Noble Book."[6] Though strongly influenced by Nasser, Qaddafi went beyond his hero in emphasizing the Islamic component of his ideology.

Qaddafi's Appeal to Islam

A series of well-publicized reforms implementing Libya's Arab-Islamic identity and orientation were instituted. In reasserting Libya's heritage, vestiges of a Christian European colonial past were suppressed. Churches and cathedrals were closed; foreign missionary activities were banned. Arabic was required in all government transactions, and Arabic names and street signs replaced their Western counterparts. Islamic measures prohibiting gambling, night clubs, and alcohol were introduced. Islamization of state and society seemed near in October 1971, when a law commission was established to review all Libyan law in order to bring it into conformity with Islam. In 1972 several Islamic laws were introduced. Canonically mandated criminal penalties ("limits" of God) were reinstated: amputation for theft, stoning for fornication and adultery. Several other Islamic regulations that affected the collection of the alms tax and the banning of banking interest were announced. However, despite the rhetoric and activity, their implementation was limited. In fact if closely examined, despite much fanfare by the Libyan government and the Western press, Islamic law remained relatively peripheral to Libyan society. However, what was becoming clearer was the distinctive brand of Islam that was being introduced. It was neither Sanusi

(Sufi) Islam nor the Islam of the *ulama* but rather Colonel Qaddafi's own, idiosyncratic interpretation of Islam.

By 1975 with the publication of Qaddafi's *The Green Book*, it had become clear that while Islam was tied to Libya's Arab nationalism and socialism, ultimately Qaddafi would define and determine Libya's identity and ideology as he also would dictate its Islamic character. *The Green Book* is a series of three small volumes: "The Solution to the Problem of Democracy" (1975), "Solution of the Economic Problem: Socialism" (1977), and "Social Basis of the Third International Theory" (1979). It is taught in the schools, required reading for all Libyan citizens, and propagated through the innumerable wall posters which seem to dominate the Libyan landscape. It is in *The Green Book* that Qaddafi presented his alternative to Western imperialism. In contradistinction to capitalism and communism, Qaddafi offered his "Third Way" or "Third International Theory" which was to provide the blueprint for Libyan society and an example to the Arab world. As he stated in a *NY Times Magazine,* interview with Oriana Fallaci, December 16, 1979, "*The Green Book* is the guide to the emancipation of man . . . the new gospel. The gospel of the new era, the era of the masses."

For Qaddafi, colonialism caused the Arabs to forget and doubt their own cultural identity and values, to become like the pagans to whom God had sent his messengers—peoples for whom religion and morality are dismissed as fables and reactionism. Both the Soviets and the West are the culprits: "Both the East and West want to corrupt us from within, obliterate every distinguishing mark of our personality and snuff out the light [religion] which guides us."[7]

To counter this threat, Qaddafi set forth a theory whose focus, he claimed, is the *Quran,* the perfect book and comprehensive guide: "We must take the *Quran* as the focal point in our journey in life because the *Quran* is perfect; it is light and in it are solutions to the problems of man . . . from personal status . . . to international problems."[8] Qaddafi asserted a continuity between Libya's new social revolution and Islam's glorious past. Though the bulk of *The Green Book* is not overtly Islamic, he drew upon the major themes of Islamic renewal and reform, similar to those found in the eighteenth and nineteenth-century reform movements. As a result Qaddafi's experiment also provides a bridge to the contemporary political revival of Islam.

Qaddafi's assessment of the Arab world's plight is cast in the categories of traditional Islamic revivalism: the decline of the community, caused by departure from religion, cured by a return to the true path of Islam. Thus, the backwardness of the Arab Islamic world is likened to the "pagan" pre-Islamic period when prophets were rejected and revelation likened to fables. It is a time of social injustice characterized by exploitation and corruption. The cause of this backwardness is departure from the true path of Islam by blindly following the dictates of Western imperialism. Muslims stand torn between two extremes: capitalism with its unbridled emphasis on wealth and power and communism which seeks to violently uproot and reshape everything. Like the revivalists of old, Qaddafi called the community to its historic, divinely mandated mission. "The time has come to manifest the truth of Islam as a force to move mankind, to make progress, and to change the course of history as we changed it formerly."[9]

But who is to undertake this grand Islamic struggle (jihad, in its fullest sense)? In the first volume of The Green Book Qaddafi maintained that "the details of the theory, its component parts and its elucidation are not my specialization . . . [but] . . . every learned person every thinker, every mujtahid [one capable of interpreting, ijtihad]."[10] This position was indicative of Qaddafi's break with the ulama who had initially supported his regime. Traditionally they alone had claimed to have the proper training and expertise to quality as interpreters of Islam. This belief had been the basis for their status and power as guardians and interpreters of Islam.

Having opened the door of interpretation wide, Qaddafi proceeded in subsequent years and in the later volumes of The Green Book to delineate the "Third Way" himself. In so doing, he has radically redefined traditional Islam and Arab socialism, stamping them with his own distinctive interpretation. Although Qaddafi had appealed to the Quran as the source of his revolutionary theory, "in it are solutions to the problems of man . . . from personal status . . . to international problems." and maintained that Libya's socialist program emanates "from the true religion of Islam and its Noble Book," specific references to Islam are conspicuously absent from the last two volumes of The Green Book.

As previously noted, The Green Book has displaced the Shariah's governance of the political and social order. Mixing populist ideological statements with a broad range of political, social, and economic experimentation, Qaddafi has undertaken nothing less than his own cultural revolution, based not on the divine guidance of the Quran or the example of the Prophet but upon the thought of

Qaddafi. Libya's new identity and ideology of popular authority were symbolized in March 1977 when the General People's Congress, which replaced the Revolutionary Command Council, changed Libya's name from the Libyan Arab Republic to the Socialist People's Libyan Arab Jamahiriya. Qaddafi resigned his position as president to become the philosopher/ideologue of the revolution. Al-Jamahiriya ("the masses") was a peoples' state. Libya became a decentralized, populist, participatory government of people's committees which control government offices, schools, the media, and many corporations. Qaddafi encouraged peoples' committees to take over Libya's embassies and seize control of its mosques. The socialist economic policy of *The Green Book* includes the abolition of private land ownership, wages, and rent in favor of worker control and participation in the means of production. Implementation of the new socialist experiment began in 1978 with Libyans who owned more than one home or apartment being forced to choose which one they wished to retain and live in. Those who were renting became owners of these dwellings. Factory workers have seized their factories and overnight became partners in this workers' revolution. Qaddafi has responded to Islamic critics of his socialist policy by appealing in general terms to Islamic social justice and by resorting to a creative interpretation of Quranic texts. In addition, the continued use of Islam for legitimation and popular support is reflected in the innumerable billboards whose slogans extol and exhort the masses such as: "Al Fateh ["the beginning," i.e., of Libya's Revolution, 1969] is an Islamic Revolution" and "The Glorious *Quran* is the *Shariah* of Our New Socialist Society."[11]

Qaddafi's Third Way

However, although Islam is involved, Libya's socialist experiment is certainly a departure from the past. Though Qaddafi is generally characterized as an Islamic fundamentalist, his use of Islam could more properly be described as modern revisionist. Indeed for some Muslims, his departure or deviation from Islamic tradition is seen as heresy. A major example of this is the place of the *Shariah* in the state. As noted in Chapter 1, Sunni jurists had accepted *Shariah* or *Shariah* governance as the practical criterion for an Islamic state. Traditional Islamic law was based on the *Quran* and Example (Sunnah) of the Prophet and provided the ideal blueprint for state and society. In contrast, Qaddafi has cast aside the traditions of the Prophet, claiming many are not authentic. Instead he maintains that the *Quran* and *The Green Book* are the basis of Libyan society. Contrary to his earlier claims in *The Green Book* itself regarding the economic, military and sociopolitical aspects of scripture, the *Quran* is now restricted to religious observances (prayer, fasting, almsgiving), while *The Green Book*, not the *Shariah*, governs politics and society. Thus, *The Green Book*, the message of Muammar Qaddafi, has replaced the traditional, comprehensive role of the Shariah.

Qaddafi set aside the traditional formulations of Islamic law distinguishing between the immutable *Quran* and those formulations or interpretations which are historically conditioned. Here he adopted the position of many Islamic modernists. However, rather than reforming the law, he replaced much of it with *The Green Book*. His confrontation with the *ulama* was forewarned in an article "No mufti, no marabits, no Shaykhs" which appeared in the official government daily newspaper *al-Fajr al-Jadid* in October 1977. Although written under another name, the article was believed to have come from Qaddafi himself. A major contention of the article is the rejection of traditional religious leaders and the authority of the *mufti* as contrary to "popular authority." In April 1978 some religious leaders at an international conference on *The Green Book*, publically criticized its socialist doctrine, specifically its assertion that "land is not private property," maintaining that such a statement was contrary to the Islamic tradition. Qaddafi defended his interpretation as consonant with Islamic social justice. Within a month, people's popular committees were "instructed to 'seize the mosques' to rid them of 'paganist tendencies' and of *imams* [religious leaders] accused of 'propagating heretical tales elaborated over centuries of decadence and which distort the Islamic religion.' "[12]

During the time that Muammar Qaddafi has been in power, Libya has undergone a series of changes as Qaddafi has put his changing theories into practice. Although varying in degree of intensity, throughout his rule, Qaddafi has used Islam to buttress his Arab socialism. The process has moved from what appeared to be a fundamentalist implementation of traditional Islamic law to the more radical reformist program of *The Green Book*. Qaddafi's experiment in redefining Libyan identity with his "Third Way" has alienated both landed and business classes and the religious establishment who have increasingly rejected his brand of Islamic politics. The *ulama* have condemned Qaddafi's "innovative" interpretations of Islam—

his rejection of the blinding force of Prophetic traditions, his substitution of *The Green Book* for *Shariah* governance, and his abolition of private property for their deviation from the Islamic tradition. While the outside world views Qaddafi as an "Islamic" leader, governing an Islamic state, for many, including Libya's religious establishment, Qaddafi's experiment in redefining Libyan identity is far from Islamic.

PAKISTAN

When Zulfikar Ali Bhutto was elected head of state in 1971 few expected that this secularist, representing the socialist platform of his Pakistan People's Party would be the initiator of Islamization in Pakistan. Most observers believed that while religious sensitivities had to be respected, Pakistan would generally continue in its political and social development along a *de facto* Western, secular path. However, several factors caused a significant revival of Islam in Pakistan's politics: a post-Bangladesh identity crisis, Arab oil, and domestic politics.[13] As a result, Islam became a major theme in Pakistan politics; indeed, by the end of Bhutto's rule, it had become the dominant theme.

The loss of East Pakistan, after a bloody civil war which led to the formation of an independent Bangladesh in 1971, caused a crisis in Pakistan that resulted in a renewed concern with questions of national identity and unity as Pakistan's founding and early history were re-examined to better understand the basis for its existence.[14] Amid the soul-searching and deliberations in national conferences, publications and the media, Pakistan's establishment as a Muslim homeland was re-examined. The popularly perceived, though vaguely defined, commitment to Islam resurfaced in politics. For many, Islam was the reason and only means to create a sense of unity that transcended Pakistan's ethnic and linguistic divisions.

Internationally, Bhutto determined to draw closer to the Arab oil countries for aid and, toward this end, progressively emphasized the common Islamic identity and bond of Pakistan with the Arab world. He embarked upon a shuttle diplomacy with the Arab oil countries. This new initiative was strikingly symbolized by Pakistan's 1974 hosting of an Islamic Summit in Lahore in 1974. The summit, attended by heads of state from around the Muslim world, provided a forum for Colonel Muammar Qaddafi who addressed throngs of Pakistanis at the Badshai Mosque in Lahore. Bhutto permitted Anwar Sadat's mediation between Pakistan and Bangladesh and a restoration of diplomatic relations in the name of Islam. The Bhutto government also initiated programs to encourage the study of Arabic and fostered an increasing number of religious conferences to which representatives from other Muslim countries were invited.

Despite all of his efforts in the name of Islam, the Jamaat-i-Islami and other religious parties led a concerted effort to defeat Bhutto. Their tactics included the raising of a substantial campaign fund—the Fund for the Protection of the Ideology of Pakistan—and the issuing of decrees against Bhutto's socialism by 113 *ulama*. In reacting to this internal political pressure from religious critics, Bhutto increasingly responded to them on their own ground—through appeals to Islam to legitimate his programs and policies. The Pakistan People's Party had established itself as a mass political party with such populist, socialist slogans as *"Roti, kapra, aur mikan"* (bread, clothing, and shelter) and *"Zamin kashtkaron ko"* (land to the tiller). Its socialist orientation and social reform policies such as nationalization and land reform were progressively equated with Islamic social justice. Phrases like *Musawat-i-Muhammadi* (The Equality of Muhammad) and *Islami Musawat* (Islamic Equality) became part of the political rhetoric of the Pakistan People's Party. A new journal, *Musawat*, (Equality) was founded which, somewhat like *Minbar al-Islam* in Nasser's Egypt, provided an organ for the Islamic justification of the PPP's policies appealing to the *Quran*, the Sunnah of the Prophet and the practice of the early Rightly Guided Caliphs.[15]

In addition, in 1974 Bhutto yielded to the decades-long campaign of religious leaders to have the Ahmadiyya declared a non-Muslim minority. As discussed in Chapter 4, many religious leaders had long maintained that the Ahmadiyya recognized their founder, Ghulam Ahmad, as a prophet and thus rejected a pillar of Islam—that Muhammad was the final Prophet of God. As seen in the discussion of the anti-Ahmadiyya riots of 1953, religious leaders viewed the Ahmadiyya as non-Muslims, and they especially objected to their holding important positions in government and the military. Bhutto approved provisions in the 1973 Constitution which required that both the president and prime minister be Muslims; the oath of office was amended to require an affirmation of the finality of Muhammad's Prophethood.

The politicization of Islam reached its zenith in the March 1977 general elections. Nine political parties joined under the umbrella of Islam to form an opposition block, the Pakistan National Alliance. The Alliance included the Pakistan Muslim League, National Democratic Party, Tehrik-i-Istiqlal, and others. However, its direction and leadership came from the Islamic religious parties: the Jamaat-i-Islami, the Jamiyyat-i-ulama-i-Pakistan (The Organization of the Ulama of Pakistan) and the Jamiyyat-i-ulama-i-Islam (The Organization of the Ulama of Islam). Although member parties spanned the political spectrum, the symbols and slogans of the Pakistan National Alliance were Islamic: "Islam in Danger" and "The System of the Prophet," i.e., an Islamic system of government. Criticisms of the Bhutto regime were carefully couched in Islamic terms. Both Bhutto's personal life style and his government were denounced as anti-Islamic. The Pakistan National Alliance pledged itself to the introduction of an Islamic system of government. The vast network of *ulama* and mosques and religious schools, seminaries were employed as centers for political organization and communications.

The strength of Pakistan National Alliance support came primarily from the middle class (traditional and modern): urban intellectuals who had supported Bhutto's early socialist platform and were now alienated by his purge of the more leftist elements in his cabinet in 1974; small traditional businessmen and merchants and members of the "new" middle class professions (teachers, doctors, clerical workers, university students and other professionals) for whom Bhutto's political and economic reforms resulted in an increased sense of powerlessness and alienation. Bhutto's political reforms had resulted in tighter control by the Pakistan People's Party of government and district level officials as primary emphasis was placed on party loyalty and connections rather than merit. Moreover, Bhutto's autocratic rule was reflected in a government that increasingly resorted to media censorship, the "policing" of its own security force, political harassment, arrests, and imprisonment.

The middle-class nature of the Pakistan National Alliance movement was reinforced by the presence and leadership of the religious parties whose traditional base of support has always come primarily from among the urban and town-based middle class. This was particularly true of Mawlana Mawdudi's Jamaat-i-Islami whose ideological and organizational input in the PNA was of major importance.

Mawdudi and most of the religious leadership had, from the

start, rejected Bhutto's socialism as un-Islamic. To this they added a critique of political and social corruption, the breakdown of law and order. In its place they called for national unity rooted in Pakistan's Islamic *raison d'être* in which Islamic brotherhood and solidarity would transcend regional, linguistic divisions. They emphasized that the only means to achieve this was a return to Islamic law which provided the blueprint for a democratic, egalitarian society based upon Islamic social justice. Such a system of government would avoid the extremes of corporate capitalism and state socialism, substitute Islamic values for their excessive materialism and secularism, counter the corruption and spiritual malaise of the Bhutto years and thus realize for the first time Pakistan's destiny as an Islamic state and society.

The Pakistan National Alliance manifesto reflected the concerns of a religious and middle class alliance. It called for the introduction of an Islamic system of government, the elimination of political and moral corruption, support for small industry and business interests, etc. Thus, in the 1977 election campaign the lines of battle were drawn between a broad coalition of political parties enjoying strong middle-class support and the new alliance of the upper and lower classes which supported Bhutto's Pakistan People's Party.

In order to counter his Islamic opposition with its popular appeals to Islam, Bhutto and his Pakistan People's Party increasingly placed themselves under the banner of Islam. As their emphasis shifted toward Islamic slogans like the equality of Muhammad or Muhammad's egalitarianism, their use of the term "socialism" had now receded into the background. The new Pakistan People's Party manifesto included provisions which promised greater Islamization of society such as a commitment to center community life more firmly upon the *Quran* and to have Friday replace Sunday as the weekly holiday.

Despite their appeals to Islam, the Pakistan National Alliance clearly did not have the votes of the people, and Bhutto and the Pakistan People's Party scored what appeared to be an impressive victory in the general elections of March 1977. However, amid charges of widespread poll irregularities, the Pakistan National Alliance boycotted the provincial elections of March 7 and renewed their agitational politics. The mosques of the country became the centers not only for Friday communal prayer but also for political agitation. The sermons concerned "Islamic politics," and a community gathered for prayer was easily transformed into a political rally and march. Responding to widespread disturbances, the Bhutto government imposed martial law and curfews. As activities of the Pakistan National Alliance increased, Bhutto sought to diffuse their appeal by announcing further Islamization measures such as the prohibition of alcohol, gambling, and nightclubs. These Islamic provisions and promises to introduce other *Shariah* laws served to reinforce the Islamic character of the conflict. Most importantly, a turning point had been reached. Islam and Pakistan's Islamic identity had re-emerged as the dominant theme in Pakistani politics in a manner and to a degree that had not been seen since Pakistan's establishment.

The Martial Law Regime of Zia ul-Haq

The anti-Bhutto movement came to an abrupt halt with the bloodless military *coup d'état* which brought General Zia ul-Haq to power on July 5, 1977. As Chief Martial Law Administrator and President, Zia ul-Haq appealed to Islam to legitimate his *coup* and subsequent rule, based upon a commitment to implement the Nizam-i-Mustapha (System of the Prophet) or, as it is more commonly called, Nizam-i-Islam—the System of Islam. Bhutto's downfall was attributed to his un-Islamic behavior. He was progressively discredited and, after a controversial trial, executed for murder on April 4, 1979, amid worldwide appeals for clemency.

General Zia ul-Haq, in many forums, declared his commitment to "transform the country's socioeconomic and political structure in accordance with the principles of Islam," as reported in *Dawn*, September 30, 1977. Toward that end the Islamic Ideology Council was reconstituted and its scope broadened to serve as the President's chief advisory council for introducing a more Islamic system of government, for the Islamization of state and society. Three areas of immediate concern were targeted: the Islamic taxes, an interest-free economy, and an Islamic penal code. Zia's military regime forged an alliance with the Pakistan National Alliance. Some parties like the Jamiyyat-i-ulama-i-Islam refused to participate. However others, especially the Jamaat-i-Islami and Jamiyyat-i-ulama-i Pakistan, accepted the opportunity to advise and assist a government that had taken up the banner of the system of Islam. Individuals noted for their strong commitment to Islam, especially members of Mawdudi's Jamaat-i-Islami were appointed to such cabinet positions as the Ministries of Law, Religious Affairs, Information, Production and Planning.

In December 1978, the time of the Islamic New Year, the president proclaimed Pakistan's new beginning in an address entitled "Measures to Enforce Nizam-i-Islam". In addition to declaring the intention of his government to introduce reforms in the areas which were under study by the Council of Islamic Ideology, Zia announced the creation of *Shariah* Courts to determine whether or not specific existing laws were repugnant to Islam. In February 1979, Zia formalized the commitment of his government to the system of Islam with his promulgation "Introduction of Islamic Laws." Appealing to the traditional Islamic belief that Islam is a total way of life, this document announced a series of reforms in worship, law, economics, and education. Since that time Islamization has continued to be a prominent part of Pakistan's politics and life. Islamic measures and proposals affecting politics, law, economics, education, and culture have been introduced.

Politics

Politically, Islam has been used throughout Zia's rule as the source of legitimation. Although Zia had originally promised elections within ninety days of his July 1977 *coup*, elections in Pakistan have been twice postponed—in October 1977 and again in November 1979. The primary reason cited in 1979 for the cancellation of elections and the outlawing of political parties was doubt about whether Pakistan's Western-based political system was Islamic. These questions were referred to the Islamic Ideology Council, a government-appointed body which includes religious leaders as well as experts in banking, economics, and law.

These actions produced broad-based opposition, the Movement for the Restoration of Democracy which include not only Bhutto supporters but also many of the Pakistan National Alliance members who found themselves now disenfranchised and their political parties declared "defunct." Both secular and religiously oriented parties joined together in demanding the end of martial law and restoration of the political process through elections. Even religious leaders like Mian Tufail Muhammad, successor to Mawlana Mawdudi as Amir of the Jamaat-i-Islami, emphasized that martial law rule is not Islamic. They argue that the current government cannot claim to be an expression of the System of Islam since the head of an Islamic state should be chosen or elected by the people and is, himself, subject to the

Shariah or sovereignty of God's rule. Although the Jamaat-i-Islami had always been considered close to Zia's government and had not joined the Movement for the Restoration of Democracy, by spring 1984 it called for a united political front to oppose martial law and campaign for the restoration of democracy.

Zia ul-Haq is criticized for placing his martial law regulations above even the *Shariah*. Whereas the only criterion or norm guiding the Shariah courts should be the *Quran* and Sunnah, in fact, General Zia exempted his martial law regulations as well as matters of taxation and banking from the court's purview. The creation of the Federal Advisory Council as an interim parliamentary assembly and its Islamic designation as a *Majlis-i-Shura* has not allayed critics who charge that it is not Islamic and is but another tactic to delay elections. Many religious leaders assert that Islamic government is not military rule and that in an Islamic state members of the parliament should be elected not appointed by an unelected military ruler.

Law

Zia ul-Haq's Islamization program has included the introduction of Islamic measures, affecting substantive law and the judiciary. Under the current martial law regime, the 1973 Constitution has been "augmented" by a series of martial law regulations, such as MLR 48 and 49 which ban political parties and prohibit newspapers from political commentary and criticism. In effect, with the dissolution of the National Assembly, these martial law ordinances constitute the only legislation possible and thus Zia ul-Haq as Chief Martial Law Administrator is the sole lawmaker. Islamic laws have been introduced through a series of proclamations in the areas of fasting, prayer, penal law, and economics.

Public observance of fasting during Ramadan, one of the Five Pillars of Islam, has always been expected in Pakistan. Actual observance has varied significantly, subject to personal conscience and to peer pressure. Under the present government, the state now has the power of public enforcement. Public consumption of food or drink and smoking during Ramadan are punishable by a sentence of up to six months. Prosecutions have occurred under this new legislation. In addition, dance and musical productions have also been curtailed during Ramadan.

As noted previously, under Bhutto's government, Friday replaced Sunday as the weekly holiday. The Islamic System of Zia has continued this practice, the government also issued ordinances requiring that workers be provided with the time and a suitable place to perform the required daily prayers. Companies which conduct business on Friday were required to close during the noon hour to permit workers to attend Friday communal prayers at a mosque.

The most prominent and, at times, controversial area of legal reform has occurred in Pakistan's Penal Code—in particular the imposition of *Quranically* or prophetically prescribed punishments for drinking, theft, adultery, and false accusation, i.e., bearing false witness regarding sexual crimes. The Pakistan Penal Code was amended so that punishments of imprisonments and/or fines for *Quranically* prescribed crimes were replaced by amputation of the hand for theft, stoning for adultery, and flogging for fornication and drinking. However, public flogging for drinking violations and other *Quranically* prescribed crimes have been restricted both due to internal criticisms as well as to adverse publicity in the international media. Amputations have been ordered by the court, but none have occurred since physicians have refused to perform them. A sharp controversy has surrounded the imposition of stoning for adultery. Although ordered by the courts, such verdicts were appealed to the Shariah Court and declared un-Islamic. The Shariah Court was reorganized to include three *ulama* among its members and its jurisdiction expanded so that the court could review its previous decisions. Subsequently, the Federal Shariah Court reversed itself with conservative members arguing that stoning although not based on a *Quranic* text, is rooted in Prophetic tradition. Defenders of this provision argue that this severe punishment is to serve as a deterrent to the most blatant violations of public morality and that normally conviction will be rare since Islamic law requires four eye witnesses to the act itself.

Shariah Courts

In 1978 the government announced the creation of Shariah Courts. These courts differ from the traditional Islamic legal system where judges applied *Shariah* law. Pakistan's Shariah Courts are essentially courts which determine whether or not a specific law is contrary to the *Shariah*. The court's jurisdiction was to review petitions from individuals, the Federal or provincial governments which challenged any law as repugnant to Islam, i.e., the *Quran* and the

Sunnah. However, the court is barred from reviewing laws in three areas (the constitution and martial law ordinances, family law and fiscal laws). *Shariah* Bench decisions can be appealed to the Appellate *Shariah* Bench of the Supreme Court. Laws or provisions found to be un-Islamic are amended through legislative action taken by General Zia ul-Haq.

Since their inception the *Shariah* Courts have reviewed a broad spectrum of suits ranging from challenges to the legitimacy of Pakistan's Constitution and law to the acceptability of cinema, from the stoning of adulterers to government-enforced land reform. Moreover, the court has continued the work of the Islamic Ideology Council in reviewing all of Pakistan's Legal Codes to identify and rectify those aspects or provisions that are un-Islamic. Islamization of law is not seen as totally replacing Pakistan's Anglo-Muhammedan Legal System with classical Islamic law or developing a new system but rather purifying its current system of un-Islamic provisions.

Other changes have subsequently been introduced in the judiciary: the introduction of *qadi* courts and the establishment of a Department of Public Morality (Ihtisab). A bill (Qazi Courts Ordinance, 1983) establishing *qadi* courts was approved on February 20, 1983 by the Federal Council. Qazi courts would replace local and district courts, i.e., existing civil and criminal courts. They are seen as a further step in the establishment of an Islamic system of justice. Since judges will apply Islamic law, many will be recruited from the traditional religious schools and from the graduates of the Islamic University. As with the Shariah Courts, critics of the proposed system have included the legal profession as well as certain women's organizations. The Bar Councils' convention held in September 1982 rejected the *Qazi (Qadi)* Courts Ordinance (*Dawn Overseas*, September 17–23, 1982). The Department of Ihtisab reinstitutes the traditional Islamic institution of supervisor of public behavior and markets who will investigate charges of mal-administration against government ministers, agencies and corporations.[16]

Economics

Islamic economic measures have been an integral part of Zia's Islamization program affecting questions of private property, taxation, and interest.

The introduction of an alms tax and agricultural tax as well as interest-free banking have been the more substantive and controversial measures. A Zakat Fund was created in 1979 with substantial financial assistance from Saudi Arabia and the United Arab Emirates. Collection and distribution of the alms tax is managed by a multi-tiered elected administrative (organization) system. A wealth tax of 2½ percent is levied on all income and assets in excess $200 and is deducted directly at the source, i.e., directly from bank accounts and other financial assets such as investment shares, annuities, and insurance.

Criticism of the alms tax and agricultural tax measures has come from various quarters. Some resent the government's taking over what is regarded as a private obligation before God that enables Muslims to look after needy family and friends. The current system is perceived as the government's bureaucritization of a personal, charitable duty, which is now subject to mismanagement and misappropriation. The Shii community objected vociferously to the alms tax order since, according to their law, the alms tax is not compulsory on capital and trading money. The government yielded with legislation which permits a Muslim to obtain an exemption if he states that the alms tax is not enjoined by his faith and law.

The agricultural tax on productive land, finally implemented in May 1983, was set at 5 percent.[17] The tax, while compulsory, is paid voluntarily and monitored by committees that randomly sample the landowners in their districts.

The most potentially far-reaching Islamic economic change was the abolition of interest. Early in his administration Zia ul-Haq committed himself to the abolition of the "curse of interest."[18] In January 1981 interest-free banking accounts were introduced on a voluntary basis in all 7,000 branches of Pakistan's nationalized commercial banks. Under a system called Profit/Loss Sharing, the depositor and the bank enter into a partnership in which both share in the profit or losses. Money is invested in a selective portfolio, some of which consists of government-owned companies which are secure and whose profitability is known. The Profit/Loss Sharing System is optional and applicable to Savings and Fixed Deposit (time deposit) accounts.

Introduction of an interest-free economy has proven more difficult than the implementation of individual economic measures. Indeed, as early as May 1980 a special Committee on Islamization appointed by the Finance Minister had cautioned in its report, "An

Agenda for Islamic Economic Reform," issued by the Pakistan Institute of Development Economics, that "the Islamic rejection of interest is in effect a rejection of the entire capitalist system: an interest-free economy is in fact an exploitation-free economy" (p. v). The Committee stressed that the abolition of interest must be part of a far more comprehensive and complex process, the development of a complete economic system without which an interest-free economy would neither be possible nor effective:

> The abolition of interest is part of a fundamental restructuring of the whole spectrum of production, consumption, and distribution relationships on the Islamic lines. However, the search for such a system must be gradual to let the interaction between theory and practice . . . produce an economic system which corresponds to the overall vision of an Islamic economic system. (p. vi)

Zia ul-Haq's government has not adopted this more comprehensive outlook. Instead, it continues to advocate and pursue a fragmented, *ad hoc* gradualist policy of Islamic economic reform often more rhetoric than substance, which tends to satisfy none of its critics.

Education

Education and cultural reforms provide the final area of Zia ul-Haq's Islamization program. They attempt to resolve Pakistan's decades long identity problems, to overcome ethnic and regional factionalism by establishing a common national identity and ideology firmly based on the twin pillars of Islam and Pakistan. A series of changes, real and symbolic, have been introduced to underscore the government's commitment to strengthen Pakistan's national identity through a reaffirmation of her Islamic-Pakistani identity—to produce what Zia ul-Haq has called a new generation wedded to the ideology of Pakistan and Islam. An ever-burgeoning series of regulations and programs involving areas ranging from language and dress to mass media and education have been introduced and enforced. Urdu has replaced English as the medium of instruction in schools and has assumed a more prominent place in public life, in the government and media as Pakistan's national language. General Zia called upon all Pakistanis to wear national attire during working hours. Civil servants, university professors, and businessmen were to trade their suits for traditional attire. While there was initial compliance, especially in government offices and schools, there was also widespread resistance. Increased emphasis on Pakistani and Islamic identity and fraternal ties with Arab-Muslim countries has resulted in an increased emphasis on Arabic in education and the renaming of cities, streets, and public facilities: Iqbal Open University, Quaid-i-Azam ("the Great Leader" reference to Muhammad Ali Jinnah) University, and Feisalabad (a city named for Saudi Arabia's King Faisal).

Throughout government literature on Islamization, in the statement and ordinances promulgated by Zia ul-Haq, the Ideology Council, the *Shariah* Courts, or in reports by special committees such as the Panel on Islamic Economics and Banking, there is an emphasis on the importance of Islamizing society because an Islamic outlook and attitude will assure awareness, appreciation, and compliance with Islamic regulations. The mass media and education have become major foci for the implementation of the Islamization of society by government as well as traditional religious forces. Critics have viewed such actions as simply religious censorship and obscurantism. Virtually all TV and radio broadcasts are in Urdu, programs on national/Islamic history and culture are prominent in radio, TV and in print. At the same time, censorship of movies, TV commercials, and restrictions on coverage of "un-Islamic" activities have increased sharply. Ironically, the emphases on Islam and Pakistani identity have sometimes come into conflict. For example, more traditional religious leaders have attacked public performances and media coverage of national dance and music programs as un-Islamic activities.

Islamization of the informal means of education has been accompanied by reforms in Pakistan's formal educational system as well. Islamic studies courses are now required at the university level as well as in pre-university education. The Department of Education has for several years been engaged in reviewing curricula and textbooks both to eliminate un-Islamic materials as well as to revise and develop curricula and books that foster Islamic-Pakistani values.

No single institution better symbolized the Islamization of education than the Islamic University established in 1980 in Islamabad. Its faculties and their curricula, according to the Islamic University Ordinance, issued in 1980, were to assist in the implementation of the religious and cultural program of Islamization: "Islam enjoins upon the *Ummah* [community] to establish a just and humane world order . . . the purpose of education is to produce people who are imbued with Islamic learning and character and capable of meeting economic, social, political, technological, physical, intellectual and aesthetic needs of the society." The purpose and goal of the new Islamic University were to fuse Pakistan's dual or parallel systems of secular and religious learning "so as to provide an islamic vision for those engaged in education and to enable them to reconstruct human thought in all its forms on the foundations of Islam" (p. 6).

Women

A final area effected by Islamization is the status of women. Islamization has caused increased apprehension among many professional women. Fearing that government policies and the increasingly vocal protestations of conservative religious leaders would lead to increased restrictions and loss of any gains in women's rights, organizations such as the Women's Action Forum in Karachi were created. Viewed by conservatives as simply a small Westernized elite, professional women's associations have organized conferences, led public demonstrations, and lobbied for women's rights. Increased emphasis on national dress and covering the head with a veil or scarf are viewed as symbolizing a reinforcement of traditional, regressive attitudes and customs toward women which have rendered Muslim women second-class citizens. Veiling and seclusion, although often a practiced norm in Pakistani society, are rejected as un-Islamic historical accretions which are contrary to the reformist spirit of the *Quran* and Muhammad.

Pakistan, like many other Muslim countries, is a society in which seclusion as well as the wearing of the long veil covering the body have been very much in practice. Until a few years ago public separation of the sexes in buses, in banks, in education, and in many offices was commonplace. The continued strength of *"purdah* [seclusion] mentality"* regarding women's modesty among lower and middle classes today is witnessed by increasing debate in the newspapers as to whether a sari is Islamic, by incidents in which women with uncovered heads have been reprimanded even accosted in public, the banning of women's hockey before mixed audiences, the issuing of *fatwas* by religious leaders, declaring that women may not hold political office. Moreover, the example of the post-revolutionary Iranian Islamic government's actions regarding women's status—from dress to employment to the repeal of Iran's Family Protection Act with its reforms in marriage, divorce and inheritance—have reinforced women's fears that Pakistan's *ulama*, who have been vocal in their public mosque and media statements, will continue to follow a similar path. Conservative religious leaders have called for the repeal of Pakistan's *Muslim Family Laws Ordinance* of 1961. The Islamic Ideology Council had itself found that three provisions in the *Family Laws Ordinance* were un-Islamic and had recommended their repeal.[19]

Three other government measures have caused continued concern among women's groups: proposals for separate women's universities, the introduction of *Qadi* Courts and the revision of Pakistan's *Law of Evidence Act*. Women's universities are viewed as acquiescing to conservative religious pressures for separation of the sexes in society. Critics fear that women's universities will lend credibility to the belief that Islam requires such separation of the sexes. Indeed, women were originally excluded from the new Islamic University. Although finally admitted to the University, they are educated in separate facilities. Thus, many women find reason for their concern that Islamic education will be equated with separation of the sexes.

The establishment of *Qadi* Courts reconstitutes religious courts manned by judges drawn from the *ulama*. Given the conservative character of the majority of religious authorities and their tendency to simply turn to the world view of classical Islamic jurisprudence, with a minimal recognition of the need for reinterpretation, serious difficulties on women's issues are anticipated.

For many women the revision of Pakistan's Law of *Evidence Act* confirmed their worst fears. The draft submitted by the Islamic Ideology Council, supported by the vast majority of religious leaders and finally passed, implemented the traditional Islamic legal viewpoint that the testimony of two women equals that of one Muslim male.

Conclusion

Islamization in Pakistan has travelled a rocky road. When Zia ul-Haq assumed power in July 1977, both because of his own religious belief and the climate of Pakistani politics, he committed his regime to the implementation and enforcement of an Islamic system of government to legitimate his rule and to provide a basis for national identity and unity. Greeted with skepticism by some and with enthusiasm by many, the process thus far has led to frustration, disillusionment, and opposition.

The political aspirations of both secularists and traditional religious factions have been thwarted. The Pakistan National Alliance parties soon discovered that it had won a Pyrrhic victory. National and provincial elections were postponed as rule by martial law was extended; within two years the Pakistan National Alliance parties, like all political parties, were banned. All this had been done in the name of Islam. Perhaps the most fundamental questions which have arisen from Pakistan's recent experiment in Islamization are: "Whose Islam?" and "Why a negative Islam?"

Religious leaders, in particular, who initially applauded and supported the government's commitment to the establishment of an Islamic system of government, have become increasingly disillusioned. Participation in the government has given way to opposition. Many religious leaders are critical of the slow pace of Islamization. They had expected and demanded full and immediate implementation of Islamic measures such as Islamic taxes and interest-free banking.[20] What they deemed a one-year process in 1977 when Zia came to power is still incomplete. Of equal importance Zia ul-Haq and not the *ulama* nor religious parties has ultimately been the final interpreter of Islam. Islamic regulations have but one source—Zia ul-Haq; even the *Shariah* Court's authority is circumscribed by the Chief Executive. Zia's martial law regulations are not subject to its jurisdiction. The court's decisions must be endorsed by Zia before they can take effect.

"Whose Islam?" is for many tied to a related question: "Why a negative Islam?" The Islam which Zia ul-Haq's regime has implemented is criticized as simply one of restrictions, *Quranically* prescribed punishments, taxation, and political control—all in the name of Islam. Broad criticism from many quarters focuses on the government's "manipulation" of Islam to postpone elections outlaw political parties, censor and suppress dissent. This quandry underscores a dual problem that has confronted Pakistan (and many other Muslim countries) throughout its existence: an inability to agree on the content of Islamic belief and the need for substantive reinterpretation/reform. Pakistanis have found it easier to rally under the umbrella of

Islam in opposition movements, e.g., against British and Hindu rule or, more recently, against the Bhutto regime, than to agree upon what Islam and an Islamic state are.

A continuation of Pakistan's inability to achieve any consensus in theory or practice regarding the Islamic nature and character of the state was demonstrated by a debate in the media in which more than one hundred religious leaders, politicians, military officials, and intellectuals discussed the nature of an Islamic state. The positions ranged from advocating dictatorship to popular democracy, from a one-party to a multi-party political system.[21]

Islamization has also exacerbated problems of religious sectarianism—both between Sunni and Shii as well as among Sunni Muslims themselves. Although no statistics are kept, the Shii constitute perhaps 25 percent of the population. Estimates range from 5 percent to 25 percent. Historically, religious differences have resulted in clashes between the two communities. The current Islamization program has, again, underscored religious differences and their ability to split society. Initial Islamic measures like the alms and agricultural taxes and the imposition of *Quranically* prescribed penalties brought objections from the Shii community who complained that their law school (Jafari) differed in its prescriptions from the Sunni Hanafi based draft laws. Thus, Islamization did not simply mean the implementation of Islamic law in their lives but of Sunni legal interpretations in particular. In July 1980 some 15,000 Shii marched in a demonstration in Rawalpindi against compulsory alms taxes. Violence and bloodshed ensued. After a prominent Shii religious authority resigned from the Islamic Ideology Council, a special subcommittee of three Sunni and three Shii *ulama* was established to iron out the differences. Although the government amended the *zakat* ordinance to exempt anyone who believes compulsory deduction of alms tax is against his law school, tensions continue. In March 1983 there were several clashes between Sunni and Shii. A number of people were killed; a curfew was imposed; and the Iranian Consul General was asked to leave the country due to his role in inciting the mob.

Of equal significance are the religious differences among Sunni Muslims which are often overlooked by analysts more familiar with the Arab world. Pakistani Sunni Muslims distinguish themselves according to their school: Deobandi, Brelevi, Wahhabi, Ahl al-Hadith, etc. If anything, the resurgence of Islam in Pakistan has meant not only greater emphasis on its Islamic character but also a proliferation of religious literature, much of which emphasizes sectarian differences in belief and practice. *Dawn Overseas* reported on February 3, 1983, that the provincial governments had been directed to prohibit mosque sermons "against the faith of one sect or the other." These differences, coupled with the lack of hierarchical structure in Sunni Islam, have historically been a major factor in the failure of religious groups to unite and work constructively in addressing Pakistan's Islamic identity.

IRAN

Although the anti-Shah movement in Iran in 1978 startled Western observers, beneath the seemingly secure surface upon which Iran's ship of state sailed, there had been strong currents of discontent and opposition. Oil wealth, an ambitious modernization program administered by an enormous bureaucracy, the largest and best equipped army in the Middle East, and an effective secret police were the foundations of Pahlavi power and security. Yet development programs, royal patronage, repression, and official corruption proved incapable of containing growing discontent with an increasingly authoritarian state. The much touted success of the Shah's White Revolution proved less impressive upon closer examination. Despite impressive gains in health, education and agricultural reform, a disproportionate amount of the benefits from Iranian reforms went to the elites of the society. Modernization had perhaps increased their number but it also continued the pattern of concentration of wealth at the top. At the same time, the real improvements and gains of socioeconomic development did not meet rising public expectations nor significantly change the lot of many. While the literacy rate rose from 26 to 42 percent, "fewer than 40 percent of the children completed primary school, the teacher-student ratio in public schools deteriorated, only 60,000 university places opened each year for as many as 290,000 applicants, and the percentage of the population with higher degrees remained one of the lowest in the Middle East."[22]

The fruits of modernization were visible in major cities and in the lives of the upper and middle classes. Its impact upon village life was more problematic. Ninety-six percent of the villages remained without electricity. Iran had once been agriculturally self sufficient; by the mid 1970s more than $1 billion was spent per year on imported products. As in many parts of the Middle East, modernization and urbanization resulted in the migration of villagers to the city and the proliferation of urban slums. The potential advantages of migration to the city were often offset by the breakdown of the extended family and a deterioration in the quality of life—shortage of housing, over-crowded dwellings, congested streets, unemployment, etc. As Er-vand Abrahamian has observed: "For these millions, most of whom had been forced out of the villages into the new shanty towns, the oil boom did not end poverty; it merely modernized it."[23] The socioeco-nomic realities of the Shah's modernization program were exacer-bated by regional/ethnic tensions which grew out of resentment over the unequal distribution of development projects to preferred major cities like Teheran. Finally, many in the new middle class professions were frustrated by a system which made them totally dependent upon the government. Despite their education, professional positions and favorable economic status, most remained politically powerless under a monarchy that had become progressively autocratic. Con-stitutional rights and protections, parliamentary rule, a political party system were subverted by a government of decrees and secret police.

Both liberal democrats and leftists were equally threatened by a growing monarchical absolutism. Discontent with the fast pace of modernization and imperial autocracy contributed to the de-velopment of a religio-cultural alliance of traditional religious leaders and lay intellectuals which had developed during the 1960s and early 70s. For the religious classes, Pahlavi rule had come to mean the erosion of their status and sources of revenue, the undermining of their ideology, institutions and values, the imposition of an alien (Western Christian or secular) way of life. At the same time even among those who had benefited from Western style educations, many had become gravely concerned about the influence of the West, especially the United States, upon Iranian politics and society. America through its CIA had orchestrated the Shah's return from exile to Iran in 1953. Since that time, American advisers had played a major role in the training and development of Iran's military and secret police as well as her economy. Military and economic depen-dence were matched by the progressive westernization of Iranian education and society. Religious and lay shared a common concern about cultural alienation due to what the secular intellectual, Jalal al-Ahmad, called "Westoxification" or "Weststruckness," the indiscrimi-nate borrowing from and imitation of the West.

The danger of Western cultural imperialism was joined to fear of Western political domination. By 1978 there were 41,00 Americans in Iran. The growing American diplomatic, military, and corporate presence, and the very nature of development programs, which were based upon Western models of socioeconomic change, fueled fears of a loss of national autonomy and identity. The preservation and revival of Irano-Islamic culture became a common concern and rallying point. Iran's Shiite Islamic religious and cultural heritage provided an ideal framework for both a meaningful critique of the status quo as well as an authentic source of pride and identity, a sense of history and values. Interpretations of the meaning and implications of reclaiming Irano-Islamic identity, however, varied greatly.

The prevailing mood among the regime's opposition prior to 1978 had been one of reformism not revolution. Progressively, confronted by a political order that enforced its will and countered its opposition not by constitutional means but by military and police force, the coalition broadened its membership as well as its goal and became a political revolution. Reform of a corrupt system was seen to necessitate removal of its source or foundation, the Pahlavi monarchy. The religious-lay alliance included a diversity of positions. While the opposition shared a common concern and diagnosis of the disease ("Weststruckness" and authoritarian rule), their understanding of the nature of the cure—symbolically represented as a return to Islam—varied markedly.

Jalal al-Ahmad was a leading intellectual and literary figure in Iran. The son of a religious scholar, his studies at a local religious school were followed by an urban university program where he learned and was influenced by Western thought. He had been a member of the Tudeh (Communist) Party for several years. However, his acceptance of the scientific and technological aspects of modernization became tempered by his wariness and finally bitter criticism of the cultural danger of Western influence: "I say that [Weststruckness] is like cholera. . . . It is at least as bad as sawflies in the wheat fields. Have you ever seen how they infest wheat? From within. There's a healthy skin in place, but it's only a skin, just like the shell of a cicada on a tree."[24]

Like most countries influenced by colonialism, Iran had become the blind progeny of the West: relying on Western sources, judging by Western standards, dependent upon foreign advisors and consultants. He believed that the result of this total dependence on the West was loss of identity: "We're like a nation alienated from itself, in our clothing and our homes, our food and our literature, our publications and, most dangerously of all, our education. We effect Western training, we effect Western thinking, and we follow Western procedures to solve every problem."[25]

Iranians were cut off from their historical roots: the core of their society, culture and tradition. For Jalal al-Ahmad Iranian options were not simply limited to either the Westernization of society or the rejection of modernization by retreating to the past. Instead, he advocated a third alternative based upon her Irano-Islamic cultural tradition. Islam was the unifying force in Iran. Though a secularist, he had become convinced that Iranians must turn to their Islamic heritage for the foundation stones of national identity: ideology, sense of history, and values. It alone enjoyed wide public acceptance and appeal and could be used effectively to mobilize the populace. Similarly, though critical of the conservatism of the clergy, he recognized the role they might play in mass mobilization given the respect they received from the great majority of the public. As we shall see, the potential which Jalal al-Ahmad saw in Islamic ideology and religious leadership for mass mobilization later became the basis for the broad based religio-political opposition movement that dethroned the Shah.

The secular intellectual indictment of Westernization and the call for a continuity of modern Iran's identity and culture with its past was a primary agenda for religiously oriented lay and clerical ideologists as well as men like Mehdi Bazargan, Ali Shariati and of course the Ayatollah Khomeini.

In the same year that Jalal al-Ahmad's *Gharbzadegi* appeared, 1962, Mehdi Bazargan (b. 1907) delivered a lecture "The Boundary Between Religion and Social Affairs," on the relationship of religion to politics. Bazargan, a French-trained engineer with a strong Islamic commitment, had been jailed in 1939 for his opposition to the Shah's religious policies. In 1961 he and the Ayatollah Taliqani (1910–78), who had both been active members of Prime Minister Mossadeq's National Front, organized the Liberation Movement of Iran. It sought to bridge the gap between modern, secular, and traditional religious Iranians in working toward a more Islamic state and society. Arrested in 1962 for his opposition to the Shah, Bazargan was released in 1969. In 1979 he became the provisional Prime Minister of the Islamic Republic of Iran. He is viewed as a founder of modern Iran's Islamic movement.

Bazargan's political activism was inspired by his Islamic commitment. His orientation is reflected in the titles of his speeches and booklets: "The Causes of the Decadence of Muslims," "Islam, the Dynamic Religion," "Mission and Ideology," "The Relationship of Religion to Politics." Bazargan was especially effective because he combined a traditional religious outlook and vocabulary with modern concerns. Bazargan appealed to the relationship of religion to politics and society in Islam as embodied in the unity of God, Muslim belief that Islam is a way of life, the joint role of Muhammad as prophet-statesman, and the activities of the early Shii Imams. He spoke the language of the *ulama* and could utilize his credibility with them to criticize the political neutrality of many religious leaders. Bazargan argued that recognition of the interrelatedness of religion and politics in Islam should move the *ulama* to become actively involved in politics in order to bring about the renewal of Islamic society in Iran.

The socialist inclinations of Jalal al-Ahmad and the Islamic reformist spirit of Bazargan were combined in Dr. Ali Shariati, whose revolutionary Islam was at once more appealing to secularists, left-ists, and, in particular, Iranian students who often found the tradi-tionism of their religious leaders unconvincing and the secular modernism of many professors disorienting.

Ali Shariati (1933–77) incorporated many of the reformist cur-rents of his times: opposition to the Shah, rejection of Westernization, religious revivalism and social reform. Shariati was born in a village near Mashhad, in eastern Iran. His father, Muhammad Taqi Shariati, was a scholar-preacher, traditionally trained but reformist in outlook. The father served as the model and formative influence upon his son's religious and sociopolitical outlook: "My father fashioned the first dimensions of my spirit. It was he who taught me the art of thinking and the art of being human . . . I grew up and matured in his library, which was for him the whole of his life and family."[26]

Shariati received his early education in Mashhad. During his high school years he became active in his father's youth center, the Center for the Spread of Islamic Teachings, which sought to propa-gate Islam among Iranian youth, to communicate the relevance of Islam to contemporary Iranian life.

There was an educational vacuum in Iranian society. Tradi-tional religious leaders and their seminaries had developed a siege mentality in the face of the Shah's modernization reforms with its imposition of Western, secular curricula. At the same time many of the university professors had adopted a Western, secular outlook. Young Iranian students were caught between their traditional reli-gious upbringing and modern educational world view. It was this segment of Iranian society, in particular, to which Shariati devoted his life's work. In the late 1940s, Shariati and his father joined the Movement of God Worshipping-Socialists which attempted to synthesize Shiism with European socialism.[27] Father and son were also active in Dr. Mossadeq's nationalist movement and the abortive *coup* in 1953.

After graduation from the Teacher Training College, Shariati taught elementary school. It was during this time that he discovered a second hero or model for Islamic life—Abu Dharr al-Ghiffari. Abu Dharr had been a companion of the Prophet Muhammad who later denounced the wealth and corruption of caliphal court life and championed the rights of the poor. As such, he represented for Shariati and indeed for many contemporary Muslim social activists who emphasize Islamic social justice or Islamic socialism. For Shariati, Abu Dharr symbolized Islamic opposition to corruption and the concentration of wealth.

In 1959, Shariati went to Paris, where from 1959–1965 he studied Islamic history and sociology and earned a doctorate from the Sorbonne. His knowledge of traditional Islamic sources was now supplemented by the ideas of Emile Durkheim, Max Weber, Ché Guevara, Albert Camus, and Franz Fanon. As during his early years in Iran, the years in France contributed to his development both intellectually and politically. It was the time of the Algerian and Cuban revolutions. Shariati was attracted by and translated the writings of Guevara and Fanon. At the same time he was active during the early 60s in the Liberation Movement of Iran which had been founded by Mehdi Bazargan and Ayatollah Taliqani and edited *Free Iran.*

From his return to Iran in 1965, Shariati was viewed by the Shah's government as a threat. He was imprisoned for his antigovernment activities in Paris and then, after his release, was denied a teaching post at Teheran University. Although he finally obtained a position at the University of Mashhad, his popularity with students and his innovative ideas brought him into conflict with both the conservative *ulama* and the pro-monarchist administrators at the university.

In 1967 Shariati moved to Teheran where he became a leader at the Husayniyah Irshad Religious Center in 1972. Husayniyahs were places for the commemoration of Husayn's martyrdom. As such the Center symbolized Husayn's righteous struggle and martyrdom against the oppression and social injustice of the Umayyad Caliphs. For Shariati, it also symbolized the contemporary situation of the Iranian people. The impact of Shariati's lectures was almost immediate. Thousands came to hear him speak; six thousand students attended his summer classes. The original center had to be expanded and plans were made to establish similar centers outside Teheran. More than 100,000 copies of his lectures and writings were published and distributed.[28] The enormous success of his lectures in winning a wide following among students, intellectuals, and the left caused the authorities to denounce him as an "Islamic Marxist" and finally to imprison Shariati and close down the Husayniyah Irshad in 1973. After eighteen months in solitary confinement, Shariati was released and restricted to his village, Mazinan, under close surveillance. Finally, in 1977 the government permitted him to leave Iran for England. He died shortly after his arrival in England of an apparent heart attack at the age of forty four. His supporters suspected SAVAK of foul play.

Shariati was an innovative Islamic thinker who stood in sharp contrast to the traditional religious interpretation of the *ulama* and the Westernized, secular outlook of many university professors. Influenced by modern Islamic reformers like Jamal al-Din al-Afghani and Muhammad Iqbal, he emphasized the dynamic, progressive, scientific nature of Islam and the need for a thoroughgoing reinterpretation of Islam to reverse the retrogressive state of Islam and revitalize the Muslim community. Shariati combined Islamic thought with Western social scientific language in trying to provide an indigenous Shii ideology for sociopolitical reform. In doing this, he risked the wrath of the Shah, who called him an "Islamic Marxist," as well as the criticism of many religious leaders who viewed his syncretistic, innovative interpretation of Islam as an unwarranted departure from tradition.

Shariati's lectures and publications reflect the Irano-Islamic issues of his times: "Reasons for the Decline of Religion", "The Machine and the Captivity of Machinism," "Man Without Self—Two Concepts of Alienation", "A Revolution in Values," "Tawhid, A Philosophy of History." He began with the denunciation of "Weststruckness": "Come, friends, let us abandon Europe; let us cease this nauseating, apish imitation of Europe. Let us leave behind this Europe that always speaks of humanity, but destroys human beings wherever it finds them."[29] However his "return to Islam" was not based upon the medieval Islamic world view of conservative *ulama.* He distinguished scholastic, institutionalized Safavid Islam from Alid Islam, the true, dynamic, revolutionary message of Shii Islam: "Original Shiism was an intellectually progressive Islamic movement as well as a militant social force, the most committed, most revolutionary Islamic sect."[30] The doctrine of Divine Unity provides the intellectual foundation for all the affairs (religious, political, economic, social) of society. Shariati preached what may be termed a liberation theology which combined a reinterpretation of Islamic belief which incorporated modern sociological language with the Third World socialist outlook of Franz Fanon and Ché Guevara. However, he differed with Fanon's rejection of traditional religions and instead insisted that the defeat of Western imperialism in Iran required the reclaiming of her national, religious cultural identity, a reclaiming of Iran's Islamic roots.

For Shariati, the revolution in Iran had two fundamental aspects: national identity-unity and socioeconomic justice. Only this dual program could address a politically subjugated and economically exploited Iran, caught in the grips of: "world imperialism, including multinational corporations and cultural imperialism, racism, class exploitation, class oppression, class inequality, and *gharbzadegi* [Weststruckness]."[31] But who is to lead such a movement and what Islamic ideology should be followed?

Although Shariati, like Khomeini, spoke of the Imam as the guide of the community, he believed the leadership for the reassertion of Iran's political and social revolution would come primarily from religiously minded lay intelligentia rather than the *ulama*. In general, Shariati criticized the religious leaders for having been coopted by the Safavids in allowing the dynamic, revolutionary ideology of Shiism to become an establishment religion, bureaucratic and supportive of the status quo. As a result, Islam's dyamic ideology had become institutionalized, leading to the gap between Islam and the social realities of Iran. Traditional Islam under the *ulama* had become mired in a fossilized past and scholastic manuals, and had become the popular, fatalistic opiate of the masses. It had ceased to be a social force, effectively addressing the changing realities of society. Thus the decline of Muslim society was due not only to Western imperialism but the retrograde state of the religious establishment.

Shariati called for a "scientific" approach to Islam in order to recover the spirit of early Islam which was a socially revolutionary movement. His call for a "scientific" examination of Islam and his use of modern sociological terminology appealed to modern educated Iranians, especially the younger generation who felt caught between past upbringing and modern Western ideas. It restored cultural pride and confidence. At the same time his anti-Western critique and his use of Islamic sources and beliefs resonated with the world view and vocabulary of the majority of Iranian—traditionists as well as modernists. However, Shariati's methodology was clearly reformist.

Influenced in particular by Muhammad Iqbal's *The Reconstruction of Religious Thought in Islam*, Shariati emphasized the dynamic character of Islam: of the individual Muslim and the Muslim community. Islam is dynamic, progressive, scientific, indeed, revolutionary. Starting with the doctrine of unity of God, he maintained that this was not only a theological statement about the monotheistic nature of God but the unity of all creation. God's rule and guidance (Islam) extends to politics and society. This fundamental Islamic belief had been compromised by the Safavid coopting of religion and the religious establishment's cooperation with Safavid rule. Islam had become an establishment religion supporting oppressive governments rather than in continual revolt as it should be. Too often the *ulama* had become government advisers or succumbed to political quietism rather than protectors and activist leaders of the people, guarding against compromise, denouncing the oppression of rulers, true warriors of Islam.

Shariati's social doctrine began with the belief that the ideal social order established by the Prophet Muhammad, was a system based on the unity of God. However, this too had been subverted by imperial governments with their feudal systems based on class consciousness and economic exploitation. As such Iranian society was not the society envisioned by Islam but rather based upon polytheism (i.e., giving ultimate allegiance to anything other than God). For Shariati, true Islamic society was to be a classless society which rejected destinctions based upon tribe, class, or personal status.

Nowhere was Shariati's innovative method of interpretation and his revolutionary, sociopolitical understanding of Shiism more evident than in his explanation of the meaning and significance of the expectation *(intizar)* of the Imam as the Mahdi, or rightly guided one. With the absence or seclusion of the twelfth Imam, religious leaders had acquiesced to the *de facto* separation of religion and politics since they had accepted the legitimacy of temporal rulers or monarchs during the absence of the Imam. Political quietism resulted as the community passively awaited the future coming of the Mahdi and the messianic age of justice. Shariati believed that such a de-politicized Shiism subverted the revolutionary character of true Shiism. True expectation is an active striving to realize social justice, motivated by the messianic hope and promise of the Mahdi. This is the sense in which all Muslims are called to be holy warriors. Muslims find themselves "plundered, tortured, hungry, oppressed and discriminated against." *Intizar* is God's promise of victory to Islam: "He had promised the wretched masses they would become leaders of mankind; He had promised the disinherited they would inherit the earth from the mighty." Shariati concluded: "Belief in the final Saviour, in the Shii Imams and the Twelfth Imam, means that this universal Revolution and final victory is the conclusion of the one great continual justice-seeking movement of revolt against oppression."[32]

Ali Shariati did not establish or lead a specific activist organization. Instead he influenced a broad range of Islamically oriented reform minded Iranian youth, some of whom established their own organizations. Among the more prominent was the Mujahideen-i-Khalq (The People's Soldiers), a secret revolutionary organization often denounced by the Shah as "Islamic Marxists." Shariati's interpretation of Shii Islam, as a revolutionary ideology whose goal was a socially just society, was adopted by the Mujahideen as the basis for a social revolution to create a "Tawhidi," Islamic socialist system. Although part of the united Islamic opposition to the Shah, after the revolution initial cooperation with the Ayatollah Khomeini would give way to active, violent opposition to conservative *ulama* power and control of the government. Mujahideen assassination of government officials would be countered by Khomeini's denunciation of the Mujahideen as non-Muslims and an equally violent purge by government forces.

Khomeini

If Shariati was the ideologue of the Iranian revolution, Ayatollah Khomeini was its living symbol and architect. As discussed earlier, although Khomeini was not among the most senior ayatollahs, he had vigorously spoken out against the Shah's policies during 1963–65, been imprisoned several times, and finally exiled. From his exile, Khomeini continued his criticism of the monarchy. During the 1970s as the Shah became increasingly autocratic and used the military and SAVAK to silence his critics, only the religious establishment was able to remain relatively intact. Although the Shah had moved against individual religious leaders and his educational and land reform policies had weakened the religious establishment, yet the religious establishment retained its independence. First the sheer number and distribution of religious scholars and local religious leaders as well as the more than 20,000 mosques scattered throughout every village and city, made effective government control impossible. Second, the religious establishment retained a good deal of financial independence. In addition to religious endowments, they received the wealth tax for the poor and religious tax on annual income which Shii Muslims are expected to contribute to religious authorities.

Khomeini shared with Mawlana Mawdudi of the Jamaat-i-Islami and Hasan al-Banna of the Muslim Brotherhood's condemnation of Westernization, Western imperialism, and Israel: "the foul claws of imperialism have clutched at the heart of the lands of the people of the *Quran*, with our national wealth and resources being devoured by imperialism . . . with the poisonous culture of imperialism penetrating to the depths of towns and villages throughout the Muslim world, displacing the culture of the *Quran*." The Shah's recognition of Israel and Iran's shipment of oil to Israel came under blistering attack as well: "The sinister influence of imperialism is especially evident in Iran. Israel, the universally recognized enemy of Islam and the Muslims, at war with the Muslim peoples for years, has, with the assistance of the despicable government of Iran, penetrated all the economic, military, and political affairs of the country; it must be said that Iran has become a military base for Israel which means, by extension, for America."[33]

Throughout his exile in Iraq and then in France, Khomeini became the symbol of opposition to the Shah. He continued to function as a guide to his followers in Iran and, thus, to receive revenue for his activities from religious taxes. With such support from his Iranian followers, Khomeini continued to speak out and finance a movement against the Shah's regime. Copies of his writings and speeches as well as tape casettes were smuggled into Iran and circulated. Khomeini had several advantages over other opposition leaders or groups. Since he was outside Iran, he had the freedom and independence to say exactly what he thought without fear of intimidation or imprisonment. His appeal to religion could attract a broader based constituency than the nationalists whose opposition was based upon secular principles.

During the 1970s Khomeini's position moved sharply from that of a critic calling upon the Shah to reform his government to that of an opposition leader, denouncing an illegitimate, un-Islamic government. In Islamic terminology Khomeini ceased to call upon the

Shah as a Muslim ruler to repent, i.e., stop his wayward behavior and return to a more faithful following of God's path; instead, he increasingly condemned the Shah and his government as anti-Islamic, as a regime based upon unbelief, and thus the object of *jihad*. In the 1940s in *Revealing of the Secrets*, Khomeini had attacked the autocratic policies of Reza Shah but given a qualified acceptance to monarchy. By 1971, in a message to those on pilgrimage at Mecca, he stated unequivocally: "Islam is fundamentally opposed to the whole notion of monarchy." In that same message Khomeini denounced Iran's monarchy: "God only knows what disasters the Iranian monarchy has given rise to since its very beginning and what crimes it has committed. Crimes of the kings of Iran have blackened the pages of history. It is the kings of Iran that have constantly ordered massacres of their own people and had pyramids built with their skulls."[34]

During 1970 Khomeini had occasion to lecture on the nature of government in Islam and the role of the *ulama*. These lectures, delivered at the seminary in Najaf, Iraq, were later published under the title of *Islamic Government*. Rejecting monarchy, Khomeini argued for the supervision of the government by religious authorities and even their direct rule. Like Ali Shariati, Khomeini believed that absence of the Imam did not mean Shiite political quietism. Muslims were not to wait for the return of the Imam in order to live in an Islamic state and society. Islam and politics were inseparable, and so there should be an Islamic government. Such a government could take a number of forms. In the case of a temporal ruler, the Islamic character of the government is determined by *Shariah* rule. The *Shariah* provides the blueprint for state and society which the executive is to protect and safeguard and the judiciary to apply. The legislative branch of government is not necessary since only God can legislate and Muslims already possess His law. What is necessary is the *Shariah's* implementation in place of the man-made foreign codes which they have adopted. Khomeini differs sharply here from Mawlana Mawdudi and the Muslim Brotherhood both of whom maintain that Muslim society must first be made truly Islamic before Islamic law (especially its penal laws) can be fully implemented. In contrast, Khomeini maintained that the immediate implementation of Islamic law is the means to bring about the reformation or renewal of Islamic society. In this Khomeini's position was similar to that of Islamic revolutionaries in Iran and Egypt who advocate the overthrow of corrupt, un-Islamic governments and the Islamization of society through the imposition of *Shariah* rule.

Khomeini's view on Islamic government would have remained academic had the political situation in Iran not deteriorated so rapidly and the Shah's repressive policies not only silenced but provided a common cause for a broadly based resistance movement. With the widespread suppression of his critics: intellectuals, journalists, politicians, liberal nationalists, socialists, Marxists, Shii Islam provided the most viable banner for a united opposition. Khomeini, who had been forced to move from Iraq to Paris, because of his forced exile by the Shah, his increasingly vitriolic condemnation of the Shah, and his call for a new political order which included a constitutional government and socio-economic reform, became the symbol and center of opposition. Iranian dissidents studying or living in Europe and America like Abol-Hasan Bani Sadr, Sadeq Ghotbzadeh, and Mansur Farhang gathered around him.

Khomeini believed that the establishment of Islamic governments faced formidable obstacles: "the imperialists, the oppressive and treacherous rulers, the Jews, Christians, and materialists are all attempting to distort the truths of Islam and lead the Muslims astray."[35] In 1970 Khomeini had spoken of an Islamic Revolution whose realization might take centuries; even he could not foresee the events that would rapidly bring about the revolution of 1977–79, the downfall of the Shah, and his triumphant return to Iran to establish the Islamic Republic of Iran.

An "Islamic" Revolution

As opposition mounted within Iran, Shii Islam emerged as the most viable vehicle for an effective mass movement. Islam provided a common set of symbols, an historic identity, and a value system which was non-Western, indigenous, and broadly appealing. It offered an ideological framework within which a variety of factions could function. Moreover, the religious leadership had remained untainted, having not cooperated with the government. It also provided some hierarchical organization and leadership in its charismatic ayatollahs. A number of them—the Ayatollahs Khomeini, Talleqani, and Shariatmadari—had suffered under the Shah for their opposition to the government. Moreover, Islamic lay reformers like Shariati and Bazargan enjoyed the respect of many, especially of an alienated and increasingly militant younger generation. The *ulama*-mosque system provided a natural, informal nationwide communications network. The thousands of mosques, scattered throughout every city and village in Iran, became the foci for dissent, centers for political organization and agitation. Mosques offered a sanctuary; the Friday sermon became a political platform; and religious figures represented a vast reservoir of grass roots leadership. Shii Islam offered an ideological view of history that gave meaning and legitimation to an opposition movement. Shii Islam is a religion of protest with an ideology and symbolism well suited to protest and opposition.

Unlike Sunni Islam with its sense that early success and power were signs of God's favor, for Shii Islam, history documents the persistent denial or frustration of God's will regarding leadership of the Islamic community. As noted previously, the Shii ("the Party" of Ali), believe that Ali, the cousin and son-in-law of Muhammad, had been designated by Muhammad as his successor. However, his right of succession as leader was denied by the Sunni majority of the Islamic community who accepted the selection/election of Abu Bakr as successor to the Prophet. The martyrdom of Husayn at Karbala in A.D. 680 was of special significance, providing the paradigm for the Iranian revolution. It symbolized the role of Shii Islam as a protest movement in which a small righteous party struggled against the overwhelming forces of evil. Thus Shii Islam, the religion of the vast majority of Iranians, provided the ideology and symbols for a popular revolutionary struggle. For many Shii the Shah and his overwhelming military army, like Yazid's army, represented the evils of corruption and social injustice. Like Husayn and his forces, the righteous had a religious right to revolt against this modern Satan and undertake a holy war to restore the reign of goodness, equity, and social justice to make Iran a true Islamic territory. Toward this end, self-sacrifice and even death were to be freely accepted, for to die in God's struggle was to become a martyr and win eternal reward.

Under the umbrella of Islam, heterogeneous groups in the political spectrum, from secularists to Islamic activists, from liberal democrats to Marxists, joined together. They marched behind banners that symbolically declared their three options: USA (West), hammer and sickle (USSR), and Allah. Crossing out the first two options on their banners, they rejected the West and Russia and chose the third, the more authentic, Iranian/Islamic alternative. However, while there was a common purpose—opposition to the Shah and a desire for a more indigenously rooted modernity—the religious and political outlook and agenda of the various groups were quite diverse. Some wished to reclaim their Iranian identity or selfhood, through a more conscious incorporation of their cultural heritage, its history and its values, within Iran's modernization. For many, the Islamic alternative, symbolized by the name Allah, meant a return to Islam, the establishment of an Islamic state and society.

Among the Islamically committed, there were sharp and distinctive differences in their interpretations of Islamic identity and ideology. Nowhere was this clearer than in the juxtaposition of banners depicting the Ayatollah Khomeini and Dr. Ali Shariati in street protests and homes. The former emerged as the leader of the revolution and the latter served as its ideologue. Khomeini, the conservative religious authority, looked to Islam's traditional past, the manuals of medieval Islam. Shariati and other Islamic modernists represented a far more innovative, reformist approach, viewing Shii Islam in a more radically creative, revolutionary, manner.

The year 1977 was a turning point in contemporary Iranian history, the onset of the revolution of 1977–79. Like the uprisings in 1963, the high point of political agitation in 1978 would occur during the holy month of Muharram. Several events in particular caused the seething but contained forces of political opposition to erupt into mass, public demonstrations in the streets which were to spread across Iran and eventually bring down the government. In November 1977 the police tried to break up a session of what had been a series of peaceful poetry readings at Aryamehr University, sponsored by the Writers' Association, an organization of leading writers and intellectuals who were critical of the regime. The more than 10,000 students and participants poured out of the packed hall into the streets, shouting anti-regime slogans. In the clash that followed, one student was killed, seventy injured and one hundred arrested.[36] This police action precipitated a mass of student strikes that shut down major universities in Iran.

Two months later two additional incidents occurred which brought public political protest to a climax. In January 1978 a seminarian who had been granted sanctuary was killed by government forces. As in the Tobacco Rebellion, religious sanctuary was used to publicize political protest as well as seek protection. Although the regime had often chosen not to respect religious sanctuary during the previous decade, the climate had changed. The government's ability to simply control or repress its opposition had been weakened both because of external pressures regarding human rights and, much more importantly, the growing galvanization of diverse groups and factions, united by their common opposition to the monarchy. Moreover, given the Islamic identification of anti-Shah forces, the violation of sanctuary took on an added religio-political significance.

However, the event which sparked a long round of demonstrations and violence was the government's attack in January 1978 upon the *ulama* and Khomeini in particular. On January 7, a newspaper article entitled, "Iran and the Black and Red Reactionaries" denounced the religious leaders as "black reactionaries" in league with international communism. Moreover, "the article also charged that Khomeini was really a foreigner who in his youth had worked as a British spy, led a licentious life, and to top it all, had written erotic Sufi poetry."[37] The pattern of protest was one which became familiar. The *ulama*-merchant leadership closed down their establishments and 4,000 demonstrators took to the streets, chanting "we don't want the Yazid government" and "we demand the return of Ayatollah Khomeini."[38] The police moved in, and, in the ensuing clash, students were killed and injured. What became known as the Qum massacre was followed by a series of public demonstrations which were originally called to peacefully commemorate such events by closing down the universities and the bazaars and attending mosque services.

While most demonstrations remained peaceful, in Tabriz (February 18, 1978), Yazd (March 29, 1978), and again in Qum (May 10, 1978) demonstrators rioted when fired upon by police, army tanks and helicopter gunships. Protestors attacked symbols of the royal family and its "modernized-Westernized" state: police stations, statues of the Pahlavi monarchs, luxury hotels, liquor stores, movie houses. Increasingly, the chanting slogans of the crowds became more militant: "Death to the Shah," "Glory to Husayn," "Husayn is our guide, Khomeini is our leader," "Cast out America", "We desire an Islamic Republic". The Shah was the new Yazid, the devil incarnate; Khomeini was the representative of the martyred Imam Husayn. The battle had been joined between the "pagan" Pahlavi usurper regime and the "forces of Islam." Events came to a head in Teheran on "Black Friday." On September 7, more than 500,000 demonstrators had gathered to protest the imposition of martial law by royal decree. On Friday, September 8, approximately 75,000 people staged a sit-in demonstration in Jaleh Square. When the military and police were unable to break up the crowd, the crowd was directly fired upon by helicopter gunships in the air as well as tanks and soldiers on the ground.

Black Friday was a turning point in the revolution. It united the opposition and radicalized and mobilized the masses. The opposition, secular and religious, regardless of political outlook and orientation, united to an unprecedented degree with Khomeini as its symbol. Islamic ideology, symbols and the *ulama*-mosque infrastructure formed the core of the revolution and in this sense Iran's revolution became an Islamic revolution, i.e., cast in an Irano-Islamic mold and idiom. This development was demonstrated by the use of Islamic symbols. Believer and unbeliever, liberal constitutionalist and radicals, traditionist and modernist could be heard by the hundreds of thousands throughout the major cities and in villages proclaiming in defiance throughout the night "Allahu Akbar!" the traditional Islamic battle cry—God is most Great. Similarly, women who had worn modern attire now joined with their more traditional sisters in donning the veil as a symbol of protest against a monarch whose modernization program had once attempted to ban the veil.

During the months that followed Black Friday a wave of strikes swept across the country, threatening to paralyze the government. Schools, universities, banks, railroads, airlines, mass media, government offices, oil fields, mines and many industrial plants were affected as white and blue collar workers, traditional and modern middle classes, city dwellers and rural peasants swelled the ranks of the opposition and engaged in political action. In December, the month of Muharram, the religious symbolism and emotions which surround the commemoration of Husayn's martyrdom were once again fused with contemporary political realities as religious processions became protest demonstrations. In Teheran the Ashura procession drew almost two million people who called for the overthrow and death of the Shah, the creation of an Islamic government and the return and leadership of Khomeini. On January 6, 1979, the Shah, buffetted by widespread dissent and violence, unable to count on a military whose soldiers were defecting, and finding his American patrons wavering in their support, left Iran.

The Islamic Republic of Iran

Iran's revolution brought together a diverse cross-section of religious and secular lay leadership, social classes, and political parties as well as guerilla movements. For historical and cultural reasons, Islam had emerged as the most effective means for mass organization and mobilization. Thus, the revolution occurred under the umbrella of Islam: employing a Shiite ideology, religious symbols, mosque centered organization/communications network. Though the anti-Shah forces were many and varied in religious and political orientations, the Ayatollah Khomeini had emerged as both the symbol of resistance and in time its principal leader and spokesman. Yet many Iranians were not prepared for what was to unfold during the first days and years after the establishment of Iran's Islamic Republic. Most were unaware of Khomeini's views on the nature of government and politics and its relationship to Iran. His criticisms and denunciation of the Shah and his call for a new, just, political and social order had been in religio-cultural categories not unlike those of many other critics of the Shah. His advisers in Paris and in the early days after he returned to Teheran included men like Abol Hasan Sadr and Sadiq Ghotbzadeh, Mansur Farhang, and Ibrahim Yazdi, modern laymen influenced by the outlook of Ali Shariati. Moreover, although the opposition had a common enemy (the Shah, Pahlavi despotism, and foreign control) and a common purpose (a more just and egalitarian government), there had been no agreement upon the particular form of government or even its leadership. These were revolutionary times. Few, other than Khomeini's colleagues and students, were familiar with his writings on the nature of Islamic government and the rule of the expert in Islamic law. Indeed, few foresaw the control which he and the *ulama* would exert in their creation of a "clerical" Islamic government.

In his writings on Islamic government, Khomeini argued from the requirement that the true Muslim ruler must be noted for his "comprehensive knowledge, justice and moral character" to the possibility of direct rule by Islamic legal experts themselves. This could be accomplished either by a group of jurists or even by a single individual. Moreover, he asserted that such guardianship or government by a jurist is similar to that exercised by the Prophet Muhammad. The jurist would have the same authority to govern and administer though, of course, not the same status as Muhammad. Few had taken much note of Khomeini's interpretation of Islamic government and the rule of the legal expert. The implications of this doctrine were only to be realized during the post 1979 period when Khomeini asserted his role as guardian or overseer of Iran's government.

Khomeini, like Mawdudi and the Muslim Brotherhood, did not provide a detailed model of an Islamic government. Instead, he spoke of general principles and specific traditional Islamic institutions which provided the basis for an Islamic state. For Khomeini both revelation and reason made it clear that if an Islamic state was necessary in the time of the Prophet for the realization of God's Will, it would continue so until the end of time. Moreover, the very nature of God's revealed law (the *Shariah*) "furnished additional proof of the necessity for establishing government, for they indicate that the laws were laid down for the purpose of creating a state and administering the political, economic, and cultural affairs of society."[39]

From its inception in February 1979, the provisional government of the new Islamic Republic of Iran reflected the impending struggle between moderates and militants. The former represented by lay Islamic moderates such as Mehdi Bazargan, Abol Hasan Bani Sadr along with some religious leaders, and the latter dominated by conservative *ulama*. Institutionally, the moderate/militant split was embodied in Iran's "dual government"—the Bazargan cabinet and the clerically controlled Revolutionary Council.[40] The *ulama* prevailed. Their dominance of the political system was symbolized by the resignation of Bazargan in November 1979 and executive rule by the Revolutionary Council.

In the meantime the *ulama* dominated the Council of Experts and drew up a constitution (ratified in November 1979) calling for the "Rule by the Jurisconsult," the Ayatollah Khomeini, assisted by a Council of Guardians to be chosen by Khomeini and the Supreme Judicial Council.

Elections followed a similar course. Although Bani Sadr was elected Iran's first president in January 1980, the *ulama* controlled the Islamic Republican Party which won the majority of seats in the parliamentary elections. They were able to consolidate their power by controlling the new cabinet which replaced the Revolutionary Council and by impeaching Bani Sadr (June 1981). Since that time the *ulama* have maintained control of the government: executive, legislative and judicial.

Overseeing Iran's government is the Ayatollah Khomeini as its Guardian. Upon his death a successor will be selected by the clerically dominated Council of Experts. The *ulama* control the cabinet and president of parliament. The Islamic Republican Party holds most of the seats in parliament. Most importantly, since Islamic law has been declared state law, the *ulama*, as the traditional interpreters and guardians of the *Shariah*, control the Supreme Judicial Council which oversees the judiciary. They fill political posts or appoint those committed to their theocratic, ideological interpretation. A Ministry of Islamic Guidance oversees the press and media.

Iran in the early 1970's appeared to be a state well on the way to becoming a modern, powerful, stable nation under an enlightened Pahlavi ruler. A corps of modern elites appeared to be growing rapidly and assisting in achieving the economic, social, educational and military transformation of traditional Iranian society as symbolized by the Shah's White Revolution. By the late 1970's Iran's western, secular path to a modernized future came to a dead end. Pahlavi's reign was abruptly terminated as Iran's peacock throne fell before a popular revolutionary movement led by a bearded Islamic cleric. The monarchy with its political and social corruption and its puppet like ties to the United States and Israel was to give way to an independent, Islamic republic which would implement a more democratic and socially just society.

Post-revolutionary Iran has witnessed the replacement of the Shah and his secular elites by the Imam as Guardian and his conservative religious colleagues. The coalition which brought about the revolution has disintegrated as not only Pahlavi officials but all who differed with the new "clerical autocracy", Islamic and Marxist dissidents alike, were silenced. Women and religious minorities as well as a wide variety of political and intellectual dissidents have felt the swift arm of Islamic justice as meted out by revolutionary guards and courts. Prisons were again filled, trials and executions often occurred in such summary fashion that the Ayatollah Khomeini himself intervened and warned against such extremes. The Islamic Republic's first prime minister, Mehdi Bazargan, resigned in disgust; Bani Sadr, its first elected president, fled to exile in France; Sadeq Ghotbzadeh, who had held a number of government posts, including that of Foreign Affairs Minister, was executed for his participation in an alleged plot to assassinate Khomeini.

All had been protégés of Khomeini and brought into office with his blessings. Those religious leaders who have not accepted Khomeini's doctrine of "Rule by the Jurist" have been hounded and harrassed by fellow clerics. The Ayatollah Shariatmadari, a senior ayatollah revered for his learning and piety, was himself defrocked in spring 1982. At the same time conservative *ulama* have consolidated their power and control of the government, parliament, the judiciary and the media. The Iran-Iraq war and the continued guidance of Khomeini has, for the time being, deferred serious popular examination and consideration of the nature of Iran's Islamic Republic and the issues which it raises.

EGYPT

In 1981 Anwar al-Sadat, the self-styled "Believer-President," was assassinated by Muslim militants in the name of Islam. This was the climax of a turbulent period of "Islamic politics" during the Sadat period. Anwar Sadat had come to power in 1970, succeeding Gamal Abd al-Nasser. At first, Sadat seemed content to rule in the shadow of Nasser, as was symbolized by the placement of his picture in public places and government offices alongside of, not in place of, Nasser's. However, by 1971 he began to assert his own policy and move against his Nasserite and socialist opponents with the inauguration of his Rectification program or "Corrective Revolution." The Arabic terms chosen to describe the twin bases for this new orientation had strong Islamic connotations—*iman* (faith) and *ilm* (knowledge, the traditional designation for religious disciplines). In his own way Sadat was continuing Nasser's use of Islam to enhance his political legitimacy.

Sadat's Use of Islam

Sadat had a reputation for personal piety; the callus on his forehead from repeated prostration in prayer attested to it. He also, at one time, had close ties with the Muslim Brotherhood. Sadat cultivated a public image as a pious Muslim ruler. President Sadat appropriated the title "The Believer President" much as caliphs had once taken the title "Commander of the Faithful." As Hasan Hanafi, an Egyptian professor and Islamic activist, has observed:

> President Sadat has been given the title "the Believer-President." He is always called by his first name Muhammad. He is shown in the mass media in his white *jallabiya*, going to the mosque or coming out of it, with a rosary in one hand, Moses stick in the other, and with a prayer mark on his forehead. . . . He murmurs in prayer, closes his eyes and shows signs of humility and devotion. He begins his

speeches with "In the name of God," and ends them with *Quranic* verses signifying modesty and asking for forgiveness."[41]

All official pronouncements began with the traditional religious invocation, "In the name of God, the Merciful and Compassionate." Sadat also increased Islamic programming in the media and Islamic courses in the schools and universities. In Cairo, a city of some forty thousand mosques, the government built a thousand additional mosques. Sadat also cultivated his relationship with religious leaders of popular and official Islam. Sufi orders were permitted to function freely in public. The bastion of "official Islam"—al-Azhar University—became an object of special financial support, undertaking an expansion program that included new buildings and satellite provincial campuses. By the late 1970s Sadat could count on support from leading Azhar religious scholars and the Shaykh of Al-Azhar (Abd al-Rahman Bissar) for many of his policies: the Egyptian-Israeli peace treaty, Muslim family law reforms, criticism of Islamic "extremist" movements. Sadat's control of religion was enhanced by the creation of a Deputy Premier for Religious Affairs and a ministry of Religious Endowments and Al-Azhar Affairs which administered religious endowments, paid salaries for some religious functionaries, and, in time, tried to control the topic and content of mosque sermons.

The Egyptian-Israeli war of 1973 was given a special and transcendent religious significance by Anwar Sadat. It was waged during the holy month of Ramadan. Whereas Nasser had employed the secular motto "Earth, Sea, and Sky" in the '67 war, Sadat used *Allahu Akbar!* the opening words of the call to prayer and the traditional Islamic battle cry. *Allahu Akbar!* was on the lips of Egyptian troops as they stormed across the Suez Canal. The Islamic character of the war and the miraculous nature of Egypt's success was strikingly attested to by military participants: "I swear *'Allahu Akbar!'* was written in the sky. During the crossing as we looked up, Allahu Akbar was vividly written across the sky."[42]

The war itself was in every sense portrayed as a *jihad;* religious language and symbolism were freely employed. As a result, Egypt's success in penetrating Israeli positions was seen as an Islamic victory. Sadat emerged a Muslim hero.

Sadat's encouragement of religious revivalism included a more liberal attitude toward Islamic groups, in particular the Muslim Brotherhood and Islamic university student organizations. This was done to counter the influence of pro-Nasser secular leftists. Shortly

after Sadat assumed office, Muslim Brothers who had been imprisoned since the 1965 abortive *coup* were released; those in exile were
permitted to return to public life in Egypt. Religious publications such
as *al-Dawa (The Call)*, run by Muslim Brothers, were permitted in
1976. Edited by Umar Talmassani, a Muslim Brother sentenced under
Nasser to fifteen years imprisonment in 1965, it soon achieved a circu-
lation of 100,000. At the same time, Sadat encouraged the creation of
Islamic student associations to challenge Nasserite leftist student organizations. Between 1975 and 1979 the Islamic groups captured student elections at major universities. However, they soon became
more independent and critical of the Sadat government, and in 1979
were outlawed by presidential decree.

Sadat's support of religious revivalism began to show strains
by the mid 1970s. Government use of Islam did not necessarily mean
an ability to fully control Islamic issues or organization. The greater
profile of Islam in public life led to more discussion and agitation for
increased application of Islam in state and society. The "Islamic
euphoria" after the "victory" of 1973 had confirmed for many that
Islam offered the strength, pride, and sense of history which should
serve as the core of Egyptian national identity. The "return to Islam"
had expressed itself in many ways: increased mosque attendance,
adoption of Islamic attire by men and women, a proliferation of religious literature and tape cassettes of sermons, a burgeoning of Islamic organizations. A significant proportion of the younger
generation (university students and recent graduates) became involved in this Islamic revival. By 1974 the Sadat government began to
feel the strains from the politicization of religion. Two major examples
are the debate over implementation of the *Shariah* and the anti-
government activities of Islamic militants.

During the 1970s several committees of al-Azhar religious
scholars had been established to facilitate the application of the
Shariah in Egypt. The legislative committee of the People's Assembly
and the Committee on National Security had called for the introduction of *Shariah* law. In 1977 a resolution to that affect was introduced
but then shelved. On December 15, 1978 a joint committee of National Assembly legal experts and al-Azhar religious scholars had
been established to pave the way for the implementation of the
Shariah. The net effect of the drawn-out discussion regarding implementation of the *Shariah* was years of debate and controversy in
the National Assembly and especially in the press as secularist, Islamic modernists and religious conservatives argued about the feasi-

bility of making the *Shariah* the law of the land. For the Muslim Brotherhood and younger Islamic militant organizations, introduction of the *Shariah* was the first and essential step in establishing an Islamic state in Egypt. From their point of view, Sadat's failure to do this for so many years was inexcusable.

Opposition Movements

From 1977 onwards Islamic criticism and opposition to Sadat grew. Anwar Sadat's appeal to religion and support of Islamic organizations began to backfire as these organizations took on a life of their own. They increasingly asserted their independence and pressed for substantive Islamic changes, condemning what they judged an opportunistic control and use of Islam by the Sadat government. In response the Sadat government became more autocratic. When food riots racked Cairo in January 1977, Sadat cracked down on the left and communists as well as other opposition groups, among them the Jamaat al-Muslimin (the Society of Muslims), more popularly known Takfir wal Hijra (Excommunication and Emigration).

The Takfir was one of a number of militant Islamic organizations which had sprung up after 1967. The humiliating defeat, loss of Jerusalem (the third holiest city of Islam), and the loss of the West Bank were taken as clear signs of a politically impotent, inept, and corrupt system of government. The Western, secular model of government had failed; Muslims' only hope was a return to their Islamic alternative. While the older generation of Muslim Brothers had moderated their voices during the early Sadat years, this new generation of Islamic militants, some of whom had been younger members of the Brotherhood, espoused a more aggressive, anti-government strategy. Because they developed as secret societies, little notice was taken until they began to engage in violent, anti-government acts. In April 1974 a group called Muhammad's Youth (Shahab Muhammad) or the Islamic Liberation Organization attempted a *coup d'état*. It seized the Technical Military Academy in Cairo but was prevented by government forces from carrying out its plan to assassinate President Sadat. Eleven people were killed and twenty seven wounded. The Takfir wal Hijra dramatically drew attention in July 1977 when they kidnapped Husayn al-Dhahabi, an Azhar shaykh and former Minister of Religious Endowments, who had been a strong critic of Takfir. When their demands for the release of imprisoned compatriots were not met, al-Dhahabi was executed. In the nationwide crackdown that followed, 620 members were arrested and 465 were tried before military courts.[43] The leaders of both Muhammad's Youth and the Takfir were executed and members imprisoned by the Sadat government. Although the groups were suppressed, many simply went underground and became active in other militant groups such as the Jund Allah (Soldiers of God) and Jamaat al-Jihad (Holy War Society) which by late 1977 became very active. Despite government surveillance and prosecution, militant groups grew and their violent activities multiplied.

Ideologically, Islamic militants are heavily indebted to Sayyid Qutb and Mawlana Mawdudi. They interpret their call for an Islamic revolution and *jihad* quite literally. Force and violence are accepted as part of their liberation struggle. While differences exist, there is a good deal of agreement in the ideological framework of Islamic militant organizations: Among their major beliefs are:

1. Muslim's have a God-ordained purpose and vocation, i.e., submission to and realization of God's will.

2. God's will governs both individual and community life.

3. The correct path or divine blueprint for society or *Shariah* is contained in the *Quran* and Sunnah.

4. Islam is a total way of life which embraces religion and politics, state and society.

5. They demand an Islamic state, the Rule of God on Earth.

6. Therefore, it is imperative that the *Shariah* be implemented, replacing existing Western-inspired legal codes.

7. They condemn the Westernization of Muslim society and its models for modernization because they have failed and are thus responsible for political corruption, economic decline, social injustice, and spiritual malaise, just like the pre-Islamic period of ignorance.

8. They believe that a crusader mentality, neo-colonialism, and the power of Zionism have resulted in a Western Judeo-Christian conspiracy which pits the West against the East.

9. Since the legitimacy of Muslim governments is based on the *Shariah*, governments such as Egypt which do not follow the *Shariah* are illegitimate. Those guilty of unbelief, "atheist states", are a lawful object of *jihad*.

10. Muslims are obliged to both overthrow such governments and to fight those Muslims who do not share the "total com-

mitment" of militants. Like the Kharijites in early Islam, militants regard such persons as no longer Muslims but rather unbelievers.

11. *Jihad* against unbelievers is a religious duty. The life and goods of an infidel are forfeit.

12. Non-Muslims are no longer considered "People of the Book" but rather "unbelievers." Thus non-Muslim minorities such as the Copts are persecuted.

13. The official *ulama* are rejected for their tendency to downplay the meaning of *jihad* as armed struggle and simply reduce it to striving to lead a moral or virtuous life. They have succumbed to the West and been co-opted by the government.

14. The majority of mosques which are state supported and controlled are places of unbelief since God's will and the Prophet's teachings are not upheld there.

But who are these militants—uneducated peasants ignorant of the modern world, rejecting modernization in order to bury themselves in the past? The leadership of Takfir wal Hijra and Muhammad's Youth had combined an early traditional religious upbringing with a modern education. Salih Siriya, founder of Muhammad's Youth, had earned a Ph.D. in science education. Shukri Mustafa, founder of Takfir wal Hijra, held a B.S. in agricultural science. Both had been members of the Muslim Brotherhood and imprisoned. Mustafa had, in fact, been imprisoned from 1965 and was among those released in 1971 by Sadat. Though Siriya and Mustafa honored the memory of Hasan al-Banna and Sayyid Qutb, they believed that the Brotherhood had drifted away from its early commitment; many of its members had been broken, mellowed or burned out. Therefore, each had begun to develop their own organizations during the late 60s and early 70s. The primary source for members was Egypt's younger generation. Religiously concerned students and recent university graduates were recruited from local mosques, schools and universities and organized into secret cells. Most members had come from villages and towns and migrated to such cities as Cairo, Alexandria, and Asyut. Many were educated, highly motivated members of the lower middle and middle class. As one investigator has concluded:

> The typical social profile of members of militant Islamic groups could be summarized as being young (early twenties), of rural or small-town background, from middle and lower middle class, with high achievement motivation, upwardly mobile, with science or engi-

neering education, and from a normally cohesive family. It is sometimes assumed in social science that recruits of "radical movements"
must be somehow alienated, marginal, anomic, or otherwise abnor-
mal. Most of those we investigated would be considered model
young Egyptians.[44]

Separated from their families and village communities, these
young Egyptians were exposed in heavy doses to the "new ways" of
city life. Here they encountered vividly the realities of modern Egyptian life: the wealth and high life-style of the rich, contrasting with the
overcrowded ghettos; poverty and massive unemployment, Western
dress and social (especially sexual) mores on the streets and in the
media vs. traditional Islamic values regarding women and the family.
While the freedom and delights of city life may prove seductive for
some, for Islamically-minded young Egyptians cut off from the identity and support system of their rural backgrounds, modern Egyptian
life often produced a sense of alienation. Islamic organizations offered a new sense of community. They were an Islamic society organized into cells called families. More importantly, their community
was based upon an Islamic ideology which provided a critique of their
society and an agenda for radical change, rooted in their traditional
religious world view.

The organization and leadership of Islamic organizations
reflected the temperament and styles of their leaders. Mustafa, the
"commander of the society of believers," ran the Takfir as a highly
disciplined organization, strictly controlled and "guided" by its Amir.
Like Muhammad's Youth, Takfir viewed contemporary Egyptian society as un-Islamic, a domain of unbelievers. So, like the Prophet
Muhammad who, when faced with the unbelief of Mecca, had emigrated to Medina, the Takfir set up its own "rightly guided" communities working, studying, and praying together. Its goal was the
establishment of a separate community of true believers in Egypt.
Like the Muslim Brotherhood and Pakistan's Jamaat-i-Islami, there
were gradations of membership. Full members were expected to de-
vote themselves totally to the work of the community, leaving their
jobs, family, and former friends behind. Total commitment was expected. The ideal was martyrdom, i.e., a willingness to give up everything even one's life, in their struggle for Islam. The Amir demanded
unquestioning obedience. Errant members might be excommunicated
and/or punished. While members of Muhammad's Youth were

equally militant, well organized, and disciplined, they were governed
more democratically by an executive council which relied on consultation rather than one man rule. Thus, despite Siriya's personal belief
that such an action was premature, the council had decided to seize
the Military Academy and assassinate Sadat.

During the late 1970s, Sadat's critics became increasingly
more vociferous. The political, economic, and social tensions in Egyptian society were fast reaching the boiling point. In January 1977 Cairo
was convulsed by food riots which the government blamed on Marxists and leftist. The government's response was swift and strong,
arresting many opposition leaders including members of Islamic militant organizations like the Takfir. Sadat undertook several new
policies to bolster the Egyptian economy: an open door (al-infitah)
economic program and pursuit of a peace treaty with Israel (Camp
David). Both proved unpopular. For many, the open door policy simply meant greater Western (especially American) economic involvement and influence which would line the pockets of multinational
companies and Egyptian elites rather than address the basic economic
and social problems in Egyptian society. As the best of Egyptian produce was shipped to Europe and the oil-rich Gulf states and Egyptian
workers offered subsidized imported foods, critics might well ask:

> How can the peasant, the hard working Egyptian fellah, maintain
> his dignity when, after sweating in the hot sun all day long he has to
> stand in line only to receive a frozen American chicken? . . . As he
> sits in the evening with his family to watch the TV that his son has
> purchased from the fruits of his labor in Saudi Arabia, the intrigues
> of J. R. Ewing and Sue Ellen in *Dallas* strip him of what is left of his
> legitimacy as a culture bearer in his own culture. Between programs,
> he is told in English that he should be drinking Schweppes or in
> dubbed Arabic that he should use deodorant, and that all his prob-
> lems are caused by having too many children—a total package of
> imported ideas.[45]

Camp David was viewed by Egyptian critics, as well as most
Arab Muslim governments who broke diplomatic ties with Egypt, as
a unilateral capitulation to Israel and, by extension, its American
patron.

Sadat's foreign minister resigned, public criticism rose, Islamic critics denounced the action as the treasonous act of an "unbe-

liever." The criticism of the government was not lessened by al-Azhar's endorsement of Sadat's peace initiation. Rather it confirmed the belief that the religious establishment had become a puppet of the regime. Throughout Egypt demonstrations were organized, especially by Islamic student associations at university campuses. Although the Muslim Brotherhood had initially been cautious in its responses, by March 1979 it published a call "to follow the example of Iran and to wage holy war against Israel."[46]

Islamic critics were further outraged by Sadat's unilateral implementation of controversial reform measures in Muslim family law by presidential decree during a parliamentary recess. Similar reforms had been attempted on numerous occasions, including the early 1970s, only to be shelved. The new measures, such as those expanding a wife's grounds for divorce and her maintenance rights, were regarded as a pet project of Sadat's wife, Jihan Sadat. Islamic critics viewed these reforms as representing a "Western model" of womanhood as inappropriate and objectionable as Western models of political and economic development. Family law reforms were viewed as an "attack" on traditional Muslim family law that would weaken family ties and lead to the sexual permissiveness of the West. The fact that Sadat managed to obtain the support of his appointee, the Rector of Al-Azhar, did nothing to assuage Islamic critics. The Muslim Brotherhood, through publications such as *The Call*, and militant Islamic organizations attacked the reforms as anti-Islamic.

As opposition to Sadat became progressively more widespread and aggressive, he responded defensively and repressively. Sadat's leadership style had been symbolized by his self-description which he drew from two traditional titles: "the Believer President" and "the head of the family." As dissent mounted, Sadat became the authoritarian father who knew what was best for his family and community and expected unquestioned support and compliance. Sadat demanded what he himself had been to Nasser, yes men or sycophants. He had silenced the Communists and leftists and now moved against other critics—intellectuals, lawyers, university professors. His real battle, however, was with a burgeoning Islamic opposition. The Muslim Brotherhood and Islamic student organizations, which he had encouraged, had taken on a life of their own and became as outspoken as other Islamic militants.

While the official Islamic establishment of al-Azhar could be marshalled for public support and while the Western media portrayed an enlightened and popular Egyptian first family, preachers in many of Egypt's mosques bitterly denounced the Sadat government and its policies: "open door," Camp David, family law reform, the admission of the Shah of Iran, and Sadat's denunciation of the Ayatollah Khomeini and Iran's Islamic revolution.

During 1979–80 Sadat took additional measures to silence his critics. In February 1979, shortly after the Shah's overthrow, in a speech at Alexandria University, Sadat warned that religion and politics were separate spheres. Moreover, he declared to members of his National Democratic Party: "Those who wish to practice Islam can go to the mosques and those who wish to engage in politics may do it through the legal institutions." (*Egyptian Gazette*, February 2, 1979.) This statement was taken by his Islamic critics as further proof that Sadat, "the Believer-President," was in fact an unbeliever.

Sadat criticized the Muslim Brotherhood for becoming "a state within a state."[47] University student Islamic organizations were banned by presidential decree. Finally, in September 1981, the government cast a wide net over its reputed opponents, arresting and imprisoning Muslim Brothers and other members of militant Islamic organizations, university professors, political opposition leaders, Muslim preachers, journalists, and writers. Approximately fifteen hundred people were detained. Publications of both his secular political and Islamic opposition were banned. Those imprisoned were as diverse in their religious and political positions as in their professions. Indeed, the Islamic militants among them would have rejected many of their fellow prisoners as Marxists, atheists, leftists, and Muslim "backsliders."

Like the Shah, Sadat combined autocratic rule and identification of Egypt with his personality and will: "Sadat the dictator was becoming the State itself and the Sadatization of Egypt was expressed in almost every song on radio and television. . . . Two processes were at work: . . . a Sadatization of Egypt on the one hand and a deification of Sadat on the other—the rebirth of the Egyptian pharaoh."[48] Sadat's indiscriminate crackdown in September and his pharaonic style only served to broaden popular discontent and opposition among moderate Egyptians.

On October 6, while reviewing a parade commemorating Egypt's successes in the 1973 War, Anwar Sadat was assassinated. Although initially attributed to the Takfir wal Hijra, it soon became evident that the Jamaat al-Jihad (Holy War Society) was responsible. Al-Jihad had developed from the survivors of Muhammad's Youth's abortive *coup* in 1974.[49] Those who had escaped or were released scattered and took up residence in Upper Egypt (Asyut, Minya, Fayyum) as well as in Cairo and Giza. In time separate groups grew up around a local leader. Members came primarily from the lower middle and middle classes, rural migrants who had come recently to the cities. The leadership could best be described as young, devout, educated, committed, but disillusioned and increasingly disaffected with Egyptian society, finding it politically corrupt, economically unjust, and spiritually lax.

Al-Jihad recruited its membership from those young people who were observed at university mosques and private mosques. The latter had proved especially important in development of Islamic movements, providing recruits and sympathetic supporters. During the 1970s the number of private mosques had doubled from approximately 20,000 to 40,000 so that out of 46,000 mosques in Egypt only 6,000 were controlled by the Ministry of Religious Endowments. Private mosques dotted the neighborhoods of cities and towns where they served the vast majority of the Egyptian people. More importantly, such mosques and their preachers were independent, financially and politically, unlike the state-supported mosques whose staffs and sermons came under government control. As the situation in Egypt became more radicalized in the late 70s, Sadat's support from the official Islamic establishment and the government-controlled media was often seriously undermined and offset by the fiery sermons in private mosques delivered by his Islamic critics. Such mosques provided natural meeting places and organizational centers for Islamic militants.

Al-Jihad also extended its influence through the establishment of religious societies, such as those for *Quran* study and social centers. The latter provided food, clothing, and assistance in obtaining housing. In particular, religious fraternities were created at universities to assist students with free books, tutoring, and housing.

During the late 1970s al-Jihad's centers grew and often clashed with Egyptian security forces, especially in Asyut, Minya, and Alexandria. Despite arrests, government surveillance, and harassment, their strength was not diminished but rather increased. In 1980 a central consultative committee was established, bringing together, in a greater organizational unity, the leaders of the various factions. However, it was not until March of 1981 that the leadership of al-Jihad moved beyond isolated attacks and confrontations with the government to plotting an overthrow of Anwar Sadat. Among the leading figures to emerge during this process were: Muhammad al-Farag, Colonel Abbud al-Zumur, Lieutenant Khalid Istanbuli, and Shaykh Umar Abd al-Rahman. They reflected a civilian, military, and religious alliance and character. As noted previously, al-Farag was in many ways the ideologist of al-Jihad. Colonel al-Zumur and Lieutenant Istanbuli were primarily responsible for the recruitment, planning and execution of the assassination.[50] Shaykh Abd al-Rahman was, in many respects, the religious advisor for al-Jihad. He issued decrees which provided religious legitimacy for al-Jihad's actions.

The assassination of Anwar Sadat followed quite logically from the ideology of al-Jihad. Like other militant groups, it was strongly indebted to the writings of Hasan al-Banna, Mawlana Mawdudi and, most especially, Sayyid Qutb. This is clearly reflected in Muhammad al-Farag's brief tract, "The Absent Obligation" (i.e., *jihad*). A former Muslim Brother who had become disaffected by its moderate posture, al-Faraq, draws heavily on the ideology and world view of al-Banna, Mawdudi, and Qutb, taking them quite literally and following their thoughts regarding the required Islamic revolution to their logical conclusion. At the heart of al-Jihad's message and mission was the call to "true believers" to wage holy war against Egypt's un-Islamic state and its leader, Anwar al-Sadat. Al-Jihad's goal was the establishment of an Islamic state, a society governed by the *Shariah*. However, to achieve this, given the decadent state of Islamic society, *jihad* is required. Since Muslims find themselves living in what is in effect a non-Islamic territory, abode of war, armed struggle is necessary to establish once again a Islamic territory. Al-Jihad advocated a caliphal form of government in which the just leader would govern according to the *Shariah*. The *ulama* are faulted for their cooperation with the government and their encouragement of a quiescent Islam through their interpretation of *jihad* as primarily personal struggle to lead a virtuous life. The Muslim Brotherhood are also found wanting. Their moderate tone in working for the gradual Islamization of society in order to bring about an Islamic state is seen as unrealistic. The condition of Egypt was viewed as so far gone that radical surgery was required. According to the revolutionary logic of *al-Jihad*, power must be seized. An Islamic state must be established in order that in following Islamic law instead of Western law, an errant Egyptian society might be Islamized.

CONCLUSION

The 1970s proved an explosive and turbulent period in the history of Muslim politics. Seemingly stable governments were deeply shaken and several Muslim rulers forcibly removed from office through *coups d'etat* or assassination. While such events were in themselves not all that unusual, the substantial re-emergence of Islam's role and function in politics was surprising to many. Islamic ideology, symbols, religious leaders, and organizations took on a level of importance that moved Islam from the periphery of political life to center stage. Qaddafi, Bhutto, Zia ul-Haq, and Sadat used Islam to strengthen their political legitimacy and make their policies more acceptable. At the same time, political opposition in countries like Iran, Pakistan, Egypt, and Saudi Arabia also took an Islamic form. Islamic activists used Islam as a measuring stick against which established governments were judged autocratic, politically corrupt, economically unjust and spiritually and morally debilitated. Religious and secular opposition leaders found a tentative unity in the condemnation of a common enemy and an appeal to their shared, deeply-rooted Islamic identity and culture. Disillusionment with Western political and cultural hegemony, along with the relative effectiveness of an Islamically styled opposition due to its mass popular appeal, its pervasive institutional presence, and independent sources of income and support made Islam a natural rallying point for anti-government groups. Under the umbrella of Islam, dissidents organized; they cast their critiques and agendas for reform in Islamic language and rhetoric. Tactics ranged from rallies, sit-ins, and demonstrations to violent, terrorist attacks and assassination.

While the 1970s may be viewed as a time of renewed Islamic power and pride, the appeals to Islam and the very form of the Islamic alternative itself varied significantly. Similarly, implementation of Islamic alternatives in countries like Libya, Pakistan, and Iran have raised many issues.

6

Issues and Prospects

ITHIN SEVERAL DECADES, the modern Middle East has undergone major political and socioeconomic changes. From Morocco to Pakistan, European colonialism was terminated and newly independent Muslim states pursued the process of nation building. Most Muslim nations took modern western states as their models for political and socioeconomic development. In addition, Israel was created and with it has come decades of warfare in Palestine creating both an international political problem as well as an Islamic issue.

For many Muslims, the early 1970s signaled an important turning point in modern Muslim history. The centuries-long decline of Islamic fortunes seemed reversed by the Egyptian "victory" over Israel in the 1973 war and by the Arab oil embargo. The attention of the West was drawn to an Arab/Islamic world whose new-found oil wealth transformed its geo-political and strategic significance. The restoration of success, pride and self-confidence was accompanied by a significant revival in Islamic practice and politics. The re-assertion of religio-cultural identity in public as well as personal life has become a major factor in contemporary Muslim life and politics at the national and international levels. During the 1980s, the force of a politicized Islam continues to assert itself in public life. Egypt's *al-Jihad* assassinated Anwar Sadat in 1981. President Hafiz Assad's government ruthlessly levelled much of Homa (1982), its third largest city, to suppress Syria's Muslim Brotherhood. Other Islamic radical groups calling themselves *al-Jihad* took credit for the terrorist attack against American troops in Lebanon (October 1983) and similar car bomb

211

attacks in Kuwait (December 1983). In 1983 Saudi Arabia, Kuwait and other Gulf States established a commission to study and develop a unified code of Shariah law. Algeria and Tunisia have cracked down on Islamic activists. In Turkey, voters rejected the ruling military junta's preferences and elected Turgut Ozal prime minister. In the last pre-junta elections, Mr. Ozal had been a candidate for the "Islamic", National Salvation Party (NSP) whose deputy leader is his brother, Korkut Ozal. From the Sudan to Malaysia, Islamic leaders have been given cabinet level positions, and regulations in banking, and insurance as well as new Islamic laws have been introduced.

The resurgence of Islam has challenged many of the presuppositions and expectations of development theory. Modernization for the Muslim world has not necessarily followed the general wisdom of western political theories by resulting in the progressive secularization of state and society.[1] While a minority elite class accepted and implemented a western secular worldview along with its ideologies and values, the majority of the Muslim population has not truly accepted and internalized a secular outlook.[2] Daniel Crecelius' observation regarding Egypt, which is second only to Turkey in its pursuit of Westernization, is true for much of the Islamic world: "Most studies on the process of modernization or secularism recognize the necessity for all systems by which man lives, the psychological and intellectual no less than the political and economic, to undergo transformation. We do not find this change in Egypt, whether at the level of state or society, except among a small minority of Westernized individuals. Traditional beliefs, practices, and values reign supreme among Egypt's teaming village population and among the majority of its urban masses. It should be emphasized that adherence to tradition is not confined to any single class or group of occupations, but is characteristic of a broad spectrum of all Egyptian social classes."[3]

Ironically, the technological tools of modernization have often served to reinforce traditional belief and practice as religious leaders who initially opposed modernization now use radio, TV, and print to preach and disseminate, to educate and proselytize. The message of Islam is not simply available from a preacher at the local mosque. Sermons and religious education from leading preachers and writers can be transmitted to every city and village. As any visitor to the Muslim world is quick to observe, the message of Islam has become an integral part of daily media programming and an available commodity in inexpensive pamphlets, books and cassette tapes sold in the kiosks and book stalls.

Modernization has not led to the triumph of secular political and economic ideologies. Liberal nationalism, Arab nationalism/socialism, capitalism and Marxism have, in fact, come to be viewed as the sources of Muslim political and economic failures. Disillusionment with political rulers and deteriorating socio-economic conditions have translated into a repudiation of "foreign" systems which, like any inappropriate transplant, have been rejected. Islamic activists have instead advocated a more authentic, Islamic framework for Muslim society. Though often described in monolithic terms and grouped under the umbrella of Islam, a diverse and prolific assortment of Islamic ideologies, actors, political parties and organizations have re-emerged in Muslim politics: conservative religious states (Saudi Arabia and Pakistan), radical Islamic experiments (Libya and Iran), military officers, kings, ayatollahs, state supported religious organizations and militant, secret Islamic opposition movements. All have advocated an Islamically oriented future and employed Islamic symbols and rhetoric. Islam has proven a meaningful and effective mobilizing force among modern as well as traditional Muslims. For some Islamic activists the means to achieve their Islamic goals are persuasion and gradual change; for others it is violent confrontation, armed revolution through holy war.

The adaptability of Islam to modern political conditions continues to be a hotly debated question. Despite the euphoria of the early 1970s, the realities of contemporary Islamic politics have more often led to disillusionment over unfulfilled dreams and expectations. Muslim critics of contemporary attempts to Islamize society denounce the arbitrary, self-serving use of Islam by autocratic governments in Libya, Iran and Pakistan. Muslims have thus far seemed incapable of turning great wealth into effective power nationally and transnationally. A greater divisiveness rather than a pan-Islamic unity of purpose and cooperation has plagued the "brotherhood of believers": the Iran-Iraq War, the assassination of the "believer-President" of Egypt by an Islamic organization, Sunni-Shii conflicts in Pakistan, Qaddafi's confrontation with Egypt, Chad, the Sudan as well as with his own *ulama*, the ruling from scholars of Egypt's al-Azhar University countering the Ayatollah Khomeini's condemnation of Iran's *Mujahideen* as non-Muslims, Iran's radical religious propaganda and encouragement to Shii in Iraq, Saudi Arabia, Kuwait and other Gulf States to overthrow their Sunni governments. International Islamic organizations such as the Organization of the Islamic Conference as well as Islamic governments have proven ineffectual in resolving the crises in Afghanistan and Lebanon, and between Iran and Iraq. In addition, economic polarization has occurred within and among many Muslim countries between those who have profited handsomely from an oil-based economy and modernization and their less fortunate Muslim brethren. The defenders of the "have nots" denounce economic oppression in the name of Islamic egalitarianism and social justice. For many Western and Muslim observers, the failures of a resurgent political Islam demonstrate the inherent inability of Islam to play a constructive role in modern political development. The juxtaposition of the certitude and commitment of Islamic activists with such skepticism once again raises for students of Islamic politics the questions which modern Islamic reformers, like Afghani, Abduh, Ahmad Khan, and Iqbal, have addressed since the late nineteenth century: "Are Islam and modernization compatible?" "Can Islamic history and tradition (culture) support modern sociopolitical change"? If so, "What might this Islamic future look like?" "What are the issues which accompany contemporary calls for the Islamization of state and society?"

ISLAM AND MODERNIZATION

The study of modernization in Islam is too often fraught with unwarranted dichotomies: tradition versus change, fundamentalism versus modernism, stagnation versus progress and development. For many Western analysts and Muslim secularists, Islam is a major impediment to meaningful political and social change in the Muslim world. For Islamic activists and other believers, Islam remains eternally relevant and valid. A key factor in the discussion of political modernization is the status and hold of tradition, the authority of the past, in Islam.

Despite the important place of Arab customary practice and non-Arab influences on Muslim life, during the early Islamic centuries the very meaning of tradition was redefined and standardized. This process obscured the complex, dynamic historical development of Islamic tradition with its inclusion of non-Islamic sources. Originally tribal tradition, Sunnah "beaten or trodden path", meant the accumulated wisdom or practice of Arab tribal society, passed down from generation to generation in oral law. During the early Islamic centuries this was replaced by the notion of "Islamic" tradition. All belief and practice were "Islamized" by maintaining that the Islamic community's way of life was rooted not simply in the accumulated wisdom and experience of the community but in revelation: the word of God *(Quran)* and the example *(Sunnah)* or model behavior of the Prophet. In particular, the established practice of the tribe was subsumed under and replaced by the practice or model behavior of the Prophet. Tribal *sunnah* gave way to Prophetic *Sunnah*. With the development of Islamic law, the traditional Islamic way of life was no longer simply viewed as the product of human wisdom but rather as the divinely revealed blueprint for society, the straight path *(Shariah)* of Islamic law. By the tenth century, this Islamic framework for state and society was essentially seen as determined and fixed—preserved in Islamic law, guarded and interpreted by the *ulama*. It was law that provided the statement and synthesis representing the unity and "guidance" of Islam amid the diversity of Muslim life and historical experience. Within Sunni Islam, the notion of the closing of the door of personal interpretation reflected and reinforced the general belief that the guidelines for Muslim individual and communal life had been fully determined and set forth. Henceforth, society was simply to emulate, follow the revealed guidelines of a sacred tradition. The net result was a system that effectively standardized and sanctified tradition by grounding it more directly in revelation and religious sanctions. It preserved Islamic identity and the power of the *ulama*. However, the preservation of a normative ideal was obtained at the expense of Muslim remembrance and awareness of Islam's dynamic historical development and adaptability.

As we have seen, the Islamization of state and society during the early Islamic centuries had included a process of borrowing and assimilation, through adoption and adaptation of non-Muslim beliefs and institutions. Islamic law itself was the product of reasoning and decision making by early caliphs, legal scholars, judges. In the attempt to establish its unity and authority, the classical formula for the sources of law, which later jurists accepted as expressing the development of Islam's code for state and society, emphasized its revealed character and origins at the expense of its human input. The sources of Islamic law were described as the product of revealed sources *(Quran* and *Sunnah* of the Prophet), regulations deduced through analogical reasoning based on revelation and accepted by the consensus of the community which was deemed infallible. The role of personal judgment and local customary laws was "officially" overlooked. At most, they were acknowledged as subsidiary principles of law. No wonder that Islamic tradition became fixed and sacrosanct; future generations were simply to follow the ideal pattern as comprehensively and authoritatively set forth in Islamic law. Departure from the revealed law or practice of the community, substantive addition or change, was viewed as heresy.

The sacrosanct nature of tradition in Islam, rooted in a romanticized understanding of Islamic history, is of primary significance in contemporary Islamic political development for it serves as an inspirational reality for traditionists and, at times, a major obstacle for modern reformers. There are two general approaches to Islamic renewal and reform: (1) a traditionist desire to restore the past, to replicate an early Islamic ideal; (2) a reformist call for renovation or reconstruction through Islamic (as distinct from Western) reform. Both approaches emphasize reliance on Islamic sources and distance themselves to varying degrees from the uncritical westernization of secular elites as well as the heritage of an earlier Islamic modernism such as that of Muhammad Abduh; each is viewed as too heavily influenced by the outlook and values of the West. A key difference between Islamic traditionists and reformers is their understanding and use of Islamic history and tradition as well as the degree of change that they advocate. The compatibility of Islam and modernity itself is not the issue. Most Muslims of varying persuasions would acknowledge the traditional place and acceptability of Islamic renewal and reform. Traditionist and reformer can assent to Mawlana Mawdudi's observation that "Islam needed in every age and still needs . . . groups of men and institutions which could change the course of the times and bring the world round to bow before the authority of the One, Almighty."[4] However, they disagree as to the direction, method, and the degree of change required.

Muslim Attitudes Toward Change

Four positions or attitudes toward modernization and Islamic socio-political change may be identified among Muslims today: secularist, conservative, neo-traditionist, and Islamic reformist.

Secularists advocate the separation of religion from the state. They view appeals to Islam in politics as retrogressive or inappropriate to modern political and social realities and thus they would limit

Islam to the private sphere of life. It is only the other three positions that are concerned with the implementation of Islam in public life and for whom the relationship of Islam to the sociopolitical aspects of life is an important task.

The conservative position is represented by the majority of the *ulama* for whom the Islamic blueprint for society continues to be what medieval synthesis developed during the early Islamic centuries and preserved in manuals and commentaries on Islamic law. Islam is a closed cultural system fully articulated in the past, preserved in medieval Islamic texts and valid for all ages. Religious conservatives, who constitute the majority of religious leaders, accepted as an interim measure the imposition of western, secular law since it left their "ideal blueprint" intact for implementation in a later, more Islamic, period. Since Islamic law is the divinely revealed pattern for life, it is not Islamic law that must change or modernize but society which must "return to Islam", conform to God's Will. However, when the opportunity occurs as in Iran and Pakistan and to a lesser degree in the Sudan, Egypt and Malaysia, conservatives equate an Islamic order with the restoration or following of traditional formulations of Islamic law.

Neo-traditionists, however, maintain the need, and their right to go back to the *Quran* and *Sunnah* of the Prophet in order to bring about the renewal of Muslim society. Although they value the medieval Islamic synthesis, they are not wedded to it as are the conservatives. Movements like the Muslim Brotherhood and the Jamaat-i-Islami reflect a neo-traditionist approach. While they accept much of classical law, they believe that law historically incorporated many un-Islamic practices. Therefore, Muslims must return to their revealed sources to revitalize the Islamic community. Claiming continuity with eighteenth and nineteenth century Islamic revivalists like Muhammad ibn Abd al-Wahhab and Shah Wali Allah, neo-traditionists maintain that the only authority to be followed is that of the *Quran* and *Sunnah;* they claim the right to interpret the *Quran* and Sunnah to respond to the needs of modernity. Neo-traditionists, like conservatives, reject both Muslim secularism as well as early twentieth century Islamic modernism. Islamic modernism, in its attempt to harmonize Islam and the West, is judged guilty of Westernizing Islam, sacrificing its authentic vision and voice. Neo-traditionists emphasize the complete self-sufficiency of Islam—the comprehensiveness and totality of the Islamic world view. Muslims need only look to Islam's sources to find the answers for Islamic society today. What is required is a rearticulation of Islam's eternally valid message. As we have seen, for neo-traditionists like Sayyid Qutb and Mawlana Mawdudi, Islam is the divinely mandated alternative to the materialism and secularism of Western capitalism and communism. While Westernization is rejected, selective modernization is not. Western science and technology are to be appropriated cautiously and "Islamized." However, Western values and mores are rejected for Islam has its own answers for humankind.

In contrast to religious conservatives and neo-traditionists, there are contemporary Islamic reformers. They too look to the early period of Islam as embodying the normative ideal. However, reformers distinguish more sharply between the principles and values of Islam's immutable revelation and the historically and socially conditioned Islamic institutions and practices that can and should be changed to meet contemporary conditions. Many reformers, like Ali Shariati, are Western educated but Islamically oriented. They are committed to an "Islamic modernization," i.e., a future in which political and social development are more self-consciously and firmly rooted in Islamic history and values. They learn from the West but do not wish to westernize Muslim society. Unlike the Islamic modernism of Muhammad Abduh and Ahmad Khan, contemporary reformers do not see themselves as responding apologetically or polemically to the West but rather as seeking in a more independent, indigenous and authentic manner to meet the needs of Muslim societies. They view Islamization as a process by which Islamic principles and values are reapplied to meet the circumstances and needs of a changing sociopolitical milieu. The greater implementation of Islamic law and the establishment of Islamic banks, insurance companies, the creation of Islamic universities and curriculum reform are viewed as part of this process.

As in the formative period of Islam, Islamization can include adoption and adaptation of other cultures' political and economic systems. However, whether in politics, education, economics or law, Islamically acceptable development eschews the transplanting of foreign models. Programs and policies must be appropriate to the specific needs of Muslim societies, and must either embody Islamic principles and values or, at the very least, not be contrary to Islam. Unlike early Islamic modernists, today's Muslim reformers believe that they live at a time and in political and social circumstances when specific programs may be developed and implemented not simply advocated and written about by pioneering voices.

Islamic Pioneers

Jamal al-Din Afghani, Hassan al-Banna, Sayyid Qutb, Mawlana Mawdudi, and Muhammad Iqbal paved the way for contemporary Islamic activism by alerting the Islamic community to the dangers of Western domination and arguing for a modernity grounded in Islam. They reasserted Islam's role in politics and society in a milieu dominated by secular elites and Western models of development. Despite the differences between neo-traditionists and early Islamic modernists, both were trailblazers of contemporary Islamic revivalism. They rekindled an awareness of the totality of Islam, the integral relationship of religion to all areas of life—politics, law, and society. They restored pride in Islamic history and civilization and, by extension, acceptance of reason, philosophy, modern science and technology. The contribution of these Islamic actors occurred in two particular areas: organization and interpretation.

Islamic organizations like the Muslim Brotherhood and the Jamaat-i-Islami provided the vanguard for what has developed into a more broad-based Islamic movement. They have served as the organizational models for a proliferation of Islamic societies which bring together small groups or cells of committed Muslims to live, train, and work for the transformation of society. Throughout much of the Islamic world, Muslim Brotherhoods have been established along with a host of Islamic political and social reform societies. Islamic student societies exist at most major schools and universities, often capturing student elections. Some Islamic organizations such as Pakistan's Jamaat-i-Islami, Turkey's National Salvation Party, and Iran's Islamic Republican Party contest elections. Moreover, Islamic activist leaders have, since the late 1970s, obtained cabinet level positions not only in Iran and Pakistan but in the Sudan and Malaysia. For a minority of Islamic organizations, the struggle for Islamic renewal has taken a violent, terrorist path.

Islamic pioneers, through their preaching and writings, provide an ideological interpretation of Islam that sets forth the principles and guidelines for a more authentic, Islamic alternative for state and society. Given the growing polarization in many Muslim states, the reassertion of Islam in politics, the proliferation of Islamic societies with their improved resources, a new phase of implementation and experimentation has begun. Theory has given way to practice.

Throughout the Islamic world there are innumerable conferences on Islamic politics, law, economics, education. Governments increasingly introduce Islamic laws and levy Islamic taxes. Islamic banks and insurance companies may be formed throughout much of the Islamic world and in non-Muslim countries where there are significant Muslim populations. There is a burgeoning literature on Islamic economics which itself reflects a growing sophistication in analysis. Education is a priority. Not only are new Islamic universities created and required courses in Islam introduced. More significantly, in addition to Islamic student associations at schools and universities, broader based Islamic youth organizations such as the Saudi-based World Assembly of Muslim Youth, the Islamic Student Association of North America, and the Muslim Youth Movement in Malaysia. These organizations, many of whose members are modern educated, bring together students and younger professionals (university professors, government bureaucrats, businessmen) who are committed to the implementation of more Islamic states and societies. They develop programs and materials to foster modern, Islamically oriented youth, run social centers, and where political conditions permit, engage in politics.

THE NATURE OF ISLAMIC GOVERNMENT

The widespread sentiment, discussion, and attempts to re-establish Islamic states and societies have again focused attention on the question of the nature and necessity of Islamic government. As we have seen, there was and is no single, agreed upon model of an Islamic state. The Islamic past was, in fact, quite diverse. Although the revealed material sources (*Quran* and *Sunnah* of the Prophet) of Islam and the early caliphate period are viewed by Sunni Muslims as exemplifying the Islamic ideal in which religion and power were fused in an Islamic government and delineated in Islamic law, the reality of Umayyad and Abbassid caliphal rule was often quite different from the normative vision. Indeed, many devout Sunni Muslims believe that the Islamic imperative was realized solely under Muhammad and the First Four Righteous Caliphs. For Shii, only the rule of Ali, and not the other caliphs, is acknowledged as legitimate. The imamate remained an eschatological hope to be realized when the Twelfth Imam returns as the Mahdi. The reality of Islamic history, with *de facto* fragmentation of the Islamic empire after A.D. 850 as well as the un-

Islamic character or concerns of many Muslim rulers, belie the existence of an ideal Islamic state.

The conclusion that the Islamic state/empire became a secular state, is equally unwarranted and misleading. To begin with, secularization is a modern term describing the separation of religion and state. This concept does not reflect the political reality. Throughout Islamic history the legitimacy of the ruler and the ideal blueprint of the state, whether caliphate, imamate or sultanate, continued to be official adherence to Islamic law as the basis for state and society. The caliph-sultan remained a symbol of Islamic unity; Islam continued to be operative in political notions of society and citizenship, law and judiciary, education and taxation. State institutions concerned with law, the judiciary, education, and social welfare services were administered in large part by the *ulama*. The state was often a major patron of Islam, Muslim institutions, scholars, disciplines, and sources. Thus, although Islam may not have been the guiding force in the life of its rulers, both in theory and, albeit in a more limited manner, in practice religion remained organically related to state and society. Despite changes of time and place, with their accompanying diversity of practice until the colonial period most Muslims could well believe and maintain that, however imperfect, they lived in an Islamic state and society officially guided by the Shariah. Moreover, despite the loss of power and autonomy occasioned by colonialism and the Western secular path followed by most Muslim governments, Islam has remained a primary principle of social cohesion and identity. Its continued presence among the vast majority of Muslims explains the continued appeal to and acceptance by many Muslims of Islamic politics.

Lack of a single, concrete, historical model has led to confusion as well as a lack of consensus as to what an Islamic state is. Summarizing what we have seen, this confusion is due to several factors: (1) the Medinan ideal (the state under Muhammad and Four Righteous Caliphs) does not offer much in the way of a detailed model; (2) the later Caliphal practice of the Umayyads and Abbasids provides only a skeletal system of political institutions, taxes, etc.; (3) failure to fully establish an Islamic state led to the formulation of ideal formulae (Islamic law and political theory) which, at best, constitute a theoretical, idealized version of an utopian society; (4) the relationship of religion to the state, like most beliefs and practices and indeed revelation itself, has throughout the ages been subject to a variety of interpretations.

The process of interpretation and application of religious

truths to society is conditioned not only by the authority of past practice but also by the very socio-historical realities to which it speaks. Neither individual religious scholars and leaders nor religious organizations and institutions can escape this hermeneutical fact. Both the Umayyad caliphs and their critics appealed to Islam; Sunni and Shii, who possess the same Book and Prophet, deduced different political theories of the caliphate and imamate. Diversity of interpretation and lack of consensus are reflected in contemporary Islamic politics, in the variety of Islamically oriented states: Saudi Arabia's monarchy, Pakistan's martial law regime, Iran's clergy-run Islamic Republic, and Libya's "state of the masses". Competing Islamic visions and claims pit militant Islamic opposition movements against Muslim governments as has occurred in Iran, Pakistan, Egypt, Syria, and Saudi Arabia. However, as in the case of those who seized Mecca's Grand Mosque in 1979 or Muslim militants in Egypt and Syria, beyond denouncing "un-Islamic" regimes and general references to the need to restore the Medinan ideal and *Shariah* law, there is little consensus or specificity to Islamic militants' agendas.

The history of two countries in particular, Pakistan and Iran, exemplify the problems of agreement and definition among Islamic activists during the twentieth century. As discussed in Chapter 4, the Munir Commission's report on the anti-Ahmadiyya riots in the early 1950s noted that extensive questioning and testimony of religious leaders revealed a one-sided consensus on who was not a Muslim. The Ahmadiyya, the *ulama* were incapable of agreeing on such fundamental questions as: "Who is a Muslim" or "What is an Islamic State?" The critical nature of this problem and its implications were summarized in the Munir Report:

> Keeping in view the several definitions of a Muslim given by the *Ulama*, need we make any comment except that no two learned divines are agreed on this fundamental . . . if we adopt the definition given by any one of the *Ulama* we remain Muslims according to the view of that *alim* [religious scholars] and *kafirs* [unbelievers] according to the definition of everyone else.[5]

Similarly, as indicated in Chapter 5, in Pakistan today religious forces that were able to unite under the banner of Islam in an opposition movement, have been unable to achieve any consensus regarding the nature of Pakistan's Islamic republic.

Iran's Constitutional Revolt of 1905–11 and the Islamic Revolution of 1979 provide striking examples of a reversal of Islam's unifying role once an opposition movement moved beyond the common object of concern, beyond Islamic rhetoric to the formulation and implementation of government institutions and policy. During the Constitutional Revolt of 1905–11, conservative religious leaders insisted upon full implementation of the *Shariah* and rejected liberal constitutionalist adoption of a Belgian based constitution with religious clauses and a "supreme committee" of interpreters who would assure that no law was contrary to the *Shariah*. So, too, in post revolutionary Iran conservatives and liberal constitutionalists again divided when clerics rejected the liberal constitutionalist option and instead implemented a clergy dominated state based upon the governance of the experts and *Shariah* rule.

Contemporary Islamic revivalism with its movement beyond talk of Islamization to actual implementation has highlighted a variety of issues regarding the relationship of Islam to modern politics. In its most general sense Islamic activists call for the introduction of a more Islamically oriented way of life in Muslim states—an Islamic order. In its more general sense, it means "Muslim" states whose inspiration and general orientation are derived from Islam. More particularly, the ideal is to establish "Islamic" states in which religion and politics are integrally related, politically, economically, legally, socially. The ideological foundation of an Islamic state is the belief in the absolute unity, sovereignty, and totality of God's will for humankind. The organic relationship of religion to all areas of life is viewed as distinguishing the Islamic community from Christiantiy as well as Western secularism and communism. Islam is to provide the ideological basis for both individual and communal life, for state and society. This Islamic alternative is referred to as an Islamic order or system or the system of Muhammad. Given the lack of a specific, agreed-upon authoritative model for an Islamic state, Islamic activists, organizations and governments have had to address a number of issues among them: the nature of Islamic government, political institutions, and international relations.

Early twentieth century Islamic activists, Afghani, al-Banna, Qutb, Mawdudi, Iqbal, were pioneers, ideological visionaries rather than practitioners. Their writings on Islamic government and institutions tend to be sketchy, dealing more with general principles and ideals rather than specific details. There is some general agreement regarding certain required features: (1) the state is the means by which an Islamic order or way of life is fostered and regulated. (2) The Islamic state is primarily a community of believers bound by a common faith and commitment to their divenely mandated mission to obey God and spread his just rule and governance throughout the world. (3) The consensus of the community is the source of authority regarding the particular form of Islamic government as well as the selection and removal of the head of state. (4) Based upon Quranic prescription (*Quran* 42:38 and 3:159) and early Islamic practice, the ruler must be selected or elected. This may occur through direct elections or indirectly by representatives of the people, a consultative assembly. These may be a group of community leaders or an elected parliament. (5) The ruler is to govern according to and assure implementation of the *Shariah* to which ruler and ruled alike are bound. (6) The ruler is required to consult with representatives of the people. However, he is not bound to follow their advice. (7) The checks on the ruler's power are the limits of the *Shariah,* an indpendent judiciary, and the right of the people to remove an unjust ruler.

In light of these general principles as well as recent Muslim writings and state practice, a preliminary assessment can be made regarding the ideology and political institutions of an Islamically oriented state and the issues raised by such a process.

Islamic State(s)

There is some agreement regarding what is not an Islamic government and less regarding what is. Most Muslims agree that hereditary succession, monarchy, dictatorship, and military rule are not Islamic although historical circumstances may require such interim forms of government. Thus, in recent times, the monarchies of Saudi Arabia and of Iran, the military government of Pakistan and the increasingly dictatorial policies of Anwar Sadat, became easy targets for Islamic critics.

Historically Islam has had a strong executive exemplified by Muhammad and the early caliphs as well as medieval sultans and shahs. Sunni notions of the caliphate and Shii doctrines of the imamate also envision a strong central authority. Within the limits of the *Shariah,* the caliph or Imam retains final political, administrative, military, and judicial authority. Contemporary Islamic political activists, though still retaining a strong executive, tend to provide some checks on the ruler's authority, such as elections (direct or indirect) of the head of state, the formation of a parliament as a modern version of the caliph's advisory councils, and the subordination of the ruler to the *Shariah*. Yet, for Islamic leaders like Mawlana Mawdudi and the Ayatollah Khomeini, the head of government remains quite powerful since, for all practical purposes, he controls the government. He must consult with the parliament but is not necessarily bound by their decisions. He oversees the appointment of the judiciary and military leadership. Furthermore, there is a sharp difference between Sunni models of Islamic government and the Shii model of the Ayatollah Khomeini. Sunni Muslims do not advocate a theocracy, governed by the *ulama*. They emphasize *Shariah* (what some call a nomocracy) governance with the *ulama* serving as advisers. For Khomeini, as noted previously, the legal expert is the ultimate guide of a government dominated by clerics. It should be noted that this is not *the* Shii model but *a* model of government because many Shii, including the Ayatollah Shariatmadari and Mehdi Bazargan, would restrict clerical input to an advisory rather than governing role.

The ideological orientation of an Islamic state is reflected in Islamic activists' expectation and demand that governments be led by the most virtuous, observant Muslims. In societies in which the governments are often viewed as corrupt, autocratic regimes, such moral idealism has proven attractive. Not only neo-traditionists like Egypt's Muslim Brotherhood and Pakistan's Jamaat-i-Islami but Islamic reformers subscribe to the position that "the prevailing criteria of political merit for the purposes of candidature for any political office revolves on moral integrity as well as other relevant considerations. All this would, no doubt, influence the form and spirit of accession to positions of power."[6]

This moral idealism is extended to the process of candidate selection, especially the ruler. Candidates should not actively seek office or undertake a modern political campaign. Rather, an independent nominating committee would select these best of men.

Most Islamic leaders and organizations espouse some form of democratically elected national assembly with legislative powers. However, for most conservative *ulama* and neo-traditionists the assembly or parliament is in the final analysis a consultative body. Although the *Shariah* is law and therefore the assembly technically has no legislative function, in fact it is permitted to pass additional or supplementary legislation in areas not covered by the Shariah provided these regulations do not contradict established Shariah principles. Most Muslims advocate some kind of committee of religious experts to advise the parliament in the drafting of legislation. However, the place of the *ulama* has become a disputed question. The classical view of legal development is that Islamic law is the province and product of the *ulama* in particular the legal scholars of the early law schools. They alone are seen as having the requisite learning to function as interpreters of the law. This is the rationale for committees who are to advise the elected assembly (most of whom are lay, not religious leaders of the community), and to assist in resolving jurisprudential problems in draft legislation. However, many Islamic modernists, in order to justify lay input in legislating as well as to limit the powers of the *ulama*, whom they regard as out of touch with modern realities, have challenged the status, power, and scope of *ulama* authority. They recall that in Islam, all Muslims are equal and have a direct relationship with God. There are neither sacraments nor clerical intermediaries. There should be no clergy or clerical class in Islam. They argue that the title *ulama* (plural of *alim*, "learned") simply means one who has knowledge or is an expert. Modernists argue that this title belongs properly not to a specific clerical group or class but to any Muslim who is qualified. The issue is raised subtly by Dr. Hassan Turabi, leader of Sudan's Muslim Brotherhood, former Attorney General and current presidential adviser on foreign affairs:

> The *ulama* should have a role in this procedure [parliamentary deliberations or legislation] . . . not as the ultimate authority determining what the law is, but as advisors in the *shura* [assembly] to enlighten the Muslims as to the options which are open to them. What do I mean by *ulama*? The word historically has come to mean those versed in the legacy of religious (revealed) knowledge *(ilm)*. However, *ilm* does not mean that alone. It means anyone who knows anything well enough to relate it to God. Because all knowledge is divine and religious, a chemist, an engineer, an economist, or a jurist are all *ulama*. So the *ulama* in the broad sense, whether they are social or natural scientists, public opinion leaders, or philosophers, should enlighten society.[7]

Islamic Law

Since *Shariah* rule is the *sine qua non* of an Islamic state, law reform is a fundamental issue in the Muslim world today. During the colonial period, western inspired legal codes replaced much of Islamic law in most Muslim countries. The major exception was Muslim family law. Family law, which includes laws governing marriage, divorce, and inheritance, has always enjoyed pride of place within the *Shariah*, reflecting the centrality of the family in Muslim society. Throughout Islamic history, although caliphs and sultans might circumvent other areas, family law was the one area of the *Shariah* that remained enforced. Similarly, despite modernization of law during the eighteenth and nineteenth centuries, it was not until the post-World War I period that change in this sensitive area of Muslim life first occurred in Egypt and after World War II in many other Muslim countries. Even then, unlike previous legal reform which introduced modern legal codes, reform in Muslim family law was accomplished through selective changes in traditional Islamic law. The process of legal change did not reflect widespread societal change so much as the desires of modern elites. Governments imposed reforms from above through legislation. Though attempts were made to provide an Islamic justification or rationale, as we saw in our discussion of the debate surrounding Pakistan's *Muslim Family Laws Ordinance* of 1961, the religious establishment objected to this tampering with the law. It was an incursion into an area of Muslim life which religious scholars, not politicians or bureaucrats, had developed and controlled. They denounced reforms as a further erosion of the *Shariah* through an introduction of western, and thus un-Islamic, regulations and values by parliamentary bodies composed of non-experts.

Despite lack of religious and popular support, modernizing elites, who constituted a small percentage of the population, enacted family law legislation from Morocco and Tunisia to Indonesia. While some reform minded religious leaders supported change, the more conservative majority did not. Most were content to bide their time until a more favorable period when Islamic law might again be implemented.

Modern Islamic legal reform has been directly challenged by the contemporary resurgence of Islam. Khomeini's Islamic Republic has repudiated Iran's *Family Protection Act* and conservative *ulama* in Pakistan have called for the repeal of *the Muslim Family Laws Ordinance*. Demands for a return to the *Shariah* are common in many parts of the Muslim world. Countries as different culturally as in degree of modernization and westernization as Egypt, the Sudan, Libya, Iran, Pakistan and Mauritania have declared the *Shariah* as the source of law. As we saw in the previous chapter, many have enacted Islamic legislation enforcing traditional Islamic penalties for theft, alcohol consumption, fornication and adultery. Even more have curbed gambling, night clubs and cinemas. Even Muslim governments like the Sudan and Malaysia which have significant non-Muslim populations have introduced Islamic legislation.

The real issue in law, as in sociopolitical change in general, is the continuing question of how much change. How much change is required and how much departure from tradition is legitimate. Conservatives see no need; neo-traditionists who accept *ijtihad* in principle, reinterpret sparingly in practice. Islamic modernism created a climate for the acceptance and Islamic legitimacy of reform, but failed to provide an agreed upon method to render such change. As a result the resurgence of Islam in politics and society has been a process of revivalism rather than reconstruction through reinterpretation and reform. This orientation is especially evident in issues regarding women's status and the rights of non-Muslims in an Islamic state.

Women's Rights

All sane, male, adult Muslims are entitled to citizenship, to vote and to hold office in Muslim states. In recent decades, Muslim women in modernizing Muslims states have been given the right to vote and to serve in government. However, there is growing concern that contemporary Islamic revivalism will reverse these gains. The return of Islam has more often included a return to the veil with increased emphasis on the separation of sexes and the restriction of women's role in public.

Although the veiling and seclusion of women in Islam is not based upon revelation but rather is borrowed from non-Islamic sources, the practice has, like many others, become so embedded in tradition that it came to be viewed as integral to Islam. Thus, Mawlana Mawdudi could write:

> People have tried their very best to prove that the present form of Purdah was a custom in pre-Islamic communities, and that the Muslims adopted this custom of ignorance long after the time of the Holy Prophet. The question is: Where was the necessity of carrying out this historical research in the present of a clear verse of the *Quran*, the established practice of the time of the Holy Prophet, and the explanations given by the Companions and their pupils? Obviously this trouble was taken in order to justify the objective of life preva-

lent in the West. For without this, it was not possible to advocate the Western concepts of "progress" and "civilization" that have got deeply fixed in the minds."[8]

After the Iranian Revolution, women who had donned the veil as a symbol of opposition to the Shah and because of the anonymity it afforded in public anti-government demonstrations, were demonstrating in March 1979 against the compulsory wearing of the veil. Though the regulation was rescinded, veiling was made compulsory in government and public offices in the summer of 1980. In addition, coeducation has been banned. Women judges have lost their positions; women are barred from the judiciary and legal professions. Similarly, as noted in the previous chapter, Islamization in Pakistan has included implementation or advocacy of traditional Islamic measures regarding dress, the separation of the sexes, and legal rights.

Non-Muslim Minority Rights

The revivalist mood and orientation or resurgent Islam has also raised concerns about the status and rights of non-Muslims. In recent years tensions and clashes between Muslim and non-Muslim communities have increased: the Copts in Egypt, Bahai and Jews in Iran, Chinese in Malaysia, Christians in the Sudan.

Although Muslim-Copt relations in Egypt had been relatively calm, during the 1970s the situation slowly altered with a series of communal disturbances. As Egyptians were returning to their Arab-Muslim heritage, the Coptic community underwent a similar revival, returning to their Coptic monastic heritage under the strong leadership of their patriarch and bishops. The spirit of the renewal is summarized in the declaration: "All authentic service begins and ends with the Church. [9] Tensions mounted between two increasingly militant communities. The conflict escalated and took on a national dimension in 1977 when a bill was introduced in parliament to reinstate the death penalty, the traditional Islamic punishment, for apostasy from Islam. The draft legislation was directed at Copts who, unable to divorce their wives according to their own religious tradition, converted to Islam and then, after the divorce, returned to Christianity. Public protests against the proposed legislation were led by Pope

Shenouda III, the Coptic leader, and stopped only after Sadat's government declared its opposition to the bill. Tensions between Muslims and Copts continued with incidents involving church bombings, stonings, disruption of Christian celebrations and harrassment of Coptic students at universities in Cairo, Alexandria, and Asyut. In April 1980 Pope Shenouda called off public Easter celebrations in protest. In June 1981 a major Muslim-Christian confrontation in Cairo took eighteen lives and required riot police. For many Copts Islamic revivalism with its push for more *Shariah* law and a greater popular religious enthusiasm threatens their legal rights, religious freedom, and personal safety.

Muslim-Bahai confrontations, like Muslim-Ahmadiyya conflicts in Pakistan, have a long history. As discussed in Chapter 4, during the late 1950s the *ulama* had mounted a campaign against the Bahai when they considered apostates from Islam. The dome of Teheran Bahai center had been destroyed and the religious authorities tried unsuccessfully to persuade the government to pass legislation which would have suppressed the Bahai and dismissed its members from public office. After the Revolution of 1979 the Bahai again came under heavy attack: there religion has been declared illegal, property seized, and many have been imprisoned and executed. Although government officials insist that Bahai have been punished for political crimes and not religious reasons, the rights of non-Muslim minorities in an Islamic State remains an unresolved issue.

According to Islamic law, non-Muslims belonged to a second class of citizens, the protected, who constituted their own community. In exchange for their allegiance to the state and payment of a poll tax, they are free to practice their faith and are governed by their religious leaders and laws in matters of worship, private life, education, and family laws. Most Muslim states have granted equality of citizenship to all regardless of religious faith. However, the contemporary resurgence has resurrected pressures to reassert legally the often widespread, traditional attitude toward non-Muslims which, though changed by modern legislation, has remained operative in the minds and outlooks of many Muslims. This attitude is further reflected in the extension of new Islamic public laws such as the banning of alcohol to non-Muslim citizens in the Sudan, Iran, and Pakistan.

Non-Muslim minorities face another potential limitation in Islamic states. Given the state's Islamic ideology, many now ask: "Should non-Muslims be permitted to hold key government positions?" In most contemporary Muslim states, with the exception of the head of state or prime minister, citizens regardless of faith may hold office. This modern, liberal, secular approach is contested in many quarters today by those who argue that the state's Islamic ideology requires a commitment to Islam. This would preclude non-Muslims from holding key posts in government, the legislature, judiciary and military which formulate and implement the ideology of the state. Despite modern constitutional reforms, Islamic organizations like the Muslim Brotherhood and the Jamaat-i-Islami and many religious leaders have continued to teach and preach a restricted role for non-Muslims. In Pakistan, the 1953 anti-Ahmadiyah riots in the Punjab had been caused by Muslim demands that the Ahmadiyya be declared non-Muslims and that Zafrullah Khan and other Ahmadi government officials be dismissed from office. Similar demands and confrontations continued to occur for decades. In Iran, Islamic opponents criticized the Shah for permitting Bahai to occupy important government and military positions. In both Pakistan and Iran, the Islamic opposition eventually succeeded. Pakistan declared the Ahmadiyya a non-Muslim minority and the Islamic Republic of Iran has suppressed the Bahai faith.

In practice, in many Muslim countries non-Muslims have been absent from top posts in government. This is due not only to their limited numbers but also to government recognition and acceptance in practice of widely held traditional attitudes toward the place of non-Muslims in an Islamically oriented state. Finally, radical Islamic organizations today reject non-Muslim involvement in government both as contrary to Islam and, in the case of Christians, because of their past ties with Christian, European colonial powers and their continued association with the Christian West.

The tendency toward a strong executive, coupled with restrictions that flow from the Islamic ideology and commitment of the state, has led critics to speak of Islam's totalitarian or autocratic nature.[10] Islamic advocates themselves, though arguing that the principles of consultation and consensus indicate Islam's democratic spirit, do distinguish between Western and Islamic democracy since the political ideology of an Islamic state is God, not man centered. This orientation does include guidelines or limits. Sovereignty belongs to God alone; the *Shariah* is law. All additional or supplementary laws and state policies must be formulated within the limits of the *Shariah;* that is, they may not contradict it. Therefore, legislation is not based solely on the popular will. Actions proscribed by the *Quran* and *Sun-*

nah can never be introduced no matter how popular. To those who view such a political system as autocratic or totalitarian, Muhammad Natsir, a former Indonesian prime minister and leader of the Islamically oriented Masjumi Party, would respond: "Islam is not one hundred percent democracy, neither is it one hundred percent autocracy. Islam is . . . Islam."[11]

NATIONALISM AND PAN-ISLAM

The current reassertion of Islam in politics, with its emphasis on Islamic identity and ideology, has implications for international relations as well as domestic politics.[12] The agendas and actions of radical Islamic groups, combined with statements by many traditionalist leaders directly challenge existing political structures, in particular the nation state itself. Many condemn not only specific political regimes but also nationalism as un-Islamic. They reaffirm the pan-Islamic ideal of the unity and solidarity of a supranational community. The tendency of Islamic revivalism to look to the Medinan ideal and the traditional belief in a pan-Islamic caliphate would seem to reinforce this expectation. Both traditionalists like Mawdudi and Islamic modernists like Iqbal had repudiated nationalism as a tool used by colonialism, as Iqbal said, "to shatter the religious unity of Islam in pieces."[13] However, political realities and the passing of time have, in fact, tempered the normative ideal for many Muslims. Modern states even with their once artificially drawn boundaries, have become an accepted fact of life for most.

The trend in both self-styled Islamic states and in Muslim states is to supplement acceptance of the nation state with support for pan-Islamic cooperation, more than political unity. Saudi Arabia seeks and exercises influence over other Muslim states and Islamic organizations while guarding its boundaries and national identity jealously. Although Libya has had a number of abortive unions with other Arab countries, these were to foster Qaddafi's brand of Arab nationalism. Qaddafi's engagement in international Islamic politics has been aimed at enhancing his stature and promoting his revolutionary beliefs not in uniting the community. Khomeini, despite his pan-Islamic statements from time to time and support for revolutions in other states, is primarily an Iranian Shiite national leader. the Iran-

Iraq war, despite Khomeini's Islamic rhetoric, is more a result of Arab-Persian historic rivalry. Though some Sunni Muslim activists admire and wish to emulate Khomeini's in toppling a Western oriented and supported regime, few would unite under the leadership of a Shiite ayatollah. The traces of Sunni-Shii historical differences run deep. Pakistan, like many other Muslim states, willingly courts development assistance from Arab oil countries, but not political union.

Finally, major international Islamic organizations, like the Organization of the Islamic Conference, retain their nation state orientations while pursuing greater Islamic cooperation. Indeed, one could argue that, as has long been the case, there continues to be a great gap between normative vision and political reality. Whatever agreement Muslims muster in closing ranks when faced by threats from non-Islamic countries is in the nature of an opposition movement whose unity soon passes and is displaced by a return to national self interest. Neither the Palestine problem nor recent Islamic political issues like Afghanistan and Moro Muslim separatism in the Philippines have produced an effective transnational Islamic front. Lebanon, the Iran-Iraq war, and Libyan-Saudi differences counter the images of a united Islamic world.

The passing of time has brought about a gradual transformation in which the sharp dichotomy between a pan-Islamic supranational ideal and modern nationalism has been softened. Though the Western modern concept of nationalism and the nation state adopted by Muslim political elites seem initially Islamically unacceptable, the seeds for an Islamic adaptation or Islamization of nationalism are present. Objections to modern nationalism were primarily a reaction to the continuation of Western imperialism through the displacement of Islamic institutions by Western, secular models. For some, nationalism represented the further division and weakening of an already debilitated Islam before a militant, colonial West. It undermined Islamic solidarity and unity of the community, replaced God's sovereignty with ultimate allegiance to the nation, and its implicit secularism reduced Islam to the private sphere of life. Yet a case for a more Islamically acceptable nationalism can be made. Islamic modernists like Afghani, Rida and Iqbal had realized the necessity for some acceptance of nationalism while continuing to speak of pan-Islamism as the source of Muslim's most basic identity, solidarity and strength. For most, actual political union remained at best a future goal: "In order to create a really effective political unity of Islam, all Moslem countries must first become independent, and then in their totality they should range themselves under the caliph. Is such a thing possible at the present moment? If not today, one must wait." Muhammad Iqbal reflected a more pragmatic revolution which many Muslims today have come to espouse: "God is slowly bringing home to us the truth that Islam is neither Nationalism nor Imperialism but a League of nations which recognize artificial boundaries and racial distinctions of reference and not for restricting the social horizon of its members."[14]

Different language, tribal and ethnic groups have always existed under the umbrella of Islam. In the *Quran* God declares: "We . . . made you into tribes and nations" (49:13). Muslims have long recognized the political force and sociological reality of local or national identity as well as a more basic, universal supranational pan-Islamism. As Fazlur Rahman notes: "This 'nationalism', therefore, is not averse to a wider loyalty and, in face of a non-Muslim aggressor (as we have often witnessed during this and the preceding century) the two sentiments make an extraordinarily powerful liaison." However, for many Muslims such local or national group sentiment must be subservient to a broader Islamic identification and commitment. It must also eschew a secularism that would reduce Islam solely to the private sphere of life. The problem occurs when: "this primitive 'nationalism' comes to be formulated as a political ideology and is transformed into a nation-state claiming sovereignty and demanding paramount loyalty."[15]

Modern liberal nationalism is objectionable more for its Western, secular origin and orientation than its organization of Muslims in modern states. The general climate is one that seeks to reformulate or reconstruct the nation state rather than to replace it, to make it compatible with Islam. The process is one of Islamization.

ISLAMIZATION

Appeals to Islamization again underscore the revivalist vs. reformist differences among Islamic activists. The term is used by both traditionist and reformers to describe the method by which more Islamically oriented states are to be implemented. However, their use of the term differs. For traditionist, Islamization is primarily the reintroduction of past institutions and practices with little adaptation or change, e.g., veiling of women, separate facilities for men and women, traditional Islamic laws and punishments. Reformers understanding of Islamization is more faithful to history, recognizing the creative process by which Islam developed. They see themselves as continuing a dynamic process that is as old as Islam itself. Muslims borrowed freely from the cultures that they conquered, adopting and adapting political, legal, social, and economic practices as long as they were not contrary to Islam. Therefore Islamic systems of government and the *Shariah* were not simply based upon *Quranic* and prophetic guidelines, but those ideas, practices and institutions, from Arabia, Byzantium and the Sasanid empires, which did not contradict Islam and were adopted or modified. While traditionists take great pains to emphasize the total self sufficiency of Islam, reformers insist that while some past law and institutions may be valuable, new circumstances and problems require new solutions formulated in light of *Quranic* principles and through selective borrowing. This will result in "Islamic modernization" not simply wholesale Westernization.

Sadiq al-Mahdi, Oxford educated grandson of the Sudanese Mahdi, and a former Prime Minister, is representative of a reformist approach. He describes Islamization as separating Islam from the traditionist formulation of Islam, which is based upon a historically conditioned understanding of the *Quran* and Sunnah. The purpose of Islamization is to separate modernization from Westernization. The goal is to establish a synthesis which is both Islamic and modern.[16] Given this view of the historical conditioning of past Islamic practice, he can declare that there is no single Islamic political or economic system but historical applications of Islamic political and economic injunctions.[17] Similarly in law, "Even the most specific injunctions, injunctions which have been explicitly specified by holy texts are contingent upon conditions which permit a high degree of flexibility. Thus the canonical punishments known as *hudud* (e.g., amputation for theft) . . . are associated with elaborate conditions which allow circumstantial considerations to qualify their application."[18]

Another reformist understanding and approach to Islamization or Islamic sociopolitical change is taken by Hasan Turabi:

> Any form or procedures for the organization of public life that can ultimately be related to God and put to his service in the furtherance of the aims of Islamic government can be adopted unless expressly excluded by the *Shariah*. Once so received, it is an integral part of Islam whatever its source may be. Through the process of islamiza-

tion, the Muslims were always very open to expansion and change. Thus, Muslims can incorporate any experience whatever if not contrary to their ideals. Muslims took most of their bureaucratic forms from Roman and Persian models. Now much can be borrowed from contemporary sources, critically appreciated in the light of the *Shariah* values and norms, and integrated into the Islamic framework of government.[19]

The Islamic reformist task would require think tanks of Muslims to develop models appropriate to differing conditions of Muslim societies. It would also require experimentation. However, given the traditional orientation of the majority of religious leaders and the Muslim masses, the tendency of Islamic experiments has been fundamentalist, exemplifying the distinctly different visions and orientations of traditionists and modernists.

Education

The key to resolving the problem of tradition and change is education. Traditionally, education and religious scholarships have been the province of the *ulama*. In the past religious schools trained the leaders of society; however, as we have seen in the nineteenth and twentieth centuries, many Muslim countries introduced secular education alongside the ulama's traditional religious education. This existence of two parallel systems has actually caused a bifurcation of Muslim society. Despite some curriculum reform, the traditional system remains relatively isolated from the mainstream. Government funding priority has been given to secular schools which provide the training and academic degrees for prestige positions in a modern society (engineering, medicine, law, journalism). Graduates of religious schools, with predominantly traditional educations, continue to serve as religious leaders or teachers. However, they are often ill-prepared to understand and respond to the demands of modernity. Most are unable to provide created reinterpretation of traditional values, the religious leadership required in modern society. On the other hand, modern elites trained in Western oriented secular schools are well versed in modern disciplines but often lacking in the true awareness of their tradition necessary to make changes that are sensitive to the history and values of their cultural *milieu*. As a result,

Western models and presuppositions have been adopted by modern elites. Opportunities to render change reflecting some continuity with the past have gone unrecognized as well as unrealized. Thus, both traditional and modern elites have failed to provide a new synthesis that clearly provides some continuity between tradition and modernity.

Too often the Muslim world has seen, on the one hand, an elite minority convinced that they must forge ahead regardless of the obscurantist opposition of religious leaders and, on the other, a religious leadership suspicious of and resistant to an alien process—modernization—characterized as Western secularist, materialist, and godless. To date, the religious leadership is seen as an obstacle to change while the Western secular Muslims and their governments are conveniently blamed for the social and spiritual ills of society.

The bifurcation of education and the consequent training of two separate mind-sets or outlooks (traditional and modern) is clearly illustrated in the contemporary Islamic revival. The demand for more Islamically-oriented states requires a reexamination of political, social, legal, and economic institutions as well as of the principles and values which inform them. If secularists have denied the necessity, let alone feasibility, of undertaking such a task, the religious leadership has generally proven incapable of it. More conservative religious leaders tend to be fixated on the past. They view tradition not so much as a source of direction and inspiration but rather as the very map to be followed in all its details. Conservatives fail to distinguish between revealed, immutable principles and historically-conditioned laws and institutions that were the product of the early jurists' human reason.

Moreover, the hold of tradition is to be found in a more hidden form among those who advocate reinterpretation and change in principle but who, when pressed on specific changes, often reflect a "*taqlid* mentality," a tendency to follow past practice reflexively. Thus, when religious forces gain power (Iran) or influence (Pakistan) or become more vocal in calling for the Islamization of society (Egypt), the Islam many advocate and/or introduce is that of the past not simply in its revealed principles but often in its derivative prescriptions and forms.

Yet, we must avoid the too over-simplified distinction between intransigent traditionists and reform-minded modernists. The tendency of the more tradition bound to view their understanding of Islam as definitive has not precluded actual change. The very process of preserving and passing on a religious tradition requires interpretation and application thus contributing to Islamic change. The study, preaching and interpreting of Islam by individual religious scholars and teachers as well as it implementation occur in changing social contexts. Diversity results from the very fact that normative Islamic ideologies espoused in a particular time and place are themselves the product of both the carriers and the contexts.[20] Thus, for example, while all Muslims are bound by Islamic law, yet its overall unity incorporated a diversity in practice which reflects differences in juristic reasoning as well as the customs of the diverse geographic areas in which the law developed. So, too, today traditional, beliefs, practices and institutions take on new meanings in the teachings of even the most orthodox. The Ayatollah Khomeini's interpretation of government by the jurist and Zia ul-Haq's implementation of Islamic measures, though ostensibly justified as a "restoration," of past practice are viewed by others, both traditionists and modernists, as innovative interpretations. The application of Islamic history and values to modern concerns and deeds have produced fresh interpretations or extensions of Islamic concepts. Consultation and consensus are used to Islamically legitimate modern parliamentary forms of "Islamic" government. In the name of Islam, constitutionalism, democracy, parliamentary forms of government have been adopted and rendered Islamic. Muslims, drawing on a rich and diverse tradition, reconstruct an ideologized Islam: a systematic, integrated ideology encompassing politics, law, economics, education. As a result, most conservative, neo-traditionists and Islamic reformers accept "Islamized" versions of modern government and administrative organizations.

Differences in Islamic visions are accompanied by profound disagreements regarding the implementation of Islamic rule. For the vast majority of Muslims, the resurgence of Islam is a reassertion of cultural identity, formal religious observance, Sufi practice, family values, and morality. The establishment of an Islamic society is seen as requiring a personal and social transformation which is a prerequisite for true Islamic government. Effective change is to come from below through a gradual process of change brought about through the implementation of Islamic law. For the majority of Muslims, the process is one of social transformation through reform. Yet, an increasingly significant minority view the societies and governments in Muslim countries as so hopelessly corrupted that violent revolution is perceived as the only effective method. Their pagan (un-Islamic) societies and their leaders, who are regarded as no better than infidels, must be eradicated. Islamic revolutionaries reject not only the political, economic, and social status quo but also the religious establishment. In most countries the *ulama* and Sufi leaders are regarded as having been coopted by their governments. Therefore both established political and religious elites, in whose hands power is concentrated, must be overthrown. Power must be seized by a new Islamically committed leadership, the *Shariah* imposed, a deviant society restored to its divinely revealed path and thus governed Islamically. Radical revolutionary groups have remained relatively small in membership. However, the number of groups continues to proliferate. Though effective in political agitation, disruption, and assassination, they have generally not been successful in mass mobilization.

CONCLUSION

In many parts of the Islamic world, Muslims stand at a crossroads. Although independent states for several decades, the political legitimacy of many Muslim governments is far from established. To the extent that incumbent governments fail to satisfy the political and economic needs of their societies and to pursue a path of modernization which is sensitive to their Islamic heritage, they will remain in a precarious position in which stability is based more often than not on authoritarian rule and force. If Muslim governments strive to achieve a new synthesis providing some continuity between the demands of modernity and their Islamic tradition, then a broad range of possibilities stretch out before them—from a conservative, fundamentalist to a more reformist state and society. The possibilities are many. While the outcome indeed will vary from country to country depending upon political, social, and economic variables, the process itself is inevitable because it involves national identity as well as religious understanding and commitment.

$\mathcal{N}$otes

CHAPTER 1

1. Bernard Lewis, *The Arabs in History* (New York: Harper Torchbooks, 1966), p. 62.

2. Marshall S. G. Hodgson, *The Venture of Islam*, 3 vols. (Chicago: University of Chicago Press, 1974), 1:209.

3. Fred R. Donner, *The Early Islamic Conquests* (Princeton: Princeton University Press, 1981), p. 269.

4. Lewis, *Arabs*, pp. 67–68.

5. Reuben Levy, *The Social Structure of Islam* (Cambridge: Cambridge University Press, rpt. 1971), p. 299.

6. N. J. Coulson, *A History of Islamic Law* (Edinburgh: Edinburgh University Press, 1964), p. 28; Levy, *Social Structure*, p. 334.

7. See John L. Esposito "Law in Islam," *The Islamic Impact*, edited by Yvonne Y. Haddad (Syracuse: Syracuse University Press, 1984), Chapter 4; Coulson, *History of Islamic Law*, Chapter 3.

8. Hodgson, *Venture*, 1: p. 252.

9. Laura Veccia Vaglieri, "The Patriarchal and Ummayad Caliphates," *The Cambridge History of Islam*, edited by P. M. Holt, Ann K. S. Lambton, and Bernard Lewis (Cambridge: Cambridge University Press, 1978), 1A: 103.

10. Fazlur Rahman, *Islam*, 2nd ed. (Chicago: University of Chicago Press, 1979), p. 79.

11. See Yvonne Y. Haddad, ed., *The Islamic Impact* (Syracuse: Syracuse University Press, 1984).

12. Norman Itzkowitz, *Ottoman Empire and Islamic Tradition* (Chicago: University of Chicago Press, 1971), p. 3.

13. Erwin I. J. Rosenthal, *Political Thought in Medieval Islam* (Cambridge: Cambridge University Press, 1958), p. 27.

14. H. A. R. Gibb, *Studies in Islamic Civilizations* (Princeton: Princeton University Press, 1982), p. 45.

CHAPTER 2

1. See John O. Voll, "Renewal and Reform in Islamic *Tajdid* and *Islah,*" *Voices of Resurgent Islam,* edited by John L. Esposito (New York: Oxford University Press, 1983), Chapter 2.

2. Barbara Daly Metcalf, *Islamic Revival in British India, 1860–1900* (Princeton: Princeton University Press, 1982), pp. 56 ff.

3. *Ibid.*

4. See Aziz Ahmad, *Islamic Culture in the Indian Environment* (Oxford: Oxford University Press, 1964), pp. 209–17.

5. As quoted in John O. Voll, "The Sudanese Mahdi: Frontier Fundamentalist," *International Journal of Middle East Studies* 10 (1979): 159.

6. P. M. Holt and M. W. Daly, *The History of the Sudan: From the Coming of Islam to the Present,* 3rd ed. (Boulder, Co.: Westview, 1979), p. 95.

7. Hodgson, *Venture,* 3: 136.

8. *Ibid.,* p. 152.

9. See Metcalf, *Islamic Revival,* pp. 46 ff. for a discussion of differing interpretations of this *fatwa.*

10. The Hijrat movement in India had inspired more than 30,000 Muslims to migrate to Afghanistan, clogging the Khyber Pass. See Gail Minault, "Islam and Mass Politics: The India Ulama and the Khilafat Movement,"*Islam and Political Modernization,* edited by Donald E. Smith (New Haven: Yale University Press, 1974), pp. 178–79.

11. Albert Hourani, *Arabic Thought in the Liberal Age, 1798–1939* (Oxford: Oxford University Press, 1970), p. 41.

12. As quoted in *Ibid.,* p. 48.

13. *Ibid.,* p. 194, and Sylvia G. Haim ed., *Arab Nationalism* (Berkeley: University of California Press, 1976), p. 21 ff.

14. Daniel Crecelius, "The Course of Secularization in Modern Egypt," *Islam and Development: Religion and Sociopolitical Change,* edited by John L. Esposito (Syracuse: Syracuse University Press, 1980), p. 60.

15. For a fuller analysis of Afghani see Hourani, *Arabic Thought,* Chapter V, and Nikki R. Keddie, *Sayyid Jamal al-Din "al-Afghani": A Political Biography* (Berkeley: University of California Press, 1972).

16. Aziz Ahmad, *Islamic Modernism in India and Pakistan, 1857–1964* (London: Oxford University Press, 1967), p. 126.

17. Hourani, *Arabic Thought,* p. 109.

18. See Wilfred Cantwell Smith, *Islam in Modern History* (Princeton: Princeton University Press), pp. 47–51, and Hourani, *Arabic Thought,* Chapter V.

19. Also referred to as the Manar Movement, after its journal, *Al-Manar.*

20. *Ta'ammulat* (Cairo: Dar al Maarif, nd), pp. 68–69, translation in John J. Donohue and John L. Esposito, eds. *Islam in Transition: Muslim Perspectives* (New York: Oxford University Press, 1982), p. 70.

21. *Ibid.*, p. 71.

22. *Ara wa ahadith fi al-wataniyya wa al-qawmiyya* (Views and Speeches on Nationalism and Patriotism) (Cairo: Mahbaat al-risala, 1944), p. 20.

23. Fazlur Rahman, *Islam*, 2nd ed. (Chicago: University of Chicago Press, 1979), p. 227.

24. Aziz Ahmad, *Islamic Modernism*, p. 34.

25. As quoted in Rahman, *Islam*, p. 267.

26. "Lecture on Islam" Donohue and Esposito, eds., *Islam in Transition*, p. 42.

27. *Ibid.*

28. Chiragh Ali, *The Proposed Political, Legal and Social Reforms in the Ottoman Empire and Other Mohammedan States* (Bombay, 1883), p. 118.

CHAPTER 3

1. Hourani, *Arabic Thought*, p. 227.

2. *Al-Manar wal Azhar*, p. 179, in *ibid.*, p. 226.

3. Malcolm H. Kerr, *Islamic Reform: The Political and Legal Theories of Muhammad Abduh and Rashid Rida* (Berkeley: University of California Press, 1966), p. 190.

4. *Al-Manar*, 3 (Cairo, 1900), p. 172, 290–92.

5. *Ibid.* 33 (Cairo, 1933). Translated in Donohue and Esposito, eds., *Islam in Transition*, pp. 57–58.

6. Nadav Safran, *Egypt in Search of Identity* (Cambridge, Ma.: Harvard University Press, 1961), p. 83.

7. Rashid Rida, *al-Wahabiyyun wal Hijaz* (Cairo, 1926), p. 47.

8. Kerr, *Islamic Reform*, p. 187.

9. *Taamulat*, as translated in Donohue and Esposito, eds., *Islam in Transition*, pp. 70–71.

10. *Ibid.*, p. 71.

11. *Ibid.*, p. 72.

12. *The Future of Culture in Egypt*, excerpted in Donohue and Esposito, eds., *Islam in Transition*, p. 74. Subsequent citations to this volume will be carried in parentheses in the text.

13. *Al-Islam wa usul al-hukm* (Cairo, 1925); translated into French by L. Bercher, *L'Islam et les bases du pouvoir*, in *Revue de etudes islamiques* 7 (1933): 353–91; 8 (1934): 122–63; selections translated into English as "Islam and the Bases of Authority," in Donahue and Esposito, eds., *Islam in Transition*, pp. 29–37.

14. For summaries of Abd al-Raziq's position and the controversy see Hourani, *Arabic Thought*, pp. 183–92, and Leonard Binder, "Ali Abd al-Raziq and Islamic Liberalism," *Asian and African Studies* 16, no. 1 (March 1982): 31–58.

15. Muhammad Rashid Rida, *al-Khilafa* (Cairo: Manar Press 1923). French translation: *Le Califat dans la doctrine of Rashid Rida*, tr. by H. Laoust (Beirut, 1938).

16. Ali Abd al-Raziq, "Islam and the Bases of Authority," Donahue and Esposito, eds., *Islam in Transition*, p. 30. Subsequent citations will be carried in parentheses in the text.

17. *Our Decline and Its Causes* excerpted in Donohue and Esposito, eds., *Islam in Transition*, p. 61. Subsequent citations will be carried in parentheses in the text.

18. "Muslim Unity and Arab Unity," Donohue and Esposito, eds., *Islam in Transition*, p. 69. Subsequent citations will be carried in parentheses in the text.

19. Abd al-Rahman al-Bazzaz, "Islam and Arab Nationalism," Donohue and Esposito, eds., *Islam in Transition*, p. 84. Subsequent citations will be carried in parentheses in the text.

20. David and Marina Ottoway, *Algeria: The Politics of a Socialist Revolution* (Berkeley: University of California Press, 1970), p. 30.

21. David C. Gordon, *The Passage of French Algeria* (New York: Oxford University Press, 1966), p. 30 n. 58.

22. See L. Carl Brown, "The Islamic Reform Movement in North Africa," *Journal of Modern African Studies* 2 (1964): 55–63.

23. See Jamil Abun Nasr, "The Salafiyya Movement in The Religious Bases of the Moroccan Nationalist Movement," *St. Antony's Papers, No. 16, Middle Eastern Affairs No. 3*, edited by Albert Hourani (London: Chatto and Windus, 1963), pp. 90–105.

24. John Waterbury, *Commander of the Faithful: The Moroccan Political Elite* (New York: Columbia University Press, 1970), p. 48.

25. As cited in Gordon, *French Algeria*, p. 24.

26. *Ibid.*, p. 50.

27. Bernard Lewis, *The Middle East and the West* (New York: Harper Row, 1964), and Joseph Desparment, "Les Guides de l'opinion indigene en Algerie," *L'Afrique Francaise* (1933): 11–16.

28. Mangol Bayat, *Mysticism and Dissent* (Syracuse, New York: Syracuse University Press, 1982), pp. 15–20.

29. Ann K. Lambton, "Quis Custodiet Custodes?" *Studia Islamica* 6 (1956): 133.

30. See E. G. Browne, *Persian Revolution of 1905–1909* (Cambridge: Cambridge University Press, 1916) and Hamid Algar, *Religion and State in Iran 1785–1906* (Berkeley: University of California Press, 1969).

31. Nikki R. Keddie, *Iran: Religion, Politics and Society* (London: Frank Cass, 1980), p. 41.

32. See Ann K. S. Lambton, "Persia: The Breakdown of a Society," *The Cambridge History of Islam*, p. 465. See also "Persian Political Societies 1906–1911," *St. Antony Papers, No. 16, Middle East Affairs* 3 (London, 1963): 41–89.

33. Hamid Algar, "The Oppositional Role of the Ulama in Twentieth Century Iran," *Scholars, Saints, and Sufis*, edited by Nikki R. Keddie (Berkeley: University of California Press, 1972), p. 234.

34. Algar, *Religion and State*, p. 252.

35. Shaykh Fazl Allah Nuri, "Refutation of the Idea of Constitutionalism,"

translated by Abdul Hadi Hairi, *Middle Eastern Studies* 13, no. 3 (October 1977): 329; excerpt in Donohue and Esposito, eds., *Islam in Transition*, pp. 292–96.

36. Donohue and Esposito, eds., *Islam in Transition*, pp. 289, 288.

37. Gail Minault, "Islam and Mass Politics: The Indian Ulama and the Khilafat Movement," *Islam and Political Modernization*, edited by Smith, pp. 170–171.

38. Al-Hillal, vol. 1, no. 4, as quoted in M. U. Haq, *Muslim Politics in Modern India* (Lahore: Book Traders, n.d.), p. 83.

39. S. Abul Hasan Ali Nadwi, *Islam and the World* (Lahore: Muhammad Ashraf, rpt. 1967), p. 139.

40. Abul Ala Mawdudi, *Nationalism and Islam* (Lahore: Islamic Publications 1947), p. 10.

41. Aziz Ahmad, *Islamic Modernism*, p. 186.

42. *Struggle for Independence: 1857–1947* (Karachi: n.p., 1958), App. IV, p. 14.

43. *Ibid.*, p. 18.

44. Jamil-ud-din Ahmad, ed., *Speeches and Writings of Mr. Jinnah* (Lahore: Muhammad Ashraf, 1952), I:177.

CHAPTER 4

1. Stanford J. Shaw and Ezel Kural Shaw, *History of the Ottoman Empire and Modern Turkey*, Vol. 2 (Cambridge: Cambridge University Press, 1977), p. 375.

2. Don Peretz, *The Middle East Today*, 2nd ed. (New York: Holt, Rinehart and Winston, 1971), p. 160.

3. Howard A. Reed, "Attaturk's Secularizing Legacy and the Continuing Vitality of Islam in Republican Turkey," *Islam in the Contemporary World*, edited by Cyriac K. Pullapilly (Notre Dame, In.: Cross Roads Books, 1980), p. 331.

4. Kemal H. Karpat, "Modern Turkey," in *The Cambridge History of Islam*, pp. 562–63.

5. G. L. Lewis, "Turkey," in "Islam and Politics," *The Muslim World* 56, no. 4 (October 1966).

6. Serif Mardin, "Turkey," *Islam in the Political Process*, edited by James P. Piscatori (Cambridge: Cambridge University Press, 1983), p. 134.

7. *Ibid.*, p. 144.

8. For background information on the early history of Saudi Arabia see John L. Burckhardt, *Notes on the Bedouins and Wahabys* (London: Henry Colburn and Richard Bentley, 1831); H. St. John Philby, *Saudi Arabia* (Beirut: Librairie du Liban, 1968); and George S. Rentz, "Muhammad ibn Abd al-Wahhab (1703–1792) and the Beginnings of the Unitarian Empire in Arabia," Ph.D. dissertation (University of California at Berkeley, 1948).

9. James P. Piscatori, "The Formation of Saudi Arabia: A Case Study in the Utility of Transnationalism," *Ethnic Identities in a Transnational World*, edited by John Stack (Westport, Ct.: Greenwood Press, 1981). Also see "The Iraq-Najd Frontier" *Journal of the Central Asian Society* 17 (January 1930): 85–90, and George Rentz, "Wahhabism and

Saudi Arabia," *The Arabian Peninsula: Society and Politics,* edited by Derek Hopewood (London: George Allen and Unwin, 1972), pp. 64–65.

10. Ronald R. MacIntyre, "Saudi Arabia," *The Politics of Islamic Reassertion,* edited by Mohammed Ayoob (New York: St. Martin's Press, 1981), p. 13.

11. James P. Piscatori, "The Roles of Islam in Saudi Arabia's Political Development," *Islam and Development,* edited by John L. Esposito (Syracuse: Syracuse University Press, 1980), p. 134.

12. As quoted in Yvonne Y. Haddad, "The Arab-Israeli Wars, Nasserism and Islamic Identity," *Islam and Development,* edited by John L. Esposito (Syracuse: Syracuse University Press, 1980), p. 239, n. 23.

13. *The Islamic Pact: An Obvious Trick* (Cairo: Supreme Council of Islamic Affairs, n.d.), p. 50.

14. David Holden and Richard Johns, *The House of Saud* (New York: Holt, Rinehart and Winston, 1981), p. 512.

15. The following analysis is based upon my "Pakistan: Quest for Islamic Identity," *Islam and Development,* edited by John L. Esposito (Syracuse: Syracuse University Press, 1980), Chapter 8.

16. Leonard Binder, *Religion and Politics in Pakistan* (Berkeley: University of California Press, 1961); E. I. J. Rosenthal, *Islam in the Modern National State* (Cambridge: Cambridge University Press, 1965), pp. 181–281; Fazlur Rahman, "Islam and the Constitutional Problems of Pakistan," *Studia Islamica* 32, no. 4 (December 1970): 275–87.

17. *Constitution of the Islamic Republic of Pakistan* (Karachi: Government of Pakistan, 1956), Part I, Art. 1. Subsequent citations form this document are in parentheses in the text.

18. *Report of the Court of Inquiry Constituted under Punjab Act II of 1954 to Inquire into the Disturbances of 1953* (Lahore: n.p. 1954), pp. 231 ff.

19. As quoted in M. Ahmed, "Islamic Aspects of the New Constitution of Pakistan," *Islamic Studies* 2 (June 1963): 262.

20. *Ibid.,* Appendix C, p. 283.

21. *Report of the Commission on Marriage and Family Laws* as excerpted in Donohue and Esposito, eds., *Islam in Transition,* pp. 201–202. Subsequent citations given in text.

22. For a detailed analysis see John L. Esposito, *Women in Muslim Family Law* (Syracuse: Syracuse University Press, 1982), pp. 83–101.

23. Sharough Akhavi, *Religion and Politics in Contemporary Iran* (Albany: SUNY Press, 1980), pp. 42 ff.

24. *Ibid.,* p. 38.

25. Ervand Abrahamian, *Iran Between Two Revolutions* (Princeton: Princeton University Press, 1982), p. 259.

26. Sharough Akhavi, "Shii Social Thought and Praxis in Recent Iranian History," *Islam in the Contemporary World,* edited by Cyriac K. Pullapilly (Notre Dame: Cross Roads Books, 1980), p. 183.

27. Hamid Algar, "The Oppositional Role of the Ulama in Twentieth-Century Iran," *Scholars, Saints, and Sufis,* edited by Nikki R. Keddie (Berkeley: University of California Press, 1972), p. 247.

28. *Ibid.*, p. 247.

29. In Fayez Sayegh, "The Theoretical Structure of Nasser's Arab Socialism," *St. Antony Papers*, No. 17, Middle Eastern Affairs, 4 (London: Oxford University Press, 1965), p. 13.

30. Gamal Abd al-Nasser, *Egypt's Liberation: The Philosophy of the Revolution* (Washington, D.C.: Public Affairs Press, 1955), pp. 86–87.

31. Morroe Berger, *Islam in Egypt: Social and Political Aspects of Popular Religion* (Cambridge: Cambridge University Press, 1970), p. 47.

32. Shaykh Mahmud Shaltut, "Al-Ishtirakiyya wal-Islam" (Socialism and Islam), Donohue and Esposito, eds., *Islam in Transition*, p. 99.

33. *Ibid.*, p. 101.

34. *Ibid.*, p. 102.

35. See, for example, a *fatwa* on land reform in *ibid.*, pp. 197–99.

36. Daniel C. Crecelius, p. 234 #30.

37. As quoted in Guenter Lewy, "Naseerism and Islam," *Religion and Political Modernization*, edited by Donald E. Smith (New Haven: Yale University Press, 1974), p. 270–71.

38. As quoted in Christina Phelps Harris, *Nationalism and Revolution in Egypt* (The Hague: Mouton, 1964), p. 144.

39. *Ibid.*, p. 145.

40. Richard P. Mitchell, *The Society of the Muslim Brothers* (London: Oxford University Press, 1969), p. 9, 14.

41. For my interpretation of Sayyid Qutb, I am especially indebted to Yvonne Y. Haddad, in particular her "Sayyid Qutb: Ideologue of the Islamic Revival," *Voices of Resurgent Islam*, edited by John L. Esposito (New York: Oxford University Press, 1983), Chapter 6, and "The Quranic Justification for an Islamic Revolution. The View of Sayyid Qutb," *The Middle East Journal* 37, no. 1 (Winter 1983): 14–79.

42. Muhammad al-Ghazzali, *Our Beginning in Wisdom* (Min Huna Nalam), translated by Ismail R. al-Faruqi (Washington, D.C.: American Council of Learned Societies, 1953), p. 54.

43. Sayyid Qutb, quoted in Haddad, "Sayyid Qutb," *Voices of Resurgent Islam*, edited by Esposito, p. 73.

44. *Ibid.*, p. 74.

45. *Ibid.*, p. 70.

46. Hasan al-Banna, "Min al-qadim: Ittijah al-nahda al-jadida fi al-ulam al-Islami," translated excerpts in Donohue and Esposito, eds., *Islam in Transition*, p. 78.

47. Nadav Safran, *Egypt in Search of Political Community* (Cambridge, Ma.: Harvard University Press, 1961), p. 209.

48. Sayyid Qutb, *Khasais*, in Haddad, "Sayyid Qutb," *Voices of Resurgent Islam*, edited by Esposito, p. 74.

49. *Ibid.*, p. 76.

50. *Ibid.*

51. *Ibid.*, p. 71.

52. Hasan Ismail Hudaybi, *al-Musawwar*, as quoted in Mitchell, *Muslim Brothers*, p. 258.

53. For an introduction to Mawdudi's development and thought see Charles J. Adams, "Mawdudi and the Islamic State," *Voices of Resurgent Islam*, edited by John L. Esposito (New York: Oxford University Press, 1983), Chapter 5, and Adams, "The Ideology of Mawlana Mawdudi," *South Asian Politics and Religion*, edited by Donald E. Smith (Princeton: Princeton University Press, 1966), Chapter 7.

54. Abul Ala Mawdudi, *Tarjuman al-Quran* (November–December 1938), p. 48.

55. Abul Ala Mawdudi, "Political Theory of Islam," *The Islamic Law and Constitution*, edited by Khurshid Ahmad (Lahore: Islamic Publications, 1977), 6th ed., p. 130.

56. Abul Ala Mawdudi, "The Islamic Law," *ibid.*, p. 5.

57. Adams, "Mawdudi and the Islamic State," *ibid.*, p. 116.

58. Abul Ala Mawdudi, "First Principles of the Islamic State," *The Islamic Law*, edited by Khurshid Ahmad, p. 23.

59. *Ibid.*

60. Mawdudi, "Political Theory of Islam," p. 159. Subsequent citations noted in text.

61. Mawdudi, "First Principles of the Islamic State," p. 214.

62. Mawdudi, "The Islamic Law," p. 66.

CHAPTER 5

1. *Islamic Resurgence in the Arab World*, edited by Ali E. Hillal Dessouki (New York: Praeger 1982). Mohammed Ayoob, ed., *The Politics of Islamic Reassertion* (New York: St. Martin's Press, 1980), and Edward Mortimer, *Faith and Power* (New York: Random House, 1982), and John O. Voll, *Islam: Continuity and Change in the Modern World* (Boulder, Co.: Westview, 1982). For case studies see John L. Esposito, ed., *Islam and Development* (Syracuse: Syracuse University Press, 1980), and John L. Esposito, ed., *Voices of Resurgent Islam* (New York: Oxford University Press, 1983).

2. See John J. Donohue, "Islam and the Search for Arab Identity," *Voices of Resurgent Islam*, edited by John L. Esposito (New York: Oxford University Press, 1983), Chapter 3, and Ali Merad, "The Ideolozisation of Islam in the Contemporary Muslim World," *Islam and Power*, edited by A. S. Cudsi and Ali E. Hillal Dessouki (Baltimore: Johns Hopkins University Press), Chapter 3.

3. Donohue, "Islam and the Search for Arab Identity," *Voices of Resurgent Islam*, edited by Esposito, Chapter 3.

4. For Qaddafi's use of Islam, see Lisa Anderson, "Qaddafi's Islam," *Voices of Resurgent Islam*, edited by John L. Esposito (New York: Oxford University Press, 1983), and Lisa Anderson, "Religion and Politics in Libya," *Journal of Arab Affairs* 1, no. 1 (Autumn 1981), Ann Mayer, "Islamic Resurgence or a New Prophethood: The Role of

Islam in Qadhdhafi's Ideology," *The Arab World*, edited by Ali E. Hilal Dessouki (New York: Praeger, 1982).

5. Lisa Anderson, "Qaddafi's Islam," p. 136.

6. "The Libyan Revolution in the Words of Its Leaders," *The Middle East Journal* 24 (1970): 208.

7. Muammar al-Qadhdhafi, *The Green Book*, excerpted as "The Third Way," Donohue and Esposito, eds., *Islam in Transition* (New York: Oxford University Press, 1982), p. 103.

8. *Ibid.*

9. *Ibid.*, p. 105.

10. *Ibid.*, p. 104.

11. For a useful summary of Qaddafi's socialist program see Raymond H. Habiby, "Muammar Qaddafi's New Islamic Scientific Socialist Society," *Religion and Politics in the Middle East*, edited by Michael Curtis (Boulder, Co.: Westview, 1980), Chapter 18, p. 247.

12. Anderson, "Qaddafi's Islam" p. 143.

13. William L. Richter, "The Political Dynamics of Islamic Resurgence in Pakistan," *Asian Survey* 19, no. 6 (June 1979): 547–57.

14. See, for example, Waheed-uz-Zaman, ed., *The Quest for Identity* (Islamabad: Islamabad University Press, 1973).

15. Philip E. Jones, "Islam and Politics Under Ayub and Bhutto: A Comparative Analysis," unpublished manuscript (Madison, Wi.: Seventh Conference on South Asia, November 1978).

16. "News from the Country," *al-Mushir* (Rawalpindi) 23, no. 3 (1981): 115.

17. *Zakat and Ushr Ordinances, 1980* (Islamabad: Government of Pakistan, 1980), p. 33.

18. *Introduction of Islamic Laws: Address to the Nation by President General Zia-ul-Haq* (Islamabad: Government Printing Office, 1979), p. 16.

19. For an extended treatment of Muslim family law reform in Pakistan and its methodological problems, see John L. Esposito, *Women in Muslim Family Law* (Syracuse: Syracuse University Press, 1982), especially Chapter 3.

20. See, for example, the comments of Mawlana Ahmad Noorani, President of the JUP, in *Dawn*, October 2, 1979, p. 3.

21. The author wishes to acknowledge his debt to Mumtaz Ahmad for this information.

22. Ervand Abrahamian, *Iran: Between Two Revolutions* (Princeton: Princeton University Press, 1982), p. 447.

23. *Ibid.*, p. 448.

24. Jalal-Al-e-Ahmad, *Garbzadegi* [Weststruckness], translated by John Green and Ahmad Alizadeh (Lexington, Ky.: Mazda Press, 1982), p. 11.

25. *Ibid.*, p. 59.

26. Ali Shariati, as quoted in *On the Sociology of Islam* (Berkeley: Mizan Press, 1979), p. 17. For Shariati's life and thought, see Abdul Aziz Sachedina, "Ali Shariati: Ideologue of the Iranian Revolution," *Voices of Resurgent Islam*, edited by John L. Esposito.

27. Ervand Abrahamian, "Ali Shariati: Ideologue of the Iranian Revolution," *MERIP Reports* 102 (January 1982), p. 25.

28. Dr. Ali Shariati, *Man and Islam* (Houston, Tx.: Free Islamic Lit., 1980), p. xi.

29. As quoted in Shariati *On the Sociology of Islam.*

30. Ali Shariati, *Intizar Madhab-i-itiraz,* translated by Mangol Bayat, in Donohue and Esposito, eds., *Islam in Transition,* p. 297.

31. As quoted in Abrahamian, *MERIP,* p. 26.

32. Donohue and Esposito, eds., *Islam in Transition.*

33. "Message to the Pilgrims," *Islam and Revolution: Writings and Declarations of Imam Khomeini* translated by Hamid Algar (Berkeley: Mizan Press, 1981), p. 195.

34. *Ibid.*

35. *Islamic Government, ibid.,* p. 127.

36. Abrahamian, *Iran,* p. 505.

37. *Ibid.*

38. *Ibid.*

39. *Islamic Government,* in Khomeini, *Islam and Revolution,* translated by Algar, p. 43.

40. For this discussion of clerical control of Iran's government, I am especially indebted to Shahrough Akhavi's "Islam and Public Life in Iran" presented at the Asia Society's "Islam and Public Life in Asia Conference," March 25–27, 1984, Airlie, Virginia.

41. Hasan Hanafi, "The Relevance of the Islamic Alternative in Egypt," *Arab Studies Quarterly* 4, nos. 1 and 2 (Spring 1982,) p. 63.

42. As cited in Fadwa El Guindi, "Religious Revival and Islamic Survival in Egypt," *Middle East Insight* 2, no. 1 (November–December 1981).

43. Saad Eddin Ibrahim, "Islamic Militancy As a Social Movement: The Case of Two Groups in Egypt," *Islamic Resurgence in the Arab World,* edited by Ali E. Hillal Dessouki (New York: Praeger, 1982), p. 118.

44. Saad Eddin Ibrahim, "Egypt's Islamic Militants," *MERIP Reports* 103 (February 1982): 11.

45. Fadwa El Guindi, "The Killing of Sadat and After: A Current Assessment of Egypt's Islamic Movement," *Middle East Insight* 2, no. 5 (January–February 1982): 21.

46. *Middle East International* 95 (March 16, 1979), p. 2.

47. Louis J. Cantori, "Religion and Politics in Egypt," *Religion and Politics in the Middle East,* edited by Michael Curtis (Boulder, Co.: Westview, 1980), p. 86.

48. Fadwa El Guindi, p. 23.

49. I am indebted in my analysis to a prepublication copy of Hamied N. Ansari's "The Islamic Militants in Egyptian Politics," *International Journal of Middle East Studies* 16, no. 1 (March 1984): 123–44.

50. *Ibid.,* p. 134.

CHAPTER 6

1. For examples of the conventional wisdom see Manfred Halpern, *The Politics of Social Change in the Middle East and North Africa* (Princeton, N.J.: Princeton University Press, 1963), and Gabriel Almond and G. Bingham Powell, *Comparative Politics: A Comparative Approach* (Boston: Little, Brown, 1966), and Donald E. Smith, *Religion and Political Development* (Boston: Little, Brown, 1970).

2. Michael C. Hudson, "Islam and Political Development, *Islam and Development*, edited by John L. Esposito (Syracuse: Syracuse University Press, 1980), esp. pp. 7 ff.

3. Daniel Crecelius, "The Path of Secularization in Egypt," *ibid.*, pp. 68–70.

4. Abul Ala Mawdudi, *A Short History of the Revivalist Movement in Islam* (Lahore: Islamic Publications, 1973), p. 33.

5. *Report of the Court of Inquiry Constituted under Punjab Act II of 1954, to Inquire into Punjab Disturbances of 1953*, p. 218. See also Muhammad Munir *From Jinnah to Zia* (Lahore: Vanguard Books, n.d.), especially pp. 38–73.

6. Hassan al-Turabi, "The Islamic State," *Voices of Resurgent Islam*, edited by John L. Esposito (New York: Oxford University Press, 1983), p. 248.

7. *Ibid.*, p. 245.

8. S. Abul A. la Mawdudi, *Purdah and the Status of Woman in Islam*, translated and edited by al-Ashari (Lahore: Islamic Publications, 1972), pp. 200–201.

9. *Matta al-Maskin*, as quoted in "The Coptic-Muslim Conflict in Egypt. Modernization of Society and Religious Renovation," *CEMAM Reports* (Beirut: Center for the Study of the Modern Arab World, 1976), p. 34.

10. As Mangol Bayat concludes in "Islam in Pahlavi and Post-Phalavi Iran: A Cultural Revolution?" *Islam and Development*, edited by John L. Esposito (Syracuse: Syracuse University Press, 1980), p. 106.

11. Deliar Noer, *The Modernist Muslim Movement in Indonesia* (London: Oxford University Press, 1973), pp. 287–88.

12. See James P. Piscatori, "Islam in the International Order," *The Expansion of International Societies*, edited by Hedley Bull (Oxford: Oxford University Press, 1984).

13. Muhammad Iqbal in *Speeches and Statements of Iqbal*, edited by Shamloo (Lahore: Muhammad Ashraf, 1948), p. 224.

14. Muhammad Iqbal, *The Reconstruction of Religious Thought in Islam* (Lahore: Muhammad Ashraf, 1968), p. 159.

15. Fazlur Rahman, *Islam*, 2nd ed. (Chicago: University of Chicago Press, 1979), p. 227.

16. Sadiq al-Mahdi, "Islam—Society and Change," *Voices of Resurgent Islam*, edited by John L. Esposito (New York: Oxford University Press, 1983), p. 239.

17. *Ibid.*, pp. 236–37.

18. *Ibid.*, p. 238.

19. Hassan al-Turabi, "The Islamic State," pp. 249–25.

20. Dale F. Eickelman, "The Study of Islam in Local Contexts," *Asian Studies* 17 (1982): 12.

Bibliography

Abrahamian, Ervand. *Iran Between Two Revolutions.* Princeton, N.J.: Princeton University Press, 1982.

Ahmad, Aziz. *Islamic Modernism in India and Pakistan, 1857–1964.* Oxford: Oxford University Press, 1967.

———. *Studies in Islamic Culture in the Indian Environment.* Oxford: Oxford University Press, 1964.

Ajami, Fouad. *The Arab Predicament.* New York: Cambridge University Press, 1982.

Akhavi, Sharough. *Religion and Politics in Contemporary Iran.* Albany, N.Y.: SUNY Press, 1980.

Algar, Hamid, tr. *Islam and Revolution: Writings and Declarations of Imam Khomeini.* Berkeley, Ca.: Mizan Press, 1981.

Algar, Hamid. *Religion and State in Iran 1785–1906.* Berkeley, Ca.: University of California Press, 1969.

Anderson, James Norman. *Islamic Law in the Modern World.* Westport, Ct.: Greenwood Press, 1976.

Ayoob, Mohammed, ed. *The Politics of Islamic Reassertion.* New York: St. Martin's, 1981.

Bayat, Mangol. *Mysticism and Dissent.* Syracuse, N.Y.: Syracuse University Press, 1982.

Berger, Morroe. *Islam in Egypt: Social and Political Aspects of Popular Religion.* Cambridge: Cambridge University Press, 1970.

Chelkowski, Peter J., ed. *Taziyeh: Ritual and Drama in Iran.* New York: New York University Press, 1979.

253

Coulson, Noel. *A History of Islamic Law.* New York: Columbia University Press, 1978.

————. *Conflicts and Tensions in Islamic Jurisprudence.* Chicago, Il.: University of Chicago Press, 1969.

Curtis, Michael, ed. *Religion and Politics in the Middle East.* Boulder, Co.: Westview, 1982.

Dessouki, Ali E. Hillal, ed. *Islamic Resurgence in the Arab World.* New York: Praeger, 1982.

Donner, Fred R. *The Early Islamic Conquests.* Princeton, N.J.: Princeton University Press, 1981.

Donohue, John J., and Esposito, John L., eds. *Islam in Transition: Muslim Perspectives.* New York: Oxford University Press, 1982.

Eickelman, Dale F. *The Middle East.* Englewood Cliffs, N.J.: Prentice-Hall, 1981.

Enayat, Hamid. *Modern Islamic Political Thought.* Austin, Tx.: University of Texas Press, 1982.

Esposito, John L., ed. *Islam and Development.* Syracuse, N.Y.: Syracuse University Press, 1980.

Esposito, John L., ed. *Voices of Resurgent Islam.* New York: Oxford University Press, 1983.

Esposito, John L. *Women in Muslim Family Law.* Syracuse, N.Y.: Syracuse University Press, 1982.

Evans-Pritchard, E. E. *The Sanusi of Cyrenaica.* New York: Oxford University Press, 1949.

Fernea, Elizabeth, and Bezirgan, Basima, eds. *Middle Eastern Muslim Women Speak.* Austin, Tx.: University of Texas Press, 1977.

Fischer, Michael M. J. *Iran: From Religious Discourse to Revolution.* Cambridge, Ma.: Harvard University Press, 1980.

Gellner, Ernest. *Muslim Society.* New York: Cambridge University Press, 1981.

Gibb, Hamilton A. R. *Mohammedanism: An Historical Survey,* 2nd ed. New York: Oxford University Press, 1953.

————. *Studies on the Civilization of Islam.* Princeton, N.J.: Princeton University Press, 1982.

————, and Harold Bowen *Islamic Society and the West.* Oxford: Oxford University Press, 1960.

Gilsenan, Michael. *Recognizing Islam: Religion and Society in the Modern Arab World.* New York: Pantheon, 1983.

Goldschmidt, Arthur, Jr. *A Concise History of the Middle East,* 2nd ed. Boulder, Co.: Westview, 1983.

Haddad, Yvonne Y. *Contemporary Islam and the Challenge of History.* Albany, N.Y.: State University of New York Press, 1982.

————, ed. *The Islamic Impact.* Syracuse, N.Y.: Syracuse University Press, 1984.

Haim, Sylvia G., ed. *Arab Nationalism.* Berkeley, Ca.: University of California Press, 1976.

Hodgson, Marshall S. G. *The Venture of Islam,* 3 vols. Chicago, Il.: University of Chicago Press, 1974.

Holt, P. M., and Daly, M. W. *The History of the Sudan: From the Coming of Islam to the Present,* 3rd ed. Boulder, Co.: Westview, 1979.

Holt, P. M., Lambton, Ann K. S., and Lewis, Bernard, eds. *The Cambridge History of Islam.* New York: Cambridge University Press, 1977–78.

Hourani, Albert. *Arabic Thought in the Liberal Age 1798–1939.* New York: Cambridge University Press, 1983.

Hudson, Michael C. *Arab Politics: The Search for Legitimacy.* New Haven, Ct.: Yale University Press, 1977.

Iqbal, Muhammad. *The Reconstruction of Religious Thought in Islam.* Lahore: Muhammad Ashraf, 1968.

Itkowitz, Norman. *Ottoman Empire and Islamic Tradition.* Chicago, Il.: University of Chicago Press, 1980.

Jafri, J. H. M. *The Origins and Early Development of Shii Islam.* London: Longmans, 1979.

Johnson, Nels. *Islam and the Politics of Meaning in Palestinian Nationalism.* London: Kegan Paul, 1982.

Keddie, Nikki R. *Iran: Religion, Politics and Society.* London: Frank Cass, 1980.

————. *Roots of Revolution: An Interpretive History of Modern Iran.* New Haven, Ct.: Yale University Press, 1981.

————. *Sayyid Jamal al-Din "al-Afghani": A Political Biography.* Berkeley, Ca.: University of California Press, 1972.

————. ed. *Scholars, Saints, and Sufis.* Berkeley, Ca.: University of California Press, 1972.

Keddie, Nikki, and Beck, Lois, eds. *Women in the Muslim World.* Cambridge, Ma.: Harvard University Press, 1978.

Kerr, Malcolm H. *Islamic Reform: The Political and Legal Theories of Muhammad Abduh and Rashid Rida.* Berkeley, Ca.: University of California Press, 1966.

Lambton, Ann K. S. *State and Government in Medieval Islam.* Oxford: Oxford University Press, 1981.

Lapidus, Ira M. *Muslim Cities in the Later Middle Ages.* Cambridge, Ma.: Harvard University Press, 1967.

Lassner, Jacob. *The Shaping of Abbasid Rule.* Princeton, N.J.: Princeton University Press, 1980.

Levy, Reuben. *The Social Structure of Islam.* Cambridge: Cambridge University Press, rpt. 1971.

Lewis, Bernard. *The Middle East and the West.* New York: Harper and Row, 1968.

———. *The Emergence of Modern Turkey,* 2nd ed. New York: Oxford University Press, 1968.

———. *The Muslim Discovery of Europe.* New York: Horton, 1982.

———. *The Arabs in History.* New York: Harper, 1966.

Lisbesny, Herbert. *The Law of the Near and Middle East.* Albany, N.Y.: State University of New York Press, 1975.

Malik, Hafeez. *Sir Sayyid Ahmad Khan and Muslim Modernism in India and Pakistan.* New York: Columbia University Press, 1980.

Martin, B. G. *Muslim Brotherhoods in Nineteenth Century Africa.* New York: Cambridge University Press, 1977.

Metcalf, Barbara Daly. *Islamic Revival in British India, 1860–1900.* Princeton, N.J.: Princeton University Press, 1982.

Minai, Naila. *Women in Islam.* New York: Putnam, 1981.

Minault, Gail. *The Khilafat Movement.* New York: Columbia University Press, 1982.

Mitchell, Richard. *The Society of Muslim Brothers.* New York: Oxford University Press, 1969.

Mortimer, Edward. *Faith and Power.* New York: Random House, 1982.

Mottahedeh, Roy P. *Loyalty and Leadership in an Early Islamic Society.* Princeton, N.J.: Princeton University Press, 1980.

Nashat, Guity, ed. *Women and Revolution in Iran.* Boulder, Co.: Westview, 1983.

Peters, Francis E. *Allah's Commonwealth.* New York: Simon and Schuster, 1974.

Pipes, Daniel. *In the Path of God.* New York: Basic Books, 1983.

Polk, William R. and Chamber, Richard L., eds. *Beginnings of Modernization in the Middle East: The Nineteenth Century.* Chicago, Il.: University of Chicago Press, 1968.

Rahman, Fazlur. *Islam and Modernity.* Chicago, Il.: University of Chicago Press, 1982.

———. *Islam,* 2nd ed. Chicago, Il.: University of Chicago Press, 1979.

Rodinson, Maxime. *Muhammad.* New York: Pantheon, 1980.

Rosenthal, Erwin I. J. *Political Thought in Medieval Islam.* Cambridge: Cambridge University Press, 1958.

Safran, Nadav. *Egypt in Search of Political Community.* Cambridge, Ma.: Harvard University Press, 1961.

Saunder, J. J. *The History of the Mongol Conquests.* Boston, Ma.: Routledge and Kegan Paul, 1971.

Savory, Roger M. *Iran under the Safavids.* New York: Cambridge University Press, 1980.

Schacht, Joseph. *An Introduction to Islamic Law.* New York: Oxford University Press, 1964.

Shariati, Ali. *On the Sociology of Islam.* Berkeley, Ca.: Mizan Press, 1979.

Shaw, Stanford J., and Shaw, Ezel Kural. *History of the Ottoman Empire and Modern Turkey,* vol. 2. Cambridge: Cambridge University Press, 1977.

Siddiqui, Kalim, ed. *Issues in the Islamic Movement.* London: The Open Press, 1983.

Smith, Donald E. *South Asian Politics and Religion.* Princeton, N.J.: Princeton University Press, 1966.

————, ed. *Religion and Political Modernization.* New Haven, Ct.: Yale University Press, 1974.

Smith, Jane, ed. *Women in Contemporary Muslim Societies.* Lewisburg, Pa.: Bucknell University Press, 1980.

Smith, Wilfred Cantwell. *Islam in Modern History.* Princeton, N.J.: Princeton University Press, 1957.

Al-Tabataba'i, Muhammad H. *Shi'ite Islam,* 2nd ed. Albany, N.Y.: State University of New York Press, 1979.

Trimingham, J. Spencer. *The Sufi Orders in Islam.* New York: Oxford University Press, 1973.

Vaglieri, Laura Veccia. "The Patriarchal and Ummayad Caliphates," in *The Cambridge History of Islam,* edited by P. M. Holt, Ann K. S. Lambton, and Bernard Lewis. Cambridge: Cambridge University Press, 1978.

Voll, John Obert. *Islam, Continuity and Change in the Modern World.* Boulder, Co.: Westview, 1982.

Von Grunebaum, Gustave E. *Classical Islam.* Winchester, Ma.: Allen and Unwin, 1970.

Waterbury, John. *Commander of the Faithful: The Moroccan Political Elite.* New York: Columbia University Press, 1970.

Watt, W. Montgomery. *Islamic Political Thought.* New York: Columbia University Press, 1980.

————. *The Formative Period of Islamic Thought.* New York: Columbia University Press, 1973.

————. *Muhammad: Prophet and Statesman.* New York: Oxford University Press, 1974.

Index

Haddad, Yvonne, 240, 245–46
Hadith, 9
Halpern, Manfred, 250
Hamdard, 87
Hanafi, Hasan, 198, 249
Hanafi law, 19, 34
Harris, Christina Phelps, 246
al-Hasa, 101
Hasan, 7
Hashimite clan, 3
Hijaz, 89, 101
al-Hikma, 70
al-Hillah, 86, 87, 244
Hodgson, Marshall S. G., 40, 240, 241
Holden, David, 245
Holt, P. M., 241
Holy War. See jihad
Holy War Society (Jamaat-al-Jihan), 202
Holy War Society, The (al-Jihad), 134
Homa, leveling of, 211
Hopewood, Derek, 245
Hourani, Albert, 241, 242
House of Saud, 109
Hudabiyya, 36
Huda Sha-arawi, Madame, 50
Hudaybi, Hasan Ismail, 247
Hudson, Michael C., 250
Hudud, 235
Hulaqu, 22
al-Hursi, Sati, 71
Husayn, 7, 11, 65; martyrdom of, 110, 191, 194; tomb of, 34; Yazid's rout of, 27
Husayniyah Irshad, 184
Husayniyah Irshad Religious Center, 183
al-Husri, Sati, 70
Hussein, Taha, 69
Ibn Khaldun, 27, 28
Ibn Taymiyyah, 19, 34
Ibrahim, Saad Eddin, 249
Idris, King, 38, 155, 156
Imam, 11, 100, 186; seclusion of, 81
Imam Husayn, 83
Imamate, 220; institution of, 80

India, 38, 40; British control of, 51; Caliphate movement in, 87–89; Central Caliphite Committee of, 89 Kanpur incident in, 86; religious school in, 86; struggle for independence of, 88; ulama of, 90; Indian Congress party, 90, 92
Indian Mutiny of 1857, 51
Indian National Congress, 85, 87, 89, 91
Indian nationalism, 57, 90, 92, 142
Indian Subcontinent, 51–54, 85–92; British in, 40; separation of Hindus and Muslims, 91–92; ulama in, 85
Indissoluble Link, The (al-Urwa al-wuthqu), 48
Indonesia, 40
Inheritance, 56
Institute of Higher Arab Studies, 71
Institute for Muslim Minority Affairs, 108
International Center for Research in Islamic Economics, 108
International Islamic News Agency, 108
International Students Association of North America, 220
Iqbal, Muhammad, 54, 89–92, 144, 186, 219, 223, 234, 250; repudiation of nationalism, of, 232
Iran, x, xv, 21, 120–25, 178–98; aid to Shah of, 153; American advisers in, 179; American hostages in, ix; American presence in, 121, 124; Bahai in, 231; communism in, 122; Constitutional Revolution of 1905–11, 83; education in, 121; Family Protection Act of, 227; harassment of ulama in, 125; Islamic Republic of, 194; Islamic Republican Party of, 219; land reform in, 123, 124, 187; Liberation Movement in, 183; literacy rate in, 178; martial law in, 193; Ministry of Education in, 121; monarchical absolutism in, 179; Muslim family law under Shah of, 121; occupation of during World War II, 121; opposition to Westernization in, 180; poverty in, 179; radical religious propaganda of, 213; religious sanctuary in, 192; religious taxes in, 188; repeal of Family Protection Act of,

Epilogue to Revised, Second Edition

UPDATE: PAKISTAN, IRAN, AND EGYPT

Pakistan

$\mathcal{E}$ VENTS IN PAKISTAN have unfolded dramatically since 1984. In December 1984, General Zia ul-Haq called a surprise national referendum: "To approve policies to conform the nation's laws with Islam and the peaceful transition of power to elected representatives." Although ostensibly to ask voters if they approved of his Islamization program, Zia linked a "yes" answer with retention of the presidency until 1990. Despite an opposition boycott led by the Movement for the Restoration of Democracy (MRD), charges of election irregularities, and a low voter turnout (the government claimed a 50 percent turnout; unofficial estimates were 15–20 percent), a majority voted in the affirmative. Thus, martial law was lifted after seven years, but not before amendments were passed to the 1973 Constitution to preserve Zia's ultimate power as president, incorporate many of the martial law regulations promulgated during Zia's rule, and exempt from future prosecution those associated with the martial law system. In February 1985 national and provincial elections were held on a nonparty basis. By the end of 1985, martial law had been terminated and civilian rule restored. In January 1986, a civilian government headed by Prime Minister Muhammad Khan Junejo, whom Zia had selected the previous March, took office. Press censorship was lifted, and political parties were permitted to function with some restriction.

The return to civilian rule did not bring stability. The MRD continued to press for free elections on a political party basis and for General Zia to resign as army chief of staff in order to be a true civilian president. In April 1986 Benazir Bhutto, daughter of Zulfikar Ali Bhutto, returned to Pakistan to challenge Zia's regime. Zia and the military did not miss the message in the record crowds that greeted Benazir Bhutto, many of whom were there to voice opposition to Zia's rule rather than solely to support Bhutto. Benazir, however, has thus far proven incapable of effectively organizing a united opposition.

The Zia/Junejo government has also been challenged by ethnic and religious conflicts: Baluchs and Pathans have clashed in Baluchistan; Sindhis and non-Sindhis have battled the Sind; sections of Karachi have been devastated by a series of ethnic riots between Pathans and Muhajirs; Sunni tensions continue to explode from time to time in Karachi, Lahore, and Islamabad. At the same time, many of the ulama and traditional religious parties have become more vocal in their criticisms of the government's failure to adequately and expeditiously implement an Islamic system of government. These concerns were reflected in two attempts at legislative reform. In July 1985 two Jamaat-i-Islami members of the Senate introduced the Shariat (Shariah) Bill which was to require that all laws be brought within the purview of the shariah. The move proved unpopular to the government, to many non-government organizations, including the Women's Action Forum, and to Shia organizations, and was referred to committee. More serious is a proposed amendment (the Ninth Amendment) to the constitution which would expand the jurisdiction of the Federal Shariah Court to include family laws. While more conservative religious organizations favor the bill, more liberal leaders worry that such a change could lead to repeal of or changes in existing marriage and family laws such as Pakistan's Family Laws Ordinance of 1961 and to the passage of laws discriminatory to women, especially since the ulama will play a greater role as judges on the Court. Pakistan has returned to civilian government and somewhat moderated the pace of its Islamization programs. However, though unable to mount a unified movement, a variety of opposition forces continue to challenge the rule of Zia ul-Haq.

Iran

At one level, Iran's revolution has been successfully institutionalized. The clergy and/or their supporters control key government positions and institutions. Purges (of political organizations, the military, judiciary, educational institutions, and government bureaus), control of the media, and intimidation of dissident clergy have severely restricted the opposition. The six-year-old Iran-Iraq war, while devastating in its human and economic tolls, has provided an excuse for Iran's serious economic problems, minimized criticism of the government, and mobilized support for the regime. Beneath the surface, internal divisions exist. Iran's strength has come from its manpower advantage (three times the population of Iraq) and strong religious motivation to fight and die for Iran/Islam in its holy war. Patriotism and martyrdom have been fused effectively to a degree that has often astonished outside observers. Yet, the prolonged war, with no end in sight and heavy casualties (approaching 250,000) that have touched most families, has taken its toll. Important differences also exist among Iran's top leaders.

While the leadership in Iran remains united in its desire for a victory in the war with Iraq, differing tendencies prevail in domestic and international policy due to factionalization within the political elite over power and policy issues such as dealings with the West, promotion of revolution abroad, land reform, and nationalization. Though the situation remains somewhat fluid, differing groups have crystallized among clerical leaders. Among the more powerful are those led by Hojjat al-Islam Hashemi Rafsanjani, the speaker of Parliament, and Ali Khomenei, Iran's President, versus that of Ayatollah Hussein Ali Montazeri, Khomeini's designated successor, and Prime Minister Mir Hussein Musavi. The arrest in October 1986 of Mehdi Hashemi, the brother of Montazeri's son-in-law and head of the bureau charged with exporting Iran's revolution, was a sign of internal differences and political jockeying for power. More significant was the revelation that Robert MacFarlane, former U.S. National Security Adviser, had met with Rafsanjani and that the United States had sold arms to Iran for the release of American hostages held in Lebanon.

The mullahs of Iran have proven equally divided over socioeconomic reforms. For supporters of Iran's revolution, the goals were not only political and cultural but also social and economic. Social justice, the redressing of the oppression of the poor, the disinherited, were popular revolutionary themes. While criticism of the Shah's

Western-inspired modernization program had once provided a common ground, post-revolutionary attempts to implement an Islamic model for socioeconomic development have revealed substantial differences of opinion among clergy. Islam has been used to justify both state control of the economy and private-sector freedom. Competing Islamic interpretations have resulted from differences in juristic interpretation and conflicting class interests. While all accept the authority of Islamic law, some insist that answers must be found or based upon explicit texts in traditional Islamic jurisprudence, i.e., past legal interpretations or regulations. Others argue that new problems require new interpretations of God's revelation.

Confusion and indecision have characterized much of the attempt to institute substantive social reform. A majority in parliament have attempted to implement a social revolution to improve the lot of the urban poor, farmers, and villagers through state control of the economy and thus restriction of the private sector and free enterprise. A series of laws were passed to limit the private sector: to control prices and markets; to nationalize many industries and banks, foreign trade; to expropriate urban land for use by the poor and homeless; to undertake major land reform through the redistribution of the agricultural lands of absentee landlords to peasant farmers. Merchants, who had been a major source of financial support for the revolution, and landowners (who include clerical leaders) were among those who were strongly opposed to such measures and lobbied politicians and senior clerics. The Council of Guardians (a committee of clerical experts in Islamic law who determine whether or not a parliamentary law is Islamically acceptable) has rather consistently vetoed much of the reform legislation.

Although Ayatollah Hussein Ali Montazeri has been selected as the Ayatollah Khomeini's successor, Montazeri does not command the same respect or possess the same authority. During the post-Khomeini period, competition for power among Iran's leadership will heighten the deep differences of opinion and policy that already exist.

Egypt

When Hosni Mubarrak became President in October 1981, he pursued a path of greater political liberalization and tolerance in contrast to the repression which had characterized the late Sadat period. Mubarak released the 1,500 political prisoners arrested during Sadat's last month in office, consulted with opposition leaders, permitted open debate and criticism of government policies, and allowed trials of those who had benefited from corruption and exploitation during the Sadat era. Even religious critics of the government were given public outlets, permitted to voice their objections in the media and press, and to publish newspapers. At the same time, Mubarak was firm in crushing a fundamentalist outburst in Assyut, executing Sadat's murderers and trying those arrested in connection with the assassination.

Internationally, while committing himself to the peace process, Mubarak struck a more independent position vis-à-vis Israel and the United States and sought to re-establish ties with moderate Arab states. While pledging Egyptian cooperation in the Camp David peace process, Mubarak called for Israeli withdrawal from Lebanon and further talks regarding the autonomy of the West Bank and Gaza, and he condemned Israel's bombing of Palestinian camps in Tunis, U.S. downing of an Egyptian plane carrying the *Achille Lauro* hijackers (both in October 1985), and the U.S.–Iranian arms deal for American hostages held in Lebanon (December 1986).

Under Mubarak, Islamic organizations have pursued a number of courses. The Muslim Brotherhood has continued to make headway as a moderate group working within the political system. In the national elections of May 1984, the Brotherhood formed an alliance with the New Wafd party which won 12.7 percent of the seats in the People's Assembly. Mubarak's liberalism was tested when Egypt's courts acquitted 174 of those militants tried for the Sadat assassination. The professions of those released revealed the potential appeal of radical groups: members of the presidential guard, military intelligence, security, civil servants, radio and television workers, and university students and professors. The militants' defiant chants from behind prison bars reflected deep-seated fears regarding Egypt's dangerous dependence upon a host of "enemies": "Holy war against lackeys, Jews, Christians, and atheists" and "No to America and no to Israel."[1]

These unresolved tensions were played out in a number of ways: continued clashes between Copts and Muslims such as those in Fayoum where Coptic shops and property were burned. In February 1985, a broad coalition of demonstrators burned an Israeli flag to protest the "normalization" of relations with Israel.[2] While Mubarak dealt firmly but fairly with such incidents, by the summer of 1985, when a spectrum of religious organizations and opposition parties resurrected the call for Islamic law, he began to show signs of over-reaction similar to that of his predecessor. For Islamic activists, application of the shariah is the litmus test for Islamic orthodoxy, one which Sadat had ultimately failed. Mubarrak's response was un-characteristically harsh and reminiscent of Sadat's excesses. He banned a mass march on Parliament planned by its supporters, broke up subsequent rallies led by popular religious leaders like Shaykh Hafez Salama, and threatened to reinstitute Anwar Sadat's plan to na-tionalize all private mosques, thus bringing them under government control. Sadat's attempt to do this during the last month of his rule had been a clear indication of his recognition that these independent mosques were often the centers and sources of popular criticism of the regime. Mubarrak's more aggressive and confrontational policy ran the risk of both emphasizing his fear of religious extremism and uniting oppositional forces.

The mood of Egypt's opposition, both nationalist and reli-gious, and a growing anti-American sentiment was evident in De-cember 1985 when a disturbed border policeman, Suliman Khater, killed seven Israeli tourists in the Sinai. Opposition newspapers, political parties, and Islamic leaders like Shaykh Hafez Salama de-fended this action against the "enemies of the nation." Ibrahim Shukry, leader of the Socialist Labor Party, reflected the mood when he declared his support for "this young man who has removed the shame from Egypt after Israel has bombarded the P.L.O. headquar-ters in Tunisia and after the Americans have hijacked the Egyptian plane [referring to the *Achille Lauro* incident]."[3]

While open confrontation between Islamic militants and the government has been muted, they have nevertheless continued to grow and to exert pressure. Although the National Assembly vetoed implementation of a codified Islamic law, it promised to review all laws to assure their conformity with the shariah and to expand reli-gious education. An unexpurgated edition of *A Thousand and One Nights* was banned under Egypt's pornography law as constituting a threat to the moral fabric of society. Alcohol is now banned in most non-tourist areas and draft laws have been submitted to ban alcohol completely as well as fine all who eat or smoke in public during Ramadan. Islamic student organizations have become more ag-gressive at campuses in Assyut, Minya, Cairo, Alexandria. Their demands range from an Islamic revolution to the implementation of Islamic law, separation of the sexes in classes, and banning of western music. The continued growth of militant activism within the army and middle classes was underscored in December 1986, when Egyptian authorities arrested thirty-three activists, including four military officers, charged with plotting to wage a holy war to overthrow the government. They were alleged to be connected to al-Jihad, Sadat's assassins.

Mubarrak's Egypt continues to face hard times. The economy is in dire straits. State revenues have plummetted due to the slump in oil prices. Foreign worker remittances have been cut by $3 billion, tourism has fallen sharply due to fears of regional terrorism, and Egypt's foreign debt is $38 billion. Unemployment is high, affordable housing remains abysmally scarce. While Egypt is pressured by the United States and the International Monetary Fund to lift or readjust its food and fuel subsidies and rent controls which will have a serious impact upon the poor, the high life and conspicuous consumption of luxury goods by an enormously wealthy few who have benefited from Egypt's "open door" *(infitah)* policy underscores the widening gap between a rich minority and the poverty of the masses. At the same time, Egypt is heavily dependent upon U.S. aid—an economic dependency whose political implications have become an increasing issue and source of anti-American sentiment. While Egypt has been readmitted to membership in the OIC and attempted to reintegrate itself more fully in the Arab fold, the Mubarrak government continues to be criticized for its strong ties with the United States and its relations with Israel. The dismal economic situation and the failure of the Mubarrak government to provide strong political leadership provides a fertile ground for its Islamic and leftist critics, among others, to grow and constitute a serious challenge to the regime's future stability.

SUPPLEMENT: THE SUDAN AND LEBANON

The Sudan

On April 5, 1985, the military dictatorship of Jafar al-Numayri was toppled by a *coup d'etat* after sixteen years of rule. For a number of years Numayri had struggled to maintain his government and enhance his legitimacy through his self-proclaimed Islamic revolution in the Sudan. His public commitment to Islamize Africa's largest country resulted in Islamic laws, courts, punishments, and taxes that propelled this Arab socialist state far down the road to becoming a self-proclaimed Islamic state.[4]

Numayri's Turn to Islam

Personal as well as political factors had influenced Numayri's espousal of an Islamic direction in his life and government. During the 1970s, Numayri had become increasingly more religiously observant, abstaining from alcohol, gambling, and carousing. He began to frequent Sufi celebrations and to seek the private counsel of local Sufi shaykhs or pirs. At the same time, Numayri's public statements frequently emphasized a holistic understanding of Islam, similar to that espoused by the Sudan's traditional Islamic organizations, the Ansar or followers of the Mahdi and the Muslim Brotherhood, which had both asserted Islam's integral relationship with all aspects of public and private life. In 1976, Numayri issued a directive to government officials to refrain from drinking. He even wrote a book, *Why the Islamic Way*, about his increased emphasis upon Islam in which he called for the application of Islamic law in the Sudan.[5]

A variety of factors can be identified to explain Numayri's public espousal of Islam. The appeal of Islam offered Numayri a new way out of a deteriorating situation. It was consonant with his leadership style, had continuity with the Islamic character of Sudanese political history and social culture, and thus had the potential to consolidate popular support among the Sudan's 70 percent Muslim population. Throughout his regime, Numayri had ruled through a variety of alliances—leftist, military, tribal, or religious—which he used only for as long as was necessary, shifting from one partner to another to avoid any becoming too strong in its own right.[6] His strength was in maintaining a balance between building alliances and keeping potential rivals disorganized and relatively weak. However, a series of events during the 1970s had progressively narrowed Numayri's political options. An abortive communist *coup* in 1971 made Numayri resolutely anti-leftist. His own brand of Arab socialism had failed as a national ideology, proving itself unable to garner popular domestic support. The Sudan's economy had deteriorated; its national debt had spiraled out of control. Responding to pressures from the World Bank and the International Monetary Fund, the Sudan had lifted government subsidies on staples such as bread and sugar, causing popular anti-government demonstrations and food riots in 1979 and again in 1982. Insurrection grew in the predominantly non-Muslim south, and Numayri continued to be challenged by the National Front, an alliance of national Islamic organizations, led by Sadiq al-Mahdi, the great grandson of the Sudanese Mahdi and a former prime minister.

In the early 1980s, Numayri moved against the growing political fragmentation in the south. He dissolved the regional government in the south and imposed a military regime, completely discarding the Addis Ababa Accords of 1972 which had brought a ceasefire to the seventeen-year civil war between the predominantly Arab Muslim north and the non-Arab, non-Muslim south. Guerrilla warfare escalated under the Sudan People's Liberation Movement (SPLM), led by Colonel John Garang, an American-trained Ph.D., and supported by Libya and Ethiopia. The Muslim government of the north was viewed as dominating the south politically and exploiting its economic resources. Numayri used the rebellion in the south to strengthen his ties with Western allies, in particular the United States. Maintaining that the SPLM were Marxists supported by Libya and Ethiopia, he reinforced the perception of the Sudan as a bulwark against communism in Africa in order to press for increased military aid from the United States.

While Numayri's turn to Islam troubled many, it had potential popular appeal among the Sudan's Muslim majority. The Sudan has had a rich Islamic past. It was central to two major Islamic states, the Funj sultanate (1504–1820) and Mahdist state (1811–98). Many regard the Mahdist state as the origin and paradigm of the modern Sudanese nation state. The Mahdist movement in particular left a legacy not only of Islamic identification with the state, but also of Islam's role as an anti-colonialist force and an integral component of Sudanese nationalism and independence due to its revolt against Ottoman-Egyptian rule (1820–81) and Anglo-Egyptian rule (1899–1955).

Moreover, Islam continues to be both a pervasive social and cultural presence, a source of identity, ideology, and values. It has been a major source of local and national leadership and has inspired Islamic organizations and parties such as the Ansar, Khatmiyya, and Muslim Brotherhood. Even more secular-oriented nationalists paid homage to the Sudan's Islamic past and to its Mahdist tradition as the origin of Sudanese nationalism. In addition, Numayri's regime, like many other Muslim states during the 1970s, looked to oil-rich Arab states and companies for loans and investments. Numayri's approach was similar in this regard to that of Pakistan's Zulfikar Ali Bhutto (and his successor General Zia ul-Haq) who strengthened their case for aid from Saudi Arabia and other Gulf states by fostering greater Islamization.

The appeal to Islam both resonated with popular Islamic sentiments and coopted many of the themes of Numayri's major national Islamic opposition, the National Front, with its emphasis on Islamic symbols and rhetoric, criticism of the Westernization of society and culture, condemnation of communism, and assertion of the primary importance of Islamic ideology and law.

The Front represented the major national Islamic organizations/banned political parties: the Ummah (Ansar) party of Sadiq al-Mahdi, the Democratic Union Party (Khatmiyya) of Sharif al-Hindi, and the Islamic Charter Front (Muslim Brotherhood) of Hassan al-Turabi. In 1977, Numayri signed a formal agreement of National Reconciliation with Sadiq-al-Mahdi, the leader of the Front. However, the major benefactor of National Reconciliation and its most cooperative participant was the Muslim Brotherhood. While the others remained more aloof, the Brotherhood joined the government. After more than two decades, much of which was spent in opposition, the Muslim Brotherhood had become part of the political establishment.

The Muslim Brotherhood was founded in 1954. Although inspired by Egypt's Muslim Brotherhood, it is an autonomous organization. From its creation, the Brotherhood advocated the establishment of an Islamic political and social order through the adoption of an Islamic constitution based upon the Quran and the introduction of Islamic law. The Brotherhood offered an Islamic alternative for traditionally raised Muslims who had then gone on to receive modern educations. Rejecting the Westernization of society and secularism, it advocated a modern state and society more firmly rooted in Sudan's Islamic faith and heritage.

The Brotherhood came to prominence during the mid-1960s aided by Dr. Hassan al-Turabi, who had returned from France with a doctorate in international law, had become Dean of the Law School at Khartoum University, and was then elected Secretary General of the Brotherhood in 1964. When a civilian government, strongly influenced by the left, came to power in October 1964, the Brotherhood mobilized popular support behind its call to eradicate communism and to introduce an Islamic constitution under the banner of the new

Islamic Charter Front Party. The Brotherhood participated in the creation of the National Front and its efforts to overthrow Numayri's
Communist-supported regime. Under Turabi, a brother-in-law of
Sadiq al-Mahdi, the Brotherhood assisted the Ansar's abortive revolt
at Aba Island in 1970. While Sadiq went into exile in Britain, Turabi
and some of his followers were imprisoned from 1969 to 1977.

The fortunes of Turabi and the Brotherhood were reversed in
1977. Unlike other members of the National Front, the Muslim Brotherhood showed little hesitation in accepting the fruits of National
Reconciliation, greater involvement in the political process. The strategy of the Muslim Brotherhood had been to bring about gradual
change from below, from within the system. Their work on campuses
and among educated professionals was aimed at changing society
through the development of a new elite who would enter and influence all sectors of education, the professions, and government. While
the long-range goal might be the creation of an Islamic state under a
suitable Muslim leader, the Brotherhood was content in the short run
to establish itself as a recognized political force or pressure group
which any government, whatever its orientation, would have to take
seriously. Thus, whether Numayri was sincere or not, Turabi could
view Numayri's new initiative as offering an opportunity for the
Brotherhood to be in a position to influence government policy directly. Their alliance was motivated on both sides less by a meeting of
the minds than by political expediency as later events will illustrate.

From 1978 onwards the Muslim Brotherhood was closely associated with the Numayri regime. Turabi became the Sudan's Attorney General. Muslim Brothers secured senior appointments in the
cabinet and government ministries (law, education, religious affairs),
in the judiciary, and the Sudanese Socialist Union (SSU), and they
won a substantial number of seats in the elections for a new People's
Assembly in 1980. Their strength in government was complemented
by a continued expansion of their control or influence over such non-
governmental institutions as universities, student and professional
organizations, mosques and cultural centers, and a burgeoning system of Islamic banks and insurance companies. By 1980, the Islamic
Trend Movement, the student wing of the Brotherhood, controlled
student unions in every university except Juba University in the
south. In the early 1980s, throughout the Sudan, student government
elections were dominated by Islamic issues, and invariably Muslim
Brotherhood candidates proved most successful. Student politics
spilled into the streets as Islamically oriented students led marches,

chanting "Non-western, non-eastern, Islamic 100 percent" in support of the Muslim Brotherhood and Islamization.[7]

Numayri's Islamization Program

Islamization of the Sudan intensified on September 8, 1983, when Jafar Numayri declared that the Sudan would be an Islamic republic and issued an official decree for the application of the shariah in the Sudan. Numayri proclaimed an "Islamic revolution" which would have an impact on politics, law, and society.

That the Islamization program in the Sudan was very much "Numayri's Islam" is illustrated both by the process itself and by Numayri's handling of alternative national Islamic leaders and organizations. More than 20 laws and assorted regulations and policies were hastily formulated, with little or no consultation with the Attorney General's office or the Chief Justice. They were issued by presidential decree, not legislative action. Their implementation and application were equally erratic, dependent upon Numayri's presidential decree and special "decisive justice courts," not by the Sudan's duly established judiciary.

Numayri curtailed the powers of the Sudan's courts by introducing "decisive justice courts," purportedly to provide swift adjudication and justice in criminal cases. Thousands were arrested and brought before government-appointed judges whose courts often functioned like military tribunals, employing Islamic punishments such as flogging, quite liberally, for a variety of crimes. In May 1984, European-style dancing was banned when a nightclub owner was sentenced to twenty-five lashes for permitting heterosexual dancing that was judged contrary to Islam.[8] While the courts were admittedly swift, there were often grave differences of opinion as to their independence and to the quality of justice that they dispensed.

In the socioeconomic sphere, new guidelines were enacted for taxation and banking. The *Zakat* Tax Act of 1984 replaced much of the state's taxation system with an alms tax which was supposed to become the major source of revenue. The Sudan now joined a number of self-styled Islamic governments, like Pakistan and Iran, in passing legislation that empowered the state to levy, collect, and distribute the *zakat*.

Numayri's stated intention to convert all of the Sudan's banks into interest-free institutions was an especially controversial economic reform. The Sudan already had five such banks, including the Faisal

Islamic Bank which had close ties with the Muslim Brotherhood. The move to an Islamic banking system in the Sudan, as in Pakistan and Iran, was to be the first step in basing the entire economy on Islamic principles. These policies greatly disturbed many in the Sudan as well as foreign interests, in particular U.S.–based multinationals operating in the Sudan.

Numayri skillfully used Islam to direct, and thus control, Islamic revivalism within the Sudan and to enhance his political legitimacy by appropriating a religio-political status. At the same time, he weakened the power of Hassan Turabi, whom he had seen as a competitor, by replacing him with a more subservient Attorney General. Turabi was made Presidential Adviser for Foreign Affairs, a less influential though important-sounding position. Numayri also took action against Sadiq al-Mahdi who, upon returning from exile in 1982, was first placed in "protective custody" and then imprisoned. Sadiq had always represented a formidable challenge to Numayri. With the greater emphasis upon Islam, Sadiq's direct descent from the Mahdi and his leadership of a national Islamic organization threatened Numayri's own attempt to enhance his legitimacy through an appeal to Islam. Moreover, Sadiq had been critical of Numayri's Islamization program, maintaining that the introduction of the shariah was premature, that society had to be prepared for its introduction.

To enhance his own status as an "Islamic" political leader, Numayri used flamboyant public acts in 1983, such as his release of a reported 13,000 prisoners to give them a "second chance" under Islamic law, to dramatize the new Islamic order. Similarly, he supervised the destruction of alcohol, worth $11 million, pouring it into the Nile in a public demonstration and media event that gained both national and international attention. In May 1984, he required that senior members of the government, judiciary, military, trade unions, and the Sudanese Socialist Union (SSU) perform the *baya*, pledging their allegiance and loyalty to him, acknowledging him as a Muslim ruler guided by the Quran. The *baya* ceremony, combined with his Islamic laws and creation of "decisive justice courts," were fundamental expressions of his appropriation of Islamic leadership and legitimacy to justify authoritarian rule. Indeed, Numayri planned to declare himself Imam, the religio-political leader of the state. However, on July 11, 1984, Numayri was unexpectedly rebuffed by the People's Assembly when it postponed a vote on a series of amendments which would have ratified his Islamic laws and his religio-political status.

Initially, Islamization had proved popular in the north. Many felt that the crime rate and corruption were on the decline. Public floggings and amputations drew large supportive crowds. However, Numayri's use of Islam to expand his power and justify an increasingly repressive regime, erratic decisions of "decisive justice courts," and the indiscriminate use of flogging undermined his image at home and abroad. The Ansar, Republican Brothers, Khatmiyya, secularists, and southern opposition leaders continued to oppose Numayri's Islamization program and, at the same time, to strongly regard the Muslim Brotherhood as the architects of Numayri's program. Even conservative Muslim states like Saudi Arabia became concerned about a negative image of Islam and Islamic justice as international media coverage of a seemingly endless number of floggings and amputations increased.

Throughout 1984, the Sudan's political and economic situation continued to deteriorate. In July, a new opposition coalition, the National Salvation Front, was formed by the Ansar, Khatmiyya, Sudanese Communist Party, and others. Their program included civil rights, especially for non-Muslims, retention of the shariah as a source of legislation, and the abolition of laws that were regarded as not truly Islamic. Although John Garang participated in the discussions, he refused to join unless complete secularization was accepted. Political instability was exacerbated by the continued deterioration of the economy. The Sudanese pound had been devalued five times in the previous three years. The effects of the famine in Ethiopia (more than 1.2 million refugees) and within the Sudan were inescapable. The United States froze $114 million in economic aid in December 1984, siding with the IMF in pressing the Sudan to introduce economic reforms in order to control its spiraling deficit of $9 billion debt.

Numayri responded by a series of reforms which tempered his Islamization program. He discontinued the steady stream of floggings and amputations in the north, backed away from his plan to divide the south, and gave assurances that shariah would not be implemented there. As Numayri moderated his push for Islamization, talk of an imminent introduction of an interest-free Islamic economy also subsided. The *zakat* tax was abolished and income tax restored.

In January, amidst growing criticism of Islamization, Numayri selected an easy target, the Republican Brothers, to symbolize his intention of silencing his critics and to rally popular Muslim support. Masking authoritarianism in the guise of being the protector of Islamic orthodoxy, he arrested, tried, and executed the seventy-six-year-old founder and leader of the Republican Brothers, Mahmud Muhammad Taha, for apostasy. Taha had opposed sectarian politics and attempts to implement Islamic law. Many Muslims—including the Ansar, Muslim Brotherhood, and the local Sufi leaders—had long regarded Taha's religious claims and his reinterpretation of Islam as not simply liberal reformism but heresy.

In March 1985 Numayri continued his attempt to salvage his tottering regime, answer his critics, and direct blame for the Sudan's ills away from himself. He followed his long-established pattern, co-opting potential rivals into a government coalition and then repudiating them, by moving to eliminate the Muslim Brotherhood as a political force and making it a scapegoat for the failures of his regime. In a statement to reassure his American allies as much as assuage the Sudanese populace, Numayri claimed to have thwarted a *coup* by the Muslim Brotherhood whom he charged were armed by Iran in order to overthrow his pro-American government. Numayri dismissed all members of the Muslim Brotherhood from the government and the SSU and ordered the arrest of two hundred of its leaders, including Hassan Turabi.

The removal of Brotherhood leaders from key positions and new government "reforms" were a response to the U.S., Egypt, and Saudi Arabia as much as to his domestic critics. Indeed, they occurred immediately after the visit of Vice-President George Bush and a U.S. delegation. The timing was such that both within the Sudan and in the Arab world, reports maintaining that among the four conditions Bush presented for lifting the freeze on American economic aid were discontinuation of Islamic criminal punishments *(hudud)* and dismissal of Islamic fundamentalists from the government and its institutions. The other two alleged points were halting contacts with Libya and accepting the economic reforms demanded by the IMF. The fact that Bush ended his visit by announcing resumption of U.S. aid and that a team from the World Bank left for the Sudan the following day appeared to confirm U.S. responsibility for Numayri's new initiatives. This perception was reinforced in late March when the Sudan's government, yielding to IMF and U.S. pressures, lifted subsidies upon staples, an act which proved to be the undoing of the Numayri regime.

The lifting of subsidies on bread and fuel offered Numayri's critics a rallying point which enabled them to transcend their differences. A coalition, the "Spring Movement," of trade unions, professional organizations (doctors, lawyers, engineers), and political parties, had an issue which united them in opposition to Numayri and which could be used to mobilize popular support. They demanded Numayri's resignation. Hours after Numayri left the Sudan on March 27 to meet President Ronald Reagan in Washington, his military and security forces were battling demonstrators in the streets. On April 4, more than 20,000 demonstrators marched through the streets of Khartoum chanting, "Down with one man rule" and "Down with the USA." On the morning of April 5, general Abdul Rahman Siwar al-Dhahab, a senior officer, led a military *coup* which brought sixteen years of the Numayri regime as well as its Islamic experiment to an abrupt and bloodless end.

The transitional military government of Siwar al-Dhahab included a predominantly civilian cabinet and promised elections by March 1986. Once again the major traditional political forces dominated: the Umma Party led by Sadiq al-Mahdi, the Democratic Unionist Party (DUP) associated closely with the Khatmiyya order, and the Islamic National Front (INF), an alliance forged by Hassan Turabi of the Muslim Brotherhood. Because the Umma and DUP had remained aloof from Numayri, with their leaders often living in exile in Britain or Libya, they were freed from the INF's political handicap of past alliance with Numayri. While Turabi and the Muslim Brothers had once thrived as an opposition party, their connection with Numayri now made them, in the eyes of many, the symbol for the excesses of Numayri's Islamization program. In contrast, Sadiq al-Mahdi, an outspoken critic of Numayri's sharia experiment, was able to emerge from prison to rally his traditional Ansar supporters and at the same time build a coalition of support, projecting the Umma party as a centrist, pluralistic party.

In April 1986 the Sudan held its first multi-party election in eighteen years. The Umma Party won 99 seats, the DUP took 63 and the INF captured a surprising 51 seats. Although Turabi lost his bid for a seat in the National Assembly, the INF swept 23 of the 28 seats reserved for university graduates, and also demonstrated its ability to win in areas other than their usual urban, professional constituency. The DUP joined with the Umma party to form a coalition, with Sadiq al-Mahdi returning to power as Prime Minister of the Sudan. Turabi and the INF constitute the major opposition party.

Sudan's Islamic experiment under Jafar al-Numayri may be viewed as an irrational aberration, or it may be regarded as a logical response, given Numayri's personal disposition and the historical and political realities of the Sudan. Numayri's return to stricter Islamic observance also brought him into line with the Islamic, Mahdist tradition of the Sudan which had combined Sufism with Islamic political activism and government. In many ways, Numayri attempted to enhance his legitimacy and popular support by forging his own neo-Sufi, Islamic state. He cultivated relations with local Sufi leaders and diffused the opposition from national Islamic organizations by appealing to Islam and incorporating the Muslim Brotherhood within the government. If the followers of Sadiq al-Mahdi ultimately remained aloof, other branches of the Ansar did not. Because of the erosion of his support in the south, Numayri attempted to mobilize the Muslim masses behind him. The introduction of Islamic laws were a prelude to his plan to religiously buttress his regime by establishing himself as the religio-political leader of an Islamic state.

The experience of the Muslim Brotherhood underscores the thorny and precarious position of modern Islamic organizations in this process. Working for change within the system but frequently in opposition to the regime often leads to government repression. However, the alternative of cooperation in exchange for representation and influence within the government, though initially attractive, can often result in losses that greatly outweigh potential gains. Short-term influence in the government by the Brothers was offset by a "guilt by association." Ultimately unable to control Numayri, the Brothers came to be viewed as the primary source for all of Numayri's Islamization measures and actions. As a result, he could attempt to use the Muslim Brotherhood as a scapegoat for the excesses and failures of his regime. Moreover, in the post-Numayri period, the Brotherhood had to struggle to regain its credibility and support. In contrast, Sadiq al-Mahdi's opposition and imprisonment under Numayri enhanced his credentials, made him more effective in coalition building, and enabled him to emerge victorious in national elections to become the Sudan's Prime Minister.

Lebanon

Shii Politics in Lebanon

Ironically the two Middle East countries most torn apart by violence and civil strife since the mid-1970s were among those regarded as the most stable, modernizing, and Western oriented—

Lebanon and Iran. In the aftermath of the Iranian Revolution, Lebanon has also become a major theatre for Shii political activism, a battlefield where Shii organizations have struggled against other Lebanese militias, Israeli troops, and Western presence, particularly American military and civilian personnel.

Lebanon offers the second most-potent example of militant Shii politics. Since the late 1970s, organization as such as AMAL and Hezbullah have mobilized Shii Muslims into protest and revolutionary movements. As a result, a religio-political community, long dominated by Maronite Christians and Sunni Muslims within Lebanon's sectarian system of government, has become a formidable force in Lebanese politics.

Like Iran, the emergence of Islam in Lebanese politics was the product of political and socioeconomic factors combined with an effective charismatic religious leadership which skillfully used key beliefs and symbols to organize and enlist popular support. However, in contrast to Iran, the Shii of Lebanon had long been a religious minority community, predominantly rural, poor, disorganized, and lacking an effective clerical organization or hierarchy.

The Shii of Lebanon existed in a state whose stability was based upon the delicate balance of confessional political organizations and parties and their militias. Lebanon's post-independence sectarian system of government, a legacy of the French Mandate, was based upon an informal agreement, the National Pact of 1943, which institutionalized the relative population strengths of the dominant religious communities as found in the 1932 census. Key positions in the government, cabinet, parliament, bureaucracy, and military were distributed along confessional lines. Constitutionally, Lebanon is a parliamentary republic with a strong presidency. Its top leadership consists of a Maronite President, Sunni Prime Minister and Shii Speaker of the Chamber of Deputies.

Lebanon's capital, Beirut ("the Paris of the Middle East"), reflected strong foreign influence from its boutiques and banks to its leading universities—the French Jesuits' Université St. Joseph and the American University of Beirut (formerly the Syrian Protestant College). Within this context, the Shii were the most politically, economically, and educationally disadvantaged group in the country, a distant third to the better-organized and more prosperous Maronite Christian and Sunni Muslim communities. Shii disaffection with their lot had resulted in emigration abroad, in particular, to West Africa and the Gulf. However, during the 1970s, Shii grievances increasingly took the form of politicization and involvement in a number of multi-confessional leftist and Communist groups such as the Syrian Socialist National Party, the Baath Party, and the Communist Party of Lebanon. Within this context the first Shii-based movement emerged due in large part to a rather remarkable personality, Imam Musa Sadr.

Musa Sadr and Amal[9]

As the Ayatollah Khomeini became the living symbol of Iran's revolutionary movement, so too Imam Musa Sadr, an Iranian-born and Qum-educated cleric, became the embodiment of Shii aspirations and militancy in Lebanon. Musa Sadr had come from Iran to Lebanon in 1959 at the invitation of the Shii community in the southern city of Tyre. By 1969 he had emerged as the leading Shii cleric in Lebanon as confirmed by his election as chairman of the government's newly established Supreme Shii Council. During the early 1970s Musa Sadr led a series of demonstrations and general strikes to demand reforms to redress socioeconomic injustices and to dramatize Shii concerns in the South regarding the Israeli military threat. Increasingly, he called upon the dispossessed of Lebanon to organize and fight against the social injustices that they suffered. In 1974 he founded the Movement for the Dispossessed (Harakat Mahrumin). It was identified as a movement for the emancipation of Lebanon's oppressed people, its disinherited, from domestic and international domination and exploitation. Although not restricted to Shii, implicit in its language, symbolism, and leadership was an appeal to Shii identity and a sense of community solidarity rooted in its history and religious heritage. Shii Islam was employed to provide an ideology of social protest and struggle against tyranny, disinheritance, and social injustice. Early Shii suffering at the hands of the Caliph Yazid, the Imam Husayn's murderer, was equated to the exploitation and discrimination suffered by Shii under the Lebanese confessional system.

Like the Ayatollah Khomeini, Musa Sadr was a charismatic figure who cultivated his religious persona, often identifying his situation with that of the great Imams of early Islam, Ali and his son Hussein, and aligning his role with the spiritual and leadership qualities of the Imam. He did not discourage or prevent his followers from calling him Imam. Musa Sadr became a cult hero whose portrait and posters could be found everywhere in homes, taxis, village squares, schools, mosques, and at demonstrations and rallies. Like Khomeini, his role as a symbol or focus for Shii political activism was captured in slogans such as "Our blood and our souls are yours, Imam."[10]

The goals of the movement were true parity: confessional equality which reflected the new demographic realities of Lebanon, increased political power, and a more equitable distribution of wealth and educational opportunities. Thus, political and socioeconomic reforms—from government posts and civil service jobs to irrigation projects, schools, and hospitals—were demanded. The movement denounced domestic domination and condemned Israel as the chief external enemy, a direct threat to the peace and security of southern Lebanon. Attendance at the movement's rallies was a testimony both to popular identification with its agenda and to Musa Sadr's personal charisma. The movement often drew 75,000 to 100,000 people, easily eclipsing its leftist competitors.

As civil war loomed in 1975, Musa Sadr, following the lead of other communities, created a military wing or militia, the Lebanese Resistance Battalions (Afwaj al-Muqawimah al-Lubnaniyah), whose acronym, AMAL, means "hope." However, AMAL remained a relatively small organization, one of a number of outlets for an increasingly politicized Shii youth. Four events between 1975 and 1982 profoundly affected the politics of Lebanon and contributed to growing Shii radicalization. These were the 1975 Lebanese Civil War, the disappearance of Imam Musa Sadr in 1978, the Iranian revolution of 1979, and the Israeli invasions in 1978 and 1982.

Despite demographic changes which had resulted in a Muslim majority in Lebanon, Lebanon's Christian-dominated government remained inflexible during the 1970s, refusing to redistribute power more equitably. The Shii in particular had grown from 18 percent of the population in 1968 to 30 percent (approximately one million today), to become the largest community in Lebanon. The influx of thousands of Palestinians, driven out of Jordan by King Hussein in 1970–71, and their substantial presence in the south, exacerbated an already fragile political atmosphere. The PLO's strength was such that it threatened to become a state within a state, dominating the Shii villages of the south. The PLO used southern Lebanon as a base for its operations against Israel.

Shii found themselves actually caught in PLO-Israeli crossfire, their autonomy and security endangered as their territory became a battleground between entrenched PLO forces and Israeli commandos. In 1975 Muslims, frustrated by government intransigence and the failure to provide a redistribution of power based upon the new proportional population, withdrew their cooperation from the National Pact. The result was a civil war between Christian and Muslim militias and the de facto partitioning of Lebanon into Christian and Muslim regions. Israel's 1978 invasion of southern Lebanon (the Litani operation), with the consequent loss of Shii lives and destruction of their homes and property, realized Shii fears as it brought "an active [Israeli] campaign of air attacks, raids, kidnappings and house bombings."[11]

While the Lebanese civil war had eclipsed the development of AMAL, the disappearance of Imam Musa Sadr in 1978, during a visit with Muammar Qaddafi in Libya, breathed new life into AMAL. Although many believed that Musa Sadr died in Libya, his disappearance fit nicely with the traditional Shii doctrines of martyrdom and the occultation of the hidden Imam. The Iranian Revolution of 1978–79 reinforced this religio-political legacy and interpretation. It was a witness to the power of Shii ideology to produce a religiously based movement for social protest and change. In the popular mind, the Imam Musa Sadr became a religious hero and paradigm, a worthy descendant of Imam Husayn and the Hidden Twelfth Imam, who is in seclusion but will return. In the interim, the Shii community would continue to fight on. Thus, Musa Sadr's disappearance provided AMAL with a symbol of martyrdom and a messianic hope, an effective rallying point for an embattled Shii community.

The discrediting of Qaddafi caused by the disappearance of Musa Sadr, coupled with Iran's example and influence, turned many Shii away from Arab leftist nationalist ideologies. Students and a rising class of professionals and businessmen offered a fertile ground for recruitment. Financial support came both from within the country and from prosperous members of the Shii diaspora in West Africa and the Gulf.

In 1980 Nabih Berri (b. 1938), a lawyer and long-time AMAL member, gained control of AMAL. Under Berri's leadership, AMAL has been a Shii nationalist organization, pursuing the redressing of Shii grievances while accepting the framework of a united, Arab multi-confessional Lebanon, a parliamentary republic with a free economic system. It does not speak of Shii dominance or an Islamic state but of full equality and parity for Lebanon's disinherited community. At the same time it has pursued a pragmatic approach in its relations with the Lebanese government and Western powers, in particular the United States.

1982: A Turning Point

Israel's invasion of Lebanon in June 1982 to eradicate the PLO precipitated further radicalization in the Shii community as witnessed by the emergence of Islamic AMAL and Hezbullah. At first Shii responses to the Israeli invasion were mixed. In southern Lebanon, Israeli troops were greeted with flowers, welcomed as liberators from the PLO whose military presence and dominance had led to Shii-PLO clashes. However, as the Israelis settled in, they increasingly came to be viewed as an army of occupation. Shii flowers were replaced by growing armed resistance against this new oppression. In Beirut, the massacre of Palestinians and Lebanese in the Sabra and Shatila camps by Christian Phalangist fighters, with Israeli complicity, shocked and outraged Sunni and Shii alike both within Lebanon and throughout the Muslim world. It contributed significantly to the further radicalization of many hitherto moderate Palestinians as well as Lebanese Shii youth. As a result of the Israeli invasion and the massacres, 1982 became another watershed in the tumultuous politics of war-torn Lebanon. It contributed to the rise of more radical Islamic organizations like Hezbullah and Islamic Jihad and to a wave of anti-Americanism. The U.S. government was regarded as a partner with Israel, approving Israel's invasion and continued occupation, and a major supporter of the regime of President Amin Gemayel, which radical Shii regarded as an unrepresentative, intransigent government.

As Shaykh Fadl Allah, a noted Shii cleric, observed: "Israel, with the approval of the U.S., invaded Lebanon. The invasion was based on an American decision and American help. Beirut was destroyed and thousands of people were killed by Israeli forces. We consider, the ordinary people consider, [and] if you take a poll you will see that everybody considers the U.S. responsible for what happened. The presence of the Multinational Force was perceived as an umbrella protecting the regime, protecting Israel, not protecting the people."[12]

Nabih Berri's leadership of AMAL was challenged in July 1982 by Husayn Musawi (b. 1945-), a member of AMAL's command council. When Berri formed an alliance (the Committee of National Salvation) with the Christian Phalangist President of Lebanon, Bashir Gemayel, and the Druze leader, Walid Jumblatt, Musawi broke with Berri, charging that AMAL had collaborated, in effect, with Israel. Musawi rejected AMAL's secular nationalist objectives as un-Islamic and, following Iran's example, advocated an Islamic republic for

Lebanon. He withdrew to the Shii center at Baalbek in the Beqaa Valley where he established Islamic AMAL. Baalbek had become a center for militants. Hezbullah was already active there with the support of 1,000 newly arrived Revolutionary Guards (Pasdaran) from Iran. Musawi, who has repeatedly defended the use of violence as a means to achieve his goals, has been linked to the bombing of the U.S. Embassy in April 1983 and of the U.S. Marine barracks and French military headquarters in Beirut in October 1983. In recent years, Islamic AMAL appears to have become a military arm of Hezbullah.

Hezbullah ("Party of God")

Progressively during the 1980s, the influence of AMAL has been challenged by the more radically oriented Shii movement, Hezbullah.

Born in Baalbeck in the wake of the Iranian revolution, Hezbullah came to prominence as a response to the Israeli invasion of 1982. Pro-Iranian Lebanese Shii clerics and their mosques provided the critical core leadership and centers. They were assisted by local students and professionals, as well as Iranian Revolutionary Guards. Sermons, lectures, films, and media materials from Iran were employed in training programs which indoctrinated and prepared this new generation of holy warriors. By the summer of 1983, Hezbullah had spread to the Shii suburb of Beirut that surrounded the U.S. Marine headquarters near Beirut Airport. Its presence was further solidified when it joined forces with AMAL in the February 1984 Shii takeover of West Beirut.

Organizationally, Hezbullah, like AMAL, lacks the formal structure associated with political parties. It is a loose confederation of smaller groups or cells and individuals. Today it is located in Shii neighborhoods, villages, and towns in the Beqaa Valley, Beirut, and southern Lebanon. Hezbullah provides a more radical Islamic alternative to AMAL, regarding violence as the necessary means of defense against U.S. influence and Israeli occupation. The American military presence was regarded not as a peacekeeping force but a support and protection for Lebanon's unrepresentative, oppressive Christian government. The location of the Marine headquarters in a Shii area symbolized occupation, not peacekeeping. Similarly, given France's strong political and cultural influence as the protector of Lebanon's Christian community and its former rule during the Mandate Period, French UN forces were equally disdained. In April 1983 the U.S. Embassy was bombed and in October 1983, suicide attacks against the U.S. and French military compounds left 300 dead. These acts have been attributed to radical groups like Hezbullah, Islamic AMAL, and Islamic Jihad.

Although he denies a leadership role, the spiritual inspiration or guide of Hezbullah appears to be Shaykh Fadl Allah. Born of Lebanese parents and educated in the Shii holy city of Najaf in Iraq, he emigrated to Lebanon in 1966 where he quickly established himself as a major Shii religious authority, known for his religious scholarship and exemplary life. In addition to a multi-volume commentary on the Quran, he is the author of a number of other works, including *Islam and the Logic of Force*. Shaykh Fadl Allah's political significance grew during the 1980s both as a result of his outspoken sermons and his influence upon Hezbullah. Today, he is the most highly regarded scholar and spiritual guide among Lebanese Shii and enjoys significant influence in the Gulf as well.

Fadl Allah maintains that there is little difference between Sunni and Shii, and he also advocates interconfessional tolerance. Although he favors an Islamic state governed by shariah law and accepts the concept of clerical rule *(wilayat al-faqih)*, Fadl Allah maintains the current conditions in Lebanon are not right for an Islamic Republic. At the same time, Fadl Allah emphasizes that Lebanon's Islamic Republic will not be a mere replica of Iran's but rather be suited to the Lebanese context. While rejecting random violence, Fadl Allah does, however, accept the use of force when necessary, regarding it as self-defense. "I call for the liberation from colonialism. I call to fight colonialism. If colonialism oppresses the people, the people should fight it. But to say that I lead people to do violent acts—no. The American administration should understand that it itself is leading people towards violence. . . . Their problem is that they see the tragedy in the reaction to their action but they do not see the tragedies created by their action . . . oppressed people cannot always behave in a reasonable manner. Reason cannot face up to a rocket."[13]

Shaykh Fadl Allah's popularity and influence and the deteriorating situation in Lebanon have fanned the growth of Hezbullah and forced Nabih Berri and AMAL to compete with Hezbullah's more militant and Islamic image. Hezbullah's very name, Party of God, and its orientation have made it a natural focal point for other militant organizations. By 1984–85 the Islamic AMAL, the Hussein Suicide Squad, Jund Allah or the Army of God, and the Islamic Resistance Movement had become part of Hezbullah's fluid organization. Moreover, Hezbullah may indeed be the source for the most radical of all organizations, Islamic Jihad.

The Islamic Jihad Organization (Munazzamat al-Jihad al-Islami)

Given the secretive nature of Islamic Jihad, little can be said about this shadowy group. Other than taking credit in phone calls for bombings and kidnappings, no individuals have claimed to be or have been definitely identified as members. Some observers believe that it is a single organization; others maintain that Islamic Jihad is a convenient label for uncoordinated terrorist attacks by commandos associated with Hezbullah. The common thread is an undefined commitment to create an Islamic state, an agreement regarding the major obstacles (America, Israel, France, pro-Western Muslim, governments such as Saudi Arabia and Kuwait, and the Lebanese government), and a common belief that it is a religious duty to eradicate these "enemies of God."

These common elements, rather than any organizational center or headquarters, may link Lebanon's Islamic Jihad with similar organizations in the Muslim world. Islamic Jihad had been linked to or has politically taken credit for the kidnappings of Americans and others in Lebanon, the bombing and suicide attacks against American and French installations, the hijacking of a Kuwaiti jet and the murder of two American passengers in December 1984, the attempted assassination of Kuwait's ruler in May 1985, and the hijacking of TWA 474 (June 1985) among others.

Lebanon's Islamic Jihad, like Hezbullah, is linked both to Iran and Syria. In addition to Husayn al-Musawi and Shaykh Fadl Allah's contacts with Iran and the Revolutionary Guards in the Beqaa, the Supreme Council of the Islamic Revolution in Teheran provides both financial support and religious and military training at camps located in Iran and Syrian-run camps in the Beqaa Valley. The Iranian connection was clearly evident in the case of David Dodge who, as acting president of the American University of Beirut, was kidnapped in July 1982 and spent the last months of his captivity in Iran.

Although Israel had entered Lebanon to score a decisive victory in its war with the PLO, the equation has changed radically. The Israeli-PLO war was transformed into an Israeli-Shiite War in the south. Israeli occupation and policies contributed to a further deterioration and radicalization, leading Israeli statesman Abba Eban to observe: "If it turns out that all we have done is traded the hostility of

7,000 Palestinians for the hostility of 700,000 Shiites, then I think we will have made a very poor trade."[14] The very villages that had welcomed Israeli troops as liberators now became the battleground for full-scale guerrilla warfare between Israeli troops and Shiite villagers.

The confrontation reached explosive proportions in April 1985, when more than 750 Lebanese prisoners, mostly Shii, were moved from Ansar prison camp in Lebanon to Atlit, Israel, in apparent violation of the Geneva Conventions. U.S.–Shii relations reached their nadir when, in March and April 1985, the United States vetoed resolutions condemning Israel's "Iron Fist" policy and the transfer of prisoners, respectively. These actions, coupled with an event near Shaykh Fadl Allah's home in Beirut—a car bomb explosion that killed twenty and injured eighty and was attributed to a CIA–influenced Lebanese group—led to the hijacking of TWA 847 and the taking of American hostages in exchange for those Lebanese held in Israel.

As was evident throughout the negotiations, Nabih Berri, the more moderate-pragmatic leader of AMAL, sought to establish his leadership by gaining control of the hostages from their more militant kidnappers. Yet, he did not have the clout to free them without help from the Syrians, allies of Iran. Berri's moderation and his connections with the U.S. (he held a green card and members of his immediate family live in Detroit) undermined his credibility. Since that time, as the situation in Lebanon has deteriorated, AMAL and Hezbullah have been locked in an ongoing struggle for support in the south. While AMAL's membership has significantly exceeded that of Hezbullah, Hezbullah's more strident, aggressive orientation has proven very attractive to Shii villagers battling Israeli occupation forces and the South Lebanese Army (SLA), a Christian militia armed by Israel. Hezbullah cells have grown steadily around local Shii clerics or mullahs who lead the resistance. Posters of the Ayatollah Khomeini seem ubiquitous and the wearing of the *hijab* (veil) more common.

AMAL and Hezbullah also differ in their dealings with the PLO. Ironically, although AMAL had received early training from Fatah, it is now engaged in fierce battles with the PLO in the Palestinian camps of Beirut. In contrast, Hezbullah has tended to ally itself with returning PLO in the south while AMAL wants to keep them out. Despite the deployment of the majority of Israeli forces to Israel in June 1985, more than 1,000 Israeli military advisers along with the Israeli-supported Maronite Christian militia, the South Lebanon Army (SLA) of General Antoine Lahad remain often locked in combat with the Lebanese National Resistance, a coalition of opposition forces which include the Islamic Resistance Movement led by Hezbullah. Popular Shii resistance to continued Israeli occupation in the south provides the scene for a bitter struggle between AMAL and Hezbullah for followers, amidst growing radicalization. AMAL's pragmatic policy of limited restraint toward Israel is steadily losing ground to the more combative stance of Hezbullah.

Lebanon's central government remains powerless and in disarray. Israel's southern policy is unchanged; the U.S.'s Middle East policy is confused and further discredited by its abortive attempt in 1986 to obtain the release of American hostages from Lebanon through arms sales to Iran. Syria and Iran continue to be influential actors. The political mix in Lebanon remains combustible and with little hope for an early resolution to civil war. Indeed, partition is a growing reality.

SUMMARY

The examples of the Sudan and Lebanon reinforce several themes seen throughout this volume. First, the role of Islam in Muslim politics is not monolithic but reveals a rich diversity of interpretations and policies. Second, this diversity is determined by the interplay of religious ideology and politics; that is, Islamic ideologies are conditioned by social, political, and economic realities. Third, this dialectic affects the nature of government usages of Islam as well as the moderate versus radical orientation and agenda of Islamic organizations. Fourth, the responses of Islamic organizations to their own governments and to foreign powers (in particular the superpowers) are strongly determined by the experience or perception of government policies and actions, not necessarily by an inherent animosity or predeliction for violence.

NOTES

1. *The New York Times*, October 1, 1984.
2. Robert Bianchi, "Egypt: Drift at Home, Passivity Abroad," *Current History* (February 1986), p. 73.

3. John Kifner, "Egyptian Opposition Lionizes Guard Who Killed 7 Israelites," *New York Times,* December 27, 1985.

4. I have drawn on materials from my "Sudan's Islamic Experiment," *The Muslim World* 76 (July/October 1986): 181–201. I am especially indebted to my colleague, John O. Voll, for information contained in his *The Political Impact of Islam in the Sudan* (Washington, D.C.: Unites States Department of State, 1984), and for his comments.

5. *Al-Nahj al-Islami li madha* (Cairo: al-Maktab al Misri al-Hadith, 1980).

6. Bona Malwai, *The Sudan* (New York: Thornton Books, 1985).

7. *Sudanow* 7 no. 12 (December 1982): 5.

8. *The Arab News,* May 31, 1984.

9. For insightful studies see Richard Augustus Norton, *Amal and the Shia: Struggle for the Soul of Lebanon* (Austin: University of Texas Press, 1987), and Fouad Ajami, *The Vanished Imam: Musa Sadr and the Shia of Lebanon* (Ithaca: Cornell University Press, 1986).

10. Salim Nasr, "Roots of the Shii Movement" in *MERIP Reports* (June 1985), p. 14.

11. R. Augustus Norton, "Harakat AMAL—The Emergence of a New Lebanon Fantasy or Reality," *Islamic Fundamentalism and Islamic Radicalism* (Washington, D.C.: House Committee on Foreign Affairs, 1985), p. 347.

12. George Nader, "Interview with Sheikh Fadl Allah," *Middle East Insight* (June/July 1985), p. 19.

13. *Ibid.*

14. Thomas L. Friedman, "Israel's Dilemma: Living With a Dirty War," *The New York Times Magazine,* January 20, 1985, p. 42.

ISLAM AND POLITICS

was composed in 10-point Linotron 202 Palatino and leaded two points
by Coghill Book Typesetting Co.;
with display type in Legend by Dix Typesetting Co., Inc.;
printed by sheet-fed offset on 50-pound, acid-free Glatfelter Eggshell Cream paper stock
Smythe-sewn, and bound over binder's boards in Columbia Bayside Vellum,
also adhesive bound with 10-point Carolina laminated covers,
by Maple-Vail Book Manufacturing Group, Inc.;
and published by

SYRACUSE UNIVERSITY PRESS
SYRACUSE, NEW YORK 13244-5160